FROM EQUALITY TO INEQUALITY

Social Change among Newly Sedentary Lanoh
Hunter-Gatherer Traders of Peninsular Malaysia

How does inequality emerge in previously egalitarian societies? This question has occupied generations of anthropologists since the nineteenth century. In spite of the various theories explaining processes leading to inequality and the development of social complexity, we still have a limited understanding of the problem. This is partly because research has focused primarily on exogamous factors, and partly because the process of emerging inequality has been notoriously difficult to study empirically.

In this book, Csilla Dallos presents the results of ethnographic fieldwork among the hunter-gatherers in Peninsular Malaysia that addresses these issues. It provides rich empirical data on the effects of internal processes deemed significant in developing inequality, such as sedentism, integration, leadership competition, self-aggrandizement, marginalization, and feuding of kinship groups. By studying and interpreting social change in this previously egalitarian community of Lanoh forager-collectors, Dallos argues that, to understand emerging inequality, and to integrate anthropological models of equality and inequality, scholars need to review the conception of politics in small-scale egalitarian societies. Based on her findings, the author proposes a new model of developing inequality, one that is congruent with the principles of complexity theory.

(Anthropological Horizons)

CSILLA DALLOS is an associate professor in the Department of Anthropology at St Thomas University.

ANTHROPOLOGICAL HORIZONS

Editor: Michael Lambek, University of Toronto

This series, begun in 1991, focuses on theoretically informed ethnographic works addressing issues of mind and body, knowledge and power, equality and inequality, the individual and the collective. Interdisciplinary in its perspective, the series makes a unique contribution in several other academic disciplines: women's studies, history, philosophy, psychology, political science, and sociology.

For a list of the book published in this series see page 337.

CSILLA DALLOS

From Equality to Inequality

Social Change among Newly Sedentary Lanoh Hunter-Gatherer Traders of Peninsular Malaysia

UNIVERSITY OF TORONTO PRESS
Toronto Buffalo London

© University of Toronto Press Incorporated 2011
Toronto Buffalo London
www.utppublishing.com
Printed in Canada

ISBN 978-1-4426-4222-5 (cloth)
ISBN 978-1-4426-1122-1 (paper)

∞

Printed on acid-free, 100% post-consumer recycled paper with
vegetable-based inks.

Library and Archives Canada Cataloguing in Publication

Dallos, Csilla, 1963–
From equality to inequality : social change among newly sedentary
Lanoh hunter-gatherer traders of Peninsular Malaysia / Csilla Dallos.

(Anthropological horizons)
Includes bibliographical references and index.
ISBN 978-1-4426-4222-5 (bound).   ISBN 978-1-4426-1122-1 (pbk.)

1. Indigenous peoples – Malaysia – Social conditions.   I. Title.   II. Series:
Anthropological horizons

GN635.M4D34 2011   305.89'928   C2010-907616-8

This book has been published with the help of a grant from the Canadian
Federation for the Humanities and Social Sciences, through the Aid to
Scholarly Publications Program, using funds provided by the Social
Sciences and Humanities Research Council of Canada.

University of Toronto Press acknowledges the financial assistance to its
publishing program of the Canada Council for the Arts and the Ontario
Arts Council.

 Canada Council   Conseil des Arts
for the Arts   du Canada

 ONTARIO ARTS COUNCIL
CONSEIL DES ARTS DE L'ONTARIO

University of Toronto Press acknowledges the financial support of the
Government of Canada through the Canada Book Fund for its publishing
activities.

Contents

Maps and Figures

Maps

Figures

Tables

Preface and Acknowledgments

These days, I teach, and as I consider how this book took shape, I think of my students, novice researchers struggling with their material at different phases of project completion. This book came together eventually, but, as anyone who has ever worked with ethnographic material can attest, there were times when its realization was far from obvious.

This book is the outcome of nearly fifteen years of thinking and it has benefited from the help of numerous individuals and institutions. It began at the University of Toronto, when I approached my Master's supervisor, Professor Shuichi Nagata, for advice on my final research project. He handed me two articles, James Woodburn's 'Egalitarian Society' and a paper by Robert Dentan on Senoi Semai, asking if I would be interested in tackling the issues raised by these authors. I was, and this marked the beginning of my connection with the Orang Asli, the indigenous people of Peninsular Malaysia, as well as my relationship with Shuichi Nagata, who has remained my mentor over the years and to whom I feel more gratitude than I can ever express.

Or did this project start even earlier, when I signed up for my first course in cultural anthropology as an undergraduate at the University of Toronto with Richard B. Lee, whose lectures were steeped in his captivating work with the !Kung. It is to him that I owe my fascination with hunter-gatherers and their role in anthropological theory. I carried these interests with me when I transferred to McGill University, where I enrolled in a doctoral program. I owe a great deal to my thesis supervisor, Jérôme Rousseau, who initiated me into the problematic of social inequality, and to the legendary archaeologist Bruce Trigger, who engaged me in discussions on social evolution. During these years, my conversations with Jérôme about complexity theory turned to ways in which it could address postmodern criticisms of evolutionary thinking and thereby rescue social evolutionism from obsolescence.

When, after this conceptual preparation, it came time to decide where I would conduct my dissertation research, I had little doubt in my mind that it would be among the Orang Asli of Peninsular Malaysia. I was still uncertain, however, of exactly where and with whom I would be working. To narrow my choices, I travelled to Malaysia for a short visit, where Geoffrey Benjamin was kind enough to discuss with me potential research sites. It was Cornelia van der Sluys, however, who literally grabbed me from a hotel in Kuala Lumpur and took me to Upper Perak, where she introduced me to the Lanoh of Tawai and Air Bah. I cannot begin to describe how important this gesture was for the success of my project. It was an introduction by a trusted friend, guaranteeing that I would receive a warm welcome into the community when I returned a year later.

The dissertation (Dallos 2003) resulting from this fieldwork was put aside for some years while I grappled with the challenges of teaching. While my doctoral thesis contained the core of the argument outlined in this book, it took many further months to shape it into its present form. Though this book is based on ethnographic work, it is not 'framed as ethnography' in the sense that its primary goal is not to present 'a picture of a group of people' (Wolcott 2008: 44, 66). Instead, it builds on ethnographic data to develop a theoretical argument about hunter-gatherers, social change, egalitarian societies, and their role in social and human evolution. This, I believe, is where its main utility lies, both for students and professional anthropologists.

Above all, I would like this book to be a useful educational resource. I not only hope that readers find it beneficial in furthering their understanding of the indigenous hunter-gatherers of Southeast Asia, but also that they appreciate the link I set out to establish between ethnographic data and anthropological theory. As I was working on the final version, I tried to envision the kind of organization and structure that would benefit my students most. For this reason, I especially recommend this book to anthropology students learning to construct arguments from ethnographic data, as well as secondary sources.

It would also be gratifying to know that this work inspires fellow researchers and colleagues to delve deeper into theories of social evolution and change, and to find ways to further develop complexity theory into a useful analytical tool in this area. Most importantly, however, I hope that this book will prompt discussions about the evolution of human culture and its relation to political structures in egalitarian society.

Finally, apart from acknowledging the role of those whose input was essential for this project, I would also like to thank several organizations and individuals whose generous help was instrumental in its completion. Funding for fieldwork was provided by the International Development Research Centre's Young Canadian Researcher Award, by the Canada-ASEAN Centre Graduate Student Travel Grant, and by McGill University Open Fellowships. This research further benefited from the help of the staff of the JHEOA offices in Kuala Lumpur and Grik, as well as from conversations with members of the mobile medical unit, Kementarian Kesihatan Malaysia, RKPBV Pejabat Kesihatan Grik. I also thank the Economic Planning Unit, Prime Minister's Department, Government of Malaysia, for granting me a research permit, and the Universiti Sains Malaysia for providing affiliation and support during my stay. I am very grateful to St Thomas University for a General Research Grant as well as for the McCain Award that has allowed me to prepare the book for publication. This book has been published with the help of a grant from the Canadian Federation for the Humanities and Social Sciences, through the Aid to Scholarly Publications Program, using funds provided by the Social Sciences and Humanities Research Council of Canada.

Apart from these institutions, this project owes much to the help of fellow researchers. I thank Wazir-Jahan Karim, Razha Rashid, Hood Salleh, Colin Nicholas, Lye Tuck-Po, and Bah Tony Williams-Hunt for their support, advice, and encouragement at different phases of this research. I am extremely grateful to Kirk M. Endicott, who did more than his share to get this project underway by offering careful comments and generous publication advice. I also thank Oie and Francis Osmund in Seremban, Roy and Pat Joseph in Penang, and the Malek family in Singapore, for providing shelter, food, assistance, and friendship. A special thanks is due to my friends and colleagues in Canada, Anne Hayhurst-Rice, Cristina Redko, Eldon Yellowhorn, Alicia Colson, Caroline Tait, André Leblanc, Santiago Mora, Craig Proulx, Peter Toner, Moira McLaughlin, Glen Harris, and Christine Varga-Harris, for their support both in the dissertation and revision phases of this work. Throughout my fieldwork, and ever since, I have benefited from the help of my friend and partner Gazaly Malek, whose pragmatism, unceasing enthusiasm, and abundant knowledge of everything Southeast Asian greatly contributed to my understanding of the region, its cultures, and its peoples. I further thank David Groves for his thorough, intuitive, and efficient editing of the manuscript. Most of all, I would like to convey my gratitude to the people of Air Bah and Tawai for enduring my clumsiness and insistent questioning with a marvellous sense of humour. I am especially thankful to Abang Alias, Abeng, Hassan, Abu, and Jamil for their unrelenting effort to teach me the ways of Lanoh, to Samsiah for her friendship, and to Abang Panjang for his special contribution to this project.

Fredericton, June 2010

FROM EQUALITY TO INEQUALITY

Social Change among Newly Sedentary Lanoh
Hunter-Gatherer Traders of Peninsular Malaysia

1 Equality, Inequality, and Changing Hunter-Gatherers

I feel that if we want to understand social change, we need concepts that allow us to observe and describe the *events* of change.

– Fredrik Barth 1967: 661

Lanoh: Changing Hunter-Gatherers

Today's indigenous peoples are undergoing unprecedented change, pressed on by the forces of economic, technological, and social development. The following study records social change among Lanoh newly sedentary forest collectors in Peninsular Malaysia. Lanoh are one of several Orang Asli groups of the peninsula (Map 1.1).[1] In spite of their linguistic and possibly ethnohistorical affiliation with Senoi horticulturists, they have always been classified as a Semang people (Evans 1937; Carey 1976).[2] This classification is based on their pre-resettlement lifestyle. Unlike agriculturist Malays of the coastal areas or horticulturist Senoi of the interior hills, Semang primarily subsisted as hunter-gatherers and collectors of forest products, although they may have sporadically engaged in cultivation as well. They likely descended from the earliest hunter-gatherer populations of the region, but as David Bulbeck (2003) has pointed out, contemporary Semang differ considerably from early pre-Austronesian hunter-gatherers who lived in the area.[3] Whereas those were generalized hunters, Semang have come to focus on small arboreal game, and their social organization has changed accordingly.

Semang social organization corresponds closely to James Woodburn's (1982) model of hunter-gatherers who have an immediate-return sys-

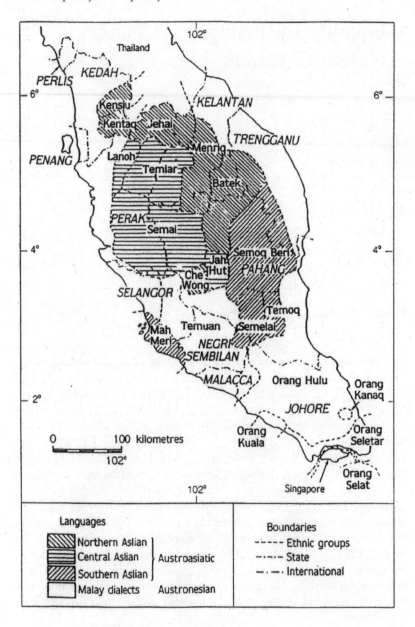

Map 1.1 Distribution of Orang Asli subgroups.
Source: Geoffrey Benjamin, in Nicholas (2000).

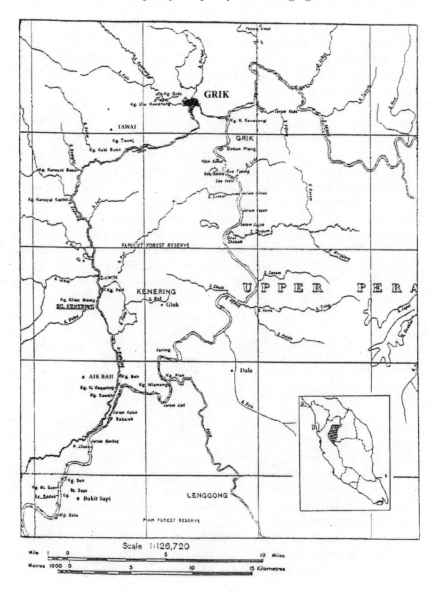

Map 1.2 The Lanoh Area, Upper Perak, West Malaysia.
Source: Map of Perak, Sheet 2, Geographical Section, General Staff, No. 4255 War Office 1942 (original published by the F.M.S. & S.S. Survey Dept. 1929).

tem of production.[4] They are mobile and individualistic, have a flexible social organization, lack permanent leadership or political centralization, and actively resist group solidarity, corporate identity, and ethnic boundaries (Schebesta 1929; Noone 1954–55; Benjamin 1986b; Nagata, personal communication). The primary form of distribution between Semang is sharing, and to repeat Woodburn, they are among the most egalitarian peoples known to anthropologists.[5] Pre-resettlement Lanoh were similarly mobile and fluid in their social organization. Like other Semang, they also participated in the forest product trade and their contact with nearby Malay villages extended over several generations.[6]

Unlike Senoi peoples, who withdrew to the interior hills in the face of Malay expansion,[7] Lanoh as well as other Semang remained in lowland areas, near Malay settlements. As noted by an early researcher of Semang, Ivor N.H. Evans, curator of the ethnographic museum of Taiping, who typically found Semang (Negrito) foraging camps near Malay (or Thai) villages, 'the Negritos ... [are] not mountaineers, or even hillmen. They like river valleys; at the most foot-hills' (1937: 11; also see Junker 2002b: 226). Lanoh in Air Bah confirmed this observation, stating:

> From the time of the first Lanoh, [we] never liked to move far away, or up to the hills.

Elaborating on this statement, an old man, Tabot,[8] added:

> Lanoh do not like to stay upland. It is not our nature to stay there. From the beginning, we have liked to stay lowland, near the water, near the river. Our traditional area is Sumpitan, Gluk, Malau, Kenering, and we do not like to go anywhere else. We do not like to go upland because it is so difficult to live upland. Why should we live like Temiar, who stay on the hill and collect water in bamboo and carry it up on their back? That's stupid. Kensiu and Kintak are like the Lanoh. They also prefer lowland. That is why the Lanoh get along with Kensiu and Kintak. Jahai are like the Temiar, they prefer the hills, but they are different in that they like to live near the water. Only Temiar ... do not like to live near water.

As is reflected in this interview excerpt, Lanoh clearly differentiate their pre-resettlement lifestyle from that of Senoi Temiar, to whom they are linked by historical ties.[9]

Before resettlement Lanoh lived as mobile forest collectors. They resided and moved within a well-defined area in the Perak Valley between the towns of Lenggong and Grik (Map 1.2). The association of Lanoh with the Perak River, the most important river route in northern Perak, is commemorated in their autonym, *səma? bloom*, which means 'people of the big river.'[10] Evans confirms this association between Lanoh and the Perak River: 'Passing now to the Negritos of the valley of the Perak River: Groups frequent the neighbourhoods of Lenggong, Sumpitan and Kuala Kenering and call themselves Semak Belum or Semak Belong, being known to the Kintak Bong and Menik Kaien as Lanoh (Schebesta's Lano) ... For the Perak River is called by them Ong Belum (or Belong), the Belum (or Belong) Water (1937: 26).'[11] In explaining the way they came to occupy the Perak River Valley, Lanoh refer to an old myth, according to which god (L. *ya?*, 'grandmother') 'pushed the mountains a little bit west, pushed the mountains a little bit east, and said, "You, [*səma?*, 'people'] stay here near the water."' The low population density of Lanoh in pre-resettlement times allowed them to spread between a few principal villages and campsites over this relatively large area.[12] From conversations with people in Air Bah one can discern five to seven commonly frequented areas. This suggests that Lanoh villages and camps in the past were small, with a population rarely exceeding thirty or thirty-five people.[13] This mobile lifestyle, which Lanoh led for hundreds if not thousands of years, however, came to an end after *Merdeka*, Malaysia's independence, in 1957.

Reconstructing this pre-resettlement history and lifestyle is not an easy task. Although contemporary indigenous groups are frequent subjects of studies of social change, anthropologists intent on actually *assessing* change over a period of time face a major obstacle: participant observation, the primary method of ethnographic data collecting, is far better suited for investigating synchronic phenomena. As a result ethnohistorical reconstruction has always been problematic in sociocultural anthropology (Tuzin 2001). My task was further complicated by the lack of previous ethnographic research done among the northern hunter-gatherers of Peninsular Malaysia (Rashid 1995: 3–4).[14]

Nonetheless, in seeking an understanding of Lanoh history, I was fortunate to be able to consult the extensive body of early material compiled by Ivor Evans, who repeatedly visited Lanoh, or 'Lenggong Negrito,' between 1910 and 1930 (1914, 1924, 1927a, 1927b, 1937). Early ethnographic work on Lanoh also includes writings by Father Paul Schebesta (1929) and Major P.D.R. Williams-Hunt (1954). For a comparative perspective, I also consulted ethnographic accounts of Semang groups (Batek, Kensiu, Kintak, and Jahai) by Karen Endicott (1979, 1981, 1984, 1999), Kirk Endicott (1974, 1979, 1984, 1988, 1995, 1999b, 2002), Lye Tuck-Po (1998, 2005), Shuichi Nagata (1997a, 1997b, 1999), and Cornelia van der Sluys (1993, 2000). In spite of these sources, however, I still lacked direct means to ascertain how Lanoh lived a hundred, fifty, or even twenty years ago.

To establish firmer ground for my propositions about social change, and to facilitate the contrast between pre-resettlement life (in the Perak Valley) and post-resettlement life (in Air Bah), I collected life history interviews with a number of individuals in Air Bah, as well as in other locations with significant ties to the village, such as Tawai and Cenawi.[15] These interviews, supplemented by earlier accounts of Lanoh life and ethnographic literature on other Semang peoples, helped me better understand the lifestyle of Lanoh prior to Malaysia's independence and provided a baseline by which to appraise social change during the post-resettlement period. Through life stories I gained insight into pre-resettlement mobility patterns, geographical distributions, priorities in subsistence and commercial activities, and the characteristics of interpersonal ties. Even more importantly, beyond recounting events, people also helped to interpret them.[16] Especially engaging were interviews with Temiar in Air Bah, whose comments highlighted discrepancies between Temiar and Lanoh world views and values.

In spite of the substantial changes the region has experienced since the end of the nineteenth century (at the height of British colonialism), the Lanoh lifestyle seems to have not changed fundamentally until Malaysia's independence. However, within the framework of the Malay nation state, the Lanoh way of life, like that of all Orang Asli, has undergone unprecedented change,[17] mainly as a result of land and resource loss, logging, deforestation, new forms of subsistence and commercial activities, involuntary resettlement, and pressures to conform to the mainstream Malaysian lifestyle and convert to Islam (Chee Heng Leng 1995; Williams-Hunt 1995; Nicholas 2000; Gomes 2007).

Regrouped and permanently resettled since the early 1980s, primarily in the village of Air Bah, Lanoh have been struggling to reconcile these changes with their cultural values and customary way of life. The first attempt to resettle the Lanoh took place under Malay administration in the early 1960s, when they were regrouped in Kampung Bal (*kampu? bal*), about a half an hour walking distance from the present-day village of Air Bah. This effort was interrupted, however, by a cholera epidemic in 1965, after which the Lanoh once again dispersed in small groups into their traditional villages and campsites. The epidemic had a devastating effect on Lanoh families and decimated their overall population. In the 1970s most of the remaining Lanoh were regrouped once again in a different location, Kampung Kling (*kampu? ?ɔŋ kəliŋ*), from where they moved to Air Bah in the late 1970s.[18]

It is unlikely that the move to Air Bah was initiated by the Lanoh because, being far from the road and water, they would consider the place extremely unsuitable for permanent settlement.[19] Instead, Air Bah was chosen by the Jabatan Hal Ehwal Orang Asli (JHEOA), the administrative agency responsible for Orang Asli affairs, as a permanent resettlement village for the Lanoh. The settlement in Air Bah was permanently developed more or less accidentally in 1984, when, one day, officers of the JHEOA arrived with building material originally intended for another Orang Asli village whose inhabitants had moved away. The JHEOA used this material to build twenty-one wooden houses and instructed the villagers, who until then had lived in Lanoh-style lean-to shelters, to move in. Air Bah's status as a resettlement village was finalized in 1993, when a two-storey mosque was erected to house Muslim proselytizers during their intermittent visits to the village.[20]

In spite of resettlement, villagers in Air Bah continue most of their pre-resettlement activities. They hunt, gather vegetables in the nearby hills, and collect forest products (albeit no longer predominantly for Malay and Chinese villagers but for large-scale buyers from the nearby town of Grik). Despite new large-scale commercial opportunities, as well as numerous government-run development and aid projects, the settlement remains comparatively 'underdeveloped.' This is due partly to the inappropriateness of the proposed programs and partly to their continued rejection by the Lanoh. Regardless, the JHEOA doggedly continues to implement development projects and to pressure Lanoh to adopt a more sedentary and agricultural lifestyle. Development projects in the village have included the promotion of vegetable and fruit tree planting as well as animal husbandry. Since 1986 the JHEOA have also organized workshops in agriculture, seminars for indigenous healers, crash courses in first aid, and even auto mechanic training in Kuala Lumpur. Other government entities, such as the Forestry Department and the Department of Agriculture, have also established training programs in agricultural production. Lanoh lack of interest in these programs has been met with threats of withdrawal of assistance. As a result of these tactics, Lanoh have come to perceive their situation as entrapment, and sedentism as a price to pay for government assistance.

Overwhelming as it may seem, however, the government's involvement in Air Bah is much less extensive than it is in larger resettlement villages, such as Dala or Kemah. Under the Rancangan Perkampungan Semula (Resettlement Program), the inhabitants of these latter villages receive complete funding not only for community administration, but also for various social and economic activities. By contrast, apart from the wooden houses and the mosque, used by the village boys to lie down, chat, nap, and escape from the midday heat, infrastructure in Air Bah consists solely of a generator, water pipes, and a public telephone. However, the generator requires a regular supply of fuel which Lanoh are unable to afford, the water pipes only intermittently carry water to the village from a nearby waterfall, and the public telephone rarely works.

Yet, in spite of the appearance of continuity and comparatively limited government interference, life in Air Bah is far removed from life in pre-resettlement times. Much of the discrepancy between pre- and post-resettlement life is a result of permanent sedentism and regroupment, but deforestation and development have further altered the villagers' livelihoods and relationships. Although vegetable collecting appears less affected, hunting is in decline, especially around the settlement. Commercial activities have been similarly affected, and the conditions of forest collecting only superficially resemble those in the past. Lanoh men, whose movements are increasingly dictated by the need to earn cash and who are increasingly involved in contract jobs, are often away from the village for periods lasting from a few days to several weeks. Additionally, because of the development of roads and public transport in Perak, Lanoh now have more contact with Orang Asli from other villages than they did in the past. Before modernization Lanoh mostly interacted with people at the boundaries of their region. Improved transportation facilities have increased communication between Orang Asli and created a network of villages centred around Grik. Atan, a resident in Air Bah explained:

> Before we had no opportunity to meet other people. Since the early 1980s, about the time we started to go to Grik, we began to meet other people.

In Grik, Lanoh are likely to meet people they would have had limited contact with in pre-resettlement times. Nowadays, a Saturday trip to Grik is a regular part of the weekly schedule of Lanoh. When in Grik, Lanoh men sell their products, meet with their friends and acquaintances from other villages, and stepping off the bus on their way home, before turning to the footpath that leads back to the village through the rubber and palm oil plantations, they stop in at the store in the Malay village of Sawa to do their weekly shopping.

This weekly shopping activity is one indication of commoditization in Air Bah. There are few immediately noticeable signs of this, because by most standards, people in Air Bah are extremely poor, and their houses are void of material possessions. Villagers continue to recycle and reuse objects, as they did in pre-resettlement times.[21] Nonetheless, acquisitiveness and a reliance on cash seem to have increased compared with the past. Fifty years ago, Lanoh wore loincloths and no shoes, used fruit acid instead of salt, grew their tobacco and rice, and lit fires using indigenous methods. Today, the average Saturday 'shopping basket' includes rice, cooking oil, sugar, coffee, tea, cans of sweetened condensed milk, biscuits, soap, toothpaste, candies, *ikan bilis* (dried fish, M.), dried shrimps, *belacan* (shrimp paste, M.), dried chili, and curry powder.

People in Air Bah attribute their consumerism to sedentism and the type of houses most of them occupy today. They are aware that in the past they limited their material possessions to accommodate frequent mobility. To the question, 'What did you bring with you when you moved in the past?' they answer:

> We had our house things. Sometimes we'd make very nice bamboo cups, which we kept. We wrapped food in banana leaves. We had our blow-pipes, and some people may have had a *parang* [machete-like heavy knife used as a tool or weapon in Malaysia and Indonesia].

People believe that since resettlement, their large, spacious, wooden houses have compelled them to purchase things they would not have bought nor even required in the past. They suggest that, even today, they only buy what they need, such as kitchen equipment and tools, and not luxury items, but that in the past they needed even less, because their houses were small. Villagers in Air Bah explained:

> [Before] we built the house, lived in it for a short while, and then moved on. Now we live in these big houses and we have to stay. Therefore, we need more things.

To 'fill up' their houses, they have begun to acquire commercial goods

such as plastic utensils, metal pots, furniture such as floor mats, clothing, and electric equipment, including radio and television sets.[22] One
indication of this acquisitiveness is the village's debt of 700 ringgit to
Indian and Patani Malay travelling vendors, who periodically stop in
Air Bah to sell medicine, plastic goods, carpets, and food, such as fish.[23]

Apart from subsistence patterns, consumer behaviour, and interethnic contact, settlement composition and population dynamics have also
changed compared with pre-resettlement times. Lanoh today intermar-
ry with Temiar more often than they did in the past: in 1998 ten out of
the twenty-two married couples in Air Bah were mixed Lanoh-Temiar.
As well, Air Bah's population is larger than that of Lanoh villages and
camps of pre-resettlement times, not only because the village was established as a result of regroupment, but also because Lanoh today often
have more children than they did in the past.[24] Instead of an average
of three children, as was customary in pre-resettlement times, Lanoh
families might now have between six and eight children.[25]

One might infer from this that Air Bah is a lively, vibrant place, but
this is hardly the case, as about half of the village's children attend a
boarding school for Orang Asli children in Air Panas, a settlement near
Grik, from where they only return during school holidays.[26] In fact,
on days when men are away, the village seems desolate and deserted.
The village's layout, architecture, and landscaping contribute to this
impression: since it originally served as a paddy-planting site, Air Bah
is almost completely void of vegetation (see Figure 1.1). Furthermore,
unlike the circular camps of the past, the resettlement has an elongated
shape, stretching along two sides of a dirt road, with the plank houses
facing each other at considerable distance. This arrangement not only
obstructs visibility but discourages interaction. In the past, small camps
and see-through lean-to shelters ensured high visibility, incessant communication, and constant participation in the lives of others.[27] Today
much remains hidden. Although people still spend considerable time
leisurely chatting together in prominent communal spots, the walls of
the wooden plank houses encourage privacy.

These changes are all substantial, but perhaps the greatest change
compared with pre-resettlement times is the disappearance of the
equality that characterizes mobile hunter-gatherers. Within a mere
generation since resettlement, inequalities have begun to emerge in Air
Bah between individuals, between households, and between kinship
groups. This development, echoing records of emerging social differentiation among changing foragers elsewhere, became my study's main
focus.[28]

Figure 1.1   Lanoh resettlement village of Air Bah, 1998.

Inequality, Integration, and Changing Hunter-Gatherers

The emergence of inequality, 'various patterns of asymmetrical relations' (Tilly 2001a: 300), in previously egalitarian societies is one of
anthropology's oldest and most enduring areas of study (Hayden
1995). Over the years, a number of competing and often incompatible
theories have been developed to explain this phenomenon (McGuire
1983; Béteille 1983, 1996; Curtis 1986; Bern 1987; Lee 1990; Hastorf 1990;
Paynter and McGuire 1991; Feinman 1995; Blanton 1995; Hayden 1995;
Arnold 1995; Earle 1997; Salzman 1999; Tilly 2001a, 2001b; Wiessner
2002; Rousseau 2006).[29] Yet, despite all the attention it has received, as
Kelly notes, 'relatively little progress ... has been made in explaining
inequality' (1991: 136, in Feinman 1995: 255). Thus, although it is a topic
of intense inquiry, a satisfying explanation for the rise of social inequality remains elusive.

One reason is that the process of social differentiation is exceedingly
difficult to study empirically (Béteille 1996: 304). Anthropologists have
generally focused on two solutions: either shifting their efforts to studying how inequality is reproduced in different contexts or reverting to
the less satisfactory comparative approach (Rousseau 2006: 4). Tuzin
reinforces this point when stating that 'the legacy of earlier scholarship
is such that there are very few ethnographic studies which trace the
changing historical experiences of a particular society in explicitly evo-

lutionary systems' (2001: 10). Faced with this fact, anthropologists have often turned to changing, newly sedentary hunter-gatherers to observe social inequality as it develops.

In light of recent debates in hunter-gatherer studies, however, such an approach requires elaboration and justification. Beginning in the 1980s, revisionist critics of earlier hunter-gatherer research have taken issue with the practice of conjectural history, which uses contemporary hunter-gatherers as analogues for historical and prehistoric societies (Trigger 1998: 163). These critics have argued that contact with neighbouring agriculturist or pastoralist societies has shaped modern hunter-gatherers' lifestyles significantly more than was previously acknowledged (Schrire 1980 and 1984: 18; Headland 1986; Galaty 1986; Denbow and Wilmsen 1986; Bailey et al. 1989; Headland and Reid 1989: 51). If this is true, then the context of social change in modern hunter-gatherers is utterly alien to hunter-gatherers of the past, and offers few tangible clues about historical change.

Revisionist critics have further pointed out that social change among contemporary hunter-gatherers occurs within nation states and their developing, industrializing, and globalizing societies. Consequently, resource depletion, land loss, forced resettlement, crowding, health problems, unprecedented legal, political, and cultural interference, and an increasing reliance on cash have placed immense stress on the social relationships of these peoples, and thus must be considered among the theoretical implications of studies on contemporary hunter-gatherers (K.M. Endicott 1979; Couillard 1980; Gomes 1986; Kuchikura 1987; Peterson 1991; Dentan et al. 1997; Nicholas 2000). Indeed, critics contend that these effects on contemporary indigenous societies are so fundamental that 'social anthropology may turn out to be only a study of acculturation' (Trigger 1998: 163).

In light of these arguments, any attempt to draw direct inferences from studies of these 'post-foragers' to historical or prehistoric processes of social change could be seen as misguided. That said, studies of changing hunter-gatherers continue to lead to testable and applicable models and insights relevant to anthropological theory, including the realm of social complexity (e.g., Wiessner 2002).[30] As Victor Turner stated, it is often during crisis that the 'less plastic, more durable, but nevertheless gradually changing basic social structure, made up of relations which are relatively constant and consistent' reveals itself (1980: 151). Similarly, I maintain that, although Lanoh have not escaped the effects of modernization and a developing national economy, a study of change within their society will still provide important lessons for our understanding of historical and prehistoric social change and the development of complex hierarchical societies.

There are a number of benefits to focusing on modern hunter-gatherers in the study of social evolution. Research among post-foragers not only provides first-hand empirical data on developing inequality, but also a chance to investigate variables considered significant in theories of social complexity. Changes in contemporary hunter-gatherer lifestyles, for example, often affect their mobility patterns and population dynamics. Since both demography and sedentism have figured so importantly in models of social evolution, researchers have continued to find it justifiable to test social evolutionary theories among newly sedentary hunters and gatherers despite the fact that the sedentism of contemporary hunter-gatherers is typically involuntary, that their aggregation is due to regroupment, and that demographic changes are generally the result of medical care and decreased infant mortality (Hitchcock 1982; Ellen 1988; Griffin 1989; Kent 1989, 1995a, 1995b; Draper 1975b, 1992; Knauft 1990; Gardner 2000).[31] Summing up the view that contemporary hunter-gatherers are useful for testing theories of social evolution, Susan Kent suggests that newly sedentary hunter-gatherers 'provide an opportunity to study sedentarization in action' (1989: 708). Donald Tuzin makes a similar argument, submitting that modern post-forager studies can add causal precision to the inexact world of inequality theory: 'Few would deny that population size and societal complexity are functionally related; but this unadorned correlation begs questions of causality, cognition, motivation, agency, and intentionality to which ethnography may have something to contribute' (2001: 6).[32]

Tuzin's argument highlights a second advantage that studies of changing hunter-gatherers can bring to theories of social change. Beyond a potential to generate empirical data on the process of social differentiation, such studies may also provide researchers with an opportunity to examine internal factors and the role of agency (Lightfoot and Feinman 1982; Hayden and Gargett 1990; Hayden 1995; Feinman 1995: 262, 273, 257–9; Rousseau 2006: 24, 36). Studies of changing hunter-gatherers have been criticized for exaggerating the effect of external factors, such as an encroaching state, while overlooking possibly important internal processes (Bender and Morris 1998: 8, 12; Bender 1990: 263; Layton 2001). Participant observation, the key method of ethnographic data collecting, is eminently suited for generating data on intragroup dynamics and the role of individual actors in developing inequality. An impressive body of ethnographic work already exists on how hunter-gatherers, on an individual level, have responded to changes affecting their mobility, livelihood, and social relationships (Barnard 1983; Myers 1988; Spielman and Eder 1994; Bird-David 1994; Burch 1994; Kelly 1995; Ingold 1999; Lee 1999; Pryor 2003). This strongly suggests that questions of inequality could benefit from the same approach.

In spite of increased interest in modern hunter-gatherers and social evolution in the past four decades, there are still insufficient data on how contemporary hunter-gatherers respond to change along the dimensions of equality versus inequality and individualism versus integration. This fact constitutes the final and perhaps most important reason why studies of contemporary hunter-gatherers can inform theories of social complexity. Christine Hastorf addresses these dimensions by posing the following research questions: on the one hand, she suggests that we study the individualism-integration dimension by asking 'how ... individuals decide to give up ... or unconsciously [lose] their autonomy to a minority of the group' (1990: 147), and on the other hand, she recommends that we inquire about the fate of ideological equality by asking 'how ... inequality [is] made acceptable in a group' (ibid.: 149). Hastorf's questions outline a realistic program of research because they address the two most important obstacles in the development of social inequality: ideological and organizational resistance.

Ideological Resistance as an Obstacle in Understanding Social Inequality

In the study of social differentiation, two models have been developed to address previous biases towards exogenous explanations. These models both focus on internal dynamics and rely on agency, albeit in different ways. According to social order models, inequality develops as stronger leaders deal with organizational difficulties in newly sedentary communities (Boserup 1965, 1981; Plog 1990; Hastorf 1990; Keeley 1991; Trigger 1998: 144–5; Rowley-Conwy 2001: 43). In contrast, conflict theories propose that inequality develops as a consequence of leaders enhancing their status through political competition (Clark and Blake 1993; Bujra 1974; Trigger 1990; Brumfiel 1992, 1994). While the models are at variance concerning the mechanism of emerging leadership, they are nonetheless in agreement concerning the importance of individual actors, especially 'self-aggrandizers' (Lightfoot and Feinman 1982; Hayden and Garnett 1990; Clark and Blake 1993; Hayden 1995).

Brian Hayden defines an 'aggrandizer' as 'any ambitious, enterprising, aggressive, accumulative individual ... who strives to become dominant in a community, especially by economic means' (1995: 18). This definition raises a serious problem: even though such aggrandizers have been identified as key to understanding social inequality, egalitarian hunter-gatherers are strongly resistant to the actions and attitudes of self-aggrandizing individuals. If, as these models assert, self-aggrandizers are crucial to the rise of inequality, how do they overcome this resistance?

It is generally acknowledged that, among all societies known to anthropology, mobile hunter-gatherers are the most equal (Woodburn 1982). In his 1982 paper, 'Egalitarian Societies,' Woodburn differentiates between two types of egalitarian societies, those with immediate-return systems of production and those with delayed-return systems of production. The latter category includes hunter-gatherers, small farmers, and pastoralists, while the former is restricted to a few mobile hunter-gatherer groups: African hunter-gatherers such as the Hadza, !Kung, and Mbuti; Southeast Asian Semang, such as the Batek; and South Asian foragers, such as Pandaram and Paliyan (ibid.: 433). Accordingly, in these groups, individuals do not possess exclusive rights to valuable assets, and 'equalities of power, equalities of wealth and equalities of prestige or rank are not merely sought but are, with certain limited exceptions, genuinely realised' (432). Woodburn concludes that these mobile hunter-gatherers are 'the closest approximation to equality known to any human societies' (431).

This equality, however, does not mean an absence of social differentiation. Indeed, current perspectives often highlight differences of age, gender, skills, and ambitions even in otherwise egalitarian societies (Flanagan 1989; Paynter and McGuire 1991; Schubert 1991: 35; Boehm 1993: 235, 227 and 1999: 252–3; Erdal and Whiten 1994: 176–7; Knauft 1994: 181 and 1991: 397; Feinman 1995: 256, 261–2; Hayden 1995: 20; Trigger 1998: 216; Wiessner 2002: 233; Rousseau 2006: 31). These elements of social differentiation in egalitarian societies seemingly present a contradiction that has elicited conflicting explanations. Some, such as Jérôme Rousseau, infer from this that it is 'impossible to make a valid contrast between egalitarian and inegalitarian societies' (2006: 31; see also Yanagisako and Collier 1987). Others, however, argue that these sources of social differentiation demonstrate clear evidence of a counteractive mechanism – an egalitarian ethos – that is applied to maintain relative equality in these societies (Cashdan 1980; Woodburn 1982; Knauft 1994).

The egalitarian ethos, or ethic, has been described as a 'culturally sustained conscious intention' (Woodburn 1982: 431–2) involving the 'moralistic suppression of status rivalry' through the 'vigilant sharing of power' (Boehm 1997: S101, S104; also see Erdal and Whiten 1994; Knauft 1994). Scholars have emphasized that, among mobile hunter-gatherers, equality 'is not neutral, the mere absence of inequality or hierarchy, but is *asserted*' (Woodburn 1982: 431, original emphasis). In these groups, as Christopher Boehm argues, 'egalitarianism does not just happen; it is *made* to happen' largely through the enforcement of sanctions and egalitarian practices (1997: S104, original emphasis; also see Lee 1979). As a result these societies develop a 'coalitionary resistance to subordination,' and followers dominate leaders, rather than the other way around (Boehm 1993: 236; also Erdal and Whiten 1994: 178). This coalitionary resistance minimizes internal social differences by 'denying any individual or group the ability to command internally or to control relations with the outside world' (Bern 1987: 212; see also Knight et al. 1999: 9; Erdal and Whiten 1994; and Wiessner 2002: 235).

Therefore, the theory of an egalitarian ethic implies that egalitarian ideology and the sanctions facilitating it need to be eliminated for inequality to develop. Many have urged that this discrepancy between egalitarian ideology and aggrandizement should be at the centre of studies investigating developing inequality. For instance, as Gary Feinman (1995: 262) has pointed out, if there is differentiation in egalitarian societies, the mechanisms that mitigate it, along with the external and internal factors that 'negate' it, are fundamental. Elizabeth Cashdan also reasons that 'inequality ... can ... be explained best not as the development of any formal organization of "ranking" or "stratification," but, rather, as the inevitable result of the *lifting* of the constraints that produce strict egalitarianism' (1980: 119–20, in Hayden 1995: 20, original emphasis).

Although erasing counterdominance would seem to be an important condition of developing inequality, research on changing hunter-gatherers does not indicate that this takes place. Many have observed that counterdominance among hunter-gatherers tends to prevail even among changing, newly sedentary hunter-gatherers (Lee 1979; Woodburn 1980, 1982; Bird 1982, 1983). Thomas Headland, observing this phenomenon among the Agta, suggests that 'one reason Agta fail [at] agriculture is because other Agta hinder any of their fellows who behave in a way they interpret as "trying to get ahead"' (1986: 416). Similarly, Woodburn argues that among both Hadza and !Kung, 'egalitarian levelling mechanisms' continue to prevent accumulation, even after sedentism (1982: 447; see also Lee 1979: 313, 409–14 and 1981: 16; Fox 1953: 248; Meillassoux 1973; Rai 1982). In 'Egalitarian Societies,' Woodburn writes: 'I would agree that the nomadic hunting and gathering societies I have discussed are even more profoundly conservative. Fluidity of local grouping and spatial mobility ... combined with and reinforced by a set of distinctive egalitarian practices which disengage people from property, inhibit not only political change but any form of intensification of the economy' (1982: 447).

Several other scholars have supported Woodburn, reporting strong resistance to inequality among contemporary hunters and gatherers (Ten Raa 1986; K.M. Endicott 1988; Headland 1987; Persoon 1989; Bird-David 1990, 1992b; Peterson 1991; Grinker 1992; Lee 1992; Rushforth 1994; Silberbauer 1996; Hewlett 1996; Lewis-Williams 1996).

Organizational Resistance as an Obstacle in Understanding Social Inequality

A similar problem emerges when considering social integration and its role in emerging social complexity. Both the conflict and social order models described above assume increased social integration at some level as a prerequisite to the rise of inequality. Mobile hunter-gatherers, however, are known not only for their assertive egalitarianism but also for their fierce individualism. Anthropologists have long commented on the fluidity and flexibility of organization in these groups. This quality has crystallized in the concept of 'individual autonomy syndrome' (Gardner 1991). The individual autonomy of hunter-gatherers has been described in two ways: negatively, as a poorly developed ability to identify with others, or positively, as self-assured independence and non-interference in others' affairs (Dentan 1968; Marshall 1979; Robarchek 1989; Woodburn 1982; Gardner 1991; K.L. Endicott 1992; Ross 1993; Norström 2001: 42–3 and 2003). Woodburn associates individual autonomy with self-sufficiency in fulfilling subsistence needs. He believes that individual autonomy is related to the fact that people in these groups are not dependent on specific others for basic requirements (1982: 434). Peter Gardner (1991), relying on a cross-cultural statistical survey, identifies and examines twelve factors that may explain the existence of 'individual autonomy syndrome,' among which are: child-rearing, generalized reciprocity, dispersed resources, variability of resources due to a lack of storage, a move from complexity to simplicity due to resource depletion, involvement in external trade, and response to inferiority experienced due to encapsulation. However, he is still unable to conclusively identify which of these is the most significant. Others, such as Nurit Bird-David and Susan Kent, have also explored this question. Bird-David (1987) examines the role of the single person among mobile hunter-gatherers, whereas Kent (1996a) points out that these hunter-gatherers often value friendship over kinship. Fred Myers sums up these observations by various anthropologists by stating that, in small hunter-gatherer groups, 'sociality is constituted largely out of dyadic relations,' emphasizing the interpersonal and interindividual, over the group (1986: 124).

The individualism of mobile hunter-gatherers presents a serious obstacle to the kind of social integration included in most theories of developing inequality. This relationship between integration and emerging leadership is more evident in social order, or functional-ist, explanations of inequality, which focus on the need to cope with managerial tasks, especially conflict resolution, after sedentism (Bose-rup 1965, 1981; Hitchcock 1982; Kent 1989; Plog 1990: 198; Keeley 1991; Rowley-Conwy 2001: 43). Kent accentuates the role of social integration when suggesting that 'sedentary societies have to discourage individ-ual variability and its consequences, or they cannot remain aggregated or sedentary' (1996a: 9). Feinman also notes that organizational chal-lenges resulting from population increases in permanent settlements may explain why group members tolerate inequalities of power: 'as integration, dispute resolution, and mutual defense become greater concerns, the willingness to endure a self-serving leader may also grow' (1995: 263).

Conflict theories of developing inequality also assume social integra-tion, although at the level of competing leaders' support groups (or factions) (Clark and Blake 1993; Bujra 1974; Trigger 1990; Brumfiel 1992, 1994). Feinman posits that 'factions form because followers perceive benefits and rewards (material, political, or spiritual) for their support' (1995: 263). Hayden, alternatively, envisions dependencies and mutual obligations between faction leaders and followers in terms of debts, proposing that 'one of the most critical questions to ask is how are bind-ing, or "contractual," debts created in transegalitarian communities' (1995: 21; also see Rousseau 2006).[33] Competitive feasts have further been suggested as primary mechanisms for achieving greater integra-tion and support for ambitious leaders (Sahlins 1958; Johnson and Earle 1987; Hayden 1995).

Even though integration is implied in both social order and conflict

models, it must be noted that scholars have occasionally identified individualistic pathways to inequality.[34] Feinman, for instance, contrasts
'corporate' and 'network' models as different pathways to inequality
(1995: 273). Hayden (1995: 18–19), similarly, differentiates between settings where subsistence is based on the work of independent families
and those where communal cooperation is necessary, claiming that
self-aggrandizement in the first case will be based on the control of
labour and in the second on control of resources. Nonetheless, most
theories of social evolution assume integration to be the first important step towards social complexity.[35] To appreciate the obstacle that
this presents to theories of inequality, we need to consider the role of
mobile hunter-gatherers in evolutionary terms.

There is a general consensus among anthropologists that, as Joyce
Marcus contends, 'humans began as hunters and gatherers. By 20,000
years ago, however, at least some of them had adopted a "delayed
return" economic strategy that involved various combinations of storage, game management, encouragement of wild plants, and exchange
systems that linked human groups into larger symbiotic networks'
(2008: 254). Since the feature that most differentiates immediate-return
societies from delayed-return societies is integration, or the presence
or absence of 'dependence on specific others' (Woodburn 1982: 439),
social evolutionary theories *should* be able to account for the way the
integration emerged. Yet, factors supporting and limiting integration
have rarely been examined in studies of changing hunter-gatherers.
Researchers have devoted considerable attention to the vertical and
hierarchical dimensions of change, but they have not focused on the
horizontal dimension of individualism versus integration. A closer look
at integration is vital because, as in the case of aggrandizement, theories of social evolution and existing data on changing hunter-gatherers
seem to contradict each other.

There are several factors that could potentially promote integration
among changing hunter-gatherers. Thomas Fricke suggests that cooperation increases when 'it becomes impossible for any individual to
combine the elements of subsistence on his own' (1990: 143). In this
light, sedentism, resource depletion, or market integration may result
in reduced subsistence opportunities, increasing mutual dependence
(Emerson 1962; Molm 1985; Das and Cotton 1988; Stearman 1989: 222).
Cultural factors, such as assimilating to a neighbouring people's values,
may also bring about increased cooperation. Alternatively, resistance to
acculturation could reinforce ethnic identities and cultural boundaries,

resulting in 'heightened group solidarity' (Kent 1995b; Boehm 1999: 255; Hastorf 1990: 173–4; Netting 1990: 59).

Yet, in spite of the numerous factors that could enhance integration among post-foragers, individualism and organizational flexibility often persist (Bird-David 1994; Thambiah 1997; Kent 1989, 1995a, 1995b, 1999). Bird-David suggests that, among hunter-gatherers, 'the band formation often persists while subsistence activities undergo diversification' (1994: 584). In Peninsular Malaysia, Ahmad Ezanee bin Mansor (1972) found that the atomistic organization of Semang in Kampong Lubok Legong is retained, especially in relation to forest activities – while the extended family gained significance in sedentary villages, the nuclear family structure reappeared whenever people returned to the forest. In studying household organization among previously mobile Bhuket hunter-gatherers of Borneo, Shanti Thambiah (1997), similarly, recorded continuing flexibility of social organization and fluid household composition. Finally, Susan Kent, who analysed social change among newly sedentary hunter-gatherers in Kutse, reports that these hunter-gatherers continue to resist social integration on the following three levels: the village, the kinship group, and the household (1989, 1995a, 1995b, 1999). Kent writes: 'The newly imposed formal interfaces between selected community members and government officials are real only to the nation-state government and not to the inhabitants of Kutse ... Lineages, clans, age-sets, or other formal kin or non-kin groups did not occur in Central Kalahari bands nor do they exist today in Kutse ... Even household membership can be fluid as individuals visit or live with friends and relatives in different camps, sharing networks, or communities' (1999: 120–4). These findings, while fascinating and perhaps reaffirming for hunter-gatherer specialists, are extremely problematic for theorists of social inequality who assume that increasing integration is the key to the development of inequality and complexity.

Thus, based on what we know of the sociality of egalitarian hunter-gatherers, it is reasonable to assume that any research that focuses on changing hunter-gatherers not only should inquire into the dimensions of equality versus inequality and individualism versus integration, but also analytically differentiate them.

Understanding Social Change in Air Bah

Assessing Dimensions of Change through the Study of Time Allocation

To explicitly address the relationship between the ideological and organizational dimensions of equality, I focused on two particular areas in my study of social change in Air Bah: time allocation and decision-making.[36] The study of time allocation has often been applied by anthropologists seeking to understand social change (Johnson 1975). By studying time allocation in Air Bah I was able to address integration at the level of the village, at the level of kinship groups, and especially at the level of households. Although time-allocation studies often take the household as their fundamental unit of investigation, this approach is hardly justified among previously mobile hunter-gatherers known for their individualism and fluid group composition. In such contexts, the household has to be treated as a theoretical concept requiring analysis and explanation. This point is accentuated by Richard Wilk (1991), who criticizes the way that 'household' is used in contemporary anthropological research; he submits that instead of using the 'household' only as a convenient unit of data collection, anthropologists seeking new theoretical insights ought to address the 'definition issue' above all. This suggestion is especially justified when inquiring into the household organization of changing, newly sedentary hunter-gatherers.

Thus, to understand Lanoh households after sedentism, I focused on individuals, as opposed to households, as the primary units of analysis.[37] This study confirmed the resilience of organizational flexibility in Air Bah. Although I selected my sample after months of observation to ensure that the people who became part of the study were truly 'permanent residents' of the village, individuals were repeatedly marked as 'absent' in my records because they were visiting relatives in Tawai, Cenawi, Bukit Sapi, Dala, or Kroh, and they would often stay absent for weeks, even months. These absences underlined the fact that Lanoh still consider visiting to be a way of life and a conscious choice, outlining the importance of maintaining wide social networks. When, for instance, the government proposed a regroupment scheme to move people from Tawai permanently to Air Bah, in spite of their close relationships, people in both villages opposed this plan, explaining that the 'Lanoh way' was to travel, 'to spend a little time here, a little time there.' Consequently, although the study resulted in over 1,200 observations with valuable data, it was affected by the frequency and duration of visits, indicating that the composition of the village was still highly fluid.

Flexible household organization has proven similarly resilient, which means that it is still extremely hard to establish what a 'typical' household in Air Bah is. Household composition is varied, depending on numerous factors, including what architectural structures people

Figure 1.2 Malay-style plank house with Temiar-style extension in Air Bah.

occupy. It is still common for people to stay in Lanoh-style lean-to shelters (*deŋ lɛʔloy*)[38] or more permanent Temiar-style structures, instead
of the large government-supplied plank houses (Figures 1.2 to 1.3).[39]
The size of houses, however, does not necessarily reflect people's status or ethnic affiliation. Instead, confirming Kent's observations among
changing hunter-gatherers in Kutse (1995a: 308), house styles in Air
Bah primarily depend on the length of occupation.[40] Newlyweds today
more often build Temiar-style houses, because they last longer than
Lanoh *deŋ lɛʔloy*. As families grow, their members may also build Temiar-style woven attachments to their plank houses and use these either
as outdoor kitchens or as shelters for certain family members, like a
widowed mother or a young childless couple.

The structures people occupy have implications for household composition as well. Households in Air Bah include people who may or
may not live under the same roof, but who live in adjacent shelters, and
who routinely cooperate with each other. The only consistent aspect
of these cooperative units is that people tend to group themselves into
matrilocal residential clusters.[41] As in the past, households often consist
of a married couple and their children, and those living in lean-to shelters retain these nuclear family units with independent hearths. Often,
however, this nuclear core is extended to include grown-up children of

Figure 1.3 Malay-style plank house with Lanoh lean-to shelters in Air Bah.

either gender, as well as their spouses. Yet, people in Air Bah tend to spend time with those to whom they feel close, who are not necessarily their conjugal family members. Additionally, unlike among other Semang (Nagata 1999), full or partial adoptions occur in Air Bah, as a result of which people often spend their time divided between several households.[42] In one household, for instance, a daughter of the family spent her nights and all her waking hours in her grandmother's and aunt's house, only returning to her parents' house for meals. These various arrangements further confirmed flexible household composition in Air Bah.

Assessing Dimensions of Change through the Study of Decision-Making

The time-allocation study verified the resilience of organizational flexibility among Lanoh in Air Bah, whereas the decision-making study revealed continuing behavioural and cognitive flexibility. The study of decision-making has long been an integral part of anthropological projects, but it has primarily involved observing and recording communal group decision processes. This is because the study of group decisions is more methodologically viable for anthropologists than the study of individual decisions, as group decisions are easier to access through participant observation. However, this focus reflects anthropology's Durkheimian bias towards the 'superorganic,' collective aspects of social life. Because of this bias, individuals, especially their mental processes, have too often been left to psychologists. Boehm, who finds the study of communal decisions eminently useful in 'clearly [identifying] values, cognitive assessments, and competing strategies,' reveals this bias when dismissing individual decisions as so '*routinized* as to appear unthinking' (1996: 770, 765, original emphasis). This statement seems to contain the assumption that intra-individual cognitive and emotive processes are less contested and thus less interesting for anthropologists to study than communal ones are. Yet, studying individual decisions may prove especially useful in learning about areas of Boehm's interests: values, cognitive processes, and competing strategies. Inquiries into individual decisions, and a theoretical distinction between individual and communal decisions, are particularly beneficial in studies of changing hunter-gatherers.

In the anthropology of hunter-gatherers, the bias towards communal decisions reflects not only the discipline's preference for collective phenomena, but also the assumed link between egalitarianism (the democratic process) and collective decisions.[43] This assumption is evident in the following statement by Boehm: 'When foragers identify an ecological, political, or social problem that threatens or concerns the entire group, they do their best to cope with it as a group' (1997: S106; also see Boehm 1996, 1999). Unfortunately, this popular view seems to contradict research of decision-making processes among mobile hunter-gatherers (Woodburn 1982; Mithen 1990: 82; Gardner 1991; Norström 2001: 42). Communal projects are few among mobile hunter-gatherers, and so individuals are rarely faced with the need to negotiate their goals. Woodburn, for instance, notes that among Hadza, 'decisions are essentially individual ones: even when matters such as the timing of a camp move or the choice of a new site are to be decided, there are no leaders whose responsibility it is to take the decisions or to guide people towards some general agreement' (1982: 444). Again, theory and reality seem to disagree, making decision-making a potentially important arena not only for learning about the sociality of egalitarian hunter-gatherers, but also for monitoring social integration and the emergence of political centralization in newly sedentary villages, where more frequent communal decision-making could be indicative of social integration and the emergence of stronger, more centralized, leadership.

By analytically separating individual and group decision processes and comparing the two, I was able to evaluate the extent to which people in Air Bah conformed to group pressures in decision-making. In this regard I found Christina Gladwin's (1989) decision-tree modelling and especially the interview process during which she establishes *criteria*, *alternatives*, and *outcomes* in individual decision-making particularly valuable.[44] I hypothesized that varied decision criteria among the group, as well as decision criteria and outcomes that differ from those of the leaders, would signal continuing individual autonomy; on the contrary, conforming to group decisions and a greater frequency of collective decision-making would indicate social integration.[45] Apart from consensus-based decisions, I measured integration through the degree of conventionalization present, marked by uniform decision criteria and a homogenization of ideas.

This measurement of integration was based on the distinction that anthropologists have developed between societies characterized by cultural conservatism and a greater role for cultural transmission and those characterized by cultural flexibility and a greater role for individual experience (e.g., Mithen 1990). Kent further stresses this difference when stating that cultural rigidity indicates the presence of institutionalized conformity 'which reduces the cultural and behavioral options open to the majority of individuals' (1996a: 8). Among immediate-return hunter-gatherers, where 'the process of "conventionalization" is weak,' personal experiences play a larger part in people's decisions (Bird-David 1996: 302). In more complex delayed-return societies, especially in those with standard methods of controlling their environments, people tend to rely on culturally transmitted knowledge in decision-making to a greater extent (Kent 1996a). Kent links the development of cultural rigidity to sedentary lifestyles, explaining that 'sedentary societies have to discourage individual variability and its consequences, or they cannot remain aggregated or sedentary' (ibid.: 9). She further predicts that among newly sedentary foragers cultural unity is achieved because emerging leaders 'have the social and political status to achieve social cohesion and unanimity' (11).

Thus, to monitor conventionalization in Air Bah, I once again focused on variation in individual decision criteria. If individualism prevailed, variation was expected in the decision criteria of individuals. If conventionalization was underway, individual decisions were expected to become more harmonized and consensual, reflecting coordinated goals and a matching value system. Greater conventionalization would manifest itself in a higher correlation between individual and public decision criteria. This distinction proved especially valuable when evaluating leaders' attempts to establish greater unity, cohesion, and cooperation among household clusters and individual members. Had I not monitored variation in decision criteria, it would have been easy to interpret these attempts, outwardly bearing the signs of communal mobilization, as increasing village integration. However, the study of decision criteria and outcomes made it clear that these attempts by village elders and leaders had very little impact in terms of conventionalization and homogenization. For the most part Lanoh in Air Bah remain individualistic and 'opportunistic' with varied and flexible decision criteria.

Although fieldwork in Air Bah reinforced the assumption that changing hunter-gatherers demonstrate considerable organizational resilience and flexibility, it failed to provide evidence in support of the second prediction, that changing hunter-gatherers would similarly resist emerging inequalities. It appears that people there resist integration far more than they are resisting inequality. While they are, indeed, aware of changes, often comparing their present and past lifestyles, as a rule their complaints are directed at crises of subsistence, rather than at sociopolitical change. Thus, villagers in Air Bah continually call attention to economic changes, difficulties in external relationships of production, and the misconduct of their fellow villagers, yet they prove utterly ineffectual in regulating the behaviour of self-aggrandizers. This lack of resistance to developing inequality directly contradicts the notion of counterdominance among egalitarian hunter-gatherers, suggesting that our notion of egalitarianism in small-scale societies needs to be re-evaluated. The alternative explanation proposed in the final chapter of this book will have important consequences not only for understanding the sociality of mobile hunter-gatherers, but also for theories of developing inequality and social complexity. Yet, before discussing the factors that pave the way to inequality in post-resettlement Air Bah, we have to clarify some points about Lanoh cultural identity: specifically, whether pre-resettlement Lanoh could in fact be classified as hunter-gatherers with an immediate-return system of production.

2 Interethnic Trade and the Social Organization of Pre-resettlement Lanoh

In the previous chapter I suggested that, in spite of their ethnohistorical affiliation with the Senoi, anthropologists have always considered Lanoh to be members of the larger Semang culture group (Schebesta 1929; Evans 1937; Carey 1976). Nonetheless, in light of indications that they might have become sedentary or semi-sedentary farmers since the turn of the twentieth century (Benjamin 1980: 31; see also Endicott 1999a),[1] the claim that pre-resettlement Lanoh social organization resembled that of hunter-gatherers with an immediate-return system of production requires further elaboration. Lanoh farming is compatible with current anthropological perceptions of hunter-gatherers' subsistence. As part of recent debates about the authenticity and cultural identity of contemporary hunter-gatherers (e.g., Schrire 1984: 18; Headland and Reid 1989: 51; Bailey et al. 1989), anthropologists have come to question the subsistence-based, ecological definitions of these peoples. Postmodern approaches have started to emphasize variety in hunter-gatherer economies (Headland 1986; Guenther 1986; Ellen 1988; Bird-David 1990; Layton et al. 1991; Guddemi 1992; Kelly 1995). As a result researchers have come to label fluctuations between farming and foraging with annual or even longer periodicity as 'mixed economies' or 'experimentation.' In recent years these labels have become widespread in describing the economy of foragers and post-foragers who simultaneously engage in hunting, gathering, and food production (Ellen 1988; Griffin 1989; Bird-David 1990; Layton et al. 1991; Guddemi 1992; Kelly 1995).

Peter Bogucki notes that 'it is entirely possible for societies at this boundary between foraging and farming to slide back and forth from one strategy to another' (1999: 202). Archaeological, historical, and ethnographic evidence seem to support this view. Mathias Guenther (1986)

Figure 2.1 Young Lanoh men in temporary forest camp.

has demonstrated historical evidence of occupational variety among hunter-gatherers. Evidence also indicates that, apart from South American groups, hunter-gatherers of Southeast Asia like the Punan and Kubu were farmers before turning to hunting and gathering (Bellwood 1985: 133 and 1999; Headland 1986; Kelly 1995; Lee 1999). In addition, several contemporary hunter-gatherers have also been observed to farm occasionally (Headland 1986; Ellen 1988; Bird-David 1990; Layton et al. 1991; Guddemi 1992; Kelly 1995; Lee 1999). These shifts between different modes of subsistence are often interpreted in the anthropological literature as part of a general 'opportunistic' strategy. Marcus Griffin, for instance, suggests that the Agta, 'living adjacent to agriculturalists, actually are opportunists, who make use of the subsistence strategy that best suits the conditions of the moment' (1984, in Bogucki 1999: 202). Kirk Endicott posits that the characteristic opportunism of foragers' economic practices in Peninsular Malaysia is a product of the encroachment of more populous and powerful neighbours (1974: 93). Going a step further, James Eder (1988) proposes that a mix of foraging and food production is a mode of subsistence in its own right. As a result of this emphasis on opportunism and variation in hunter-gatherer subsistence, several scholars have concluded that 'there is no hard-and-fast division between gatherer-hunter and small-scale farmer' (Bender 1990: 252).[2]

However plausible this reasoning may sound, it neglects to take into account the context of interethnic trade and its impact on the ability of hunter-gatherers to farm. An analysis into the effect of trade on hunter-gatherers' social organization and interpersonal, intragroup relationships will provide a more accurate view of the history of these peoples and the changes they currently face. In Peninsular Malaysia all indigenous groups, including horticulturists and agriculturists, have participated in trade in forest products to a certain extent (Dunn 1975), yet none of these groups have developed such close symbiotic relationships with Malay villagers as the Semang. Individualistic trade with Malays has led to organizational changes affecting the subsistence of these hunter-gatherer collectors, including the pre-resettlement Lanoh. In spite of their ethnohistorical ties with the Senoi, once they came to occupy the Semang economic niche, they are more likely to have developed patterns of organization that hindered their practice of swidden farming.

Ethnic Affiliation with the Senoi

In a series of papers, Geoffrey Benjamin (1980, 1985a, 1986b) explores the development and characteristics of the divisions of indigenous cultures of the Malay Peninsula. Combining archaeological, ethnological, and linguistic evidence, Benjamin deals with the emergence of the three distinct cultural patterns, Semang, Senoi, and Malay, and their variations.[3] He has argued that cultures not falling clearly into any of the three categories play an important role in defining the boundaries between them. Lanoh are one of these 'mixed' cultures which, located at the south-north division line of the peninsula, demonstrate heterogeneous values (Benjamin 1986b).[4] According to Benjamin, their way of life has been defined by three major influences: 'In northern Perak, the Lanoh are greatly influenced by the other, foraging, Semang (their closest genetic relatives), the horticulturist Temiars (their closest linguistic relatives), and the peasant Malays (their closest economic partners)' (1980: 8). It is important to record these cultural elements from a formalist perspective in order to understand the interactions between peninsular cultural patterns. However, it is even more significant to investigate them from a functional perspective to find out how these organizational patterns have affected indigenous ways of life. With Lanoh in particular, this involves examining the extent to which their earlier affiliation with the Senoi has impacted their culture and their ability to operate as Semang hunter-gatherers. Through this focus we may gain further insights into the organizational requirements of a Semang way of life. Although several attributes of Lanoh cultural prac- tices point to an earlier link with the Senoi and suggest that they prob- ably adapted to the collector lifestyle later than many other Semang groups did, there are also indications that once they started to live like the Semang, they adjusted their way of life accordingly.

The first, and perhaps most important, sign of the Lanoh relationship with the Senoi is their linguistic affiliation. The majority of indigenous languages of the Malay Peninsula belong to the Mon-Khmer branch of the Austroasiatic stock.[5] While several Semang are speakers of the Northern Aslian branch of Austroasiatic languages, Lanoh, as well as Senoi Temiar and Semai, are speakers of the Central Aslian branch of the same language family (Schebesta 1929; Evans 1937; Carey 1976; Benjamin 1980).[6] This almost certainly indicates a close relationship in the past between Lanoh and Senoi, especially Temiar.[7] In interpret- ing this relationship, anthropologists concur that the ethnic origins of Lanoh are uncertain. H.D. (Pat) Noone proposes that Lanoh might have originated from a formerly widespread population with greater dialectical diversity (1936: 52, in Benjamin 1980: 32). Benjamin is more specific and suggests that 'the proto-Lanoh speakers hived off from the farming proto-Temiars some 2000 years ago to become foragers in less densely settled areas, but originally connected to Temiar by a dialect- chain which has since almost disappeared' (1980: 32).[8]

In social relationships the affiliation of Lanoh with Senoi translates into a mix of Senoi and Semang traits. Lanoh kinship is closer to the Senoi type, with less restrictive avoidance rules (Benjamin 1980: 8).[9] Similar to Senoi, but unlike Semang, they allow joking, even marriage, between a man and his sister-in-law. Consequently, while Semang like Jahai comment on the 'lax' Lanoh intergender relationships (Schebesta 1929), Temiar in Air Bah often note how 'harsh' Lanoh avoidance rules were.

Semang and Lanoh relationships are also dissimilar in terms of how close adult siblings are to each other.[10] According to Kirk Endi- cott (1988), as well as Benjamin (1980), the conjugal family is the only consistent unit among the Semang. Although Benjamin (1980: 12–13) suggests that the preferred foster parent among Semang tends to be an older sibling rather than someone from the parents' generation, he also suggests that these sibling relations dissolve as soon as possible, since the only reliable basis for support among the Semang derives from the conjugal family. This is, however, hardly the case with Lanoh. They are extremely proud of their ability to camp in the forest in nuclear family units, and as we will see, they interpret this ability as 'bravery,' contrasting it with the Temiar's inability and unwillingness to stay in the forest in such small units. Nonetheless, sibling ties are stronger among Lanoh than those of other Semang, and the strength of these ties extends into adulthood. In the past, it was quite common for pairs of brothers to marry pairs of sisters, and the resulting couples often formed strong cooperative units that travelled, lived, and worked together, often for extended periods of time. Even today, both opposite-sex and same-sex siblingships tend to be strong in Air Bah. Brothers act as the protectors of their sisters, go out of their way to help them financially, provide moral support against their husbands, perform errands, and if no male escort is available, accompany them when travelling between villages.

Apart from linguistic affiliation and social relations, a third difference between Lanoh and other Semang relates to their belief system. Beliefs about Karei the thunder god are widespread among the hunter-gatherers of the peninsula (Schebesta 1929; Evans 1937; Needham 1964; Robarchek and Dentan 1987; Gomes 2007), and similar beliefs have been recorded in the Andaman Islands and among the Penan of Borneo (Cooper 1940; Needham 1964). Lanoh beliefs focus less on Karei and more on *ya?*, a mythical grandmother who is often identified with the sun.[11] Lanoh ritual practices are also distinct from those of other Semang. For instance, Lanoh not only perform the Semang 'blood throwing ritual,' but equally often they collect and burn hair when taboos are violated to appease Karei.[12]

Finally, the Senoi affiliation of Lanoh is also reinforced by ethnic groupings which, it has been suggested, are more pronounced among them than among other Semang (Benjamin 1980). Indeed, at different times, travellers and researchers have elicited names for several subcategories, such as *koba?, jinjeŋ, məndərəy, lepey,* and *jeram*, from Lanoh informants (Wilkinson 1926; Schebesta 1929; Evans 1937; Benjamin, personal communication). Yet, while most Lanoh, when asked, could readily name at least a few of these categories, it is difficult to find two Lanoh who would divulge the same set. Recollections of these dialect groups are uncertain and idiosyncratic, and both anthropologists and indigenous sources disagree about their number, geographical distribution, and significance.[13]

As a result of this inconsistency in recollection, subdivisions have become one of the most debated facets of Lanoh cultural identity. The ambiguity that surrounds them indicates that even if these subdivisions once had implications for social organization or group identity, they no longer fulfil these functions.[14] Evidently, Lanoh stopped maintaining these boundaries because they no longer served them in their new life circumstances. As a result of the fluidity introduced into their social organization, these boundaries have become increasingly permeable, lost nearly all of their meaning, and as with the dialect groups of Batek, no longer 'hold constant over time' (Lye 2005: xx; also see K.M. Endicott 1997). [15] This short review of Lanoh social relations and cultural practices indicates that, while pre-resettlement Lanoh differed from other Semang in several respects, they were similar to the Semang in one important way: they chose forest collecting as the focus of their economic activities. This fact has required certain organizational adjustments that likely placed limitations on their ability to farm efficiently.

The 'Mixed' Economy of Semang

The 'mixed' economy perspective of hunter-gatherers' activities emphasizes flexibility and variation; it also encourages researchers to neglect indications that some activities may be more important than others. Thus, further inquiry into the relative significance of the subsistence and commercial activities of hunter-gatherers will lead to a better understanding of the limitations that mobile foragers face when participating in 'delayed-return' activities. An example of this is the participation of Semang in farming. On the surface, Semang in Malaysia, who hunt, gather, collect forest products for sale, and engage in occasional small-scale farming, could be considered to be adherents to a 'mixed' economy.[16] However, certain characteristics of Semang farming suggest that it clashes with priorities in their lives and the organizational requirements that underpin them.

Early researchers of peninsular hunter-gatherers have documented that pre-resettlement Lanoh, like other Semang, participated in a variety of economic activities (Schebesta 1929; Evans 1914, 1924, 1927a, 1927b, 1937; Williams-Hunt 1954–55). They fished, gathered vegetables, hunted (primarily smaller animals such as squirrels, birds, and monkeys, but also wild boar and monitor lizards), and collected minor and major forest products for trade (Dunn 1975: 87). These products included rattan, *gaharu* (*Aquilaria spp.*, eaglewood, aloewood, or agarwood), timber, and tin. In addition, Lanoh supplied Malay and Chinese villagers with building material, such as *atap* (*Nipa fruticans*, used for thatching), wood, rattan, and indigenous rubber such as *gutta perca*

(*Dichopsis gutta*) and *jelutong* (*Dyera costulata*). Minor forest products that Lanoh sold or exchanged further included medicinal herbs, resin, honey, charms and aphrodisiacs, fruits, *petai* (*Parkia binladulosa, Parkia speciosa*),[17] and occasionally meat from the jungle. Finally, like other Semang, pre-resettlement Lanoh also engaged in small-scale intermittent farming of hill paddy and tapioca.

The extent of Lanoh farming depended on a number of factors, including the site with which a family commonly associated. In the past, Lanoh frequented several major sites, and individual families tended to affiliate more with certain sites than with others. Some of the main villages and campsites, Gluk, Malau, Sumpitan, Lawin, Piah, and Air Bah, were associated with hunting, others with tin mining, rattan collecting, or farming. The interview excerpt below illuminates aspects of this specialization:

Oh yes, everybody was looking for tin; Malays, Chinese, and of course Asli too, but not the people here. The Asli gang that worked with me was from Lawin. It was the Lawin gang that'd look for tin, our *puak* [clan, tribe, group, in Malay]: Musa, Musa's father. The people here [South of Kenering] were not good at that. The people here were good at working rattan, they were good at making *atap* [roof sheets, in Malay], and wood for making houses, and rattan used as ropes to tie things together. The Chinese people were buying a lot of that. People here were good at gathering firewood to be sold. They would cut it into small pieces, tie it up, carry it on their heads, go to the *kampung* and exchange for other things. The people from the village down there would give rice, fish, salt. That's what the people here were good at before. Tin, they never knew. Only our gang from Lawin knew how to look for tin.

The second factor determining Lanoh involvement in farming was ethnic affiliation. Since the Perak Valley was a meeting point of cultures and lifestyles, pre-resettlement Lanoh came to represent a variety of life ways, depending on whether they associated more with Senoi or with other Semang. East and south of the Lanoh area was home to the Senoi Temiar and Semai, while to the north were forest collectors such as Jahai, Kensiu, and Kintak. As Evans (1937: 310–13) points out, in the early twentieth century, boundaries between Senoi and Semang type cultures were fluid, especially at contact areas. Also, as testimony to their fluid social organization, Semang camps often consisted of individuals of varied ethnic and linguistic background.[18] The following excerpt from my fieldnotes recording the history of the Ijok community underlines this point:

> Kintak Bong now are in Baling and Kelian Intan. They were originally from Ijok. However, Ijok was not their traditional area either. They were sojourners. Ijok's original inhabitants were the *mandaray* Lanoh. *Sama? kiyen* were Lanoh who are now in Bukit Sapi. They used to be in Ijok too. From Ijok, the *kinta?* went to Baling, the *mandaray* to Ulu Grik and the *kiyen* to Bt. Sapi. There is no Orang Asli in Ijok now. (The abandonement of Ijok may have been the result of the Emergency relocation or intrusion by Malays.) The *kinta? boŋ* were the same as *kɛnsiw*. The community in Ijok was a troubled community. The *kinta? boŋ* were quarrelling with the others a lot. So they were told to go away. Ijok is Lanoh territory. The *kɛnsiw* are allowed to stay to live among Lanoh if they are nice [*ba?ɛt*]. These people like to play black magic. That is why they are bad. If they are nice, they are allowed to stay. They also married Lanoh and stayed if they were nice. Otherwise, they were chased away [M. *halau*]. Another informant added the following: In Ijok, there was a *kɛnsiw* group known as *mani? kayan*. They were staying at the Upper part of Gunung Ijok. The lower part of Gunung Ijok was occupied by Lanoh *mandaray*. The *kɛnsiw* part of Ijok mixed with some *kinta?* people. These three groups knew each other, but the *mandaray* did not like the other two. When the three groups left Ijok, the *mandaray* went to Ulu Grik, the mixed *kɛnsiw* and *kinta?* went to Baling and other areas.

It is also likely that pre-resettlement Lanoh emphasized their affiliation with the Senoi ideologically. The Lanoh that R.J. Wilkinson encountered denied that they were Semang, saying: 'We are not Semang ... we are Sakai of the swamps; if you want Semang you will find them on the hills behind us' (1910: 9). Today, Lanoh often look down on other Semang because of their 'Negrito' characteristics. In the following remark on the 'Negrito' appearance, a man in Air Bah distances himself from other Semang:

> I stayed in Baling for five months. I had a woman there too, but the women there don't have long hair like here. Their hair is like that of Negros, like the Negros on TV. That's why I didn't want to marry them. Their bodies are not like ours either. It's black.

Nonetheless, there is evidence that, in spite of this ideological bias towards Senoi identity, pre-resettlement Lanoh often intermarried with other Semang (Evans 1937: 41, 52, 96). As indicated earlier, past researchers often noted that Lanoh were not only culturally but also genetically (in terms of appearance) related to Semang (Evans 1937; Benjamin 1980, 1985a, 1985b, 1985c, 2003).[19] Even today, when the number of Lanoh-Semang marriages has declined, there are still people in Air Bah whose fathers were Jahai Semang.

It is likely that Lanoh who intermixed with Senoi Temiar adjusted their lifestyle and practised farming to a greater extent, while those who associated themselves with Semang adopted the lifestyle of mobile collectors. In the early twentieth century Father Paul Schebesta encountered both types of Lanoh. He describes a group at the Tanoi River living like Temiar. According to his records, this group was 'much under the influence of the Ple [mixed Semang-Temiar] [and] ... had a splendid hubi [tuber] plantation and lived in a pile hut' (1929: 63, 132).[20] At the same time, he also observed a mixed Lanoh-Jahai camp with a typically Semang character. These Lanoh were also more likely to sacrifice the extent and efficiency of their farming to competing activities, as are other Semang.

The first noteworthy aspect of Semang farming is that it is quite obviously not a priority in the life of these collectors. It is sporadic, occasional, and on a smaller scale than farming by Senoi, either Temiar or Semai. Semang do not farm regularly, nor is everyone in any given group equally involved in the activity. Second, Semang do not strive nor care very much for efficiency in farming. Lye Tuck-Po (personal communication) notes that Batek, for instance, would plant fast-growing crops and abandon their fields soon after planting, instead of 'sitting around, watching it grow.'[21] Similarly, Kirk Endicott suggests that, although Batek farm occasionally, their gardens are abandoned and their yields are 'meager' (1999b: 300). Other researchers have noted a similar Semang-like lack of interest in farming elsewhere, for example, among the Meniq hunter-gatherers of southern Thailand (Porath 2001: 125),[22] and among the Kensiu, a group of northern hunter-gatherers in Kedah, Malaysia (Nagata, personal communication). Evans maintains that, in spite of their periodical farming, forest collecting remains the Semang's first priority. He notes that 'in reality the Negrito is by nature a hunter, root digger (the latter being woman's work) and fruit gatherer and, though he practices agriculture to some extent in various parts of the country, he still retains his more primitive methods of food-getting, which, indeed, afford his main source of supply' (1937: 58).

The limitations on Lanoh farming in the past were similar to those among other Semang. Wilkinson cites District Officer Berkeley who described farming by Lanoh ('Sakai Jeram') as follows: 'They plant rice, bananas, and all sorts of things, but never plant enough, and are always in a state of hunger and want' (1910: 11). Like other Semang, pre-resettlement Lanoh also frequently abandoned their crops to pursue alternative opportunities. People in Air Bah recounted:

> Lanoh, before our grandfathers' time, didn't keep very much. They planted, took whatever they could and left the rest on the field.[23]

The Semang's apparent 'failure' to farm efficiently has invited comments from various parties, rarely as charitable as to explain these characteristics of Semang farming in terms of 'priorities.' Some anthropologists, such as Headland (1986, 1987), favour restrictive exogenous factors, such as agriculturalist neighbours that may prevent hunter-gatherers from becoming farmers.[24] Neighbouring farmers, for their part, tend to blame the 'bad attitude' of hunter-gatherers for their conspicuous failure at farming. Evans writes:

> In certain parts of the country ... the Negritos do make clearings and plant hill rice and other crops. Some Negritos ... at Ijok, Selama, Perak ... had no ground under cultivation, but one man said that he intended opening a small clearing. The local Malays spoke very scornfully of the Negritos' agricultural efforts, saying that they were too lazy to undertake the troublesome business of burning the felled jungle, and that when occasionally they did overcome their natural indolence and plant a little rice, they would probably leave the locality just before it became ripe, and everything would be eaten by birds and monkeys. (1937: 60–1)

A Temiar who left his native village, Tanjung Rambutan, to marry in Air Bah, is similarly scornful and judgmental of Lanoh farming efforts. In the following passage, he relates the similarities and differences between Temiar and Lanoh lifestyles as he experienced them when he first arrived in Air Bah twenty-five years earlier:

> When I arrived in this village, their *deŋ lɛʔlɔy* [Lanoh lean-to shelter] was smaller, not like ours. At that time, people here worked the rattan and they also made *atap* roof for sale. They didn't have rubber at the time when I came. They had land, a little bit of land, but not much because these peo-

ple kept moving from place to place, to Malau, here and there, Sumpitan, Piah. That is the problem. Over there [in Tanjung Rambutan], that didn't happen. We stayed at one place. We opened up land, decided which jungle we wanted to clear, then cleaned, burned, planted paddy, durian, rubber. There we decided where we wanted to clear land the following year, which hill ... Then we went and cleared it. That's how it is there. So there [the land] gets bigger and bigger. That's the way.

Apart from the obstacles presented by neighbouring farmers and from the foragers' own attitudes, researchers have cited organization as a factor when discussing the limitations of hunter-gatherer farming (Ten Raa 1986; Woodburn 1988; Peterson 1991). Food domestication requires not only a shift of emphasis from natural to cultivated resources, but also of organizational principles and practices, such as commitment, cooperation, and top-down organization of production. These conditions are often contrary to the mobility, flexibility, opportunism, and immediacy of mobile hunter-gatherers (Benjamin 1973; Endicott and Bellwood 1991; Dentan 1991; Sellato 1994). With this in mind, the next two sections of this chapter will examine the social organization of pre-resettlement Lanoh and its effect on their ability to farm efficiently.

Trade, Farming, and Social Integration

As discussed in Chapter 1, in anthropological literature 'immediate-return' characteristics (such as individualism, opportunism, and social flexibility) are commonly associated with a hunter-gatherer way of life (Woodburn 1982; Bird-David 1987; Gardner 1991; Burch 1994; Ingold 1999). Lately, revisionist anthropologists have also suggested that the social organization of contemporary hunter-gatherers is a consequence of forms of interethnic contact, trade most notable among them (Schrire 1984: 18; Bailey et al. 1989; Headland and Reid 1989). Unfortunately, there have been few focused inquiries into the relationship between hunter-gatherers' social organization and the types of trade most contemporary hunter-gatherers engage in. Such inquiries would result in a better understanding of the relationship between hunter-gatherers' subsistence, trade activities, and social organization. This, in turn, would result in a more realistic model of hunter-gatherers' ecology, one that also incorporates their social relations.[25] It appears that among pre-resettlement Lanoh these 'immediate-return' characteristics might have been especially beneficial in pursuing trade in forest products while

undermining social organization in subsistence activities. These findings counter essentialist ecological models of hunter-gatherers' social
relationships.

Hunting and Social Organization

It is tempting to attribute hunter-gatherer social organization to hunting
and the distribution of the natural resources that these groups exploit
(Myers 1986; Casimir 1992; Kelly 1995). Mithen (1990), for instance,
suggests that individual information gathering and individual experience among hunter-gatherers are more valuable than a standard body
of transmitted knowledge because hunter-gatherers' natural environments are more variable and uncertain than those of food producers. In
the Malaysian context, it has similarly been posited that Semang social
organization has been shaped by the needs and challenges of securing subsistence resources. Bulbeck (2003), conceding that agricultural
expansion and trade may have affected foraging strategies during the
late Holocene, ultimately attributes the atomization of Semang society
to a shift from terrestrial to arboreal game.[26] He suggests that between
4000 and 3000 BP 'hunting in coordinated groups and ambushing the
relatively dangerous ungulates apparently gave way to very small
hunting parties less likely to disturb the ever-watchful arboreal prey'
(ibid.: 148). This assumption, shared by other researchers, has injected
inconsistency into the interpretation of Orang Asli cultural patterns.
Benjamin, for example, inexplicably attributes the social organization
of Malays to trade, while that of the Semang, who are equally predisposed to trading, to natural resources:[27]

> Generally, the foraging Semang meet with *no* notable degree of concentra-
> tion in plant and animal resources in the forest depths (although some
> resources are ecotonally concentrated ...). Semang-type society thus needs
> to maintain a wide network of relations, for localized social concentration
> would usually be ill adapted to their normally foraging mode of subsist-
> ence. In Malay-type societies farming has throughout most of their his-
> tory usually been subsidiary to trading and forest collecting as the favored
> activities, and Malay trading relations have usually been concentrated
> rather than diffused, primarily at coastal ports or at upstream entrepot
> points ... This pattern of 'resource'-concentration has implied a fair degree
> of competition between different groups; so, in a sense, the fewer intra-

societal links and the more extrasocietal links there have been, the better. (1985a: 230, original emphasis)

Yet, despite this link between resource distribution and the individualism of rainforest collectors, there is *nothing* inherent in hunting that necessitates a Semang-type social organization. The Senoi, who are horticulturists, not only continue to hunt, they even pursue game that the Semang find too prohibitive. While Semang hunters typically focus on small arboreal game and avoid large prey (Karen Endicott 1979; Kirk Endicott 1984, in Bulbeck 2003), Senoi Temiar, who hunt more cooperatively and communally, have been known to bring down game as large as an elephant.[28] Lanoh hunting corresponds to this Semang pattern: although they employed a range of methods in hunting, including traps, spears, and catapults, they refrained from pursuing rhinoceros, bears, or elephants. Lanoh even consider the elephant to be their guardian (*Orang Tua*), the 'Old Man' of the forest – to disturb or provoke one is a serious offence.

If subsistence activity is inadequate to explain immediate-return characteristics among rainforest hunter-gatherers, we should look to interethnic trade as a factor. The following discussion of the relationship between trade and hunter-gatherer social organization will undertake to reveal the significant limitations and constraints that trade places on hunter-gatherer subsistence activities – both hunting *and* farming.

Trade and Social Organization

Opportunism and individual autonomy are prevailing aspects of mobile hunter-gatherers' social organization, and both have been observed in different contexts, in relation to different types of activities (Benjamin 1973; Endicott and Bellwood 1991; Dentan 1991; Sellato 1994). Nonetheless, it has been rarely asked whether these attributes are associated with any particular activity more than with others. This question is made especially significant by assumptions about the social organization of first human hunter-gatherer groups, which are still often envisioned as similar to those of contemporary mobile hunter-gatherers, those in contact with various agriculturist and pastoralist peoples. If it is the case that the opportunism and individual autonomy of these contemporary hunter-gatherers is more significant for trade than for hunting, then these assumptions about the organization of first hunter-gatherer bands can no longer be uncritically upheld by evolutionary anthropologists. It would seem that while pre-resettlement Lanoh were opportunistic and individualistic in all their pursuits, these organiza-tional strategies were key to their trade with Malays. Unlike commer-cial trade today, village trade in the past was sporadic, intermittent, and largely unpredictable and, as such, did not benefit from the cooperation of indigenous collectors.

Several researchers have pointed out that mobile hunter-gatherers' procurement strategies do not preclude 'asset consciousness' or the long-term management of resources (Dunn 1975; Feit 1992; Sellato 1994). Lanoh in particular demonstrate a pragmatic concern with the long-term management of forest resources. They would consciously ensure the sustainability of resources when setting traps, hiding and later recovering forest resources, preserving immature plants for future extraction, and repeatedly returning to fallen trees to obtain different grades of *gaharu* (fragrant agarwood). Nonetheless, as with other rain-forest hunter-gatherers (Bird-David 1994; Benjamin 1973; Endicott and Bellwood 1991; Dentan 1991; Sellato 1994; Ingold 1999), they consist-ently display an opportunistic openness to future plans, which could be interpreted as a deliberate strategy to stay non-committal and flex-ible. Often, when answering inquiries about the future, people in Air Bah use the Malay word *peluang* (possibility, chance, or opportunity) to express this strategic openness, such as in 'we'll see the opportunity … whenever opportunity arises, we'll take it.' The following recounting of an incident indicates that in forest collecting, it often pays to keep one's options open:[29]

> Once I went alone. I went to a place near Air Kala. I sat down in the jungle and I put my blowpipe at my side. Then I heard this growl. I'm not sure what it was, perhaps a tiger, but I had time to pick up a tortoise and I ran. I had stepped on it, so I picked it up and ran.

Observing a Lanoh funeral in the 1950s, P.D.R. Williams-Hunt recorded a similar display of 'opportunism':

> The procession consisted entirely of men – eighteen in all – and I was told that women never go to an interment even when a husband or child is concerned, since 'knowing the deceased, they would be too sad.'[30] As the party left the camp there was a loud wailing from the women which last-ed, at the most, two minutes – unless it was taken up again when we were

out of earshot. The interment party adopted no particular order of march, and was anything but a solemn procession; loud laughs greeted the stumbles of the bearers as they caught their feet in the undergrowth, or slipped on rocks ... The site chosen for the interment was in a patch of secondary jungle on a steep hillside near to some Malay rubber plantations and about two miles away from the camp ... The party took it in turns to dig, although at one stage work was interrupted when a large lizard appeared and most of the diggers rushed off to catch it. (1954–55: 66–7)

Although Lanoh may be acting opportunistically in most situations, in pre-resettlement times, village trade with Malays particularly rewarded frequent mobility, individualism, and behavioural flexibility. This is because collectors who were able to change their plans at a moment's notice benefited most from ad hoc, irregular requests by Malay villagers for medicine, building materials, fragrant wood, or honey. The fieldnote excerpt below shows how requests for forest resources prompt flexible responses by Lanoh collectors:

Some of the villagers were taking a break when a Chinese man from Air Kala appeared. He told the men that he wanted to buy frogs. He offered RM 12 per kg, regardless of size, and he wanted as many as they can get. Bulat, whose brother, Salim, has just arrived from Tawai to discuss family problems and who has just woken up from a nap, rushed back to his house to get his frog collecting kit. These are: big flashlight, a scoop net, packsack, *parang* (machete-like long instrument), tobacco. He rushed out of his house, just as Salim arrived with his bag. Rushing past Salim, Bulat told him, 'I'm going with Atan for frogs.' After he left, Salim complained, 'He asked me to come here to discuss family matters and he knows I am going back to Tawai tomorrow and he is going for frogs. I have not even eaten yet.' Jantan, too, changed his plans of the day and went off to look for frogs. He had promised to work with me on language tonight, but now he is gone. Altogether, six men left hurriedly to look for frogs. They went on their separate ways in pairs.[31]

Collecting such minor products further encourages the dispersal of these hunter-collectors and discourages cooperation.

This seems to contradict the contention of many researchers that information sharing is vital for hunters and gatherers (Smith 1988: 230–2; Cashdan 1990). Hugh Brody (2000: 192–3) suggests that, unlike 'societies where social ambitions and personal rivalries are systemic,' hunter-gatherers share information as they share food, because secrecy and deception would jeopardize cooperation and place them at risk. However, as we have seen, while Lanoh would certainly benefit from cooperation in hunting, it would undoubtedly have hindered them in collecting for trade. Not only were demands for forest products irregular, but several items collected by the Semang, such as *gaharu* (fragrant agarwood), or various herbs used in traditional medicine or ritual, were prestige and luxury goods, the value of which depended on their scarcity (Andaya and Andaya 1982). Such products could not be collected or extracted in large quantity. On the contrary, collecting scarce products for intermittent requests may have resulted in competition between collectors, fostering individualism and secrecy among them.

There is some contradiction in Lanoh attitudes towards companionship. On the one hand, Lanoh deeply fear loneliness and being left alone. On the other hand, as suggested earlier, they are proud of their ability to live in small units. Like hunter-gatherers elsewhere (see, e.g., Barnard 1999), Lanoh stress the importance of always going to the forest in groups consisting of an even number of people. They consider loneliness to be the most likely cause of suicide and believe that being lonely makes one susceptible to illness and, ultimately, to death. People in Air Bah said:

> When we are very lonely, our dead family members' *roway* [soul] will come and say, 'oh, you'd better come with us.' [Then] our *roway* leaves and we die.

This fear of loneliness among Lanoh may in fact be a clear indication of the atomization of their social relations. Pre-resettlement Lanoh shared with other Semang a tendency for living in small residential groups. People in Air Bah explained:

> Lanoh of those days were very good hunters and were also brave. They were not like the Temiar in those days. Temiar would go into the jungle in large groups, but the Lanoh of my grandfather's time could go into the jungle with just one family. [A group] at that time would only need to contain one adult male, one half-adult male (*setengah budak*) and two women. Others could be children. With this composition, they could go anywhere in the jungle for a long time.

Paradoxically, in spite of their concern with loneliness, Lanoh do not seem to believe that there is safety in numbers. Instead, in case of emergency, they break up into as many small units as possible. The interview excerpt below tells of their dispersion following the cholera outbreak of the mid-1960s:

> At that time, we all fled everywhere separately. We all broke up. I followed my father and we fled from the village to up there. People fled not in big groups, but in twos and threes, because you cannot flee in big groups. You cannot even talk about fleeing. You have to leave quietly. So I fled with my father and my brother quietly. Even so, we could not stay together … we all broke up. We stayed alone, or in two people like that. Two would go over there, two would go over here, that's how we were. After about three or four months, we would get together again. We met in Kuala Piah, because those from there would return there and others from another place would return to another place.

These hunter-gatherers were primarily focused with their individual well-being, with little concern for that of the group. Indeed, young Lanoh learn quickly that they are not likely to be able to count on anyone but themselves. The following account comes from a Lanoh man who, as a young boy, was left behind in the forest by his elders to fend for himself:

> Once I've almost had it. I was going for rattan near the Lawin River. There were many of us. Somebody shouted, 'Get away, get away!' I was alone then, all the others had gone. There was this rhinoceros as big as an elephant. At that time, I was small … There was this brother-in-law of mine from Malau. I thought he was brave. He had an axe with him. I thought an adult would let us kids go first (my friend, S., was there too), but he ran and left us instead. I was about 15 then.

Competition between individual collectors is particularly expressed in various rules and prohibitions against information sharing and cooperation. Although Lanoh recall having communal meetings and discussions (L. *mənuwaʔ*) in the past, these meetings were never held to discuss activity plans or decisions, but were instead occasions for people to relate their comings and goings or share their experiences. Lanoh believe that revealing plans is a taboo, the breaking of which would jeopardize one's endeavours. As a consequence, it was prudent and even expected to conceal one's intentions. The following excerpt reveals that to protect their intentions pre-resettlement Lanoh did not hesitate to mislead or deceive their group members. This excerpt recounts a family's escape from the village during the 1960s' epidemic:

> We didn't say that we were going to run, we just split. You cannot say that.
> Before running [away], we pretend that we were going fishing or we were
> going for a walk. You just bring the things you want to go with and you
> split (M. *lari*). The three of us left; my mother, my uncle, and I. We stayed
> there, away from the village. After about a month, we left for Sumpitan.
> Even then, we said, 'Oh let's take our *blaw* [blowpipe] and look for squir-
> rels' and we ran straight away. We brought fishing nets, we brought fish-
> ing traps, we got to a safe distance, we left our traps and nets and went
> straight to Sumpitan.

With such emphasis on concealing one's intentions from others, effective cooperation was likely difficult if not impossible.

It is difficult to surmise if these secrecy taboos are primarily important to hunting or to collecting for trade. To be sure, such secrecy taboos
are common among the indigenous peoples of Southeast Asia (see, e.g.,
Rousseau 1998), and they are often related to subsistence activities.
Evans, for instance, referring to Skeat and Blagden (1906 [1966], vol.
2.: 223), writes: 'A certain way of provoking the aggressiveness of the
tiger-folk is to follow after any member of the tribe who has started on a
shooting expedition in the jungle with his blowpipe, no matter whether
with the object of accompanying or recalling him' (1937: 229). Similar
taboos on information sharing in hunting also occur among Lanoh. On
one occasion, a man returned from a blowpipe trip to the forest, visibly
upset. He said he had been out since the morning, hoping to get at least
a squirrel, but the hunt was doomed when he met two other men from
the village who asked questions about the purpose of his outing.

Rules and regulations ensuring secrecy also frequently manifest
themselves in the context of forest collecting. In the following account,
people explain the repercussions of violating secrecy taboos in collecting jungle products:

> One of these taboos is that a person going into the jungle for *gaharu*
> [aloe's wood] should not announce his intention, nor could he be asked
> by anyone else. People should not know that one is intending to look
> for *gaharu*. If he was asked where he was going, his answer should be
> evasive, for instance, 'Oh, I'm just looking for fruits.' If a question is

very close, for example, someone asks, 'Are you going to look for wood today,' the taboo is broken even if he answers, 'No.' He should abandon looking for *gaharu* and do something else. As well, one cannot pass a person returning from the same activity that one is planning to carry out. For instance, if we are going to look for frogs and on our way out we meet a person returning from collecting frogs, we will not be able to get any frogs this time.

In the context of forest collecting, these secrecy taboos serve to regulate the collection of forest products by ensuring that supply does not exceed demand. Secrecy, individualism, and the dispersal of collectors guarantee that these trade items retain their value, and by extension, the value of the collector himself.[32] Secrecy taboos also affect social organization, preventing aggregation and limiting the size of collecting parties, as can be discerned from the following excerpt:

Leman came back from *gaharu* collecting. He abandoned the search for *gaharu*. He was upset. He had to return because a taboo was broken. The second night they were there, after just selecting places and trees to work on, Amat and Bintang arrived at their camp. They were loud at night, talking and said they wanted to join Leman's party. By saying that, they broke two taboos (L. *səlantap*). As a consequence, Leman decided it was not worth staying for *gaharu* because surely they would not find good *gaharu* and there might be bad luck, accident, etc. The two taboos (L. *səlantap*) broken are (1) joining a party unplanned; and (2) talking loudly at night as well as talking negatively. Amat and Bintang's arrival had not been planned, they had not been invited; Goh's party had no idea of their intention. So their intrusion was a major taboo broken, which could mean that they would not be able to find profitable *gaharu*. At the same time, Bintang and Amat, when they arrived, talked loudly. They commented negatively on their own efforts while they were at Air Boh.[33] They said they could not find wood, they were stalked by a tiger, it was not comfortable, and so they decided to come to Leman's place. So, with their negative attitudes and thoughts they symbolized a bad sign. The stay for Leman and his party would be taking a risk of some calamity, such as sickness or accident. So, Leman, his son, and Rosli abandoned *gaharu* collecting and returned to the village. Amat and Bintang remained, while Jantan, who was part of Amat and Bintang's party, had returned home from Air Boh earlier.

Thus, while secrecy taboos play a role both in hunting and in forest collecting, their effect may be more significant in collecting forest products for trade than in securing subsistence resources.

Lanoh emphasis on opportunism and individualism would have undoubtedly restrained group leadership and leaders' ability to organize and exploit the labour of others in the past. The excerpt below is an example of how mobility, flexibility, and frequent dispersal prevented permanent leadership:

> Lanoh a long time ago chose a *tok batin* [leader, headman] by consensus. If they stayed in a village together, one person, who was liked by everyone, who was good and fair, who was wise and strong was chosen as *batin*. This person would usually be the one who had helped other people. When people were sick, he would know some *jampi* [incantation]. If people did not have food, he would give them food. But sometimes, this [person] would not stay headman for a long time because people then moved a lot. When they moved and made another village or joined another group of people, there would be another headman or they would pick a new headman. If their old headman came with them, he might have remained headman. Sometimes, there were people who were very wise and respected and people would always like them and come for advice. In those days, there were, therefore, many headmen.

Pre-resettlement Lanoh seemed to have so many 'headmen' that nearly every adult man in Air Bah claimed that his father was one.

As a rule, leaders' power manifests in their influence on the decisions of others. Some of the most consequential decisions among hunter-gatherers are those that have to do with mobility; thus, communal moves are a testimony to a leader's authority. Geoffrey Benjamin notes that Temiar household clusters, defined as 'grouping[s] of two or more closely related conjugal families who live in adjoining sections of the house,' tend to move together (1979: 269–70).[34] Some authors believe that leaders are similarly capable of influencing mobility decisions among all hunter-gatherers. Boehm, referring to an account of !Kung by Richard B. Lee, writes that 'hunter-gatherers place considerable social pressure on dissenters when migration decisions are being made' (1999: 106). Contrary to these examples, however, Lanoh leaders seemed to have great difficulty in influencing people's decisions in pre-resettlement times. The next excerpt seems to confirm that Marshall Sahlins' description of a leader with limited authority – 'One word from him

and everyone does as he pleases' (1968: 21, in Benjamin 1968: 34) –
applied to Lanoh leaders as well:

> My grandfather was Goh Suli, the *penghulu* [headman]. He asked my
> father, my mother to move.
> (Q: did he ask the whole village to move?)
> He asked the whole village to move, but some people would stay longer,
> some people would go somewhere else. It was up to them.

Although the cognitive and behavioural characteristics of pre-resettlement Lanoh that I have discussed above were advantageous in fulfilling agriculturists' demands for forest products, they were serious
liabilities for activities requiring cooperation, coordination, long-term
planning, commitment, or a degree of sedentism. In other words, these
characteristics were detrimental to subsistence farming.

Farming and Social Organization

Benjamin (1980) suggests that given the common ancestry of Lanoh
and Temiar it is not surprising that Lanoh retained farming. This raises
the question of whether remnants of a more cohesive past organization
compensated at least to some degree for the impact of forest collecting
on Lanoh interpersonal relationships. We will see that Lanoh, indeed,
have made a number of concessions to facilitate successful swidden
farming. However, hard as they may have tried, the organizational
requirements of individualistic trade in the past seemed to have prevented them from farming effectively.

   Communal activities, such as religious or social events, compel people to act as a group and foster social integration. Lanoh have few such
celebrations, and with the exception of a feast held seven days after the
death of a person, all communal events relate to farming. From planting
to harvest, the paddy cycle is marked by a string of rituals and feasts.
The incantation ceremony before planting is followed by a small feast,
and the paddy harvest is similarly celebrated by a communal meal (M.
kenduri).[35] Just before harvest, a second incantation takes place to offer
gratitude to the guardian spirit of the paddy (L. *pənjagaʔ*).[36] During this
prayer, harvesting knives are collected and passed over incense (M.
kemeriyan) burned in a coconut bowl. The communal characteristic of
this incantation is underlined by an emphasis on the 'centre' (L. *kəloŋ*).

The ritual takes place in the 'middle of the middle field,' the significance of which continues throughout the cycle, as harvest commenc-
es from the same location. In addition, of the seven holes dug during
the ceremony, the middle one represents the spirit of the paddy, while
the surrounding six represent the guardian spirits. Both planning and
harvest must begin on the 'middle day of the week,' preferably in the
'middle of the month.'[37] A common fire must be lit in the 'middle of the
village.' Cooperation and the coordination of activities are stressed; for
the ceremony to be successful everyone must participate, otherwise the
spirits will be in conflict. The success of farming is further ensured by
the prohibition on any other type of work that could be undertaken by
men during planting.[38] In addition, it is strictly forbidden to consume,
trade, or exchange newly harvested rice for seven days following the
incantation. On the seventh day, again in the 'middle day of the week,'
yet another small feast takes place where people consume the harvested rice for the first time. Finally, at the end of harvest, a celebratory feast
completes the cycle, to which relatives and friends from far and wide
are invited.

Nonetheless, in spite of these rules and regulations, the organizational requirements of individualistic trade seem to have prevented
pre-resettlement Lanoh from farming effectively. Individualistic organization does not affect all subsistence activities similarly. When it comes
to hunting, for example, a lack of cooperation may limit the choices
available to Lanoh but not their overall success. Switching from larger
to smaller game allowed the ancestors of Semang to remain successful hunters in spite of their limited social integration. While hunting
big game benefits from cooperative strategies and stronger leadership,
smaller animals such as squirrels can easily be hunted even by individuals. In the case of farming activities, particularly in the absence of
complex technology, however, it is very likely that significant manpow-
er and cooperation are required for successful food production (Dentan
1968; Bah-Tony Williams-Hunt, personal communication). Benjamin is
one of the experts who suggest that 'there is a minimum of working
force below which it becomes inefficient to work the land' (1968: 30).

Discrepancies between the organizational requirements of efficient
farming and the organization of Semang farming are even more apparent when comparing the organization of Temiar and Lanoh farming.
One of the most important differences is in the strength of leadership
and in the degree of cooperation. The following complaints by a Temiar
man in Air Bah highlight these distinctions:

In my village, *gotong royong* [communal work] is easy. There is one head-man and two assistants. We over there … our *royong* is not like this. Dur-ing paddy-planting time, we would have a meeting to get people for the *royong* … the bachelors. Bachelor men, bachelor women, 'tomorrow whichever land is to be planted, you, the bachelors, all go and plant' and so we'd know that the first thing next morning is to do the headman's [land] … go to his field first. After him, whoever had a big land, we'd then go there. Like if we want to plant paddy, or anything, we see our headman's land … see if it's big. We help them … we help him, we help the three people. The *penghulu* [headman] of my old place, sometimes, he would plant ten acres. When we finish, we come back and then work on our own [land]. That's how we are, like that over there. All together, if we finish his land one day, that is finished. Next day, we go on our own, to our own field. The main thing is that we must *royong* the headman's land. That's the *adat* (custom, M.). If we are the *penghulu*, we can do what we like. That's the *adat* there. Over there, we clean the *penghulu*'s land for him, we plant, we help him because he is taking care of us. If anything happens to us, he is the one responsible. That's how it is there. We're used to help-ing each other. In the old village, everybody helped each other. You help your brothers and sisters.

These comments were corroborated by Lanoh recollections of the way they farmed in the past:

Whether we worked together or worked just as a nuclear family [L. *baka?*] … There was never much helping out between and within families. When I was young, not many people worked *royong*. Everyone did his own small land. People worked within their family.

Thus, it appears that instead of communal work, each nuclear family unit worked individually.[39]

In summary, when faced with the implications of organizational dis-crepancies between farming and collecting for trade, Semang, includ-ing Lanoh, seem to have willingly sacrificed their farming to pursue opportunities for commerce. This conclusion, yet again challenges essentialist conceptions of contemporary hunter-gatherers: although pre-resettlement Lanoh exhibited characteristics commonly associated with immediate-return hunter-gatherers, these seem to be primarily linked to trade, rather than to hunting or the distribution of natural resources. More than half a century ago Robert Murphy and Julian

Steward wrote about a 'reduction of the local level of integration' among hunter-gatherers who also participate in trade (1956: 335–6, in Headland 1986: 410–11). According to Peter Bellwood (1999: 286), Hoabinhian ancestors of Semang hunted large game, including rhinoceros, bovids, pigs, and deer. Similarly, as noted above, Bulbeck suggests that, although earlier hunter-gatherer sites in Peninsular Malaysia contain evidence of large prey species, such as elephant, bear, rhinoceros, and deer, as well as large carnivores, 'at around 4000 BP to 3000 BP ... a shift ... occurred from large terrestrial game to arboreal game' (2003: 148). This shift roughly coincided with the arrival of Austronesian-speaking populations into the region. This suggests that ancestors of the Semang switched from large game to arboreal prey either because they came to occupy a different ecological niche after the Malay expansion[40] or because their social organization, adjusted to trading with Malays, no longer allowed them to pursue larger and more dangerous terrestrial game. This further raises the possibility that Semang, including Lanoh, continue to hunt and make the diversification of their diet a priority in order to facilitate collecting for trade.

In the next chapter I hope to show that hunting carries great significance for Lanoh men. Nonetheless, whenever Lanoh speak of the relationship between subsistence hunting and commercial collecting, collecting is always considered to be a primary occupation, while hunting is seen to be a supplementary activity that supports collecting, something that one can do once in the forest 'anyway.'[41] The priority of collecting over hunting is often expressed in assertions such as:

> We hunt in small groups (two or three people). This we can continue at the same time we collect rattan, because, for rattan, we also break up into small groups.[42]

Apart from adjusting hunting to commerce, rather than vice versa, an emphasis on a diversified subsistence base also facilitates forest collecting for trade. People in Air Bah often joke that they eat everything except 'rocks, snakes, and tigers.'[43] The following fieldnote excerpt indicates that this willingness to eat whatever comes one's way ensures that collecting for trade is interrupted as little as possible:

> Bulat and Rahim found the road condition in Malau very bad, so they looked for *gaharu* instead and were lucky enough to find good [grade 'A'] *gaharu*. After this success, Bulat decided to focus on *gaharu*. This time, he

wanted to explore another area that is known for good *gaharu*, at Gunung Ijok, near Sumpitan ... This second trip attracted more interest than the first one among the men in Air Bah. Almost everyone wanted to be in his group. Several others organized separate groups. The trip to Ijok for *gaharu*, however, was a failure. Yet, it produced an unexpected result. Bulat met another rattan buyer who offered more attractive terms than Ah Kun. Bulat said the rattan there would be easy to bring to the nearby road because they would be working uphill and all they had to do is bring the rattan down one hill. At the same time, there were many old timber roads that were still in good condition. The conditions were also good in terms of food. There were a lot of monkeys and squirrels in the area. So many that Bulat's group managed to get a monkey by just using sticks and running after it. There were so many monkeys on a tree that they would throw rocks at them. The monkeys would run from tree to tree, and the one they got ran up a tree that did not have any tree nearby for it to jump to. The monkey was stoned until it ran down the tree trying to escape. They ran after the monkey and killed it with sticks. According to Bulat, although the rattan buyer would not give credit, because of the abundance of monkeys, they would not have any problem getting food. So Bulat planned another trip to Gunung Ijok for rattan collecting. This time he decided to bring his blowpipe.

This excerpt, illustrating how hunting opportunities are weighed when calculating an area's potential for forest collecting, shows that a willingness to eat 'anything' benefits those who concentrate on forest collecting for trade.

According to Benjamin (1980), the Semang way of life is the product of choice and, as such, is characterized by distinct strategies. As the preceding discussion indicates, since hunting is key to a lifestyle suited to interethnic trade, populations previously associated with farming, including the ancestors of present-day Lanoh, would have likely shifted to hunting once they found themselves in circumstances in which trade relations with neighbouring Malays proved favourable. Although this prioritization may also reflect increased commercialization, it raises the possibility that trade plays a far more important role in defining the cultural identities of rainforest collectors than hunting and gathering. This leads us back to Benjamin's (1985a) discussion of Malay and Semang cultural patterns. As mentioned earlier, Benjamin attributes the social organization of the Semang to natural resources, but that of Malays to trade. It is, however, equally possible that, like the

Malay pattern, the Semang pattern has developed in response to trade, albeit of a different kind.

The Malay cultural pattern is characterized by residential concentration and kin endogamy, while the Semang favour residential dispersal and kin exogamy (Benjamin 1985a). These differences, however, can be explained by contrasting the communal organization of farming and large-scale maritime trade among the Malays with the individualistic organization of small-scale village trade among the Semang. This difference in social integration notwithstanding, the Malay and Semang share an outer orientation, an emphasis on external ties at the expense of local context and internal relationships.[44] For Malays, this local context consists of neighbouring villages, but for individualist Semang, it is made up of their fellow group members. In the following section, I will continue to explore the implications of trade for the lives of pre-resettlement Lanoh. A lack of social integration considerably suggests that pre-resettlement Lanoh could not farm efficiently; nevertheless, the full extent of how trade may have affected Lanoh farming prior to resettlement can only be gauged by considering the impact of trade on Lanoh families.

Trade, Farming, and Mobility Patterns

As has been frequently noted, trade among rainforest hunters and gatherers is primarily associated with men (Dunn 1975: 80; Endicott 1992: 284).[45] We have relatively limited knowledge, however, of the way organizational requirements of interethnic trade affect other segments of these groups. Only by learning more about the impact of interethnic trade on women, children, and old people will we be able to understand the social organization of these collectors and the implications of trade for subsistence activities. Among pre-resettlement Lanoh, the sexual division of labour facilitated farming, but the travel requirements of trade were paramount, limiting the people's ability to farm efficiently.

Sexual Division of Labour in Farming

What does it mean that the ancestors of Lanoh 'entered the Semang niche,' and how did they reconcile their earlier way of life with their new lifestyle? We can begin to answer these questions by studying variations in the mobility patterns of pre-resettlement Lanoh. By examining the way Lanoh coped with men's frequent movements, we can determine the extent to which they had to adapt to successfully pursue a Semang way of life. It appears that male participation in forest collecting did not automatically transform Lanoh cultural practices. On the contrary, pre-resettlement Lanoh evidently succeeded in resolving the tension between male mobility and the sedentism required for swidden farming.

On the surface, Lanoh men's engagement in small-scale village trade need not have entirely excluded farming because the sexual division of labour allowed them to farm and collect simultaneously. In Air Bah the only farming work entirely entrusted to men is land clearing, which they carry out sporadically, between other engagements, from January to July. After July, however, they resume forest collecting, and all the remaining work required for farming is left to women. Taboos, rituals, and ceremonial feasts ensure that men are available when they are needed, but between July and December, women perform all farming work, such as weeding and guarding the paddy fields, as well as the follow-up processing work such as winnowing, pounding, and drying the harvested paddy. They also do most of the harvesting in December, although men help with the 'heavy-lifting,' transporting and storing the harvested crop.

This sexual and temporal division of labour was further facilitated by a 'dual' pattern of mobility. Lewis Binford identifies two distinct patterns of mobility: residential mobility, where 'entire bands move their camps in search of resources,' and logistical mobility, where 'bands stay in relatively fixed locations and send out individuals or small task groups to bring back resources' (1980, in Bogucki 1999: 93). Although these patterns have been associated with seasonal variations (Shoocongdej 2000), Lanoh seemed to have implemented them to address the contrasting requirements of forest collecting and farming. On the one hand, they established base camps, which were moved in two-year intervals, according to the requirements of swidden cultivation. On the other hand, they also maintained temporary satellite forest camps around these base camps, which were moved according to the requirements of forest collecting for trade:

> My old man would move often, not only him, but a lot of people. After paddy planting, we would move here and there, up-river. We would move very often, but it was always around Malau. When we *really* wanted to move, the whole village moved ... everybody. But when we moved often,

it was like ... from here to there, the *Patani* place [about an hour walking distance from Air Bah in the forest] ... So, during that time, from the time I was 7, we all moved to Sumpitan, Piah, and then back to Malau. When we moved to Sumpitan, to Malau, our whole village moved, our dogs, chickens.

During the two-year period, base camps were never entirely abandoned, but were maintained by women and men too old to participate in forest collecting. These old men guarded the camp and hunted small game nearby for the women and children. People in Air Bah explained:

In the old days, there would always be some ... who stayed behind to look after what they had planted, or the houses, because the others would come back. Those who stayed behind got paid by those who moved for taking care of their things ... they would get tobacco and money.[46]

In 1998 people in Tawai still practised this dual pattern of mobility. An old man who had moved from Tawai to Air Bah recounted:

In Tawai, I was often the only man left in the village with Terok. We took care of the village, women and children, when the men went away for rattan. They would go away for one or two weeks. During that time, Terok and I prepared ['standby'] our *blaw* [blowpipe] and the men left a shotgun with us and we had the dogs. When they [the men] came back, each of them would give us two–three dollars, sometimes five, and tobacco. Once, when they got very good *gaharu*, they bought me shoes.

In theory, therefore, this flexibility would have allowed men to be more mobile and women to be more sedentary, focusing on farming while men pursued forest work. The different degrees to which men and women in Air Bah were involved in farming prior to resettlement is highlighted in the following comparison between Temiar and Lanoh farming.

Temiar in Air Bah recall being taught to farm by their fathers, but Lanoh remember receiving the same lessons from their mothers instead:

LANOH INFORMANT 1: My mother taught me about food, about paddy planting, and about all the work to be done in paddy planting.
LANOH INFORMANT 2: When I was small, when I was about 7, I followed my mother to go to the field, to gather vegetables, to plant paddy, corn, and

then my mother would give me two or three corn seeds and she would dig the hole. So that's learning ... how to do things ... But paddy she did not give me for fear of the spirit of the paddy would get me, because I was too young. Other things, like tapioca and corn, I was allowed [to play with].

TEMIAR INFORMANT: My father was doing what we are doing right now. He went hunting, look for rattan, fish, planting paddy; all the things that we are doing. He planted fruit trees, made fishing nets, traps, went to look for tin. My father taught me how to find work and work the land.

It is likely that this discrepancy between the responsibilities of Lanoh and Temiar men reflects an adjustment in shifting to forest collecting for trade.

Lanoh sexual division of labour in agriculture further reinforces the anthropological perception that small-scale farming is often associated with women. Bogucki posits that 'it is possible ... that agriculture entered foraging societies as a female activity, growing out of the earlier tradition of gathering' (1999: 200). In the context of Malaysia, Frederick Dunn (1975: 80) highlights this connection between women and farming when noting that among forest collectors farming and gathering often overlap. Similarly, farming in Air Bah is more compatible with women's work than with men's work. Men's collecting, determined by demands and the maturity rate of certain resources, requires constant mobility. Thus, men not only move around to seek out requests for forest products from villagers (and today, from buyers), but rattan and *gaharu* collecting requires them also to revisit collection sites about every fifteen years, the time it takes for these resources to recover. This pattern of mobility continues to this day, as Lanoh collectors still move between twenty such main areas between Gluk and Malau. They spend about a year in one area before moving on to the next. In this way, by the time they complete the full cycle, resources previously obtained in the first sites are ready for extraction.[47] The following excerpts illustrate this connection between men's mobility and forest collecting for trade:

People moved around, but never far away ... Sometimes, people moved so that to get closer to work. Osman's father often took his family near the Lawin Malay village because he worked *attap* for the Malays.

In the old days, we moved a lot, but usually within their area, between Glok and Malau. This is because further up north it is Jahai and Kensiu country, east of the Perak River is Temiar and south is Semai. Besides, the Lanoh area was enough for us. We moved from one place to another, depending on whether there was sickness or death or we have grown tired of [the place]. But we moved always according to what kind of work they were going to do and when to do it. We would stay in Gelok, Sumpitan to pick fruits, *petai*, plant *jago?* [*jagong*, 'corn'], or here [Air Bah] to plant paddy. Then, there would be some who did not plant paddy, but wanted to mine tin, using the *dulang* method, panning method. They would go to Lawin. And then they would remember that the area they worked rattan five–six years ago must have mature rattans now and they would go there. If someone [was] asked by Malays to get wood, bamboo, and *atap* to make houses, we would move to Tawai, because there are lots of bamboo and *atap* there. So that was how people moved a lot before.

The mobility requirements of vegetable collecting are quite different from those of collecting for trade. Unlike commercial collecting, vegetable collecting requires minimal mobility. In fact, women hardly need to travel further than the nearest hill around the camp or village to collect the staple vegetables of the Lanoh diet. Additionally, the maturation rate of fast-growing mushrooms and leafy vegetables, such as water *convolvulus* and fern shoots, is much shorter than the maturation rate of products collected by men. The relative ease of gathering vegetables also allows women to undertake this activity almost daily. Longer gathering trips of about a half-day's duration only occur when special food items are needed, such as chili peppers or bamboo shoots.[48] As a result Lanoh women are able to carry out farming and vegetable collecting concurrently; they can shift effortlessly between these activities and presumably did so in the past (see also Dunn 1975). Thus, in pre-resettlement times Lanoh women who were not involved in selling forest products could easily afford to remain sedentary if they wished to do so.

In addition, Lanoh women appear to *prefer* sedentism to mobility. Unlike men, women in Air Bah never complain about sedentism and are rarely nostalgic about their previous mobile lifestyle. Sedentism appears advantageous for women in several respects. In sedentary villages women benefit from cooperation, as well as from the company of their female relatives.[49] In Air Bah today matrifilial female kin are the most important relations in women's lives. Women related this way not only spend their leisure time together, sitting under a tree, chatting, grooming, and gossiping, but they also divide chores among themselves. Women of the same household, and often those of related households, hold regular meetings during which they schedule work. Consequently, none of them spends more than a few days a week on any particular task. If one collects vegetables, another cooks, and a third washes clothes. The more adult women a family group has, the less each particular member seems to work. These advantages would have also applied in pre-resettlement times. People in Air Bah related that in the old days if families stayed together, it was for the benefit of helping each other:

> [One family would] cook a lot of rice for the whole cluster and another would do the evening meal. One family would take care of children while the other parents worked.

In more permanent villages, women would have benefited from cooperating with their female relatives not only in chores, but also in child care.

Apart from offering alternative caretakers, sedentary villages also provide more convenient child care for women than forest camps do. This is why today in Air Bah people rarely let children roam further than the nearby fields. In principle, people in Air Bah have no objections to children older than 7 accompanying them to the forest. In practice, however, contrary to still-mobile hunter-gatherers in the peninsula (e.g., Lye 1998, 2005), women gatherers in Air Bah, fearful that children could be harmed by tigers or bears, never take children with them into the forest. Moreover, it is both more efficient for them to work in all-adult groups and safer for the children to stay back in the village.[50] An additional advantage of sedentism from a woman's point of view is that in the village children do not require constant adult supervision. In contrast to forest camps, in a larger sedentary village it is easier for them to find playmates of their own age.[51] Thus, in the safety of the sedentary village, children of different age groups play together all day, effectively supervising each other.

The benefits of companionship, cooperation, and child care indicate that many women would have likely preferred sedentism to mobility even in pre-resettlement times. Consequently, the sexual division of labour in farming and mobility strategies could explain how pre-resettlement Lanoh were relatively sedentary farmers and mobile forest collectors at the same time. However, in spite of its advantages, sedentism had one major drawback for women: in all likelihood, it jeopardized their marriages. To fully assess the ability of Lanoh to engage in swidden farming, we must next consider the implications of women's sedentism for Lanoh marriages.

Trade and Women's Mobility

Given the comparative autonomy and equality of women among mobile hunter-gatherers, it is too easy to take it for granted that 'the mobility of foragers … [is] important for women' (Dahlberg 1981: 18). This assumption has prevented researchers from inquiring into women's attitudes towards mobility and sedentism, which is essential for accurately interpreting the mobility patterns of forager-collectors. It appears that, in spite of Lanoh women's preference for sedentism, in pre-resettlement times the majority of them would have opted to accompany their husbands to forest camps, because the organization and mobility required for effective trade threatened to destroy their families.

Women's sedentism in the past depended on several factors, most important of which was the strength of their marital and kinship relations and the number of children they had. As the following account indicates, women with kin support and reason to trust their husbands could afford to remain sedentary and have several children:

> Lanoh never had many children. From the time of my grandfather, they would have two, three, at most four children. My own parents had many children because they did not move a lot. When my father moved about to work from Malau to Sumpitan, my mother would always stay with the babies. Other people, however, moved together, as a family. My father always came back with sarongs for my mother. So my mother had many children and she took care of the children at most times.

Still, it is evident from life history interviews that only a few women could afford to choose this option in pre-resettlement times. As the following interview excerpt reveals, a more sedentary lifestyle implied that women would be separated from their husbands for long periods:

> So I was learning … I followed my father, and my father said, 'all right, we're going back to Kuala Piah'… Every time, we were at two places. My mother stayed there, my father was here. So I stayed here for about three to four months, then returned over there.

In the majority of cases such lengthy separation would have weakened already fragile unions.

As a rule, Lanoh marriages in the past were short-lived and ephemeral. Lanoh did not have a word for 'marriage,' nor did they celebrate marriage in any form. In describing marriage, people in Air Bah still use the expression *təg tɛɛg*, which means cohabitation, 'having slept with,' or 'having moved in' with someone. Likewise, divorce was easy, informal, and frequent. Men in Air Bah still recall the old days, when they had relationships with up to a dozen *kədɔy* (women or wives):

> I lived there for four years. I was big then, I was about 19. I had fifteen wives. I married one day or two days or one week. In those days, young men and young women married for a few days and then change and look for another husband or wife. Here no one does that anymore ... But it was not to make children. They would be married for a few days, a week, and then they would move to another person.
>
> In the old days, the people here did that. My father's time ... they did not stay married for very long. Sometimes, they just went into the jungle at night.
>
> When I came back from Baling and stayed in Lawin, I married one [woman] there, left ... I went all over the place ... married and left, married and left.
>
> (Why did you marry and then leave?)
>
> Those days were not like today. In those days, it was our life to marry many and never stay in one place.

Yet, there was more to this pattern than mere masculine philandering. It appears that Lanoh men in the past benefited economically from marrying women in several villages, because such serial monogamy helped them establish and maintain a wide network of relationships, a clear logistical advantage in conducting trade in minor forest products. This can be discerned from the life experience of Pak Lang, one of the oldest inhabitants of Air Bah. Pak Lang's life is an example of how social and economic networks overlap in the life of mobile collectors.

Pak Lang, in spite of being well over 70 years of age, remains a mobile collector. As an old man, he no longer collects major forest products, such as rattan, but engages in 'light' collecting of blowpipe bamboo and medicinal herbs. His specialty is a puzzle toy (*main tɛndroy*),[52] which he makes of rattan and sells in villages and towns wherever he goes. Pak Lang 'doesn't like to be in one place for long.' He is constantly on the move, visiting relatives in different settlements, especially women: sisters, nieces, and most importantly, daughters by several different wives. In a sense Pak Lang's landscape is made up of women. After spending some time with one, he moves on to the other. His well-being, as well as his success in trade, depends on this network of women. As he makes his 'rounds' among his female relatives, similar to the way Lanoh men revisit forest resources in intervals, he conducts his business transactions with Malay, Chinese, and Orang Asli villagers in the vicinity.

Much in the same way as Pak Lang does today, so too Lanoh men in the past, through a series of relationships with women, could have established an array of relatives, friends, acquaintances, and business contacts. This network supported their social flexibility and facilitated their participation in trade. Yet, while Lanoh men enjoyed the advantages of marrying one woman after the other, this pattern of family relations often meant hardship for women and children. Life history interviews offer a different, more dismal, picture of what it was like to be left behind by one's father:

> [My father] had two wives at that time, when I was young. He spent more time with his new wife and less with the old wife – the old wife was my mother – she died in Lawin, my stepmother died in Malau. I was about 5 at that time. [My father] was living more in Sumpitan, we were in Malau and my mother and Hitam, who was the oldest, took care of us. They did everything, [my father] did not do anything; he would come and go. Hitam took over [my father's] place. I don't know how to start … the story, my story is so sad. At that time, I was 8 or 9 years old, life was so hard, Hitam was older then, but my life was so hard. With our mother, we went to the jungle to take *ubi* [tapioca], the one with hair on it, the one the Malays called *ubi miang* [of the taro family]. After that, we'd take it home, cook it for our food, but of course it wasn't that good, we always craved rice, and then people would say, 'You want rice? Where's your father?' So we never had rice or fish … and I did not know any better, I was small then, I didn't know anything. Those times lasted until I was about 14 years old.

It is conceivable, however, that in pre-resettlement times, Lanoh women would have been able to mitigate the impact of men's strategies by accompanying them to forest camps and in their ventures in other villages.

In Tawai, where, at least in 1998, men were more involved in forest collecting than were the men of Air Bah, women still accompanied
them to forest camps whenever they anticipated being away longer
than three weeks. Although women in Tawai cited several reasons
in support of their decisions to follow their husbands, from longing
to concerns about food supplies, an important consideration was the
belief that by being closer to their husbands they could foster and maintain their marital relationship. It is likely that Lanoh women in the past
made similar decisions – freely, but not without constraints.[53]

However, if women were to accompany their husbands to forest
camps, they needed to regulate and limit their fertility. Thus, most
Lanoh women in the past likely faced a difficult dilemma: live a more
comfortable life surrounded by female relations or give up the benefits
and comforts of sedentism and travel with their husbands. The question of birth control among Lanoh reflects this dilemma. On the one
hand, children strengthened women's ties with their husbands. People
in Air Bah said that once a man had a child with a woman, he would
always consider her to be his wife and feel obligated towards her and
her children. On the other hand, children endangered marriages, often
preventing women from following their husbands.

Lanoh in the past had several reasons to limit the number of their
children, and one of the most important among these was the impact
of children on mobility. Lanoh consider three to be the ideal number
of children. In the past people planned to have an average of three
children, so that the children would be able to support each other if
something happened to their parents (also see Benjamin 1980: 12–13).
Nonetheless, critical of Malays, Indians, and Chinese, who want many
children so that they can be taken care of in their old age, Lanoh above
all think of their present needs. They believe it is easier to take care
of fewer children today than to wait for the benefits of children in the
future. Evans, who notes that 'Negrito' women had no more than three
or four children because of the 'difficulty of feeding them,' confirms
this (1937: 245–7). Apart from 'immediacy' and economic considerations, however, pre-resettlement Lanoh mainly limited the number of
their children because they were obstacles to mobility. They usually
waited for the first child to be 'old enough to carry a few things before
having another baby on their back.'

In the past Lanoh women, who firmly believe in their ability and
right to regulate their fertility, employed a variety of contraceptive
measures.[54] Men may have had preferences, but decisions about con-

traception among Lanoh were ultimately left to women. This signifies that regulating birth was strongly related to women's interests. The relationship between the use of contraception and the strength of marriages is indicated by the fact that in Air Bah, where marriages are more secure, women have stopped using contraception. In spite of men's continuing involvement in activities outside the village, marriages in Air Bah today are more enduring than they were in the past. This is quite evident as, unlike their forefathers, most middle-aged Lanoh men have been in stable marriages for as long as twenty years.[55] Even though there have been cases of adultery, abandonment and divorces are rare. This stability seemed to have enhanced women's power and influence within their marriages. Although in the past polygamous marriages were more common, today, when women say they do not want a co-wife (*ŋen jəʔdɛ nay*), they usually have their way. As well, the custom of 'borrowing' wives has declined. One woman said:

> About *pinjam* [borrowing, M.] ... Yes, people used to do that before. It means to sleep with someone's wife. If they like each other, that's fine, but it usually ended up in a conflict or fight [M. *kelahi*]. People now don't do that because women here don't like that.

Also, as the following interview excerpt indicates, in these new circumstances, women no longer seem to have the same desire to limit the number of their children as they once did:

> Lanoh before did not like to have many children, because they travelled from place to place. Thus, they used abortive and contraceptive medicine often. Now that they stay at one place, they no longer use them as often. Nowadays, the women [in Air Bah] do not take *jarang anak* [contraceptive medicine]. People here want many children. So they take another herb, for fertility, instead.

As a result of changing attitudes, as mentioned in Chapter 1, women in Air Bah often have as many as six to eight children.[56]

Thus, no matter how convenient sedentism might have been for Lanoh women, the difference between their past and present birth control needs and practices supports the conclusion that in pre-resettlement times men's mobility was paramount, ultimately determining the mobility of all: women, children, and, by association, old people:

So we lived a nomadic life. We followed our father. If our father said, 'We'll go,' then we went. We stayed for a week or two, came back, and it was just one *baka?* [family, household]. The others ... sometimes they'd come, sometimes they didn't. We left our house. When we came back, we'd stay in the same house again. If we went to a place where we didn't have a house, then we made one.

With regard to farming, this mobility pattern implied that Lanoh women, who chose to live the life of collectors, could not '[sit] around [watch the paddy] grow.'

Conclusion

In spite of the potential for Lanoh to practise farming and collecting simultaneously, the mobility requirements of collecting seem to have outweighed the sedentary requirements of farming. Together with the organizational limitations to farming discussed earlier, it appears that pre-resettlement Lanoh sacrificed and adapted all other aspects of their life to forest collecting for trade. Despite the possibility that prior to entering the Semang niche Lanoh could have been more involved in farming, and despite continuous concessions made to farming even after they shifted to forest collecting, it is unlikely that they became sedentary or semi-sedentary farmers. This is because their participation in trade with Malays resulted in organizational adjustments that were incompatible with the demands of efficient subsistence farming. Efficient subsistence farming requires a degree of social integration and sedentism, and the participation of Lanoh in village trade jeopardized both. Consequently, even if they farmed, they did so in an 'immediate-return' manner. This discrepancy between social organization and the demands of efficient swidden farming implies that there is a boundary, albeit not between farming and hunting, but between successful farming and the collecting of minor forest products for trade.[57]

In the end, one has to agree with Serge Bahuchet (1992), who has argued that relations with villagers often have a profound effect on foragers' social and spatial organization, far more than does the distribution of natural resources. These findings could stimulate further studies into hunter-gatherer social organization and its relationship to subsistence activities and interethnic contact, leading to a reappraisal of the 'mixed economy' concept among hunters and gatherers. The next question to be explored is why did interethnic trade become so important to Semang collectors that it eclipsed not only other subsistence activities but their interpersonal relationships as well? In the next chapter, I will address this question by further inquiring into the intergroup relations of Lanoh and the implications of these before and after Malaysia's independence in 1957.

3 The Changing Context of Interethnic Relations: From Power Balance to Power Imbalance

As I have pointed out in earlier chapters, the interethnic relations of hunter-gatherers have received more and more attention in recent decades (Fox 1969; Peterson 1978; Testart 1982; Galaty 1986; Schrire 1980; Denbow and Wilmsen 1986). Most scholars tend to agree that interethnic relations are consequential for the cultural identity of hunter-gatherers, but there have been few studies on how these interethnic relations change and what that would imply. By neglecting to ask these important questions about change, many have interpreted these relationships with neighbouring agriculturist and pastoralist peoples in a timeless, unqualified manner. As we shall see, contact is often understood to imply dependency, regardless of the historical context (e.g., Schrire 1984; Bailey et al. 1989; Headland and Reid 1989; Bahuchet 1992). Yet, hunter-gatherers' intercultural contacts have varying implications according to their historical circumstances: what may have been advantageous for forager-collectors a hundred or two hundred years ago may prove to be their demise today.

The significance of this extends beyond cultural identity, dealing directly with the even thornier question of cultural continuity. Although traditions, such as forest collecting, are frequently imbued with cultural meaning and hold considerable significance for indigenous identities, when these activities no longer carry the benefits they used to, it is often more prudent to explore alternatives, even if this requires abandoning practices that marked cultural identities in the past. In short, we cannot take for granted what cultural continuity may mean in any given circumstance.

The changing interethnic relationships of Lanoh illustrate the importance of this inquiry. On the surface, Lanoh participate in pretty much the same activities as they did prior to Malaysia's independence; in spite of their greater reliance on cash, they still hunt, they still gather, and they still collect forest products. However, with the changing context of interethnic relations, the meaning of these activities has altered considerably. Before independence, interethnic relations were generally based on a balance of power and implied cultural autonomy for Lanoh. After independence they entail inferior status to those of other ethnic groups and the rapid erosion of Lanoh self-sufficiency and cultural autonomy. In these circumstances, as I am going to argue, withdrawing from contact, although contrary to Lanoh practices in the past, can in fact be understood to be an act of cultural continuity; it is not only a logical response to a loss of power, but also an attempt to restore it.

Pre-independence Relations: Power Balance

As part of the extended debate in anthropology about the relationship between hunter-gatherers and their agriculturist-pastoralist neighbours, many have projected present inequalities and dependencies onto past relationships (e.g., Schrire 1984; Bailey et al. 1989; Spielmann and Eder 1994). In these models, foragers are generally seen as subordinate or inferior to farmers (Bishop 1989; Headland and Reid 1989). While earlier studies used to interpret farmer-forager relations as more egalitarian, ranging from 'symbiosis' (Peterson 1978) to 'mutual convenience' (Turnbull 1965), as a consequence of the recent debates, hunter-gatherers' relationship with agriculturists has been interpreted in a hierarchical framework, in which they were deemed to occupy a marginal, lower-class position in food producers' social systems (Wilmsen 1983, 1989; Denbow1984; Headland and Reid 1989; Spielmann and Eder 1994).[1] Revisionist anthropologists typically perceive food producers and hunter-gatherers as constituting 'exclusively defined yet interdependent forms of economic practice' (Galaty 1986: 106). In this construction, hunter-gatherer cultural identity is conceptualized with reference to the identity of neighbouring food producers (Spielmann and Eder 1994). These theories frame the relationship between farmers and foragers as one between exploiters and exploited. Roy Grinker (1992), for instance, suggests that a 'caste' system could best describe relations between foragers and food producers.

There is certainly considerable validity to revisionist interpretations of farmer-forager relationships, from an etic point of view. No social system is completely closed, and most social phenomena can be conceptualized as part of a larger system. From an external point of view, the role of hunter-gatherers in their neighbours' economies undoubtedly renders them marginal, and from this same perspective, hunter-gatherers truly do constitute a class in relation to larger society. Nonetheless, while the revisionist challenge raises a number of valid points, I would argue that this hierarchical framework results from a misinterpretation of hunter-gatherer cultural identity. As Jérôme Rousseau (personal communication) has pointed out, hunter-gatherers have certainly perceived farmers as constraints and their expansion as oppressive, yet there is no evidence that historically, and in all circumstances, hunter-gatherers have regarded farmers as superior people. Consequently, etic frameworks, such as Marxist, world-system, and dependency theories, are not necessarily applicable to past relationships between hunter-gatherers and farmers.[2]

For anthropologists, hunter-gatherer cultural identity presents a problem. Like food producers, anthropologists have similar difficulties in conceptualizing beyond the framework of their own hierarchical perception and cognition when it comes to foragers. Grinker's work (1994) illustrates this point. Analysing the relationship between Lese agriculturists and Efe hunter-gatherers, Grinker asserts that ethnic inequality between the two populations is of the same type of inequality as is found within Lese households. He concludes that 'ethnicity is tied to inequality and is constituted by the asymmetrical integration of culturally distinct groups' (1994: xii).

The same relationships, however, are often seen differently from hunter-gatherers' point of view. John Galaty underlines the discrepancy between how food producers (along with some Western anthropologists) and hunter-gatherers might perceive the same relationship, noting that the 'European classification of East African hunters as "Wandorobo" is derived from a Maasai view of their various subordinate neighbors' (1986: 115). 'Torobo' in Maasai means 'poor man,' one without cattle. However, for hunters, the same term, 'torobo,' evokes the tsetse fly, the greatest enemy of Maasai cattle. Thus, the relation that, from the agriculturists' perspective, appears hierarchical, from the foragers' perspective may seem like a more egalitarian form of association (Turnbull 1965).

Moreover, the revisionist debate over the precedence of internal versus external factors in determining the main characteristics of hunter-gatherer social organization only offers two alternatives: isolation or dependence. Hunter-gatherer social formations are seen as either the

consequence of autonomous development or domination by neighbouring peoples (Lee and Guenther 1991). Yet, as Bird-David (1988)
suggests, the question of dependency is irrelevant, inappropriate, or
anachronistic with regard to hunter-gatherer identity and cultural
autonomy. I hope to show that cultural autonomy does not necessarily
imply isolation (Bodley 1992). In fact, for hunter-gatherers in trade relations with neighbouring farmers the opposite could be true: they may
initially have engaged in these relations to establish and maintain cultural autonomy. This certainly seems to apply to Semang forager-collectors in Peninsular Malaysia. In considering power relations between
Malays and Orang Asli collectors in pre-resettlement times, the infer-
ence that a balance of power characterized the Malay-Orang Asli relationship, rather than one-sided Malay dominance, seems inevitable.

Hunter-Gatherers and Their Neighbours

In the last chapter I suggested that collecting and trading minor forest
products was so important to pre-resettlement Lanoh that they sacrificed all other aspects of their lives to this pursuit. How should this
conclusion be interpreted in the light of recent anthropological debates
about the interaction between hunter-gatherers and their food-produc-
ing (agriculturist and pastoralist) neighbours?[3] It is well accepted in the
literature on tropical forager-traders that items exchanged with agriculturists were 'integral' to hunter-gatherer economies (Junker 2002b:
207). According to this view, hunter-gatherers are dependent on agricultural populations for 'iron tools and weapons, salt, earthenware pot-
tery, lowland livestock, and marine resources' (ibid.; see also Morrison
2002b: 108). Several proponents of this view, such as Headland and
Reid (1989: 15), as well as Bailey et al. (1989), have argued that, without
trade, these foragers would have experienced carbohydrate deficiency
(Rambo 1988; Headland and Reid 1989: 15; Bailey et al. 1989). To the
contrary, others have contested these former conclusions, contending
instead that hunter-gatherers could survive in these environments
independently, without necessarily relying on the products of agriculturists (Endicott and Bellwood 1991; Brosius 1991; Dentan 1991).

   This exchange has produced several valuable arguments; however,
it is ultimately limited, as it has been too narrowly focused on the ecological and economic aspects of interactions between hunter-gatherers
and farmers.[4] As Kathleen Morrison notes, although the ecological context of hunter-gatherers in Southeast Asia is relatively well understood,

ecologically oriented studies often pay insufficient attention to 'social and political contexts' (2002a: 5).[5] A broader sociopolitical perspective provides a far more judicious framework for analysing trade relations between foragers and farmers. Analysis conceived in this framework suggests that although foragers benefit from trading with food producers, these benefits are not primarily and necessarily economic. Instead, it is likely that in the past trade enhanced the leverage of the Semang vis-à-vis their politically dominant Malay neighbours, imposing a fragile power balance between these populations. Paradoxically, however, this power balance was built on imbalance; the political strength of the Malays was offset by their greater economic need for forest products. Therefore, the equalizing effect of trade almost certainly depended on the agriculturists' greater and the foragers' lesser reliance on the economic aspects of this relationship.

Power Balance Based on Two Imbalances

Without a doubt, of the two ethnic groups, the Malays have always asserted themselves over the Orang Asli, often overbearingly so.[6] Atrocities Orang Asli suffered at the hands of Malays, even in the past, provide evidence for this dominance. For instance, until quite recently, Orang Asli were frequent victims of slave raids (Dodge 1981; K.M. Endicott 1983; Dentan 1992, 2008); although slavery was officially abolished in Malaysia in 1883, 'ordinary' (or 'true') slavery did not cease until the mid-1920s (K.M. Endicott 1983: 217–18; also see Sullivan 1982: 42; Leary 1995: 19). The threat of slave raids has not faded from Orang Asli memory. Lanoh, like other Orang Asli, recount the kidnapping of children for sale either as slave workers in mines or as servants or concubines for Malay *rajas*. People in Air Bah also remarked that these raids were often conducted through indigenous parties and that frequently Orang Asli themselves bought or stole children to be sold to Malays. Nonetheless, this fact hardly alters the impact of these atrocities, nor does it diminish the potential dangers of living so close to Malays.[7]

Malay domination over the indigenous peoples of the peninsula has been extensively explored in Orang Asli studies. Indeed, research on Orang Asli peoples often predominantly focuses on the oppressive nature of Malay–Orang Asli relations (e.g., Dodge 1981; Dentan 1992, 2008). While this focus is certainly justified today, as the Malaysian nation state has nearly completely subjugated the indigenous populations of the peninsula, it may not be entirely warranted when applied to historical relationships. In the past Malays were far more dependent on Orang Asli for access to forest products, and this allowed the Orang Asli to counter Malay influence and remain self-sufficient.

My own research among Lanoh supports the findings of Endicott and Bellwood (1991) concerning the self-sufficiency of these peoples. As the following interview excerpt indicates, Lanoh, like Batek, insist that, in pre-resettlement times, they were able to live in the forest without the goods they obtained from Malays. Admitting that they exchanged jungle products for clothes, rice, fish, salt, and tools, they also claim that they could easily have gone without these products:

> In the old days, the only difficult things to obtain were tools; a *parang* or an axe.[8] Everything else we could get from the forest. We could drink water from the river or roots. We could get paddy, tapioca, and meat for food. We did not have cooking oil; we never used it. We could get honey for sugar. We got sour fruits as a substitute for salt, for instance, *mempelam* [a type of mango, M.]. We boiled the *mempelam*. We mixed this with our meat whenever we were cooking and chilies from the forest made food taste better than salt. We got lard from wild boar when we needed it. Even now, when we run out of salt and oil, we cook like that. We did not use pots and pans. We always cooked with bamboo. We put everything in the bamboo and cooked. For fire, we would use two stones on dry twigs and grass to spark a fire. Wild tobacco, we grew.

With such a high level of self-sufficiency, Orang Asli collectors (such as pre-resettlement Lanoh) would have had limited need for items offered by Malays.

It was quite a different matter for their agriculturist neighbours, who were much more dependent on their trade with the 'forest people.' Malays relied on Orang Asli trade not only for everyday necessities, such as honey, herbal medicines, charms and other ritual objects,[9] and building materials, but also for their larger-scale, regional maritime trade (Dunn 1975: 95; Andaya and Andaya 1982; Sullivan 1982; Gomes 1991: 167). As Morrison suggests, 'minority forest products,' such as 'rattans and canes, bamboo, palms for food and thatch, incense woods, ebony, tanning and dyeing plants and woods, various gums, oils, and resins, medicinal and poisonous plants, spices, animal products, and such minerals as tin and gold … represented valuable commodities in the world market' (2002b: 124). Laura Junker further demonstrates the importance of indigenous trade for building maritime polities in South-east Asia:

> The wealth-generating exports for … maritime trading polities were pri-marily interior forest products that could only be obtained through coerc-ing intensified trade with foraging groups occupying the island interiors. While it is difficult to support the conclusion that many contemporary Southeast Asian foragers are professional traders created out of the for-eign trade demands of recent maritime trading kingdoms, ethnographic and historical analyses point to both economic and social transformations associated with the integration of foragers into non-subsistence trade sys-tems controlled by socially stratified lowland societies. (2002a: 135)

Maritime trade thus organized people from the remotest villages of the interior to the political centres and entrepôts of the coast, and participa-tion in this network likely had significant benefits.[10]

The reliance of Malays on indigenous collectors would have been compounded by their attitudes towards the forest. Several observers have noted Malays' tendency to fear and respect the forest. As recently as the late nineteenth century, travellers located Malay villages prima-rily on riverbanks. To avoid entering the forest, which they considered perilous and largely inaccessible, they relied on riverways for move-ment and transportation (Barr 1978: 9).[11] These Malay villagers, living in relative isolation, would have depended on visits by aborigines walk-ing the forest paths, and not only as trade partners. Travelling from place to place and interacting with people everywhere, indigenous forest people would have been an indispensable source of news, gos-sip, entertainment, and information for sedentary agriculturists (Mora, personal communication).

In light of the above, it is not at all surprising that Malay attitudes towards Orang Asli do not often reflect their dominant position. It is clear that Malays distanced themselves socially from Orang Asli, but it is also apparent that they regarded these forest collectors as potent and powerful, even dangerous, like the forest itself. In earlier times, appar-ently, Malays not only feared the forest, its spirits and animals but also they respected the Orang Asli for their ability to survive in such a forbid-ding place. Malays often endowed Orang Asli with mysterious powers, as Nicolas Dodge notes: 'Although the Malays may have despised the Aborigines for being as much "beast as human," they also feared them for related reasons, in particular their ability to kill at distance by magic (*menuju*) and the special potency of the Aborigine sorcerers, especially their reputed adeptness in turning into tigers' (1981: 3; also see Dunn 1975; Woodburn 1988: 37–8). This belief suggests a measure of respect towards the Orang Asli, indicative of a de facto, albeit fragile, power balance, rather than a simple hierarchical relationship.

This power balance between Malays and Orang Asli collectors is also commemorated in official political narratives, for instance, in the founding myth describing the origin of Perak State as a result of the union of a Malay trader and a Semang woman:

> According to legend, shortly after the Portuguese took Malacca (AD 1511), a trader, Nakhoda Kasim, was dispatched from Johor Lama to look for new lands for the Malacca people in exile. He settled at Tumung in the northern reaches of the Perak River and married a Semang (aborigine) in whose veins white blood flowed. The couple had no children of their own but adopted a girl discovered in a mound of foam by the river bank, and a boy sprung from the stem of a bamboo. These two married, the woman, Tan Puteh, assuming the government of the country until Nakhoda Kasim, on his deathbed, persuaded her to invite a Raja from Johor to come and rule Perak. This Raja, afterwards known as Sultan Ahamad Taj-Uddin Syah, traced his descent from the god-kings of Minangkabau, and it was his successor who fixed the boundaries of Perak and gave the state its name. (Sullivan 1982: 1; see also Juli 2003)

The power of the Semang was more than figurative. Despite their demographic inferiority, they achieved fundamentally egalitarian ethnic relations with their Malay neighbours.[12] Only this power balance can explain why, in spite of the Malays' potential to assimilate or destroy these small hunter-gatherer populations, these peoples were able to preserve their cultural autonomy while living in close proximity with Malays for so long (in some cases, for nearly three millennia). As Porath suggests, 'for the forest people … their relationship with the forest … was as much political as economic. The forest was not just a storehouse of food, but also a place to retreat against low-level encroachment by surrounding farmers. In the forest, they could keep their autonomy' (2001: 135n3). This equality does not mean that relationships between Malays and indigenous collectors were always amicable. As K.M. Endicott notes, trade between members of these populations was sometimes restricted to 'silent barter' (1983). Nonetheless, Ivor Evans suggests that

'Malays, or others, who live within the territory may be a nuisance to the Negritos, but [they do] not affect their ideas, or movements' (1937: 21). Especially considering the Malays' potential to dominate, assimilate, or entirely annihilate Semang, the cultural autonomy of these foragers through this period is remarkable, and it arguably would not have been possible without the mitigating effect of trade.

Post-independence Relations: Power Imbalance

In recent years, several excellent studies have been published about the way post-independence change has affected the indigenous peoples of the Malay Peninsula (e.g., Dentan et al. 1997; Jumper 1997, 1999; Nicholas 2000; Benjamin and Chou 2003; Gomes 2004, 2007). However, relatively few have examined how these changes have been shaped by the unique characteristics of each people. Nor have many explored how these changes have affected relations between Orang Asli groups. Both avenues of inquiry bear promise, and such studies are necessary if we are to explain why, for instance, Lanoh have lately segregated themselves not only from Malays, but often from other Orang Asli as well.

Post-independence Change: From Power to Powerlessness

The power relations between Malays and Orang Asli drastically changed in the second part of the twentieth century, especially after Malaysia's independence in 1957 (Gomes 2007). This does not mean that earlier changes, those commencing under British rule, were inconsequential. In fact, British administration interfered with Orang Asli life in multiple ways (ibid.). In 1950, during the Malayan Emergency (Communist Insurgency, 1948–1960), the British established the Department of Orang Asli Affairs (Jabatan Orang Asli or JOA), which initiated several administrative changes in the name of efficient management. These administrative changes also affected Lanoh. They not only divided Lanoh area into two jurisdictions (Malau in the north and Sumpitan in the south), but to facilitate interaction between JOA officers and indigenous groups, they also introduced the non-indigenous title of headman (Benjamin 1968). The economic development of Perak also commenced under British rule. The British encouraged the creation of plantations and industries, such as tin mining, resulting in an influx of Chinese migrant workers, thus irrevocably changing the state's ethnic and population dynamics.[13] Occasionally, British colonial administrators even directly interfered with indigenous livelihoods. Schebesta (1929: 73) describes how Captain J. Berkeley, the District Officer of Grik at the time (1923), employed a Malay intermediary, whom he had appointed as leader (*penglima*),[14] to persuade people in a mixed Lanoh-Jahai camp to plant tapioca.

Nonetheless, while these changes are certainly significant, they seem to have only marginally affected dynamics between Malays and Orang Asli. The British generally preserved the status of Orang Asli vis-à-vis other ethnic groups and, from time to time, may have even enhanced it by employing them as forest rangers. Schebesta notes that the British District Officer, Berkeley, 'employed Semang as forest guards to catch Malays, and even Chinese, stealing timber, and they were very suited to the work' (1929: 52). It would seem, then, that the British granted Orang Asli a measure of authority over Malays and Chinese, at least in some matters. More importantly, even if driven by an essentialist view of indigenous groups, British officers were often committed to preserving indigenous lifestyles in the peninsula (Holman 1984 [1953]). Thus, consequential as British interference might have been, it was negligible compared with developments after 1957, which irrevocably altered power relations between Malays and forest collectors.[15]

After 1957 the Orang Asli increasingly lost control over the forest and its resources. This course has accelerated over the past fifty years, propelled forward by the rapid economic development of Malaysia and the political and ideological turmoil of nation building. Some aspects of this process, such as the seizure of Orang Asli land, were motivated mainly by economic gain, while others, such as the pressure to convert these groups to Islam, by political fervour. These changes have led to the loss of land and resources and to a decline in demand for forest products, exacerbating the tensions between the social organization of forest collectors and the requirements of commercial collecting of major forest products or contract work (Gomes 2007).

As a result Lanoh have found themselves in an increasingly confrontational position in relation to members of majority ethnic groups, such as Malays and Chinese, as well as other Orang Asli. In this new context, with their cultural autonomy and livelihood constantly threatened, they have slid from a position of considerable power and independence to one of powerlessness and dependence. In their new status, Lanoh are also helplessly exposed to mistreatment by members of more powerful ethnic groups. No longer able to retreat to the rainforest, Lanoh in Air Bah today are changing from a people to whom interethnic contact was a top priority to a people who withdraw from the outside world and increasingly emphasize a bounded, village identity. In the remainder of this chapter I will analyse and discuss aspects of this change.

Organizational Discrepancy: The Changing Context of Interethnic Trade

In post-independence times, as resources extracted from the forest have increasingly been replaced with synthetic materials, Orang Asli have perhaps been affected most by a decline in demand for minor forest products (Dunn 1975). With modernity came zinc roofs, concrete buildings, pharmacies, clinics, and artificial food flavourings. As a result many items that Lanoh habitually collected for trade in the past are no longer needed by Malay and Chinese villagers. Demand has ceased for wax, indigenous rubber (*gutta percha*), tin, iron ore, resin (*damak* or *damar*), and construction materials (rattan, hardwood, sandalwood, and *atap* for Malay houses). Medicinal herbs and honey are also scarcely required by villagers these days. This decrease in demand has also affected the price of forest products. While Lanoh dependence on cash has grown, the price of forest products has been steadily declining. People nowadays receive so little money for minor products that they complain that such occasional collecting is no longer even worth their effort.

With declining trade in minor products, villagers in Air Bah have turned to larger-scale specialized collecting of major products like rattan. Such commercial collecting is usually conducted via Chinese middlemen (*towkay*, 'boss,' 'owner,' a loanword from Chinese). As a result of the shift from individual demands to specialized collecting, trade relations only superficially resemble those of the past. Trade relations once helped to preserve the independence of Lanoh; today they jeopardize it. During the past few decades Lanoh in Air Bah have become increasingly dependent on a few exclusive Chinese buyers, whose influence over the community has expanded as a result.

Such close relationships between Chinese or Malay patrons and Orang Asli collectors, of course, also occurred in the past. Evans describes such a relationship between Semang and Malays in the first part of the twentieth century: 'In various parts of the country, certain Malays, sometimes foreign Malays, have, by one method or another, gained an ascendancy over some Negrito groups and act as their "protectors," very much to their own advantage, for they take care that they shall be the only persons who swindle their protégés, and keep them busy cutting rattans, or palm leaves for thatch, or gathering other jungle produce, giving them in return ridiculously small payment in kind – rice, salt, cloth, etc.' (1937: 34). Nonetheless, while the shift to major products began earlier, patron-client relationships with non-indigenous middlemen have intensified more recently, primarily because of three factors.

First, as a result of deforestation, Orang Asli collectors have come to rely on middlemen for transportation. As in other parts of Malaysia, in the past thirty years, Upper Perak has witnessed an unprecedented growth of logging activity, as well as other economic development. The impact of these increased encroachments into the forests has been dev-astating to the flora and fauna of the forest. Since forest resources have become scarcer, collectors now must cover greater distances and travel deeper into the jungle to find them. The wider the range, the more diffi-cult it is to transport these resources, especially rattan, to pick-up points on foot. Although obtaining a vehicle was at the top of the wish list of people in Air Bah, even as a village, they cannot afford to buy and maintain one. As a result they rely on their middlemen to provide the trucks for moving rattan from the forest to collection points.

Second, Lanoh depend on these middlemen to serve as a buffer against outside authorities. This aspect of Orang Asli–intermediary relationships is especially crucial given the fuzzy state of licence regula-tions concerning collecting activities in the area (Nicholas 2000). Lanoh, anxious to learn about these regulations, often complain:

> We don't know about the law, we depend on the JHEOA [Jabatan Hal Ehwal Orang Asli] and others to tell us about the law.

Their attempts to find out more about licensing through official chan-nels, however, are often met with obstacles, as the following excerpt from my field journals describes:

> The headman [of Air Bah] had arranged a meeting with one of the offic-ers of the Grik JHEOA one morning at 10:30 a.m. When he arrived on time; he was told that the officer in question was not there for the day and would not be there on any of the following days. However, he was also told by the officers who were present that he would first have to write a letter requesting a rattan licence for the village, return with the letter at 11:30 a.m. at which point someone would help him. When the *penghulu* [headman] returned with the letter an hour later, he was informed that

there was no one to take the letter from him because the officer who had suggested obtaining the licence in the first place was absent. The officer relating this information added that the headman did not need a licence to collect rattan anyway. With this, the headman was sent on his way.

People in Air Bah suspect that licences cost money to acquire. They see the situation as a '"Catch-22"... Orang Asli need money to get a rattan licence and they need a licence to get money.'[16] Making full use of this contradiction, JHEOA officers often keep Orang Asli in the dark about rattan licences, allegedly for the collectors' own benefit and protection. They are aware that Orang Asli collectors require special licences to extract forest products, but they also know that obtaining such papers is beyond the means of these peoples. As a result, when it comes to enforcing licensing rules, especially when it comes to small-scale collecting, government officials often 'look the other way.' In implementing this 'fuzzy solution,' officials provide Lanoh with as little information as possible regarding the intricacies of bureaucratic requirements. Yet, however well intentioned these officers might be, this lack of transparency makes Orang Asli collectors feel uneasy and threatened, increasing their reliance on middlemen whom they perceive to be better at interpreting rules than they are, and thus capable of acting on their behalf in dealings with the authorities.[17]

Third, Lanoh collectors are compelled to work with a small group of middlemen because they have difficulties in locating and securing alternative rattan buyers. Recently, after a disagreement over prices with their regular *towkay*, people in Air Bah actively sought out other buyers on their own. Unfortunately, these potential middlemen were far less accommodating than their regular buyer. While willing to pay higher prices, they demanded larger amounts of rattan, quantities which are unfeasible for Lanoh to transport, store, and process. As a consequence, although people in Air Bah characterized their relationship with the original *towkay* as 'extremely demoralizing' (M. *patah semangat*), after eight months of futile searching, they nonetheless returned to him, accepting his lower prices.

Beyond the relative protection and reassurance provided by their *towkay*, there are also material advantages for Orang Asli in maintaining a patron-client relationship with a particular middleman. Using the village of Tawai as an example, people in Air Bah commented on the advantages of having a relationship with a 'good *towkay*':

People in Tawai don't have to run after money [because] the Tawai people have one *towkay*, Ah Kun. They sell rattan to Ah Kun, they sell *gaharu*, *petai*, fruits, frogs, turtles to Ah Kun. They work on contract for Ah Kun. Because of this, whenever Tawai people cannot work because it is raining or cannot find wood [*gaharu*] for a week, Ah Kun readily gives them credit or buys them food. So Tawai people never have to worry about credit. When Tawai has a communal feast, Ah Kun gives them a present of 300 ringgit. When Tawai wanted to build a ceremonial platform, Ah Kun provided chain saws and his lorry to carry the building material. On Chinese New Year, Ah Kun gives presents of money to people in Tawai. Which other contractor is like Ah Kun? Not even the JHEOA is like Ah Kun.

Despite the potential for mutual benefits, strong middleman-collector relationships are hard to maintain. Most of the difficulties derive from a discrepancy between the organization of individual collecting for trade and the expectations of middlemen (as well as contractors and employers). Individual autonomy, opportunism, and organizational flexibility, all greatly advantageous for interethnic trade in the past, have become a liability; today, these attributes place Lanoh in opposition to outsiders who, coming from a different tradition, demand long-term planning, commitment, and reliability.

It is evident that this relationship is different from the past interactions of Lanoh with Malay villagers at least in two respects. The first is in the regularity of contact. While the relationship of Lanoh with Malays was continuous and often extended over generations, it was also based on infrequent, intermittent contact, and thus was less binding than their interactions with professional middlemen today. Past relationships operated in quick response to unpredictable demands, and Lanoh opportunism satisfied both parties. Lanoh flexibility was preferable to Malays, who wanted forest products when they needed them but who were not prepared to deal with indigenous collectors outside of sporadic exchanges. For Lanoh, this arrangement suited them just as well. It ensured their autonomy and kept them out of long-term obligations. Thus, in the context of village trade, flexible responses were a virtue as well as a necessity. Today the same approach has become a weakness in the eyes of middlemen. Depending on a continuous and regular flow of forest products, these professionals perceive Lanoh behaviour as fickle and impulsive. In exchange for safeguarding and promoting Lanoh interests in a paternalistic manner, they expect consistency and unrelenting loyalty. Unwilling and incapable of conforming to these expectations, Lanoh today are in constant conflict with their middle-men, as well as with outside contractors and employers.

Two significant aspects of this conflict originate in discrepancies between the organizational principles of Lanoh and those of the outside world. The clash between the immediacy of Orang Asli economic strat-egies and long-term planning among Malay, Chinese, or Indian con-tractors is a constant source of discord. With the increased need for cash and the uncertainty of collecting, Lanoh often engage in contract work involving land clearing, replanting, plantation maintenance, fertilizing, irrigating, or harvesting. Although these engagements are limited in time, even these prove impractical for Lanoh, who insist on frequent payment and flexible work schedules. These preferences are in opposi-tion to those of non-indigenous contractors who, as a rule, require fixed and measurable work schedules with time frames for completion of the job. In an attempt to ensure that Lanoh complete their tasks, contractors provide cash advances or food supplies at the outset of and throughout the contract, withholding wages until the work is completed. Having a difficult time rationing supplies for the duration of the contract, Lanoh men regularly become heavily indebted to their employers, who may then compel them to stay longer to work off their debts.

Lanoh find such arrangements intolerable. They prefer to work three or four days at a time, getting paid at the end of each such period. Such intervals allow them to return to Air Bah and deliver food and money to their families. Since this is an important priority for Lanoh men, they tend to abandon any contract or wage work that fails to conform to this pattern. They simply quit and walk back to the village, which makes them notoriously unreliable in the eyes of contractors and employers.

A further source of conflict stems from deep-seated Lanoh individu-alism. While, as noted earlier, Malay villagers dealt with the Orang Asli as individuals, present-day middlemen and contractors relate to them as a group. This is at odds with the self-perceptions of Lanoh, who con-tinue to think of themselves as individuals with limited responsibil-ity and accountability over the aspirations and actions of others, and who find it problematic to operate within the collectivistic framework imposed on them by outsiders.[18] If a *towkay* (middleman) has a problem with someone in Air Bah, for example, his dissatisfaction is reflected in his relationship with the whole village. This baffles and frustrates Lanoh and strains their intragroup relations. There are similar con-tradictions with regard to the organizational requirements of contract work. In the forest, Lanoh typically work in small groups of two to four, while contract groups often comprise ten to fourteen individuals. Lanoh find it difficult to negotiate the multiple contrasting interests in such large and inflexible units.

This predicament is also reflected in the fate of work leaders among Lanoh. It has been suggested that discrepancies between past and present collecting and contract work may be eased by the emergence of stronger leadership to coordinate work and distribute wages. In the resettlement community of Kampung Lubok Legong, for instance, Ahmad Ezanee bin Mansor (1972) observed a leader gaining importance as a result of negotiating work contracts. Originally appointed by a middleman to act as an intermediary, this individual managed to transfer his influence from work leadership to various other situations, including conflict resolution.

Among Lanoh in Air Bah such a transfer of influence is unlikely in the context of rattan collecting or contract work. This is because contractors select work group leaders based on who was hired first, rather than on broader indigenous leadership principles, such as age, knowledge, and character. Consequently, these work group leaders lack the authority to instruct, command, or coordinate their peers. Apart from lacking the cultural attributes and qualifications, they are further undermined by the penchant of Lanoh for individualism and secrecy. It is quite common, for instance, for people to keep information about contract jobs and work opportunities from each other. On one such occasion, when it came to light that two men had landed an excellent contract but failed to tell others about it, people commented:

> It's all right; everyone does that. The more people one tells, the more people there are to share the money with.

It is easy to see how, under the circumstances, Lanoh work group leaders would have difficulty holding their teams together.

In addition to managing troublesome relations within work groups, contract group leaders also bear the brunt of blame by both sides for any problems or delays. One area of disagreement, predictably, is the division of money. In Lanoh work groups it is exceedingly difficult for work leaders to find a way to justly distribute the pay that they receive as a lump sum from contractors. Hard as they might try to keep track of advances and work performances, some people always acquire more advance payment and work less than others. While Lanoh do not interfere if others take advantage of the situation, in the end, they expect to be paid proportionally to their effort.[19] Whenever they feel they are being shortchanged, they invariably blame the leader.

Occasionally, it is the contract leader who hides or retains shares of the money rightfully belonging to others. Not surprisingly, such misadventures only serve to damage the popularity of would-be leaders. As a result such leadership is necessarily of short duration, rarely lasting longer than a particular contract. In Air Bah contract work follows an inevitable curve from initial enthusiasm to final disillusionment. Since work leaders have stakes in contracts, they are inclined to advocate contracts and the main contractors associated with them beyond what others consider reasonable. Time and again, when it becomes clear to everyone that a contract situation has deteriorated beyond repair, the work leader disappears for days, while others comment, 'He is hiding like a house rat.'

Lanoh within the Nation State: Mistreatment, Paternalism, and Lack of Protection

Another indication that the power of Lanoh has declined is the mistreatment they suffer at the hands of Malay outsiders. Whereas in the past the extent to which Malays dominated Orang Asli was mitigated by several factors, the nature of their relationship with individual Malays has changed from that of relatively equal trade partners to that of employer and employee. In this new context Malays no longer perceive Orang Asli as a strange but useful resource. They are now viewed as major annoyances, obstacles, and occasionally, competitors.

Additionally, the power of Malays over Orang Asli has been extended within the framework of the Malaysian nation state. In the past Malay authority was relatively weak and localized. Compared with the decentralized nature of pre-colonial Malay rule, Malays today have nearly complete political control over the country and, as a result, are better able to protect Malay interests in everyday situations. Nation building has not been a trouble-free process in this ethnically plural society, where Malays compete with economically powerful Indians and Chinese (Nagata 1974; Gomes 2007). Malays strengthened their political grip over this process by promoting Islam, Malay economic interests, and Malay nationalism. In this light individual Malays are no longer simply members of a more powerful ethnic group, but each and every one of them potentially represents the power of the nation state. Malays will frequently exploit state protection and authority in their dealings with members of other ethnic groups, especially Orang Asli.[20]

In this climate of interethnic tension and the vulnerability of Orang Asli, it is especially important that they receive protection and representation. As discussed earlier, before independence, the British not only shielded them from injustices but occasionally even empowered them vis-à-vis Malay and Chinese groups. Today, under Malay rule, the Orang Asli are unlikely to receive such protection. After independence, the JHEOA, as successor to the British JOA, was expected to take over this protective role. Although it would seem that the JHEOA treat Orang Asli with consideration in some circumstances, for instance, when waiving some minor legal requirements, in general, JHEOA policy is characterized by paternalistic condescension. When dealing with Orang Asli, JHEOA officers frequently employ a tone and approach that one would use with a child in need of patient guidance. Accordingly, the conduct of Lanoh with Malay officials and authorities is driven by a desire to avoid harassment, punishment, and humiliation. The following incident illustrates this point. One day, when Air Bah's generator broke down, some men took it apart, only to quickly reassemble it. They told me that if the JHEOA were to discover that they had tried to fix it, they would be scolded. One wishes JHEOA paternalism also extended to the *protection* of the Orang Asli from mistreatment and exploitation, this is seldom the case, however.

Although involved in many aspects of Orang Asli life, the JHEOA provides little assistance or guidance when it comes to seeking and negotiating contracts and employment. There is an official JHEOA procedure to protect Orang Asli in their relationships with employers, but it is rarely applied in actual contract situations. More often, contractors and employers come directly to Air Bah seeking contact with villagers, rather than working through official channels. As a result Lanoh are routinely cheated, insulted, and abused in their interactions with different employers.[21] The effects of such abuse are aggravated by interethnic land and resource competition, and today these have become serious sources of conflict, not only with members of ethnic majorities but with other Orang Asli as well.

Interethnic Conflict: Competition for Land

Gone are the days when the forest was inaccessible to members of dominant ethnic groups. In the past fifty years competition for land and resources has intensified in Malaysia, and although northern Perak entered development relatively late, since the 1970s large-scale construction and land development projects have been underway there as well.[22] For Orang Asli the most conspicuous implications of this development have been deforestation and land loss: by the 1980s every significant pre-resettlement Lanoh site (Sumpitan, Gluk, Malau, Lawin, and Piah) was either owned or occupied by government or private business. Not only were these sites confiscated, but the people of Air Bah were subsequently denied access to them. For example, the village near Piah was flooded during the construction of the Kenering hydroelectric dam between 1980 and 1983. In the process of developing these areas, several Lanoh burial sites were bulldozed and clearings were overtaken by nearby Malay villages.

Of all these losses people in Air Bah lament most the loss of access to the rock shelters near Lenggong, Sumpitan, to which they attach considerable spiritual importance. Early researchers of the Semang habitually reported the occupation of these by Lanoh groups (Schebesta 1929; Evans 1927a, 1937; Williams-Hunt 1954–55).[23] It appears that, in the past, Lanoh regularly inhabited at least three sections of the cave system near Lenggong. Evans writes: 'Schebesta [1929: 47] states that Negritos near Lenggong, Upper Perak, told him, though they were camping under an overhanging cliff temporarily, that they never lived "for days together in caves." This is not correct, though they never … live in dark caves, nor would they be likely to do so … I have, on at least two occasions, found the Negritos who roam between Lenggong and Kuala Kenering living in the Gua Badak (Rhinoceros Cave), not far from the little Malay hamlet of Sumpitan' (1937: 49). These caves and the surrounding areas were significant economically, as they were often associated with particular resources or activities (such as bat hunting), but they were above all important as a potential refuge and as symbols of the connection of Lanoh to their land. In the mid-1960s, for instance, following the cholera epidemic, several families sought refuge in the rock shelters near Gluk and Sumpitan.[24]

One of these in particular, Gua Kajang (*sənyoʔ kajaʔ*), bears pronounced importance for Lanoh mythology:[25]

At [the beginning of] time, the cave which is now Gua Kajang, was not a cave, but a Lanoh house, *deŋ walwaʔ*. There were people living in this *walwaʔ*; they were the original Lanoh. God, *yaʔ*, is constantly looking for

Lanoh. She wants to take them home, because they are her grandchildren (*kancɔ*). One day *ya* decided to turn the people into *cɘnɔy*, who are invisible, live at the top of every mountain, eat flowers, wear flowers, and smell like flowers. Thus, *ya* made the small river at Kota Tampan flood, so that it became as big as the sea.[26] *Taseɲ*, the shaman, had dreamt of the flood coming and urged his people to get out. So the people left, except for two, a brother and a sister, who were asleep and who were, therefore, left behind. The water came and washed into the *walwa* from one end to the other. The Lanoh *walwa* turned into stone and saved the brother and the sister. The brother and sister finally woke up when the water came. They managed to make for themselves a *perahu* [boat or canoe, M.]. So they paddled up the *ʔɔŋ bluum* [Perak River], looking for their people. They went up the hill right to the source of [*bluum*] and down and again, up to various sources of water and down again. Finally, they followed the [*ʔɔŋ bluum*] and came to a point where the [*bluum*] turned back. That is the part, which they call Air Balik. So, not being able to find their people, they returned and then they married each other and had children. Soon their children had more children and married each other. Some of them left and became other peoples of the world (like Africans; *orang negro*), Kensiu, Jahai, Temiar, Kintak. The original children have continued to live in this area and have become Lanoh. From that time, the Lanoh have been living in this area between Gluk and Malau.

Thus, Gua Kajang has special significance for Lanoh history and identity. Yet, people from Air Bah can no longer access it: Malay villagers who had previously appropriated Lanoh land around Sumpitan are now also blocking entry to Gua Kajang. I visited this cave twice during my fieldwork, at both times accompanied by Lanoh men. During our first visit there, we were approached by villagers from nearby Kampung Gelok (Gluk), who inquired whether Lanoh intended to move back to the area. By the second visit, later in the same year, they had erected a gate and barbed wire fence around the area. When asked, these villagers told us that they had taken over the site as grazing ground for their water buffalos, because, as they explained, this land 'does not belong to anyone.'

Such claims and actions by outsiders are encouraged by the ambiguous status of Lanoh land. People in Air Bah believe that their land is comprised of approximately five hundred acres in Air Bah, three hundred acres in Sumpitan, two hundred acres in Bukit Sapi, and two hundred acres in Tawai. According to the Aboriginal Peoples Act of 1954

(Act No. 134), revised in 1974, any Orang Asli land, the continuous residence of which by Orang Asli can be demonstrated for over twenty years, is protected reserve land.[27] However, except for a few large Temiar resettlement villages, such as Dala and Kemah, the dimensions of indigenous land in Perak have seldom been clarified. As with other Orang Asli, Lanoh land ownership has never been acknowledged by the government. According to officers of the JHEOA this is because Lanoh 'used to move a lot.' In reality, however, this ambiguous status is more likely a consequence of oversights on the part of past administrations. While British administrators took certain steps towards establishing indigenous land rights, formal titles and deeds were never issued under British rule. This failure on the part of the British has allowed the Malaysian government to subsequently delay the granting of titles and deeds to Orang Asli communities. In the years following independence, asserting Orang Asli property rights has become increasingly problematic due to the acquisition of land by Malay villagers, government bodies, and private plantations.

In the meantime, uncertainty concerning the status of Orang Asli land has enabled the government to subtly adjust the size of indigenous reserves without contravening the Aboriginal Act of 1954. Although the government cannot deny indigenous groups access to their reserves, it can alter the area of these reserves if it has not been legally or clearly stipulated, and this is the strategy they have often used to control Orang Asli land rights. The government, however, is not alone in trying to manipulate the size of reserve lands. Occasionally, as is evident from the incident described below, the Orang Asli attempt similar tactics in reinforcing their land claims. Unfortunately, in their case, this strategy has only sowed conflict and further exacerbated relations with government bodies and private proprietors.

Around the time of resettlement, when they still lived in Kampung Kling and used Air Bah as a paddy field, Lanoh cleared ten acres of their twenty-acre reserve land near Air Bah for paddy planting. After only one season government officials forced them to abandon this land.[28] Soon a Chinese farmer took over this land and started a vegetable farm, effectively reducing Lanoh land in the area by half.[29] Despite being certain of having ten more acres at the same location, Lanoh felt powerless; they were unable to provide evidence of the total size of their reserve land. As a result, instead of openly contesting the government's actions in an effort to reclaim this loss, they decided to clear several acres of land adjoined to their existing fields in Air Bah. While clearing this land, they cut down several *meranti* trees (a rare hardwood timber). Since this land was owned by a government plantation, upon discovering what happened, the Department of Forestry sent its officials to deal with Lanoh.

As people in Air Bah recounted, these government representatives came up to the site three times, and 'three times they were sent away.' To the officer's question, why they cut down trees that did not belong to them, the Lanoh replied:

> We are Orang Asli and we are ignorant. The Forest Department people are clever people. But we know that if we want to take the fruits of our neighbours, we have to ask them. This is our land. Nobody told us whose trees these were and who planted them. If somebody had told us that these trees were Forest Department trees, then we would have asked why they were planted here in our land. So if we did anything wrong, then we can be arrested. But we did not do anything wrong. If the Forest Department plants trees on Chinese land, on Malay land, they would have to pay rent. So had we known, we would have asked for rent as well.

Incidents like this provoke Lanoh demands for the recognition and protection of their land rights. Although no one in Air Bah explicitly claimed so, the events surrounding resettlement make it likely that Lanoh moved to Air Bah in the late 1970s to actively assert their rights over their remaining land there.

Interethnic Conflict: Competition for Resources

Orang Asli today compete with members of different ethnic groups not only for land, but also for resources, as these other groups exploit forest resources in ways that Lanoh find difficult to understand or accept. The Chinese, for example, are often involved in illegal sport hunting, and people in Air Bah often deplore how uncaring these poachers are towards the forest and its animals. As one Lanoh in Air Bah put it:

> The Chinese don't care. They will shoot anything in the jungle; tigers, elephants, wild boar, anything they find. Sometimes they don't even take the animals they injure or kill. That's very sad.

Orang Asli are also competing for forest products with Malays, as Malays in the area are increasingly abandoning farming for wage work.

In the nearby Malay village of Sawa, for instance, only a few villagers still own land, and if they do, they have either rented it to rubber plantations or plant rubber themselves. Pressed for extra income, these Malays now supplement their earnings with activities that Lanoh consider to be their exclusive domain. It has become such a common occurrence for Lanoh to cross paths with Malays looking for rattan, *petai*, fruit, wild boar, frogs, and other 'Orang Asli' products in the forest that they remarked:

> Nowadays the forest gets as crowded as the market in Grik.

People in Air Bah are exasperated by this encroachment, not only for economic reasons, but because it impinges on their cultural identity. As was discussed in Chapter 2, trading in forest products is at least as important for Lanoh as is hunting and gathering. While hunting is, without a doubt, a salient part of Lanoh culture, and, as Gomes points out, the blowpipe 'has become an important ethnic marker or symbol of Orang Asli identity' (2007: 100), trading in forest products may be even more essential for defining Lanoh identity.

Hunting among Lanoh is above all associated with masculinity. It is an exclusively male activity, and people in Air Bah consider the idea of women engaged in hunting ludicrous. Whereas women may fish with fish traps or their bare hands, or catch small animals as they encounter them during their gathering trips, they never hunt for larger game, mainly because they are forbidden to touch sharp objects, dangerous tools, or hunting weapons. Cooking meat is similarly associated with men. Women do the everyday cooking of rice and vegetables, which men admit,

> they do very well ... when it comes to cooking meat, however, women don't know how to do it well. Men know far better how to cook meat.

Furthermore, hunting above all symbolizes masculinity and male sexual power. Far from being a 'mere' subsistence activity, hunting represents challenge, fun, and excitement to Lanoh men. They say they know they could catch squirrels far more effectively with mousetraps, but they would never give up blowpipe hunting for this effortless but boring method. Hunting in Air Bah is associated with masculine strength in other ways as well: certain parts of frequently hunted animals, for instance, are linked to male potency. In particular, Lanoh attribute their superior sexual vitality to eating squirrel's penis, a secret delicacy consumed only by men.

Yet, while Lanoh see hunting as an important source of male gender identity, collecting may even be more consequential for their sense of who they are as a people.[30] Centuries of interethnic trade have shaped a cultural universe in which Lanoh are sellers, while Malays and Chinese are buyers, of forest products, and as such stay away from the forest and its resources. Lanoh think of the forest as their home, and they take considerable pride in knowing about its resources. I witnessed this sentiment when, on one occasion, a Malay man hesitantly ventured to suggest a spot where he thought Lanoh collectors could get ample rattan. At this suggestion, his Lanoh acquaintances laughed incredulously, shaking their heads in disbelief. The Malay was clearly trespassing in a realm that these collectors consider exclusively their own.

It is not surprising, then, that Lanoh tend to discuss Malay involvement in forest collecting in moral terms. Describing Malay infringement upon their activities as 'shameless' (*tak tahu malu*), they ask, for example:

Why should we become Muslim when the Malays are becoming Orang Asli, living off jungle products?

The following interview excerpt is an expression of the indignation many Lanoh feel over these developments. According to Tabot, an older man in Air Bah:

They used to call us 'jungle people' because of our work in the forest, but now [Malays] have become like us. They take frogs which is *haram* [forbidden] according to Islam. The other day I met a Malay *Haji* looking for frogs at Sumpitan. We were looking for frogs in the river. It was late and we decided to spend the night there. We were about to make a fire when we heard noises from the river. I went quietly to see what it was. Then I saw two people. One was a boy. He was carrying a sack, like a *hapə?* [backsack]. The man was in the river with a flashlight. He picked up a frog with a little net. Then I shouted, 'Hey, who is that?' Then man was shocked. He almost fell. Then I said, 'We are Asli. We are looking for frogs. Who are you?' The man replied, 'I'm looking for frogs too.' The man came out of the water and approached me. Seeing the fire we had made, he said he wanted to take a break. Then I saw he was wearing the white cap of a *Haji* on his head. I asked him, 'Are you a *Haji*?' He said, 'Yes.' Then I

Figure 3.1 Blowpipe making.

said, 'How can you look for frogs? This is *haram*. You are a *Haji*.' The *Haji* replied, 'Oh yes, this is not to eat. This is for sale. I'm not a rich Malay. I'm a poor Malay. Frogs are good money. I have already about 2 kilograms. Maybe I can get RM 40. This is all right. This is not wrong.' Then I said, 'Ah, now you are saying it's not wrong. Before, when we passed through the *kampung* (village), you, Malays, were always telling us, 'oh you are going for frogs. How can you eat such things? They are so dirty.' If the frogs are dirty, the money you get from selling them is also dirty. So, *Haji*, don't look down on us Asli. If you think we are dirty, now you are as dirty as we are. If you think you are clean, so are we.' The *Haji* was very angry.

As a result of such incidents and the pressures resulting from the loss of land and the depletion of resources, there has been a significant change in the Lanoh conception of interethnic relations. While they once emphasized openness and inclusion, Lanoh now stress boundaries and exclusion.

Implication: From Contextual to Bounded Identity

The challenges and setbacks that Lanoh face are not unique – indeed, similar problems have beset virtually every indigenous group in South-

Figure 3.2 Blowpipe maintenance.

east Asia. One would think this would encourage Lanoh, living and interacting with other Orang Asli on a daily basis, to draw closer to their indigenous neighbours, finding common cause against Malay intrusion. However, although Lanoh in Air Bah readily identify issues relating them to other indigenous groups, they find at least as many to separate them. Due to their cultural flexibility and contextual identity, they do not perceive any more commonality with Orang Asli than with members of majority groups. At the same time resource competition has driven a wedge between them and other Orang Asli, so that more and more, Lanoh are in open conflict with other Semang for access to forest resources. These factors have hindered Lanoh participation in any kind of pan-ethnic Orang Asli movement.

The Pan-Ethnic Indigenous Movement in Malaysia

Many researchers object to amassing the indigenous groups of the Malay Peninsula into one broad ethnic category. Anthony Walker (1983: 455), for example, remarks that 'Orang Asli' is primarily an administrative construct and that there is little sociological, ethnic, or historical justification for such a homogeneous identity.[31] Similarly, Colin Nicho-

las suggests that 'before 1960, Orang Asli did not exist as an ethnic category. The various indigenous minority peoples in the Peninsula did
not see themselves as a homogeneous group, nor did they consciously
adopt common ethnic markers to differentiate themselves from the
dominant population' (2000: 6). Nonetheless, the shared experiences
of indigenous populations in Malaysia have encouraged the formation
of a pan-ethnic indigenous identity. In the same work, Nicholas comments on this emerging sense of commonality: 'With increased contact
with the dominant population, it became clear to various Orang Asli
groups that they had more in common with one another than they did
with the dominant population. This was especially so since much of
this later contact was not amicable or beneficial for them' (2000: 10; also
see Dentan et al. 1997).

Frequently, upon entering into discussions with national govern-
ments, indigenous groups modify their understandings of property or
territoriality to more closely align them with those of the nation state
(Ingold 1986: 157–8). With an emphasis on aboriginal political unity,
indigenous identity is also becoming more ethnic and exclusive (Guenther 1986; Griffin 1996). As a consequence, as Fred Myers (1988) has
noted, indigenous concepts rapidly change to conform to the legal
codes of the dominant society.

Occasionally, anthropologists have assisted in the development of
ethnic identity and cultural conservation among aboriginal peoples.
George Silberbauer, for instance, criticizes the Botswana government
for not promoting ethnic identity among hunter-gatherers, remarking
that 'earlier government action and inaction have done little to foster
among Basarwa a sense of valued ethnic identity which might otherwise have enabled them to join together to absorb and adapt to ... influences while maintaining their own social and cultural integrity' (1996:
49). In the light of these concerns, some researchers consider establishing a strong ethnic consciousness in indigenous groups to be an urgent
need, and some have even introduced media, such as radio, into indigenous communities to encourage ethnic mobilization (Spitulnik 1993).

In Malaysian scholarship, researchers advocating a pan-ethnic identity usually refer to three sources of shared consciousness among Orang
Asli peoples. First, they often consider past exploitative relationships
between Orang Asli and Malays as a basis for commonality between
Orang Asli groups. It has been suggested that anthropologists' focus
on slavery, fear of outsiders, timidity, encapsulation, exploitation, and
marginalization may have contributed to emerging pan-ethnic identity,

because it aggravated the embitterment caused by these issues among Orang Asli leaders and intellectuals (K.M. Endicott 1983; Rashid 1995; Dentan et al. 1997). Second, because of the structure of Malaysian society, ethnic identity has become the central framework for political action, and most political parties are defined on the basis of ethnicity (Rousseau, personal communication). Third, researchers have noted that Orang Asli share a similar economic position: debilitating poverty and a future as landless proletariat (Karim 1995: 29).

This focus on a shared indigenous identity, however, obscures real differences between Orang Asli groups.[32] Due to different demographic representation within the indigenous movement and diversity in cultural practices and livelihoods, not all constituent groups are represented equally. Interestingly, this unequal representation mirrors earlier biases in anthropological research in the area. From the earliest stages of Orang Asli studies, some groups, such as Senoi cultivators, have received more attention than others, like the Semang. This is partly because the northern part of the country was virtually inaccessible during the Malayan Emergency (1948–1960), and partly because Semang groups are ethnographically less attractive than the Senoi. Even now, as geographical constraints have been eliminated and the area is more open for investigation, anthropology students at Universiti Sains Malaysia rarely consider it as a possible field site because it is a 'poor region' compared with other parts of Malaysia (Rashid, personal communication). This has also contributed to an unequal ethnic composition among the indigenous intelligentsia; most Orang Asli professionals, intellectuals, and native anthropologists are Senoi. Thus, compared with northern Semang, the two major Senoi groups (Semai and Temiar) are more organized, informed, and publicized minorities (Rashid 1995: 3–4), and the indigenous movement has accordingly focused more on their priorities.

The indigenous political movement is a relatively recent phenomenon in Malaysia, where the political mobilization of Orang Asli did not begin until the second part of the 1980s. This mobilization began with the establishment of two main organizations, the Persatuan Orang Asli Semenanjung Malaysia (POASM, the Peninsular Malaysia Orang Asli Association) and the Centre for Orang Asli Concerns (COAC).[33] The pan-ethnic indigenous movement in Malaysia focuses on two issues: land rights and the right to self-determination and a distinct culture. In their struggle for land and self-determination, however, advocates often subscribe to an 'oppositional culture' approach

(Cowlishaw 1988, in Keen 2001: 169), which may not particularly appeal to Semang.[34] Land is undoubtedly important for rainforest collectors like Lanoh but, contrary to Senoi Orang Asli cultivators, whose main resource is land, Semang collectors rely equally on social resources – most vitally, their relations with non–Orang Asli. As a result, unlike the traditionally more isolated and self-contained Senoi, Semang are wary of alienating mainstream society.[35] A more comprehensive view of Orang Asli, addressing the individual concerns, difficulties, and aspirations of these peoples, would greatly benefit the minority groups that are most overlooked.[36] As it stands, these northern hunter-gatherers have until recently received relatively little attention and even less assistance.[37]

Lanoh epitomize the fate of such groups. As we have seen, their social organization, facilitating their lifestyle and interethnic interactions in pre-resettlement times, is increasingly a burden in their relationships with outsiders. In addition, as a result of their greater reliance on contact with outsiders, Lanoh are perhaps even more vulnerable to mistreatment and injustice than members of larger, more organized Orang Asli minorities.

Sharing in the Fate of Indigenous Peoples

There is considerable basis for the assumption that a common indigenous Orang Asli identity would emerge as a matter of course. Much of what Lanoh have experienced during the past fifty years has instilled in them a sense of camaraderie with other Orang Asli, and even with indigenous peoples elsewhere. Modern media have greatly contributed to this unified indigenous identity, as people in Air Bah now readily recognize indigenous peoples when they see them on television. As an example, while watching the opening ceremony of the 1998 Commonwealth Games on television, residents of Air Bah identified a Maori dancer as 'Orang Asli,' commenting on his loincloth and tattoos, which they compared to those of Sarawak aborigines. When the Samoan team appeared, they became especially excited, pointing out similarities between Samoan costumes and their own traditional headdresses (*manulaŋ*).

In addition to noting similarities through visual markers, Lanoh in Air Bah are also likely to make reference to pan-ethnic aboriginal identity when contemplating the destruction of natural resources by members of dominant ethnic groups:

> In 1996, there was an eclipse of the sun and all the world's scientists came to Sabah to see the phenomenon. The earth shook from Thailand to Singapore and everybody was afraid, the Muslims were praying, the Christians were praying. The Lanoh knew why it happened. The reason was that the people of the world, the Buddhists, Hindus, Muslims, are destroying land, mountains, the sea and so the Sun was angry and shut its eyes. When the scientists used their telescope and looked into the Sun, they saw an Orang Asli covering the Sun's eyes.

As in the above remarks, environmental destruction always provokes exasperated notes of criticism in which indigenous people are portrayed as standing apart from the rest of humanity.

Finally, the social boundaries that have always existed between Orang Asli and members of other ethnic groups enhance in Lanoh the sense of belonging with other Orang Asli. As external cultural pressure mounts, especially in the form of Islamization, these ties have only grown stronger. Lanoh often make statements like the following:

> We married only Orang Asli, our mother is Orang Asli, our father is Orang Asli. Maybe our god is also Orang Asli.

Even while Malays vigorously try to convert Orang Asli to Islam, they continue to maintain a social distance. People in Air Bah think it is inconceivable that Malays would ever welcome them in their restaurants, invite them into their homes, or let Orang Asli marry their women. This continuing ambivalence on the part of Malays towards Orang Asli is also likely to strengthen pan-ethnic indigenous identity. However, in spite of this broad identification with indigenous peoples in Malaysia and elsewhere, the cultural flexibility of Lanoh has prevented them from strongly identifying with any larger ethnic category.

Cultural Flexibility, Contextual Identity, and Their Implications for Intergroup Relations

In the previous chapter I described the cognitive and behavioural flexibility that characterized Lanoh in the past. They de-emphasized ethnic markers and territorial boundaries; instead, their cultural identity reflected their priority to maintain a wide network of interethnic relationships. Admittedly, they operated strictly within the confines of the Perak Valley and, like other collectors, '[moved] their places of residence

... within well-defined subsistence zones' (Dunn 1975: 99), a circumscription that could be mistaken for territoriality. However, as Elizabeth Andrews suggests, territoriality also implies 'the exclusive use of resources or occupation of an area by means of overt defense, or some form of communication or advertisement' (1994: 82), and this does not apply to hunter-gatherers like Lanoh. According to Robert Kelly (1995), hunter-gatherers achieve stability and reliability through the diversification of their resource base rather than through strict geographical boundary maintenance. As mentioned earlier, for forest collectors, this resource base also comprises social relationships, including those with neighbouring food producers (Peterson 1978). Thus, as Tim Ingold has pointed out, '[the] territorial boundaries [of hunter-gatherers] are open, indeed their very existence is predicated upon the possibility of movement across them' (1987: 156). Likewise, the only territorial principle that Lanoh used to stress was a welcoming and accommodating stance towards those wishing to enter and explore their habitat.

In the context of Peninsular Malaysia, the relationship of Lanoh to their land resembles that of the Batek De's. Kirk Endicott relates the Batek De belief 'that the land was created for all people to use, both Batek and non-Batek, and no one has the right to exclude anyone else from living or working anywhere they wish' (1988: 113). People in Air Bah echoed this view:

> Among the Lanoh, there is no individual ownership of fruit trees in the forest or in the village. For the Lanoh, everything is free for everybody. For instance, the Temiar can come here and look for food. People who make boundaries are people who are looking for enemies because boundaries attract enemies.

This open, inclusive attitude is further reinforced by a high degree of cognitive flexibility. As discussed earlier, the malleable social organization of mobile hunter-gatherers is accompanied by a fluid, non-dogmatic set of beliefs (e.g., Brunton 1989; Kent 1996a). Similarly, Lanoh cultural flexibility is evident from the way Lanoh readily accept complexity, acknowledge 'grey areas,' and reject rigid conceptual constructs. As the following interview excerpts demonstrate, residents of Air Bah poke fun at the Malays for their uncompromising emphasis on the purity of categories:

> For the Malays, some animals are clean and can be eaten and some ani-

mals are dirty. For instance, they say deer are clean and monkeys are dirty. However, the Lanoh say, 'Everything in this world is dirty. Even the waterfall is dirty.'

When the Malay says the food you eat is not clean, I tell him: 'You throw dead cats, dogs and birds into the river. The fish eat the dead bodies. Then you catch the fish, make a nice curry of it and say, yam, yam, tasty. Now that is *halal* for you.'

This cultural and cognitive flexibility also extends to the rejection of rigid ethnic boundaries. Woodburn notes that people in mobile hunter-gatherer groups exhibit only a loose solidarity towards members of their own band. They 'often do not seem to value their own culture and institutions highly, and may ... not [be] accustomed to formulating what their custom is or what it ought to be' (1980: 106; see also Brunton 1989; Guenther 1996; Griffin 1996: 114; Shnirelman 1994: 301). Like immediate-return hunter-gatherers elsewhere, Lanoh also often downplay the importance of ethnic markers. When asked about the meaning of ornaments on their artefacts, they deny that these have any significance. Instead, they offer an entirely pragmatic interpretation: these ornaments, they say, are carved in for a 'better grip.' This de-emphasis of ethnic markers corresponds to R.O.D. Noone's (1954–55: 17–18) notes on Senoi and Semang blowpipe traders, which indicate that ethnic identity markers are more significant for Senoi than for Semang; when trading for ready-made Temiar blowpipes, other Senoi frequently expressed their dislike of Temiar ornaments and altered them to their taste, yet the Semang did not express any such concern or preference.

Evidence of Lanoh cultural and cognitive flexibility suggests that Lanoh identity in the past was 'contextual,' with an emphasis on regional, as opposed to ethnic, commonality. This openness also extended to their perception of members of different ethnic groups, including Malays, Chinese, and other Orang Asli. Their attitude towards these groups was far from homogeneous, and they did not judge individuals solely on the basis of ethnic affiliation. Even today, people in Air Bah tend to trust certain Malays or Chinese more than others depending on their history and the nature of their relationship with the community. As pointed out earlier, Lanho contacts, especially contacts with Malays and their families, often stretch over generations. For example, Din, a Malay man from Kampung Sawa had known people in Air Bah since he was a little boy, because his father, and before that, his father's father, regularly traded with them. This man came 'up' to Air Bah almost daily and considered several of the villagers to be his friends.

Apart from village Malays officers of the JHEOA often also claim a special rapport with different Orang Asli villages. Unlike other government officers, who are transferred repeatedly through their careers, those in the JHEOA usually serve in one area. As a result they occasionally develop durable relations with Orang Asli in different villages over the years. The driver for the Grik JHEOA, for example, pointed out that he not only speaks Temiar, as do many other JHEOA employees, but also he has known most of the adults in Air Bah since they were children.

Lanoh relationships are far less cordial, however, with unfamiliar Malays. As a result of permanent sedentism and restricted movement, old patterns of familiarity between Orang Asli and Malays have given way to new hostilities. The interactions of Lanoh with Malays in and around Sumpitan illustrate this point. Since resettlement, when Lanoh stopped going to Sumpitan, a whole new generation of Malays have settled in villages around the Lanoh caves. These Malays are migrants from other areas, occasionally from other states, and have grown up without any relationship with or knowledge of Orang Asli. Unlike the few old Sumpitan families, these 'new Sumpitan Malays' are often unfriendly and even overtly hostile when Lanoh pass through their village.

Finally, the following excerpt on the difference between 'Sawa Malays' and 'Tawai Malays' reveals a similar Lanoh preference for the Malays they know, rather than a blanket sentiment towards the whole ethnic group:

> The Malays of Tawai are not friendly people; they do not like the Orang Asli. It is because they are prejudiced. They are not like the Sawa people, who are all very nice. The Tawai Malays are not from Perak, but Kedah and the Kedah people are not nice.

Shifting criteria of inclusion and exclusion also become manifest when Lanoh consider who is or isn't *səma² bluum*:

> *Səma² bluum* means 'people of the Perak river' between the Tasik and Batu Dua. *Səma² bluum*, in the strict meaning of the word, includes non-Orang Asli who live in this area as well. But, within Orang Asli communities, *səma² bluum* means Orang Asli of this area, which is mostly Lanoh, just like

jahay [Jahai] of Kelantan are known as *səmaʔ kəlantan* by Lanoh and *məniʔ kəlantan* by other Orang Asli.

Such a contextual understanding of ethnic relations further implies that Lanoh do not necessarily feel more commonality with Orang Asli than with anyone else.[38] As the interview excerpt above indicates, they similarly judge Orang Asli according to familiarity, closeness, and local affiliation. These criteria are elaborated in the excerpt below:

> Other Orang Asli are not like Lanoh. For instance, if you marry a Temiar and go to their village and do not want to speak their language and go with them, they will ask you to leave. Jahai are the worst, like the Orang Asli from Kelantan. Even if you marry them, live like them, and speak their language, they would still not like you. You have to pay for everything, constantly buy them things.

Lanoh in Air Bah classify Orang Asli of Perak as follows:

(1) Upper Perak – Perak Ulu: *Jahai*
(2) Lower Perak – Perak Kuala (or Perak Bawa): *Semai*
(3) Central Perak – Perak Tengah: *Lanoh*

The further removed indigenous groups are from the 'centre,' Perak Tengah (Central Perak, represented by Gua Kajang in Sumpitan), the less likely it is that Lanoh would associate with them. It appears that, as in the following statement, Lanoh trust Malays with whom they have had a history of good relations more than Orang Asli from states outside Perak:

> Although I live in the village now, I know enough of the outside … Big cities like Singapore of course I have not been to, but I've been to Kuala Lumpur, Penang, Ipoh, Taiping, and of course, Grik. Other Orang Asli, you know at the Kelantan side, on the Johor side, they're Orang Asli too, but I don't know them. Here, in the village, we have known the people [Malays] in Kampung Sawa for a long time and they have also known us.

This contextual approach to ethnic groups undermines the assumption that a perceived commonality among Orang Asli peoples will alone be sufficient to foster a pan-ethnic Orang Asli identity. Despite a broad identification with indigenous peoples in Malaysia and elsewhere,

Figure 3.3 Gua Kajang, Sumpitan.

several issues are currently driving a wedge between Lanoh and other Orang Asli.

Competition for Resources and Bounded Indigenous Identities

Among the issues separating people in Air Bah from other Orang Asli, especially Semang forest collectors, competition for resources is perhaps the most consequential. Now that resources are becoming scarcer and less accessible, Lanoh contend not only with Malays and Chinese for forest products, but also with other Orang Asli. As they press further into the shrinking forest, they often cross paths with other indigenous collectors in search of the same products, and such competition inevitably leads to conflict. Hostilities between Orang Asli collectors may become manifest in covert actions, such as sabotaging each other's activities by lodging complaints to local authorities or stealing each other's stashed-away rattan. Once, for instance, while going to contact a buyer, Lanoh collectors left three hundred pieces of rattan cut and ready for sale at a collection point hidden in the forest. By the time they returned a few days later, the rattan was gone, taken by a rival group.

Apart from such acts of sabotage, resource competition may also lead to open animosity between indigenous collectors, as Bulat, a Lanoh man from Air Bah, recounted in the following case:

Very bad are those ... Banun people [Jahai], where Corry [Cornelia van der Sluys] stayed, don't fool around with them. It happened to us, they wanted to shoot us with their blowpipe.[39] We were working rattan near the highway, near Kelantan. We, all of us, went over there to work rattan. After that, one day, luckily we had collected one lorry-load of rattan already, like when we are going to load tomorrow, this evening they came. They confronted us and said, 'You people, you came in here. Do you have authority? Do you have a pass?' Oh, they brought many blowpipes with them. Luckily, a soldier from K[ampun]g Sawa [came]. Next evening, [the Jahai returned and] brought their friends, with their [blowpipes], and we were scared. They said if we had no authority, we had to leave. Next morning... we came down from the hill to the highway, loaded our rattan, and quickly left. Had we stayed another night, they would have finished us off. That's the place where Corry worked. Don't fool with them. If we make a slight mistake in talking to them, we are finished.

As a consequence of such incidents, 'trespassing,' an unfamiliar notion in the past, is becoming a concern today, threatening good relations between Orang Asli and contributing to the reinforcement of inter-group boundaries.

This concern is evident even in Air Bah's relationships with other villages, such as Tawai, to which it is tied by intimate social relations. Relationships between these two villages were extremely close in 1998. Not only were visits between people from the two locations an everyday occurrence, but representatives from Tawai were invited to participate in every important negotiation and mediation taking place in Air Bah. Members of the two villages attended each other's communal feasts (kɘnuyiʔ). Nonetheless, in spite of these connections, when asked whether collectors from Air Bah could go to the forest of Tawai to look for bamboo, a product absent from the forests surrounding Air Bah, people in Air Bah said:

No matter how close we are, Tawai is Tawai and Air Bah is Air Bah.

This statement, clearly contradicting the principle of free access to resources, expresses the growing incongruity between the values of the past and the circumstances of the present.

Lanoh relationships with Senoi Temiar are similarly contradictory. On the one hand, Lanoh are envious of what they perceive to be the more advantageous position of the Temiar. On more than one occasion, people in Air Bah bemoaned that, because of their superior education, Temiar were more likely than Lanoh to be employed as forest rangers:

Now Malays are taking Temiar with education, so we don't have a chance.

Lanoh also believe that Temiar in large resettlement villages, such as Dala or Kemah, are better off financially. These villages not only own a vehicle, which as indicated earlier, remains unattainable for Lanoh, but also they receive regular government subsidies. On the other hand, in spite of the obvious perks from living in such a large resettlement village, and in spite of being constantly urged by officials to relocate to one, Lanoh choose to keep their distance, and have repeatedly refused to move from their present location.

The way Lanoh see other Orang Asli affects their attitudes towards the broader pan-ethnic political movement as well. By 1998 most Lanoh in Air Bah had met with representatives of the Peninsular Malaysia Orang Asli Association only once, when they came to Grik during a recruitment drive in 1996 to register villagers in the area. On this occasion, people were asked to fill out forms and pay two ringgit for membership.[40] Responding to questions about their feelings towards the movement, people in Air Bah took the opportunity to explain their attitude towards Malays, as well as towards Orang Asli. With a few exceptions, they indicated a desire to minimize external communication. Some residents thought it desirable for Lanoh to have representation at higher political levels, where major decisions are made, if only because such representation could help further insulate them from the outside world. Others, however, said they did not want to have anything to do with outsiders, including the Orang Asli movement, whose leaders and representatives they mistrust.

Conclusion

The past fifty years have seen Lanoh shift from a relatively equal and autonomous position of power based on control of the all-important resources of the forest to a position of powerlessness and their subsequent withdrawal from interethnic contact – both Malay and Orang Asli. I considered the implication of this shift for Lanoh participation in the indigenous pan-ethnic political movement in Malaysia, and suggested that they would benefit significantly from a more differentiated view of the experiences and needs of the groups involved. I further suggested that for Lanoh, seeking cultural continuity during times of change may not necessarily mean that high mobility, forest collecting, or even hunting and gathering will be retained. Instead, Lanoh wish to restore pre-independence power relations and their cultural and political autonomy. In this light, withdrawal, while superficially a complete break from their 'traditional,' more socially connected lifestyle, can be understood as an attempt to achieve this cultural continuity. In the next chapter I will further pursue evidence of Lanoh withdrawal and discuss the rise of village identity in Air Bah. An important implication of this is the resistance of Lanoh to the values of neighbouring peoples. In fact, one of the most frequent Lanoh complaints against Temiar, and the reason people in Air Bah often avoid socializing with them, is that they consider Temiar to be more assimilated to Malay values and lifestyle. On seeing apparently 'well-to-do' Temiar in a coffee shop in Grik, Lanoh would often make the comment:

See, they already look and act like Malays.[41]

4 Withdrawal from Contact and the Development of Village Identity

When it comes to understanding social change among contemporary hunter-gatherers, anthropologists often turn to acculturation as their primary explanatory framework (e.g., Howell 1983; Brunton 1989: 677; Kent 1995b). This emphasis on acculturation rests on the reasoning that 'although force is the last argument in society, through ideology men submit freely to the social system without a permanent need for the use of force ... That is why a change of society can be brought about only when the ideological belief of both ruled and the rulers has been smashed' (Larrain 1979: 79–80). Today hunter-gatherers living within the framework of nation states are often under considerable ideological pressure, and this grants the assumption that the process of their acculturation would be almost automatic. However, while the impact of external forces on hunter-gatherers in recent years has been undeniable, this assumption makes it less likely that anthropologists focus on within-group dynamics that often critically influence the process of acculturation. This oversight has denied researchers the opportunity to develop a more differentiated view of foragers' response to social change and the chance to gain further important insights into the structure and organization of these societies. In Air Bah, with regard to these within-group dynamics, the way change affected different age groups proved especially significant. Lanoh elders have withdrawn from external contact, strengthened the village boundaries, promoted a sense of village identity, and minimized the impact of external influences. These attempts to establish internal cohesion have made it less likely that Lanoh of this resettlement village will assimilate to Malay values and lifestyle.

Elders'. Withdrawal from Interethnic Contact

Examinations of gender-specific responses are abundant in the literature on changing hunter-gatherers (Draper 1975a, 1975b; Bell 1995; Kent 1995a, 1995b; Howell 1983; Gomes 1991; Nagata 1992); however, age-specific responses have been largely and inexplicably ignored.[1] Yet, as my work with Lanoh suggests, age is a far from neutral factor in the process of acculturation. In Air Bah age has played a critical role in post-resettlement internal dynamics. People of different age groups react differently to the impact of development and the changing interethnic relations described in the previous chapter.[2] Of all the villagers, elders are the most affected by these changes, which not only impact their status but also their livelihoods. As a result they have shifted from emphasizing external contact to promoting internal cohesion in the form of village identity, village integration, and village boundaries. Elders in Air Bah are especially affected by two developments: mistreatment by and hostility from outsiders and a decline in the trade of minor forest products.

In the last chapter I described how Lanoh interethnic relationships have changed in the past hundred years, especially since Malaysia's independence in 1957, and how they are now much more exposed to exploitation from outsiders. Although everyone experiences the effects of this unwelcome change, it is especially damaging to village elders as it challenges their leadership and authority. Leadership among Lanoh is age based; consequently, Lanoh elders, middle-aged men between the ages of 40 and 60, are used to being treated with certain deference.[3] More than any other age group, Lanoh elders are far less able and willing to deal with humiliating contact with outsiders. They frequently bemoan how difficult it is to 'stomach being told what to do [or] yelled at' by outsiders. To avoid such abuse, they withdraw from external contact to engage in 'inside' work.

To appreciate the implications of this, we first need to consider the distinction between 'inside' and 'outside' work. To Lanoh, 'inside' refers to 'village work' (farming or rubber tapping) and 'forest work' (forest collecting), while 'outside' denotes contract or wage work. People in Air Bah evaluate 'inside' and 'outside' work differently. Lanoh prefer inside work to outside work for two main reasons. First, 'inside' resources are renewable. As Lanoh reason:

[with outside work] after one day, the pay is gone, you've spent it all and you don't have anything left, [but with inside work] if you go to the jungle or plant fruit trees, after one year, you still have the jungle and fruit trees.

Second, inside work implies personal freedom and involves less con-tact with outsiders. Leman, an elder, explained:

> Malays are rude and they look down on us so we have to play stupid all the time if we don't want conflict or argument. That is why most of us will not work 'outside,' but stay in the village and try collecting. We like to be free, we do not like to be bossed around, and we do not like to boss around others. It is not in our nature.

Yet, no matter how desirable it is, not everyone in Air Bah engages in 'inside work' to an equal degree.

Participation in 'forest work,' for instance, is determined by several factors. In the past Lanoh collected both major and minor forest prod-ucts.[4] As detailed above, they not only collected items sought by mid-dlemen, such as rattan or fragrant agarwood (M. *gaharu*), but also minor products, such as herbal medicines, charms, atap, or blowpipe bamboo for Malay and Chinese villagers. Men of different age groups were not equally invested in, or suited to collecting all types of products – the younger men, for the most part, focused on 'heavier' commercial col-lecting of rattan and *gaharu*, while 'light' collecting was almost exclu-sively left to the elders of the village.

This division of labour in 'forest work' exists because the collection of major products, especially rattan, requires certain traits: the physical endurance necessary for such strenuous work and the ability to con-form and be accepted by others (to be a 'popular' or desirable work-mate). These two criteria emerged as most important from the survey I conducted on how Lanoh men decide to engage in different types of work (Dallos 2003). While, as noted earlier, most men in Air Bah prefer the freedom and independence of 'forest work,' they will only under-take such work if they are confident that they can earn at least the same amount of money from forest collecting as they could from contract work. This confidence is influenced by two conditions: popularity and physical fitness. Forest work is dangerous and requires, above all, trust in the ability and character of one's partners. As a consequence, before each collecting trip, considerable lobbying takes place among the men in Air Bah, and those who have not proven themselves during previ-ous engagements are rejected. The least popular among the men have limited choices; they can either work alone or team up with similarly unpopular individuals. Often, such 'unpopular' men have no other choice but to pursue 'outside' activities.

Because of the physical demands involved, elders are also at a disadvantage. Collecting major products, especially rattan, is both dangerous and gruelling work. Rattan collectors climb trees, cut through thick undergrowth, carry heavy loads for miles across difficult terrain, and occasionally, run from predators. After the age of 40 Lanoh men switch from rattan collecting to less strenuous activities, as the physical demands of this work begin to take a toll on their health. As a response to their diminishing physical fitness, they usually develop specialized skills like blowpipe making or blowpipe bamboo collecting. They also move away from collecting major forest products to collecting more knowledge-intensive minor products such as herbs and spices, medicinals, charms, and aphrodisiacs. At this age many begin to enhance their knowledge of plants, healing rituals, and incantations to become healers and shamans (L. *səma? hala?*). As Frederick Dunn summarizes: 'Rotan [rattan] collecting is particularly arduous; this is left to younger men. On the other hand, the collectors of herbs – especially medicinals – must have knowledge and experience that can only be acquired over many years. Thus, specialized collecting which is not particularly strenuous is the province of older men – in the 40s, 50s, and beyond' (1975: 80; see also Endicott 2005). Lanoh men over 40 specialize according to their interests and abilities. Their skills typically fall into one of the three following categories of spiritual endowment: knowledge of medicines, knowledge of incantations, and knowledge and control of mysterious powers. At the lowest level of spiritual attainment is the medicine man, who is 'familiar with herbs and knows how to apply them.' At the next level is the *səma? jampi?*, the person 'familiar with incantations and how to use these in healing.' Finally, at the highest level is the shaman, *səma? hala?*, who can access the spiritual domain without any mediating device or entity.[5] An old man, Pak Lang, explained:

A healer, or medicine man, [L. *jənampi?*], is a person who has knowledge of *jampi?* [incantation, spell]. A *jənampi?* may also use herbs. Yet, a person may know how to use herbs but still not be [*jənampi?*]. A *jənampi?* knows *jampi?* as well as herbs, but his knowledge of *jampi?* is limited to common illnesses. He cannot, for instance, do elaborate *jampi?* for protection against bad luck, or to ensure good fortune, such as *jampi?* for paddy planting. A *səma? hala?* [shaman] is more knowledgeable than all of the

above people. He can *jampi?* and if he does not know herbs, he does not
need to use herbs.

In 1998, although there was no distinguished shaman in Air Bah,
there were several elders and older men who were renowned for
their specialized skills. One man, Tabot, was recognized far and wide
as the best blowpipe maker, even drawing customers from other villages. Another, Kecil, was celebrated for his knowledge of medicinal
herbs, and he took every opportunity to extend his expertise in this
area. Finally, a third one, Leman, was known for his familiarity with
old incantations: although people were aware of the limitations of his
powers, they considered him extremely clever (M. *pandai*) when it came
to performing minor services.

Thus, in the past eldership was an important and well-respected
niche in the Lanoh social order based on the possession of both spiritual
and pragmatic knowledge. Elders specialized in collecting forest products that benefited from the experience of age, and this experience was
not only appreciated within the group but valued in interethnic contact
as well. Unfortunately for them, the decline of small-scale village trade
affected this specialized, light, 'knowledge-based' collecting the most.
As a result, if they are tired of 'forest work' and weary of mistreatment
by outsiders, elders today have only one option: to focus on 'village
work' and farm, tap rubber, or otherwise make use of those resources
that are close at hand.[6]

Enhancing Village Integration and Emphasizing Village Boundaries

To fully exploit the limited opportunities that are now available to them,
elders require a greater degree of social coherence. Before resettlement
Lanoh elders considered 'village work' of secondary importance to collecting. As outlined before, forest collecting, especially of minor products, is an activity best performed individually; consequently, Lanoh
elders of past generations would have required little cooperation from
anyone else, and it is unlikely that they would have been overly concerned with the comings and goings of younger men. Now, however,
as elders' options are limited to activities in the village, they need to
rely more extensively on the help of their younger kin to clear land or
perform similarly demanding tasks. As a result elders today are stepping up their efforts to increase village integration and cooperation,
and by extension, they try to exercise greater influence over younger

Figure 4.1 Going into trance during sewing.

men. In the following pages, I describe several attempts at increasing internal cohesion, all of which can be interpreted to be part of elders' strategy to control younger males. In these endeavours they use several strategies such as exaggerating danger and external threats, preventing younger men from leaving the village, controlling the movement of women, encouraging endogamy and village boundaries, and, finally, promoting Lanoh values over Malay values and lifestyle.

Promoting Unity through the Exaggeration of External Threat

Even though Lanoh are known as peaceful, easygoing people who avoid confrontation, elders in Air Bah have more than once used an external threat to village security as a pretext to stir people's emotions and strengthen village unity. The leadership of Air Bah regularly call large meetings to deal with real (but more often imagined) threats to village security. The following perceived threats occurred during my stay in the village:

- A Patani[7] child was missing, and there was a perceived threat of being held responsible.
- A Malay woman was raped in one of the neighbouring villages, and there was a perceived threat of being held responsible.

- A Lanoh man had a sexual adventure in a Temiar village, and there was a fear of retribution.

Not accidentally, all of these incidents involved an interethnic element; an attempt to construct an 'imagined community' is a strategy akin to that of enhancing cohesion and the unity of different strata of society in nation states (Anderson 1991).

Observing the village elders' efforts to establish such 'imagined community,' one could conclude that Lanoh in Air Bah have become predisposed to organized action. However, the rhetoric used to ignite concerns and passions in villagers was never followed up by action. Its sole purpose was to create internal solidarity and depict Air Bah's leaders as capable, forceful, and decisive. Such dramatic events tended to bring the village together, but they did so only temporarily and were not at all successful in rallying the coveted support of younger men. Opting for a more direct approach, elders often interfered with younger men's work outside of the village.

Promoting Unity by Undermining Wage Opportunities

In Air Bah it is the primary responsibility of younger men to earn money, to provide for their families, and to support the community. Yet, in several instances, Lanoh elders prevented younger men from leaving the village to pursue more lucrative 'outside work.' The contradiction between this responsibility and the actions of the elders suggests a recent change in the relationship between younger men and elders. It is noteworthy that elders of the village work hard to undermine the best wage opportunities that would free younger men from under their influence for long periods, as well as those that could undermine their authority within the group.

Of all available opportunities, people in Air Bah dislike wage work the most; even contract work is preferable, as the lesser of two evils. Contract work not only implies less commitment and supervision, but it is usually better paid than wage work and allows Lanoh freedom to determine their own hours and pace. When pressed for cash, people in Air Bah may briefly experiment with wage employment. Even then they will unhesitatingly abandon it for better opportunities. They admit to being easily 'fed up' (L. *bood*) with monotonous work, poor working conditions, long hours, and low wages.[8]

Detesting and avoiding wage work as much as possible, Lanoh do not in principle object to paid employment. Before Malaysia's independence, for instance, Lanoh were regularly employed as forest guides and porters for British administrative officers such as Major Williams-Hunt and R.H. Noone. Even though they were quite critical of the demands made of them by their British employers, Lanoh seemed to have enjoyed the fact that this employment matched the mobility, flexibility, and individualism of their lifestyle. Adnan illustrated the importance of these principles by comparing working as a police ranger to working as a forest ranger. He explained that his brother,[9] who worked in another village as a police ranger,

> owes money, has no land, and is not free. So what's the point? Working as a forest ranger [game warden] is quite different. A forest ranger is in charge of an area, where he looks after trees, water, and animals, and that's easy.

Adnan's view is shared by most Lanoh, who particularly abhor wage work that imposes strict discipline or restricts their movements. Thus, when the government began recruiting Orang Asli for the Home Guard (M. *Wataniah*), a paramilitary reserve of the regular army, people in Air Bah refused to sign up. The following statements by Rudin, a younger man, clearly express Lanoh aversion to the structure, danger, and bondage of army service:

> Working for the army, you get yelled at and you cannot just walk away and leave because they put you in jail. You have to stand for hours, do sentry duty, all alone in the jungle, rain or shine. Besides, using guns is dangerous … and all this for a little money. We have seen Malay soldiers cry when they had to march through the jungle. When they stopped in Orang Asli villages, they cried. Also, I have children, so I'm not too keen on getting myself killed.

As a result Lanoh avoid outside wage employment as much as possible. With the exception of one person who worked for the Police Field Force (M. *Police Hutan*) in Kampung Dala, I did not meet anyone in Air Bah who held permanent employment.

Even outsiders have noted that people in Air Bah do less wage work than Orang Asli elsewhere. A Malay acquaintance of the Lanoh Pak Sarudin compared employment in Air Bah with that of another resettlement village in this way:

> Unlike the people here, those in Bt. Sapi work for other people outside. In

fact, they prefer working for wages. This is a difference between people in Air Bah and Bt. Sapi. The people there work for FELDA [Federal Land Development Authority], in factories, they work for timber companies and government services. As a consequence, they have more money and are able to buy goods, such as motorcycles and television sets.

The organizational strictures of wage work, however, are not the only reason that Lanoh avoid it. People in Air Bah also do less wage work outside the village than those in other Orang Asli resettlement villages because Air Bah elders dissuade and prevent them from such employment. This especially applies to younger men. On more than one occasion I overheard elders warning younger men that

> working in the village is better. Working outside is just working for wages. The things we want in order to prosper are not there.

The next two cases, in which village elders sabotage younger men's efforts to develop skills, acquire experience, and engage in interesting wage work outside the village, reinforce this conclusion. Occasionally, opportunities will arise that enable younger men to earn wages beyond the earning potential of most Orang Asli in Upper Perak. From time to time, for example, the government encourages young Orang Asli to acquire training in technical trades and become skilled workers. On one such occasion, in 1994, three young men from the village were invited by a government agency to participate in a six-month auto and motorcycle mechanic course in Kuala Lumpur. One of these younger men, Bulat, recounts his experience in the workshop:

> That course was paid by the JHEOA [Jabatan Hal Ehwal Orang Asli]. That was the only time I had that opportunity. I would have loved to complete that course, but it was like this: there were three of us; me, Anwar, and Amin. Amin left after a week. He couldn't stand it, he wanted to go back. Anwar and I stayed. After six months, I almost got a job. Actually, I was offered a job. It was from a workshop to repair old cars. I was given three days' vacation and told to come back after three days to start work. I came back to the village with Anwar. I went to his uncle, Hitam, and told him about Anwar's problems. While we were in the dormitory in Pahang, Anwar used to hang out with bad kids. Because of that, when it was time to go back, Anwar was advised not to go back. Because of this, I felt I couldn't go back either.

On another occasion, in 1998, another younger man, Rosli, was offered a job in the local tourist industry. Mr Tan, the Chinese owner of the Oasis Hotel in Penang, regularly hosted 'cultural shows' to cater to Western backpackers, featuring weekly displays of Orang Asli customs, songs, dances (*sewang*), and blowpipe demonstrations. He also employed Orang Asli in his hotel and restaurant. A former 'rattan boss' in the Grik-Lenggong area, Mr Tan mainly hired Temiar from Bukit Sapi and Dala, and people in Air Bah learned about this opportunity from their friends and relatives there. The work in Penang was attractive; it was not only considered easy, but also the pay was good (Mr Tan paid RM 1,000 for three months' labour, on top of food and lodging), far better than anything else available locally. It is not surprising, therefore, that Rosli decided to try his luck:

> When I started to work in Penang with my friend Glak, the people in the village did not like that. People started to talk about us ... all the elders here, like Hitam and Tengah and others as well. There were about four of them who were very critical of us. Especially when they heard that I had befriended a white woman in Penang. My friend told people about me. He came back to the village and told everybody here. He also gave people the phone number in Penang and people would call me there. My boss in Penang told me, 'You have to go back tomorrow or your people will be very angry with me.' I came back, just for one day, to give money to my sister. I wanted to leave the same evening. Just before I left, Anwar ran after me, caught me in the bus stop and said, 'Wait, wait, people want to talk to you.' The family of my old mother-in-law, Som, came and talked to me. They asked me to return. They wanted me to marry my present wife [another one of Som's daughters]. They offered her to me. So I came back to the village.

Rosli's tale is not only an important example of elders pressuring younger males to remain in the village; it also highlights one method by which they assert control: by manipulating their relationships with women. This is a relatively new practice. As discussed earlier, Lanoh marriages in the past were casual, and it was usually left to young people to choose their marriage partners. Unlike elders among other immediate-return hunter-gatherers, such as the Ju/'hoansi, where arranged marriages are quite common (see, e.g., Shostak 1981), Lanoh elders evidently had no influence in this area. As described by several Lanoh men, courtship among young Lanoh faced little to no outside pressure:

Before, a boy and girl met in the forest doing work together, spending time together. The boy would give food to the girl to cook. If she brings some back to the boy, it is a sign that she likes him. That night, they would meet secretly and marry [sleep together], without anyone knowing. The next day, he would let somebody know (for instance, a neighbour or close friend) who would tell people, older people and the girl's family. Only then would the boy go to the girl's family and apologize for not telling them earlier. That's about it. After that, they would live together, and he would start to build a house because then he could not go back to his family and the girl would not want to live with her family either. From then on, he would provide food, shelter, and clothing.

When we want to get married, we usually arrange it ourselves. Like I would ask a girl if she has any boyfriend or she has a man. Then I'd ask the girl to take me as her man. If she likes me and if she says, 'Yes,' I'd go and see her parents or her brothers, sisters and tell them of my intentions and that we've agreed. Once everybody knows about that, then we're married, we live together. It's not like the Malay marriage. We have our own *deŋ lɛʔlɔy* (lean-to shelter). We usually know ourselves who we like and we marry like that. It's easy.

In those days, marriage was not like today. We married when we both liked each other. She liked me and I liked her and so we got married. Her father said, 'Alright, now you can get married, since you like each other.' When I brought her back here, my father said, 'If you married her, that's fine, so you're married now.' We didn't have any feast, or anything like that. I just made a house and we lived here.

As the last excerpt implies, the situation has changed. Today elders exercise much more control over marriages. Part of this control arises from JHEOA policy, which requires formal registration for all Orang Asli marriages. Under these rules, the *penghulu* (headman) of Air Bah is now expected to inform the JHEOA and the *Kathi* (Muslim religious authority administering marriage) of any upcoming marriage. For this to happen, a young man must first inform the *penghulu* of his intentions. The *penghulu* in turn needs to consult with the families of the prospective couple, announce the engagement to the village, and formally notify the JHEOA and the *Kathi*. Although Lanoh in Air Bah rarely abide by these new rules, and most marriages are still conducted in the 'old way,' people cited a few cases of young couples having been

Table 4.1 Gender Differences for Time Spent outside the Village

Observations	Men n (%)	Women n (%)
Total	623 (100)	646 (100)
'Inside'	374 (60)	467 (72)
'Outside'	249 (40)	179 (28)

'caught in the Muslim trap.'[10] In addition, elders can use and have used this new script to apply pressure on younger men. As was shown earlier, they now occasionally exert their influence by trying to control and manipulate marriages within the community. As we will see, this has also had an effect on the status and treatment of women within Air Bah that varies from the situation in other villages.

Promoting Unity through the Control of Women

It is not surprising, in light of earlier discussions on female sedentism, that women in Air Bah have more limited contact with outsiders than men do. To some extent this discrepancy stems from the lifestyle of Semang peoples and to some extent from changes that all Orang Asli are experiencing. Yet, while women in Air Bah share certain roles and expectations with Orang Asli women in other villages, men in Air Bah place greater emphasis on protecting women's sexuality and shielding them from the outside world than Orang Asli men do elsewhere.

Table 4.1 shows the difference between the amount of time men and women in Air Bah spent outside the village during my fieldwork. In this table, observations made 'inside' the village area (the village and surrounding fields) are contrasted with instances when the person could not be directly observed because she or he was 'outside' the village in town, on contract, in the forest, or visiting relatives in other villages at the time of the survey. Even though Lanoh consider 'forest work' to be an 'inside' activity, for the purposes of this comparison, forest work is included in the 'outside' category because it often involves contact with outsiders. As the table also indicates, to a great extent, female mobility in Air Bah is influenced by the sexual division of labour. Women are not only more restricted than men in participating in commercial collecting or contract work, but they also bear most of the burden of child care.

As noted earlier, even in pre-resettlement times Lanoh women were less involved in commercial collecting and trade than Lanoh men were. This is certainly not unique to Lanoh, as it is quite common among the forest collectors of the peninsula. Among Semang peoples, although

Table 4.2 List of Cultivars Planted by Men and Women in Air Bah

CULTIVARS PLANTED BY MEN		
gətah	rubber	(*Gutta Caoutchouc*)
təluy	banana	(*Musa sapientum*)
taɲuy	rambutan	(*Nephelium lappaceum*)
pənyug	durian	(*Durio zibethinus*)
laŋsɛd	langsat	(*Lansium domesticum*)
cɛmpɛda?	cempedak, jack-fruit	(*Artocarpus polyphema*)
limau?	lime	(*Citrus acida*)
boh maɲi?	mangosteen	(*Garcinia manggostana*)
hipay	coconut	(*Cocos nucifera*)

CULTIVARS PLANTED BY WOMEN		
hubi?	tapioca	(*Manihot utilissima*)
jago?	corn	(*Zea mays*)
cabɛy	chili	(*Piper longum*)
sə?	sweet potato	(*Ipomoea batatas*)
siyay	lemon grass	(*Andropogon choenantus*)
bəy bayam	spinach	(*Spinacia oleracea*)
bənhɛd	pumpkin	(*Cucurbita pepo*)
labo?	squash	(*Cucurbita cucutia*)
kətulo?	gourd	(*Lua cylindrica*)

both men and women collect certain types of forest products, it is the men who deal with rattan buyers and trade in forest products (Endicott and Endicott 2008: 91–4).[11] Recently, this pattern has extended to contract work. To some degree this is due to the belief among employers that women are less capable of performing physical tasks. As a result contractors are less likely to seek female labour. When they do (women in Air Bah have regular work at a nearby Chinese vegetable farm, for example), they are generally assigned lighter tasks, such as picking vegetables or tying up cucumber vines.

These constraints are reinforced by internal taboos prohibiting women from touching dangerous objects, such as blowpipes, *parangs*, or axes. While such taboos (L. *səlantap*) are common among hunters and gatherers, they have had an effect on Lanoh women extending well beyond the realm of hunting.[12] These taboos also have major implications for the division of labour in farming, for example, as they prescribe which plants can be planted by men and which by women.[13]

Table 4.2 shows a list of the cultivars planted by men and by women in Air Bah. The items in the former group are plants with hard stems that require the use of an axe, while those in the latter have softer stems, which can be worked with a knife.

These prohibitions also have implications for women seeking to

Table 4.3 Distribution of Work by Gender in Air Bah

Observation of Activities	Men n (%)		Women n (%)	
Total number of observations (work and leisure)	623	(100)	646	(100)
Work-related activities				
Contract	102	(16)	62	(10)
Farming	42	(7)	63	(10)
Commercial collecting	94	(15)	–	
Housework	–		131	(20)
Subsistence hunting-gathering	11	(2)	25	(4)
Work and leisure accompanied by child	18	(3)	228	(35)
% of observations of work without child care	(40)		(44)	
% of observations of work including child care	(43)		(79)	

engage in contract work, because they prevent them from volunteering for activities requiring the use of sharp tools. These include high-paid jobs, such as tree felling, land clearing, or house building. As a result, while men are often bombarded by contract offers, women are restricted to work at the nearby Chinese vegetable farm. Table 4.3 shows that the time women spend outside the village is likely influenced by housework and child care. While men spend a total of 31% of their time outside the village engaged in collecting (15%) and contract work (16%), women spend only 10% of their time outside the village doing contract work. Even more revealing, women perform all household tasks (20%), including the majority of child care.

This observation contradicts accounts of mobile hunter-gatherers that have emphasized male participation in child care (e.g., K.L. Endicott 1992; Endicott and Endicott 2008). In Air Bah it was quite apparent that Lanoh men and women are not equally involved. While happy to supervise infants in their leisure time, men rarely take care of sick or older children, and overall they spend far less time with children than women do. Today, when Lanoh women have more children born at shorter intervals, child care and housework greatly impede their ability to travel outside of Air Bah. The more children a woman has, the less likely is she to leave the village.

These factors are not unique to Air Bah, but affect women in all Orang Asli settlements equally. Yet, in spite of this shared context, women in Air Bah are much more restricted. Women in other communities are not only more involved in trade, but also they travel regularly to towns frequented by Orang Asli. For instance, while Batek women participate in trade less than men do, Kirk and Karen Endicott found that 'both men and women collected and traded some kinds of forest products' (2008: 91). Lanoh women, on the contrary, never participate in trade and hardly ever accompany men to sell forest products in Lenggong or Grik. Although they often manufacture brooms and woven baskets from *pandan* leaves (*Pandanus* spp.), as do other Semang women, they never put these items up for sale. In fact, apart from family visits to other villages, women in Air Bah rarely venture further than to the Chinese vegetable farm or the small general shop in Kampung Sawa, which is no more than two hours' walking distance from the village.

This discrepancy between women in Air Bah and women in other Orang Asli communities is largely due to the varying efforts of Orang Asli to insulate women from the outside world. In Air Bah men go to much greater lengths to protect women from outsiders, urging them to move and work in large groups whenever they leave the village. When working at the Chinese vegetable farm, women are accompanied at all times by younger men who act as their guardians and mediate between them and their employers. These younger men also handle all monetary transactions and distribute the women's earnings.

These precautions arise from more than simply a pragmatic concern for women's safety. Women in Air Bah are not merely afraid to be alone when outside the village; they are *expected* to be so. It is common for women to refuse to go to the fields to collect firewood, because, as they claim, they are afraid to go alone. In one example, at around 5 o'clock in the afternoon an older woman announced that she was going to the fields to plant tapioca, expecting others to accompany her. A young woman immediately responded that she was afraid to go to the fields alone at that hour. When nobody noticed, she repeated her response (*ʔiɲ tooŋ ʔiɲ cib huma? a job*) until everyone paid attention approvingly. Men in the village often comment on women's 'shyness' with similar approval. This suggests that the need for women to be protected has assumed a social role in Air Bah that is emphasized far beyond practical concerns.

Women are coached to be concerned about protecting their sexuality from the time they are young. While there is little difference in the socialization of boys and girls until about the age of 13, parents guard their daughters' sexuality from a very early age. It is quite common for parents to let little boys run around naked, for example, but girls of any age must remain covered. When asked about this discrepancy, women replied:

Well, this is the way. Little girls must wear pants. With little boys, it doesn't matter.

As they grow older, young men (if they are not already married) are allowed to move into a separate dwelling with other men. Young women, however, may not live alone under any circumstance.[14] It thus seems clear that women's sexuality is a special concern for Lanoh, requiring close attention from a very young age.

This protection of young women is further expressed in rituals. During the ritual singing session (pɘnloj), for instance, young unmarried girls are prohibited from falling into a trance because 'no one would be able to revive them.' This need to protect young unmarried women similarly is evident in rituals that take place around the shaman's ceremonial hut (pano?):[15]

> The pano? is made of bertam leaves. The [shaman] sɘma? hala? will go inside the hut ... The sɘma? hala? will start to sing praises and stories, and then he will vanish and his body will be replaced by a spirit because with his singing he is calling the spirits. During his singing, nobody outside the hut is allowed to move. The audience sits in the following manner: the first ring around the pano? are young virgin girls. The next ring is composed of women and children, and the outer ring is of men. The sɘma? hala? commences singing during which time nobody is allowed to move about because this is the time when the spirit of the sewang is coming to the pano?. Anybody who moves would obstruct the spirit from getting into the pano? and would annoy the spirit which could result in the sickness of the person who has moved. The spirit is called the tok guru's 'son.' His son would come into the pano? and replace the sɘma? hala?. The people would still see the sɘma? hala?, because his 'son' impersonates him; he takes his voice and shape. During this singing, the women, especially virgin girls, will follow the singing.

This arrangement, with young unmarried women placed in the inner, protected circle, reinforces the view that guarding young unmarried women and their sexuality is a central, ideological concern in Lanoh social life.

Lanoh fears about women's security are occasionally justified by incidents of sexual harassment by Malays, Chinese, and Indians in the past. In the light of these events, it would seem that the fixation on protecting the women of Air Bah is merely a reaction to external threats. Past attacks on women certainly live vividly in people's memories, and the increasing presence of the outside world in Air Bah could undoubtedly enhance the fear of such incidents. Yet, while women are constantly reminded of the dangers of being sexually assaulted, reactions to actual assaults are quite mild. For instance, when recounting an incident in which a young woman was raped by an outsider, people conceded:

What could we do? We just told the girl to be more careful next time.

Men in Air Bah seem more concerned with the *threat* of rape than with *actual* incidents of rape.

Indeed, instead of rape, it is just as likely that Lanoh men are primarily worried about seduction by outsiders or prostitution, an increasingly common problem in larger Orang Asli villages (Dentan 2008). This apprehension may also explain why people in Air Bah are reluctant to move to larger villages or to fraternize with Orang Asli there. In the following interview excerpt, an elder compares the virtue of women in Air Bah with women in other villages:

Women of other villages, non-Lanoh, like Temiar and even the men are promiscuous. For instance, everybody knows in Dala, Kemah, Kroh, Ulu Grik, men will not be shy or inhibited to try to seduce women, even if the women are married. The women are like that too. Even if they are married, they will go with someone they like. And the women are especially attracted to gifts and money. It is like a cattle market. Kroh is no different. When my brother Hitam was in Kroh because he was sick, I went with him for a few days. The woman of the house we were staying in, every night would go out saying that she was watching TV and come back at two or three in the morning. On weekends, she and her family would go to town. They had a lot of money, but I did not see them really working. There are a lot of outsiders in these big Orang Asli villages, Chinese timber people would come in, Malay soldiers, Indians, and they all at night will get an Orang Asli girl. Even our friend, the JHEOA driver and officer will get Orang Asli girls when they go to Dala, Kroh, or Kamah. That is why they like to go there. Once I was in Bukit Sapi. There, too, these things happen. I had an argument with the headman there. He boasted that the Chinese farmer whom the women worked for paid better than Ah Lam here. He said the women sometime get 50 ringgit each. But of course not everybody gets 50 ringgit a day. I told him that was impossible. Chinese are Chinese, they would pay the same or less to Orang Asli workers. I said that must be something else the women were doing for the Chinese farmer. He understood that I meant the Chinese farmer was allowed to seduce the women. The headman was angry. He did not believe me. But one day, some of the young men went to spy on the women. They saw, sure enough, the Chinese farmer and also one of his friends having sex with the women. They had a mat and they were doing it near the farm where there are bushes. Then the headman believed me. The village reprimanded the women and counselled them. They stopped working for the Chinese farmer. But you know, I think some of them still follow Chinese people who want to go fishing up the river. One or two women would go in their cars and stay with them the whole day. And then these women still have money to go to Lenggong on market nights and buy things. But here the women do not know how to do those things. They go to Ah Lam in big groups, they all come back together, and they only get two–three dollars, and people come to the village, the women do not run to meet them, not like in Dala. They would run to meet these men even when they are not properly dressed.

This account suggests that elders in Air Bah may for now be more successful in protecting women's sexuality than those in other villages. This underlines the link between protecting women's sexuality and reinforcing village boundaries. By limiting women's contact with outsiders elders can protect their sexuality, an instrumental factor in controlling younger men.[16] And as the elders of Air Bah have drawn the village boundaries tighter, the Lanoh have shifted from a traditionally exogamous social network to village endogamy.

Promoting Unity through Village Endogamy

In the past, in accordance with the priority of extending relationships far and wide, Lanoh emphasized exogamous marriage. Today, however, one often hears Lanoh elders say that they wish all young people married Lanoh in the village. This is hardly possible, however, because most young people in the village are too closely related to marry without violating rules of exogamy. As a necessary compromise, people today often marry Temiar. However, these Temiar are closely watched; they are not only expected to conform to village norms, but to act Lanoh as well. Lanoh seem to consider these interethnic marriages to be reciprocal exchanges. They fully accept that the children of people who marry in Temiar villages will become Temiar, but they also anticipate that children of Temiar who marry into Air Bah will grow up as Lanoh. Temiar in Air Bah are expected to facilitate this by learning the language and making a real effort to behave like Lanoh. Those violating these expectations are severely criticized. People explain:

Figure 4.2 Women's workload increased after sedentism.

> We welcome everybody. If they come to the village, we let them stay – if they are good and follow our ways. But if they don't want to live like us, we don't want them.

As an example they often brought up the case of a Temiar woman, Sitah, who refuses to learn Lanoh and keeps returning to her native village:

> She married here, but speaks to her children in Temiar ... she is Temiar, not Lanoh.

The expectation among residents of Air Bah that newcomers must learn to be Lanoh does not simply imply a new emphasis on Lanoh identity, but specifically on village identity.

Promoting Unity through Village Identity

Increasingly, the people of Air Bah have tried to monopolize Lanoh identity, excluding Lanoh of other subdivisions. In Chapter 2, I suggested that the mobile lifestyle of forest collecting rendered these Lanoh subgroups irrelevant. Today, perhaps also prompted by the frequent inquiries of anthropologists and other outsiders, these subdivisions have re-emerged, imbued with new significance as convenient categories for Lanoh elders to reinforce village boundaries. In conversations about identity, the distinction between 'real' and 'fake' Lanoh frequently came up. According to people in Air Bah, they are the 'pure' Lanoh, Lanoh *jǝram*, variously identified as Lanoh (*sǝmnam*) or Lanoh (*sakaʔ*) ('original' or 'true' Lanoh), while the rest are 'second-class' Lanoh (M. *mereka macam clas dua Lanoh*).[17] This distinction between first- and second-class Lanoh is partly geographical, partly linguistic. First, as discussed in the previous chapter, parameters of land have been gaining practical, as well as symbolic, significance as territorial and ethnic markers. As noted earlier, Lanoh identity is anchored in the Gluk-Sumpitan area and Gua Kajang, which Lanoh consider to be their spiritual and geographical centre. People in Air Bah claim that, they, the Lanoh *jǝram*, are the only ones associated with this centre (L. *kǝloŋ*), while other groups, such as the Lanoh *kobaʔ, jinjeŋ, mǝndǝrǝy*, and *lepey*, used to inhabit areas of secondary importance to the south, west, and north.[18]

Lanoh in Air Bah further distinguish themselves based on their 'proper' pronunciation of the Lanoh language, and they tend to look down on other Lanoh because of their dialects. They explained that these 'other Lanoh' have become 'mixed' as a result of their extensive intermarriage with Temiar. People in these groups not only often use Temiar, but also speak Lanoh with a 'funny accent.'[19] For those in Air Bah this proves that they are not 'real' Lanoh. In some contexts they are considered Lanoh, while in others, they are Temiar.

A third reason for assigning members of other subdivisions such inferior status is their perceived lack of historical knowledge.[20] This concern with history in Air Bah appears to run counter to past principles of instruction and learning among Lanoh. As the following remark by Atan suggests, the instruction of young Lanoh used to be every bit as practical, contextual, situational, and up-to-date as the instruction of other young Semang (see, e.g., Lye 1998, 2005):

> The adults, old people of those days, would teach us how to hunt, where to go, how to take care of ourselves in the jungle. We didn't learn about what our grandparents did or didn't do. We don't know about stories of our grandparents, great-grandparents. We never learned that.

On the contrary, today's elders strive to educate young people beyond such practical needs and concerns. One of them, Tengah, said:

> We want to tell this story [of Lanoh origins and history] to the young ones, because they don't know about it.

They also contrast their knowledge of history with the 'ignorance' of other Lanoh:

> So we have this history. The other Lanoh in the other villages don't have this history. If you ask them where they came from, they don't know.

Thus, the people of Air Bah increasingly conflate the confines of Lanoh identity with their village limits. Lanoh in Air Bah try to preserve this identity by promoting values that identify them, as well as set them apart from others.[21] Although many of these values, especially non-violence, used to distinguish Orang Asli groups from Malays, Chinese, Indians, and Westerners, people in Air Bah believe that they may be the only ones left who care about these ideals. This need to preserve their cultural identity and traditional values is perhaps the most important reason for Lanoh to resist Islam.[22]

Resisting Acculturation

It would seem that, by now, people in Air Bah have nearly completely succumbed to acculturation. They are nearly completely sedentary and rely heavily on cash, consumer goods, and modern means of transportation; they buy food in the store, and even engage in farming far more than they once did.[23] On top of all that, the majority of people in Air Bah have been officially converted to Islam since the 1970s. Since the Malay value system is strongly rooted in Islamic tradition, we can gauge Lanoh attitudes towards the Malay lifestyle by Lanoh willingness to adopt Islamic beliefs and practices. The following study of these attitudes will reveal that, in spite of great pressure to assimilate and embrace Islam, Lanoh still resist it, especially because they perceive it to be contradictory to their core value of non-violence.[24]

Pressure to Assimilate and Embrace Islam

The biggest dissatisfaction that Lanoh have concerning Malay rule is that, unlike the British, Malays are trying to change them. As Colin Nicholas suggests, the national government of Malaysia regards Islamization as a tool towards the ultimate goal of integrating Orang Asli into Malaysian society (2000).[25] As a result of this policy, over the past thirty years Orang Asli have been under constant and intense pressure to adopt an Islamic world view. This pressure not only manifests itself in visits by Muslim missionaries, but also in the occasional appearance of a religious teacher, or *ustad*, in the village.[26] The easygoing attitude of Lanoh towards these representatives has misled many Muslim visitors who, as a consequence, remain baffled by Lanoh reluctance to practise Islam.

Malay confusion about Lanoh attitudes towards Islam derives from a misperception that Lanoh are 'good and friendly' Orang Asli, willing to put up with anything. As a Malay acquaintance once put it:

> The Lanoh are very shy people who obey authorities. They are not like Malays. Malays would have objected to all those things [referring to ill-treatment], but they've just accepted everything.

On the basis of this easygoing attitude, and the fact that 'they have lived near Malays for a long time,' many believe it is only a matter of time before Lanoh completely assimilate to mainstream Malaysian society.

As a result of this conviction Malays are often willing to take the blame and give Lanoh the benefit of the doubt when Islam fails to take root. Proselytizers visiting the village interpret refusals to attend prayers as 'shyness.' They stress it is imperative that they return periodically to Air Bah to refresh people's memory and 'to make sure that [they] follow the right way, otherwise they forget.' Other Malay acquaintances of Lanoh have suggested that the Department of (Muslim) Religious Affairs is to blame for failing to instill 'proper Islamic values in Lanoh,' but that Lanoh are otherwise ready to embrace the Muslim faith.

However, these observers fail to recognize that for Lanoh a lack of outward objection does not necessarily imply acceptance. In fact, 'going along' with the wishes of others is a strategy that Lanoh, as well as other Semang, often use in dealing with pressure from outsiders. This strategy supports a behavioural flexibility that facilitates adjustments to varied and ever-changing circumstances. For instance, Nathan Porath (2001: 134) notes that Meniq, a Semang group in Southern Thailand, are quick to adapt their image to facilitate their interaction with outsiders; while known as 'Sakai' in Thailand, they stop using this designation as soon as they cross the border into Malaysia, because they understand that there this name is considered offensive and has been abolished at indigenous request.

Lanoh in Air Bah have employed similar tactics to deal with pressure to become Muslim, agreeing outwardly while resisting inwardly.[27] This is evident when reviewing the history of Lanoh conversion to Islam – and two other religions. Chronologically, the adoption of Islam in Air Bah occurred between episodes of Baha'i and Roman Catholic conversions. People converted to the Baha'i faith in 1973, to Islam in 1974, and then to Catholicism, the religion of the 'Jesus people,' in 1982–83. In all three cases material gain in the form of gifts and monetary rewards played a decisive role, as illustrated by the following account:

> One day, [two men from Air Bah] were walking down to the store to get tobacco. They ran into the *ustad* near the Chinese banana trees. The *ustad* asked them, 'Don't you want to join the religion?' They replied, 'What kind of religion?' The *ustad* said, 'The Malay religion.' At first they were not very enthusiastic, but then the *ustad* said, 'It's so easy to enter this religion. Just put your fingerprints on this paper and you get 25 ringgit.' Those people didn't have money, so when they heard they were going to get 25 ringgit, they quickly put their fingertips down and converted right on the spot, at the roadside.

Apart from financial gain, political pressure also influenced the outcome of this religious contest. This pressure often took the form of government threats. People recall that after both Baha'i and Catholic conversions, Malays entered the village threatening a withdrawal of help, as well as with arrests, if the Lanoh continued to refuse to cooperate. People in Air Bah yielded to the pressure. Elders of the time told young men who were ready to argue with Muslim proselytizers:

> Don't fight this. We'll deal with this among ourselves. Just go along.

In spite of this outward compliance, hunter-gatherers are often resistant to different aspects of change, and in many cases they have proven surprisingly resilient. While often embracing different aspects of commercial activities with ease (Peterson and Matsuyama 1991), hunter-gatherers also frequently reject certain aspects of their neighbours' technology and values (Galaty 1986: 123; K.M. Endicott 1988; Testart 1988: 12; Rushforth 1994; Lewis-Williams 1996).[28] Similarly, the apparent submission of Lanoh masks a deep resistance to Islam, as well as to Malay values and lifestyle. Irrespective of appreciable indications of acculturation, Lanoh continue to insist that on the outside we are Muslim, on the inside we are Lanoh as before. We like to be free; we don't like to follow any religion.

Below I will review reasons for Lanoh to reject Islam before I turn to the most consequential one: non-violence.

Resisting Islam

In the previous chapter I discussed a significant reason for Lanoh to continue to resist Islam and the values of their Malay neighbours. As R.E. Park (1950, in Keen 2001: 165) suggests, accommodation by the host population is one of the necessary conditions of assimilation. Malays, however, remain ambivalent towards Orang Asli. Lanoh recognize that in spite of their conversion, Malays would never accept them as equals.

Apart from this ambivalence, Lanoh struggle with several other aspects of Islamic beliefs and practices. For one, they find it difficult to deal with the notion of an abstract, transcendent god:

> It is so hard to believe when the Malays say you cannot see God, but that God is everywhere. For us, this is not a problem. We can see God. God is up there [pointing at the Sun]. The Sun makes everything grow, every animal needs the Sun.

From a similarly practical standpoint, Lanoh consider Christianity and Baha'I to be 'good religions,' because they require that a person prays on certain days of the year, and 'this is it.' Moreover, in those religions, prayer is 'easy':

> If we want to pray, we just close our eyes and pray like that.

They perceive such habits to be far more compatible with Lanoh religious rites than Islamic prayer practice. In Lanoh rites the shaman, (*səma? hala?*) would 'just sit down and take anyone on a spiritual journey (*ceŋ ceŋ baŋ cibey*).' In comparison, they find Muslim prayers inexplicably cumbersome:

> After we had been converted, proselytizers took us, Orang Asli, from all over Malaysia, to visit places like Ipoh, Penang, and Kuala Lumpur. We were paid about RM 100 for two weeks. During all this time, we had to pray five times a day. I prayed and prayed as they asked me, standing

up, bending down, standing up, bending down, and then I felt dizzy. I stood up and I saw everything in darkness. I saw the same person becoming three or four. So I said to the *ustad*, 'What kind of prayer is this? It's not making me feel good; it's making me feel sick.' Then I realized why this was happening: Muslims who had been Muslims from the time they were babies do not suffer from prayers. But people like [us], who are made Muslim when we are older and when our head is full with all kind of *haram* things, when we pray we get sick. If we don't stop, we'll end up in the madhouse in Tanjung Rambutan.

Apart from being burdensome, Islam also causes concerns for Lanoh about their sexuality. Lanoh remain distrustful of Islam because they believe that mandatory circumcision threatens their masculinity. Selling aphrodisiacs to Malays for generations has convinced Lanoh that circumcision negatively affects male sexual powers:

> *Cancaŋ* is a root to increase the sexual potential and general vitality of men. It is a secret medicine, but some people sell it for RM 5, mostly to Malays. Lanoh men do not use it because we don't need it. We can have sex two or three times a night. Malays, however, because of circumcision, have erectile problems. Chinese and Hindu men do not have problems in this area, because they have not been circumcised either. Although we have been urged to do so, we categorically refuse to be circumcised. We are afraid of the pain, but also of the loss of our sexual power.

Lanoh, proud of their sexual prowess, are extremely reluctant to sacrifice it to any religion.

Apart from the ominous threat to their sexuality, Islam's strict dietary rules further frustrate Lanoh. People in Air Bah often complain:

> Islam is difficult; you cannot eat many things. Everything is *haram*. We like to be free and eat anything.

This factor is far more exigent than a matter of principle. In Chapter 2, I suggested that variation in their diet has allowed pre-resettlement Lanoh to focus on forest collecting. This principle also applies today. While working in the forest, collectors need to hunt to feed themselves. Now, when rattan collecting sites are too far to access by foot, Lanoh frequently use public transportation to get to these locations. They are reluctant to take their blowpipes on the bus for fear that they would be accused of eating *haram* food. Not able to hunt without their blowpipes on these occasions, they need to buy food for their stay in the jungle. Since, as they point out, they 'can't afford to buy meat in the market,' this situation frustrates them. So when a Malay religious teacher criticized them for eating *haram* food, an irked Lanoh was overheard saying:

> If you don't believe us, don't come back and you can also take your mosque with you.

This warning was not made lightly. Lanoh do not feel they need Islam and the Muslim god, because they do not consider them to be improvements in any way over what they already believe.

Perhaps the most important reason for Lanoh to resist Islamic values and beliefs is that they continue to regard their values and beliefs as superior. Lanoh, like most people, claim a central place in the universe. Consequently, they often interpret Malay animosity as 'jealousy.' Lanho believe, for instance, that Malays are already praying to the Lanoh god, without recognizing it:

> The Lanoh god is called *ya?* ['grandmother,' L.] She now lives in Mecca, in the holy shrine called Kaaba, to which Muslims turn to pray. Muslims who have not been to Mecca do not know this, but those who have been there will know that the Muslim god is actually a Lanoh god. When Muslims arrive in Mecca, the Arabs there feed them monkeys and squirrels. Those who do not eat will not be allowed to enter Mecca. It is then that they realize their god is *ya?*. They can see *ya?* sitting inside the black stone. When Muslims have been to Mecca, they become nice to Orang Asli... However, Lanoh cannot go to Mecca because if *ya?* were to see them there, she would be reminded of her longing for her grandchildren. She would be sad and she would want to return. If she did that, that would be the end of the world.

This interview excerpt shows that while people in Air Bah are ready to fit Malay beliefs *into* their own world view, they are unwilling to give this latter up entirely. At the core of the Lanoh world view is the ethic of non-violence, and Malays are often seen as violating this core principle. As long as Lanoh continue to observe these non-violent norms, they remain unlikely candidates for assimilation into Malay culture and society.

Retaining Non-violence and Resisting Islam

Non-violence is widespread among Orang Asli of Peninsular Malaysia. Although Semai non-violence has been the most extensively discussed (see, e.g., Dentan 1968, 1979, 1992, 2008; Robarchek 1977a, 1977b, 1979a, 1979b), other Orang Asli similarly observe this code of behaviour. Geoffrey Benjamin, for instance, notes that 'a [Temiar] leader who allowed conflicts to come out into the open would be failing at his job' (1968: 32). Moreover, non-violence has been recorded in other egalitarian hunter-gatherer groups (Gibson 1985; K.M. Endicott 1988: 37; Knauft 1991; Kent 1993: 487; Boehm 1993: 231). As Richard Lee suggests, '!Kung men are excellent shots when hunting game, but are poor shots when aiming at each other' (in Knauft 1991: 400).

While Orang Asli non-violence has mostly been explained in terms of intercultural pressure and psychological attributes, such as child rearing (Dentan 1978, 1979, 1992, 2008; Robarchek 1977a, 1977b, 1979a, 1979b; Howell 1989), it is equally important in regulating intragroup relations. Bruce Knauft notes that in several small-scale societies 'both within and between groups, rates of aggression are low' (1991: 406). Similarly, among Lanoh, non-violence has implications both for intergroup and intragroup relations. The intergroup ramifications of non-confrontation are illustrated in the following episode that took place in Lenggong, where the narrator, the leader of a contract group, went with four others to collect their pay:

> I had just received RM 1,000 and was walking when a group of seven Malay men stopped and surrounded me, asking for the money. I was sure they would attack if I refused. The four other … [Lanoh] … did not know what to do … we were all afraid. Luckily, I saw a policeman walking towards us from some nearby stalls. The Malays fled. We were afraid to be attacked because we did not want to fight. We, Lanoh, had never fought with people before. We are not like other people, we never learned how to fight.

The excerpt above not only shows that Lanoh often choose to flee from interethnic confrontation, but also that they consider non-violence to be a quality that differentiates them from other people. Usually outnumbered, Lanoh often respond to hostile encounters with retreat. At the same time, as the next exchange indicates, non-violence is at least as important in regulating the intragroup relations of Lanoh as it is for managing their encounters with outsiders. The following exchange took place in the village, where a group of men sat together with Malays listening to the above incident. In the next excerpt, the speaker, Atan, stresses the importance of controlling one's negative emotions:

> I don't know how it feels to hit someone or be hit by someone. I've seen Malays and Chinese getting very angry, to the point that they wanted to fight with each other and I was afraid because I had never seen anyone getting angry like that here [among Lanoh] ... I never felt angry or knew how to get angry enough to want to fight with others. When I was angry before, I always felt, it's all right if that person wants it his way, I will let go.

Such self-restraint for Lanoh is not a personal attribute but a cultural construct reinforced by multiple beliefs and practices. One of these beliefs is the trial of non-violence and self-control that every soul, except those of shamans, must go through after death. Passing this test allows the soul to enter the village of death, where it reunites with departed loved ones. The test takes the form of an encounter with two dogs to determine if the deceased had acted violently in life:

> When we die, our *roway* [spirit, soul] leaves us and goes to a place called *kampu? pɛ?* [*pɛ?* is another name for god]. Here our *roway* will be met by his parents, mother and father, who died a long time ago. Before we meet our parents, on the way there, we will be met by two dogs. One of them will look very old, the other one is a beautiful young woman. There will be the dog we hit or has been killed by someone. As we pass them, the dogs will bark at the guilty ones. The dogs will call the guilty ones out and ask them what they have done. The dog will say, 'This is the man who beat me to death.' If we lie and deny, our hands will reply: 'Yes, it was me; I did it with a stick or something.' You will be taken to be punished and beaten to death yourself. So you'll be dying twice. It will take you a long time to meet your mother then.

It is likely that violence against dogs symbolizes in-group violence, an inability to curb one's temper *within* the domestic sphere of the village or camp. Apart from a taboo against hitting domestic animals, Lanoh observe other prohibitions similarly intended to keep violence out of the village and out of domestic affairs. The most important among these relate to blood (L. *dayah*).

Among indigenous peoples of Southeast Asia, beliefs and practices related to blood are common. Rodney Needham (1964) recorded a number of beliefs and rituals concerning thunder, the mockery of animals, injuring or destroying leeches, and blood sacrifice shared by Semang of Peninsular Malaysia and Penan of Borneo. In both contexts blood sacrifices are performed to appease the thunder god or atone for wrongdoing (ibid.; also see Schebesta 1929: 258). Although Lanoh do not necessarily observe all of these blood sacrifices, they do have strong taboos against blood-letting. Similar to Penan, who 'are very much concerned about any shedding of human blood, particularly of an untoward kind, and they make a great fuss when someone is cut and there is any considerable effusion of blood' (Needham 1964: 140), Lanoh prohibit the spilling of not only human but also animal blood both within and near the village. Animals must be bled out in the forest, and bleeding animals must never be carried either into the village or to the surrounding fields. Outsiders violating this taboo cause much concern for Lanoh. For instance, when a group of Chinese hunters brought a dead, bleeding tiger into Air Bah, offering its meat to the villagers, people were outraged, not only because they do not eat tiger meat, but also for the transgression. After the Chinese left, they said:

It's not for them to be afraid. The tiger's mate will take vengeance on us.

The connection between blood and danger is so strong in Air Bah that hunting and forest trips must also be abandoned at the first sign of a cut, bruise, or injury. This relationship may further help to interpret taboos against menstruating women.

Lanoh, like many people around the world, are concerned about menstruation and menstrual blood. In the anthropological literature, such concerns are commonly discussed within the framework of gender ideologies and gender relations (see, e.g., Buckley 1982; Strassmann 1992; Gottlieb 2005). Yet, sanctions against menstruating women may equally relate to the fact that, because of menstruation, women are metonymically linked to blood and, through blood, to danger and violence. If blood symbolizes violence and the goal is to prevent in-group violence, then menstruating women are a threat that cannot easily be excluded from the village. The prohibition against women touching dangerous objects, such as weapons, may be seen as a solution because, as a result of this prohibition, women are separated from potential sources of violence. The following interview excerpt summarizes different areas of sexual division of labour among Lanoh and suggests a relationship between taboos related to menstruation and other proscriptions centring on blood and bleeding:

> Women's work is women's work and men's work is men's work, but some work, men and women can interchange and help. Like, for example, women can work at Ah Lam [a Chinese vegetable farm near Air Bah, where both Lanoh men and women regularly work on contract] and do other contract work involving vegetables. Men can work at Ah Lam, but planting vegetables, men will not do. They would prepare the bamboo stakes for cucumber, and clear the land. Men will go into the forest and cut trees. Women can only collect fallen tree branches for firewood. This is because there is a taboo for women using axes and big *parang* [machete] in the forest, *especially if they are menstruating* because bad luck would fall on them. Women can take firewood from the ground. They can go into the fields, into the hills to get vegetables, weed [paddy] and make *atap* [roofing]. Men, working in the field, make the holes and level the ground using the hoe, and women place the seeds in the holes. Men can take care of children, too. Men can only cook meat from the jungle. For instance, if a man gets a monkey, he will have to singe the animal's hair, clean it, and bring it home to cook. The *blood of the animal should not fall in the village or around the house*. Women do not cook wild boar at all, and men would have to do everything. Women cook vegetables and rice. Women will also take care of drying the paddy in the sun and clearing it of bugs. When it comes to pounding the rice, both men and women can do that. Men do the buying and selling because women do not know much about the outside world.

This excerpt indicates that prohibitions on menstruating women are not very far removed from other blood-related taboos, a fact that extends to other hunter-gatherer groups. Vishvajit Pandaya, for example, suggests that 'Andamanese women, emically defined as the gender that bleeds, avoid hunting that causes animals to bleed' (1993, in K.L. Endicott 1999: 413). Considering menstrual taboos as one among several relating to blood and bleeding would also explain why, at least among hunter-gatherers, the negative perception of menstruation and menstrual blood rarely extends to the women themselves (ibid.: 416). Rather, reflecting on gender relations, these taboos may reinforce the all-important virtue of non-violence.

Yet, while non-violence is a defining value among mobile hunter-gatherers cross-culturally, it is also often the first to fall victim to social change after sedentism (e.g., Kent 1989; Griffin 2000). In Peninsular Malaysia violence and aggression have been reported even among people previously considered to be epitomes of non-violence, such as the Semai (Robarchek and Dentan 1987, Dentan 2008). On the contrary, Lanoh in Air Bah, at least for now, have retained non-violence both as an ideal and as a practice.[29]

In retaining non-violence elders in Air Bah played a particularly important role. Although anthropologists commonly acknowledge the role of elders as guardians of traditions and values in small-scale societies, they rarely consider the implications of this in studies of changing hunter-gatherers. In Air Bah people retain non-violent values because elders there are more successful at promoting these values than they have been elsewhere. This is evident in their war against alcohol. Anthropologists have long pointed to the relationship between alcohol consumption and increased in-group violence among post-foragers (e.g., Kent 1989; Shnirelman 2001: 54–5; Quraishy 2001: 203; Lee 2005), and this link between alcohol and violence is equally recognized by indigenous peoples. Like aggressive behaviour, the consumption of alcohol has recently increased in several Orang Asli settlements. People in Air Bah, however, continue to chastise those who get drunk, and elders so far have managed to keep alcohol out of the village.[30] On one occasion a young man became drunk during an outing in Grik. He was prevented from returning to the village until he sobered up the following day. Tengah, the man recounting this incident, said that he had publicly shamed the young man, refusing to travel with him on the bus while he was in that state.

The resistance of Lanoh to animal husbandry further indicates that they continue to observe non-violence. As suggested in the trial of the two dogs, violence against domestic animals is likely to symbolize in-group violence. Lanoh believe that one of the worst possible acts of violence people can commit is killing animals that they have raised.[31] Correspondingly, Lanoh do not have much use for domestic animals. Apart from dogs, cats, and chickens, there was only a pet rabbit in the village, kept by a Temiar man. People in Air Bah do not even have coconut monkeys, as some do in other Orang Asli villages. Furthermore, they refuse to restrain or confine their animals. Dogs are kept primarily for security, to alert the village of approaching wild animals like tigers. They describe dogs, like friends, as 'unreliable'; if dogs accompany people into the forest, they only do so of their own volition. Chickens are similarly unrestricted and, as a result, are often killed and eaten by cats, dogs, and foxes. Instead of consuming the surviving remainder, people just sell them to the Chinese. As people explained:

> When we use our blowpipe for a monkey to kill for food, it is all right, because in the beginning, everything had been arranged for all the people in the world, what kind of food they can get and how to get these foods. For Orang Asli, we can eat anything in the forest. That has been meant for us. When we shoot a monkey, we did not see how the monkey lived, who his family was, his babies, his parents, we do not know all that. So that is all right. But we cannot eat our chicken, dogs that we have raised from babies, fed them every day like our children. That we cannot do. It is as if we ate our children. So we have chickens, we give them to people or sell, but we do not eat them. Malays and other people eat their chicken and cattle, like eating their children. They are strange.

Such strong aversion to killing domestic animals naturally stands in the way of animal domestication. The fact that people in Air Bah continue to refuse government attempts to introduce animal domestication indicates that this apprehension remains strong. Unfortunately, government representatives are not necessarily aware of these beliefs. Over the years their contrasting attitudes towards animal domestication have led to a few truly bizarre incidents, as in the following. One day JHEOA officers appeared in the village to inquire if people wanted to raise goats. The Lanoh replied:

> 'Yes, we would love to rear goats, but we don't know how'... The officer put this down in his big book. About a year later, the JHEOA arrived suddenly with seventy-four goats. The officer said, 'Here are seventy-four goats.' They picked twelve people to be the recipients of the goats, but they said the whole village is responsible for them. So, we told them, 'All right, we'll take care of the goats, but we don't know how to take care of goats, so don't blame us if they die.' The officer replied, 'Don't worry, it's easy; if you take care of them well, the goats won't die.' With that, they left and we took care of the goats. But so many of them kept dying. From seventy-four, soon only four were left. So the last four we sold. We got about 800 ringgit and had a big *kenduri* [feast, M.]. After that, the JHEOA came and asked, 'What happened to the goats?' We told them, 'Well, we told you we don't know how to take care of goats.'

The half-disintegrated goat pen, now a permanent fixture in the village, is a testimony to Lanoh resistance to animal domestication.

A third indication that Lanoh have retained non-violence, perhaps more than many other changing hunter-gatherers, is that they distance themselves from those who they perceive to be violence-prone, and they often attribute violent acts to members of other ethnic groups. In the next interview excerpt, a man recounts his father's violence towards his mother, his brother, and himself:

> I remember when I was [about 13 years old], my father was angry with my mother, who went off chatting with some neighbours. He yelled at her to come back. When she came back home, he took a burning piece of wood and shoved it in her face. I was outside the house. By the time I came to the house, when I heard my mother's scream, she was on the floor, her face and body burned. My father would have done the same to me, but many people came to the house. I remember feeling that if I was older a man, like my father, I would have fought him.

Hearing this, others present quickly interjected that this violent man was a Temiar:

> Yes, his father was a bad man. He would only be angry with his family, but not with other people. With others, he didn't dare. He was a Temiar from Kelantan. My father was not like that.

Accordingly, Lanoh especially want to maintain a distance from Malays, whom they perceive to be the embodiment of violence. They are not alone in this belief. To all Orang Asli, Malays, and especially the Islamic authority, have long been considered violent archetypes. In the account quoted below, the Malay *haji* (a Muslim who has completed the religious pilgrimage to Mecca) is associated with the tiger, the most violent of animals. This account also shows that Malays are not the only ones associated with different species of animals.[32] People in Air Bah often use ethnic stereotypes to illustrate attributes they consider incompatible with the values of their culture, and animal portrayals reveal such stereotypes.

The excerpt is from a retelling of Lanoh history, which consists of seven cycles, with seven epochs in each cycle. The turning point at the end of each cycle is called *kəma?*.[33] At each of these points, all things change into their mirror image, humans turn into animals and animals into humans:

> The present world came to be as a result of the last *kəma?*, which made the

Lanoh the first people of all mankind. Then came White people, Chinese, Malays, Pakistani, Hindu (Tamils), and then Negroes. Before the White Man came other Orang Asli. During every *kɔma?* everything is turned upside down and opposite. Night turns into day and day turns to night. Where there is mountain, there will be lake, where there was lake, there will be mountain. Humans turn into animals and animals become humans. For instance, the Lanoh of the previous phase became elephants, some other Orang Asli, the Temiar, became snakes. The porcupine and deer are Malays turned into animals, but some Malay *Haji* turned into tigers. The Chinese became wild boar. The monkey with long arms [gibbon] was formerly a Tamil-Indian man. The siamang was formerly a Hindustani man.

This passage, connecting Malay authority with the most vicious of wild animals, indicates that Lanoh perceive at least some Malays as aggressive, hostile, and prone to violence. As long as Lanoh associate Malays' religion with what they consider to be the worst in human nature, they are not likely to embrace Islam or Malay lifestyle. Furthermore, Lanoh today often extend this judgment to other Orang Asli, whom they see as becoming more and more like Malays in their displays of aggressive behaviour. Lanoh in Air Bah posit a relationship between the decline of non-violence among Orang Asli and their assimilation to Malay values, often complaining that violence is becoming common among the Orang Asli they know:

I don't know how people could get so angry as to fight, either. Even Orang Asli from Dala and Kemah have now learned to get angry and fight. Sometimes, they fight because of women. This is so difficult to understand; how can you get so angry over women to fight? This is so stupid. Orang Asli didn't know how to be angry before. Malays, Chinese, and even British brought it into the land. This is, because these people eat animals they raise, like chicken and goats. The spirit of these animals will be sad and will make you, the person who eats his own animal, feel angry.

Lanoh in Air Bah feel that even people in Tawai are becoming more aggressive. They were shocked to learn, for example, that two young brothers in that village had pursued and killed a tiger. As discussed before, Lanoh revere tigers as the ultimate symbols of violence and avoid them if possible. Thus, the actions of these young men can be perceived as indicators of a decline in non-violent values in Tawai.

Since aggression is associated with Malays, Lanoh see Orang Asli who are becoming more aggressive as more assimilated. On one occasion, for instance, when cheated by a contractor, people said:

> Had it been Semai from Pahang, this Malay contractor would surely be in trouble. The Semai are not afraid. They are *jahat* [bad, M.].

When asked for elaboration as to the meaning of *jahat*, people clarified that they meant *garang* (aggressive, M.). One man further added, 'What can we do? We are not like that.' Thus, in terms of their continuing adherence to non-violence, Lanoh in Air Bah believe they are apart not only from members of dominant ethnic groups, but from other Orang Asli as well.

Conclusion

Changing interethnic relations and the decline of traditional, individualistic forest trade have disproportionately affected the elders of Air Bah. As a result elders have increasingly withdrawn from contact with outsiders and promoted village identity through different means. One important consequence of this is that, in spite of the pressure to assimilate, people in Air Bah continue to believe that their values are superior to other traditions and, consequently, they resist acculturation. In the next chapter I will further analyse village dynamics in Air Bah, introducing leadership competition, feuding kinship groups, and the way these divide the village. These developments, along with those described in this chapter, seem to indicate that, far from accommodating other people's values and lifestyles, Air Bah may instead be on its way to becoming an integrated and segmented village community.

5 Leadership Competition, Self-Aggrandizement, and Inequality

Age in Egalitarian Politics

Sedentism and population dynamics have always been a key feature in theories of social complexity and inequality (Boserup 1965, 1981, in Trigger 1998: 144–5; Johnson 1982; Keeley 1988; Pauketat 1996; Rosenberg 1998; Johnson and Earle 1987). It is well understood that larger, more sedentary communities not only give rise to organizational difficulties, but also increase the likelihood of conflict (e.g., Rousseau 2006). However, theorists have often neglected to pay sufficient attention to the structural attributes of egalitarian societies that shape and constrain the rise of inequality. Consequently, theories of social complexity habitually fail to identify potential self-aggrandizers in terms of their role in this structure. I contend that this neglect largely explains why the problem of emerging inequality in small-scale societies has remained unresolved.

Researchers working in egalitarian societies often wonder what needs to happen for inequality to replace equality. Richard Lee, like other proponents of the egalitarian ethic, submits that in these societies 'those falling through the cracks are supported by the group' and that, therefore, 'one of the elements of social evolution that is of great interest is how the cracks get wider. Do people fall through those cracks by neglect, or are they preyed upon?' (1990: 145). This question can be answered by giving more consideration to the structure of egalitarian politics from which self-aggrandizers emerge. In Air Bah these structural attributes explained not only why and how leadership competition, self-aggrandizement, and inequalities developed in such a short time after resettlement, but also why these changes were so readily accepted in a previously egalitarian context.

It is generally recognized that the most important structural principle in egalitarian politics is age. Among Lanoh, age plays a pivotal function in defining leadership roles in two important ways. The first of these are the *categorical age* roles commonly observed and recorded by anthropologists in small-scale societies. Lanoh do not classify age roles into age sets or a rigid generational system, neither do they have rites of passage transitioning a person between different roles; nonetheless, they observe several well-defined classes of economic and political roles for different age categories of adult men (Table 5.1).

As Table 5.1 shows, these age categories are defined by roles and expectations. 'Young men,' below the age of 35 years, are expected to get married and support their families through their earnings, mainly from contract work or 'forest work.' These younger men are not eligible for leadership roles, because leadership resides with married heads of families between the ages of 40 and 60. These middle-aged men not only have the largest families with the greatest number of dependent children, but some of their children are already married or at least of marriageable age. Therefore, these are the men in the best position to manipulate their children's marriages in service of their status. Finally, the last group, older men over 60, is also excluded from leadership positions, a point I will elaborate on further.

Yet, categorical age, while extremely important, is alone insufficient in defining leadership roles in Air Bah, because Lanoh relationships are also governed by *relative age* differences. Relative age, a concept shared by the indigenous cultures of the peninsula (although with varying restrictions and implications) (Needham 1966; Jensen 1978), is decisive in regulating people's actions in both consanguinal and affinal relationships.[1] While categorical age defines the behaviour of a group of people, relative age regulates interpersonal relations, especially those between people within the same age category. In spite of government-issued identification cards, people in Air Bah are unaware of absolute age, but they do know who is older and younger, even if the age difference is but a few months. When expressed in relationship terms, these often minor differences in age become set roles with clearly defined rights and expectations (Table 5.2).

Relative age is exceptionally suited to regulating and negotiating politics in the fluid, dyadic relationships of Semang hunter-gatherers. The relative age structure is largely responsible for the smooth functioning of interpersonal relationships, because it eliminates doubts as to how to behave towards people one is most likely to encounter and spend time with. Lanoh are deferential and respectful to those who

Table 5.1 Age Categories and Age Roles of Adult Men in Air Bah

Age Category	Age in Years	Marital Status	Age Role
Senior	60+	Married, widowed, or divorced	Apolitical. Still participates in light collecting and occasional hunting. May live off social credit if he previously earned any as an elder. Supported by younger family members, who work on his land. Often quite mobile.
Elders	40–60	Married with a few grown-up, married children	Increasingly concerned with shifting physical activities to spiritual and knowledge-based contributions. Most political; associated with leadership roles. Involved in farming and related land schemes – reluctant to work for money (although sometimes they do). Least mobile.
Pre-elders	30–40	Married with children, no married daughters or adult sons	Still mostly involved in physical work. Expected to work on own land, as well as to earn money. Men in this category are under the greatest pressure.
Just married	20–30	Newly married with young children and infants	May start to think of clearing some land, but primarily responsible for supporting own family and in-laws from income generated from forest collecting and contract work.
Single	20–60+	Any unmarried man, irrespective of age	Has no land. Works outside, supporting parents or other, older, conjugal relatives, looking for future spouse – most mobile of all.

Table 5.2 Lanoh Referential Kinship Terms

CONSANGUINAL RELATIONS

Mother	*na^ʔ*
Father	*do^ʔ*
Child	*panɨ/kon*
Elder sibling	*kəlo^ʔ*
Younger sibling	*pə^ʔ*
Child of elder sibling	*kun kəlo^ʔ*
Child of younger sibling	*kun pə^ʔ*
Parent's elder sibling	*toy*
Parent's younger sister	*mɔ^ʔ*
Parent's younger brother	*bah*
Grandmother	*ya^ʔ*
Grandfather	*ta^ʔ*
Great-grandparent	*dɔn*
Grandchildren's generation (grandchildren, their spouses, sibling's grandchildren, and great-grandchildren)	*kancɔ^ʔ*
Cousin; child of parent's younger sibling	*kancɔ^ʔ*
Cousin; child of parent's elder sibling	*kəmuɲ*

AFFINAL RELATIONS

Relationship term not marking relative age:	
Children's spouse's parent	*bisat*
Relationship terms marking relative age:	
Son/daughter-in-law	*mənsaw*
Younger brother/sister-in-law (younger brother's wife; younger brother's wife's brother; wife's younger brother)	*mənsaw*
Father/mother-in-law	*bəlo^ʔ*
Elder brother/sister-in-law (elder brother's wife; elder sister's husband; husband's elder brother; wife's elder sister)	*kənuɲ*
Spouse's elder sibling	*kənɔy*
Relationship terms marking relative age and sex:	
Younger sister-in-law (younger brother's wife; younger sister of wife/husband)	*mənəy*
Younger brother-in-law (younger sister's husband; younger brother of wife/husband)	*cənoy*

are older, and they are caring, protective, and a little condescending towards those who are younger. It emerged as a recurring theme in life histories just how important elder brothers and cousins were in the upbringing and socialization of young men. Statements like 'I learned forest work by following my elder brother,' or 'my elder brother taught me everything' were at least as common as recollections of instruction or guidance by one's father or uncle. Younger male siblings in Air Bah respect their elder brothers and cousins, and they attempt to stay physically and emotionally close to them even in adulthood. It is not uncommon, for instance, that a younger, unmarried brother takes up residence adjacent to his elder brother's house and contributes to his household. Even after they are married, younger brothers continue to consult their elder brothers on every important problem and decision in their lives.[2]

Synthesizing the effects of categorical age and relative age, the eldest of middle-aged men possess the attributes most pertinent for discussions of leadership within Lanoh society. Unfortunately, few studies have focused on middle age as a theoretically significant category in understanding emerging inequalities in small-scale societies. This omission stems from biases in life course research in anthropology, as Jennie Keith and David Kertzer (1984) note, towards studies of the young (development, norms, and transition) and old (status and treatment). These biases have in turn affected studies on the relationship between social change and age relations in small-scale societies, which similarly approach the topic from the perspective of the aged, aging, and caring for the elderly (ibid.). Yet, as Keith and Kertzer observe, 'in most human societies throughout history few people lived past 50 years' (ibid.: 47; cf. Washburn 1981; Dolhinow 1984); thus, throughout human history, 'elder' has invariably meant 'middle-aged,' rather than old men.

This problem gains further significance when examining the difference between the age roles of men and women. Researchers have found that while women's prestige curves increase as they age, those of men decline. According to David Gutmann, for instance, women become 'more autonomous, competitive, aggressive, and instrumental,' while men become 'more passive, expressive, and dependent' (1977: 303, in Keith and Kertzer 1984: 28).

A second important difference between men's and women's age roles cross-culturally is that those of men tend to be well defined and categorical, even where there are no formal generational sets (Kertzer 1979). A study of power relations in Air Bah reinforces these observations. Among women status differences depend only on relative age and remain constant throughout life. An older sister, mother, or aunt will always have power over her younger female relatives. Contrary to the case with women, the esteem of men is defined not only by relative age, but also by age categories, and it usually declines with age.[3] The status of an aging father, for instance, is typically lower than that of his middle-aged son. After handing over their land to younger relatives in exchange for care and support, old men in Air Bah seem neither involved nor interested in politics. Depending on their personality, they may even be laughed at, mocked, or ridiculed. Indeed, on occasion, old men appear to act humorously to appease their relatives, who often exhibit resentment over having to put up with and provide for them. This decline in men's status in old age has prompted Benjamin to suggest that, among Temiar, 'a man remains village leader only to the extent that he is still physically capable of undertaking the full range of subsistence activities himself' (1968: 32). Writing about Bersiak, an old Lanoh man, Schebesta remarks that although he had been a powerful shaman (L. *səma? hala?*) when he was younger, he was no longer influential by the age of 70 (1929: 71–2). It follows that in Air Bah middle-aged men and older women were the most powerful and the most influential, and alliances formed by these two classes of people are most consequential in shaping village politics.[4]

Sedentism, Regroupment, and Leadership Competition in Air Bah

While we are quite cognizant about the way factions operate in small-scale societies (e.g., Bailey 1969; Bujra 1974; Salisbury and Silverman 1977; Brumfiel 1994), there are relatively few data about how leadership competition emerges in the first place. Yet, from the perspective of theories of inequality, this is a crucial phase. Understanding which factors are essential to the development of political competition will help us establish a link between egalitarian and non-egalitarian politics. The role of sedentism has been already discussed, but in Air Bah two additional factors played principal roles in the development of leadership competition: regroupment and age.

Regroupment,[5] which increased the number of composite kinship groups, served a key function in the rise of inequality, as is evident when comparing pre-resettlement conditions with post-resettlement conditions and their implications for leadership conflict. In pre-resettlement times, the chances for leadership competition to develop would have been rather slim, because pre-resettlement Lanoh camps and villages were unlikely to contain more than one composite family group. Although on occasion family groups merged for certain activities, and the temporarily enlarged group may have consisted of several nuclear families at once, the number of extended, three-generational arrangements per settlement was limited not only by the nature of forest collecting, but also by avoidance rules.

Cross-sex in-law avoidance is a common feature of the kinship systems of Malaysian Orang Asli (Benjamin 1980, 1985a; Gomes 2007: 29). As mentioned before, Lanoh in-law avoidance is lax compared with that of Semang, but it is stricter than among Senoi.[6] In Air Bah people in avoidance relationships cannot talk to or be near each other. As among other Semang, they cannot have their shadow fall on each other. In the following account, a Temiar man from Tanjung Rambutan laments the 'harshness' of Lanoh avoidance rules:

> Our taboo is not so major over there. Here it is too much. Here you have to speak from a distance, and even then, you have to have a go-between. For example, over there, if we want to give her [a person with whom we are in avoidance relationship] some money, we put it down and leave. Then she'll come and take it. That's over there. Here you can't do that. Here you've got to give her child the money. If we touch that money she won't take it.[7]

As these rules effectively obstruct aggregation of any sort, they must be lifted during funeral feasts, harvest celebrations, or other communal gatherings. In the resettlement village continuing adherence to avoidance rules often results in awkward situations. During my stay in Air Bah car rides often required lengthy preparations and negotiations. People in avoidance relationships refused to sit next to or address each other, thus requiring others to mediate until sitting arrangements were established to everyone's satisfaction. At other times people went out of their way to steer clear of the houses of those with whom they were in avoidance relationships. It seems likely that in the past these avoidance rules would have effectively kept people apart, because in small pre-resettlement Lanoh villages and camps, the only way people could stay away from undesired interactions was if they refrained from co-residing in large groups entirely.

Avoidance rules aside, age roles would have regulated interactions even among those who were comfortable sharing a village or camp. While generational rules would have defined the category of people who could be considered for leadership positions, relative age would further narrow down this group. Consequently, although Lanoh may not have always had permanent leadership, the positions they did have were not likely to be disputed.[8] Individuals could certainly leave and join another group, but those who stayed would not have challenged the position of their leader. For instance, brothers, who would have often shared residence, would not have challenged each other, because relative age prescribed how they were to act towards each other. Within such relations, there would have been little room for conflict. As I suggested in Chapter 2, if people did indeed move away, it was less likely to assert their independence than to pursue opportunities of work or trade.[9]

Contrary to pre-resettlement villages and camps, Air Bah now contains four kinship clusters, each with its own head. This has considerably increased the probability of conflict. Most importantly, it has brought together unrelated individuals of approximately the same age who are therefore both unregulated by relative age and equally eligible for leadership positions. Two such individuals happened to be the heads of the two largest and most influential kinship groups, Kecil, the headman, and Hitam, an extremely ambitious and charismatic elder.

When they were young, Kecil's and Hitam's age did not present a problem. People recounted that before, these two men were the best of friends who went everywhere and did everything together, from courting girls to working in the forest. Their closeness in age only became a source of tension as they approached middle age and both became eligible for leadership positions. This coincided with the death of the village leader, Senin, whom everyone remembered as a wise and influential man and a powerful shaman. Following Senin's death (about two years prior to my fieldwork), Hitam started to challenge the authority of Kecil, who by that point had been the official headman of the village for more than fifteen years. Kecil was appointed headman in the 1980s after the passing of his father, who had previously occupied the position. A young man at the time, Kecil was not respected as a leader by anyone; he was elected headman mainly because no one else was willing to take on the role.

Several scholars have commented on the discrepancy between headmanship and leadership among indigenous peoples who were previously under British rule (e.g., Schebesta 1929; Benjamin 1968; Bailey 1969; Beidelman 1971). Geoffrey Benjamin contrasts indigenous leadership and headmanship in terms of the loci of authority. He suggests that indigenous leadership refers to 'those positions of authority that gain their legitimacy by virtue of their place within the nexus of internal social relations' (1968: 1), while headmanship, primarily introduced to facilitate communication between British colonial administration and indigenous groups, refers to 'those positions of authority that are held to be legitimate in relation to some locus of higher authority situated outside [indigenous] society' (ibid.). Consequently, unlike indigenous leadership, headmanship does not necessarily imply status; instead, indigenous peoples have often regarded the position as a nuisance. Frederick Bailey remarks that after British administration had introduced formal headmanship in India, in many places 'it was practical for local notables to ensure that this office went to a junior person' (1969: 74). Through this move, he suggests, de facto indigenous leaders could express contempt for alien political practices as well as ensure that elders, people with authority, did not get involved with foreigners (ibid.: 84n4).

Likewise, headmanship in Air Bah primarily implies unpleasant chores and responsibilities, including more communication with outside authorities than most Lanoh consider desirable.[10] Consequently, the role has not been particularly coveted by Lanoh elders. Instead, in the past, younger men schooled in Malay were often ushered forth to deal with Jabatan Hal Ehwal Orang Asli officials. For this reason, when Kecil's father died, no one was too enthusiastic to take on the headman's responsibility. Kecil was elected by the JHEOA by default, while the leadership of the village continued to reside with the elders of the time. In the following interview excerpt, Kecil recounts his election to the office of village headman:[11]

> (How did you become *penghulu*?)
> In 1980, when my father died, he died of sickness, nobody else wanted to be. They were looking for somebody to become headman after my father. I didn't want to claim to be a headman either.
> (Who was looking for a *penghulu*, whom did you mean by 'they'?)
> The JHEOA spent a month looking for a *penghulu*. They couldn't find anyone. Nobody wanted to be ... nobody from here wanted to be *penghulu*. I didn't want it either. Then they told me, 'You are the *penghulu*'s son.' They said, 'If nobody else wants to, you have to be the *penghulu*.' So they [the JHEOA] trained me for two months. After two months, they saw that the ways that I did things were good and then they made me *penghulu*. We went to Grik to the office for a meeting, and they put my name down in the book as *penghulu*. So that is how it is until today.

At first Kecil was not thrilled to assume the headman's duties, and following his appointment, he disappeared from the village for two years. However, this was in the early 1980s, when Kecil was still in his late 20s and early 30s. Since then, he has grown accustomed to his role.

By 1998 his headmanship and his transition to the status of an elder brought him closer to the position of village leader. This presented a challenge to Hitam, who considered himself to be the best candidate for this position.

Soon after Senin's death Hitam began to undermine and challenge Kecil's authority, often by unilaterally acting on behalf of the village, which placed Kecil in an uncomfortable position with the JHEOA. In particular, behind Kecil's back, Hitam arranged for the sale of the village's old rubber trees. Since that incident the two have not spoken to each other, and the conflict between them rapidly transformed into leadership competition.

The sale of the rubber trees has been variously interpreted by different witnesses. In the following interview excerpt someone from Hitam's kinship group recounts the tale:

> The final incident that further strained the relationship [between Hitam and the headman] occurred at the end of 1996. Hitam proposed to cut down the old rubber trees, which were more than fifteen years old and were not producing much rubber. Everyone seemed to agree, including the *penghulu*. The idea was to sell the trees for about RM 200 per acre and then replant the land with paddy and rubber trees. However, the contractor did not honour his promises. When the trees were cut, he paid between RM 100 and RM 200 per acre. Hitam was away, and so he felt the *penghulu* should have monitored and supervised the cutting operation. While the bulldozers were cutting down the trees, no one was there. The *penghulu* went into the forest. So some people got RM 200 per acre, others less, while still others did not get anything. Also, the Malay middleman ran off with some of the money and bought himself a car. People began to complain and protest about the money. It was then that the *penghulu* and [his brother-in-law, the assistant headman] began to blame Hitam. But both received full payment and maximum pay for their rubber trees. The headman received RM 1,600 and [his assistant] RM 1,000. After that, the *penghulu* and Hitam began not to speak to each other.

However, an outsider, a Malay acquaintance of the Lanoh, interpreted the same episode differently:

> The person responsible for planning and executing the deal with the contractor was Hitam. He did this without the consent or knowledge of anybody in the village. One day tractors arrived at the village and started

cutting down the trees. Hitam explained what he had done and said people would receive RM 100 per acre. Most people ended up receiving far less than RM 100 per acre. It would have remained like that, but the real price was revealed to other people in the village as a result of the *penghulu* finally talking to the contractors ... this was the beginning of the cold war between the factions in the village. Hitam raised suspicion by buying a new motorcycle soon after the incident.

Following this event the conflict between Kecil and Hitam escalated, in large part because of the structural similarity of their positions. This reinforces Jeremy Boissevain's observation that, although faction leaders often work with asymmetrical resource bases and strategies, their positions tend to be symmetrical – they are equally strong (1968: 551). The more symmetrical the positions, the more difficult it is to resolve conflict. A few years earlier a similar competition for leadership had erupted in Tawai following the death of the village leader. There, however, the asymmetrical positions of the contestants led to a speedy resolution. Unlike in Air Bah the three contestants in Tawai occupied different positions in the age structure. One of them, although well-liked, was in his early 30s, and this rendered him too young to be seriously considered for leadership. Another, who was also popular, was in his late 50s, which made him almost too old to fulfil that role. As a result, they both voluntarily removed themselves from the situation and ended up in Air Bah, while the third person, a middle-aged man in his early 40s, became headman of the village. The first two men moved easily because, being older and younger than middle age, they were not burdened by large families with a number of dependent children. Therefore, in Tawai, the structural position of competitors not only alleviated contest by routinely assigning leadership to the most age-appropriate individual, but also helped the two less likely candidates to save face and move away.

There was no corresponding resolution in Air Bah, where the two contestants were not only of the same age, but also the heads of the two largest family groups with the most extensive ties in the village. Their similar age and similar structural position resulted in a power balance that was not easy to resolve. Had one of them been able to move away, the impetus for self-aggrandizement would have been removed. However, because of their age and the demographic effects of sedentism, these two were also the most sedentary in the village.[12] As a result, these leaders became locked into their conflict which, with no alternative but intensification, rapidly escalated into full-fledged competition for leadership. A look at the kinship clusters of Air Bah demonstrates the social position of these competing leaders. Table 5.3 not only identifies kinship group/household clusters in Air Bah, indicating how categorical age and relative age interact in determining leadership within each cluster, but also shows the symmetrical position of the two competing leaders. Thus, in Air Bah, sedentism, regroupment, and age roles set the stage for leadership competition which undermined previously egalitarian social relations.

Self-Aggrandizement, Age, and Marginalization

In the rivalry that ensued both leaders applied various self-aggrandizing strategies in an effort to illustrate their strengths over the weaknesses of the other. As a result of their actions certain individuals and families in the village became increasingly marginalized. Marginalization, 'the process by which established or emerging elites create socioeconomic relations of superior versus subordinate/dependent through manipulations of labor and distributions of social resources' (Arnold 1995: 88–9, in Rousseau 2006: 22), has been extensively studied by anthropologists. However, we still have an insufficient understanding of the micro-processes involved, the role of individual actions and attitudes in creating situations in which certain people are marginalized, and how these individual actions and attitudes relate to structural attributes of marginalizers and marginalized. A better understanding of this would go a long way in resolving questions concerning the relative role of agency and structure in the social processes of small-scale societies. In Air Bah the actions of self-aggrandizers and the marginalization process relate to structural principles and attributes that have made certain individuals and families more vulnerable than others.

Leadership Competition and Self-Aggrandizement

There were several signs of self-aggrandizement in Air Bah. After the removal of the rubber trees, for instance, competing leaders dramatically raised their agricultural production. By calling a logging company to take the rubber trees out, Hitam opened up a sizable tract of arable land, and consequently, in 1998, the scale of farming in Air Bah was unprecedented. Unlike in the past when Lanoh farmed on one or two acres, in the year of my fieldwork villagers cultivated about two-thirds

Table 5.3 Household Clusters and Male Heads

Kinship group/ Household cluster	Age (above 13 years)	Marital status	Number of children	Number of married children
1 Headman's cluster	61	Widowed	1	1
	46[a]	Married	6	1
	42	Married	10	1
	39[b]	Married	11	0
	36	Single	0	0
	19	Single	0	0
2 Charismatic leader's cluster	76	Divorced	NA	NA
	45[a]	Married	9	1
	40	Divorced	0	0
	38	Widowed	2	0
	37[b,c]	Married	5	0
	36[c]	Married	0	0
	35[c]	Married	6	1
	18	Single	0	0
	18	Single	0	0
	17	Single	0	0
	17	Single	0	0
3 Older man's cluster	58	Married	8	4
	41	Married	1	0
	31	Single	0	0
	28	Married	2	0
	21	Married	1	1
	21	Single	0	0
	20	Married	1	1
4 Younger man's cluster	31[c]	Married	5	0
	25	Married	1	0
	18	Single	0	0
Loose affiliation or unaffiliated	46[d]	Married	0	0
	44[e]	Married	6	3
	31[f]	Married	5	0
	27[g]	Married	2	0
	23	Married	0	0
	24	Single	0	0
	17	Single	0	0

NA = not available
[a]Competing leaders.
[b]Temiar.
[c]Men most often excluded.
[d]This man has lost an eye in an accident. He has no children on his own, but raises four of his wife's sister's children. None of these children are married yet.
[e]Works as a policeman in PPH (Pasukan Polis Hutan, Forest Police); he has been in the force for twenty years. Although a cousin of leader no. 2, he lives in Dala or Kroh and only very rarely returns to Air Bah.
[f]Recently moved from Tawai with his family; has no close relatives on his own in Air Bah.
[g]Son of leader no. 1, son-in-law of leader no. 2; very loosely associated with each of them.

of the fifty acres of land around the village. It must be noted, however, that the majority returned to rubber planting as soon as possible, and they had begun to plant rubber seedlings collected from nearby plantations alongside their crops. That said, regardless of its transience, farming in 1998 revealed important differences in people's responses to change.[13] One of the most important among these was that, whereas all the elders in Air Bah tended to gravitate towards 'village work,' they would only self-aggrandize in the presence of a competitor.

Competing leaders saw farming differently from other elders. Unlike other elders in the village, both competing leaders raised their agricultural production beyond what was necessary for their families' subsistence. In 1998 I conducted interviews to learn about village farming production and organized respondents into three categories according to how much paddy they planted that year (Dallos 2003). The categories used in this survey – 'above subsistence,' 'below subsistence,' and 'subsistence' – were based on the villagers' classification of 'more,' 'less,' and 'just enough to eat.'[14] This survey showed that the only ones able to sustain farming at the subsistence level were Temiar members of the village, who worked on two acres of land and produced approximately ten bags of paddy per acre. Lanoh members of the village either farmed below or above subsistence. Most importantly, these interviews revealed that the people most likely to farm beyond subsistence were the two competing leaders. Both planted paddy on eight acres of land and together were responsible for more than half of the thirty acres of cultivated land in Air Bah. As well, unlike other elders, Hitam and Kecil had detailed and elaborated plans to develop their land in the future.

Indeed, competitive long-term planning is the most important feature distinguishing self-aggrandizing leaders in Air Bah from other elders. For most people in the village, immediacy is still the primary motive in most activities. When asked, 'What would you do if you had lots of money,' villagers typically respond:

> It's hard to say. Maybe buy little things for the house, and tools to make things.

These same people, when asked what they thought would be the best course of development for the village, replied in a similarly non-committal way. Mamat, a younger man said:

> We'll see what's possible and we'll do whatever we can.

Tengah, an elder replied:

> We'll see what the situation is and then decide. Well, the road needs improvement, we'll get a licence for rattan and then we'll see what is needed and we'll do that.

Finally, a third person, Jalak, said:

> We'll see the opportunity and whatever opportunity arises, we'll take it. If we get more money, we will fix the generator and the road. Look at the road. It's horrible!

Compared with these responses, both competing leaders' plans for the future were articulate, detailed, and extremely elaborate.

These competing leaders not only made plans to increase their farming productivity during my stay in Air Bah, but also to develop their land afterwards. They both expressed an interest in intensifying farming by raising capital to invest in seeds, tools, irrigation, and fertilizers in the coming years. Furthermore, they planned on improving their output in the following year by planting 'better crops,' such as bananas, vegetables, and rubber. As well, these leaders spent considerably longer hours working on their land. The following excerpt from my fieldnotes, which record the activities of Kecil during planting season, illustrates this:

> This year, [penghulu Kecil] is very determined to be productive. For instance, today most people took the afternoon off to watch a Hindi film on television (three hours long). Kecil and his family, wife and daughters, however, continued to work on their land until nightfall. This means that they break the taboo according to which nobody should work on the fields late in the afternoon (after 5 p.m.). He is not only planting rubber and paddy, but also corn and 900 banana seedlings. He said he expected his land to produce about 50–60 forty kg bags of paddy. People say one family consumes approximately one such bag a month. Whatever paddy his family does not consume, Kecil wants to sell.

For his part, Hitam's long-term designs included plans to exploit timber commercially, as well as to turn his land into a palm oil and rubber plantation.[15] When answering the question about his future plans, Hitam related the following intricate plan to develop the land belonging to the village:

With land you can have a lot of money and the Lanoh would be all right for a long time ... even our children and grandchildren. Provided we get the 600 acres that was promised as Lanoh reserve land, I want to plant golden teakwood on 300 acres. One teak seedling costs RM 5, so we would need a lot of money for that 300 acres. I would also like to plant 100 acres with rubber, 100 with palm oil, and the last 100 acres we would divide between the families for vegetables, like tapioca. Then part of the money [from aid he was hoping to get] would be used to meet the needs of the village for three years. After three years, the 100 acres of palm trees would bear fruits and so we would have income from that. Four years after that, the 100 acres of rubber would bring income and seven years after the rubber, exactly fifteen years from the day the project started, the teakwood would be ready to be sold. Three hundred acres of teakwood would bring in millions of dollars.

Uncharacteristic of immediate-return hunter-gatherers, Hitam's ideas reach far into the future. Most likely this long-term outlook is rooted in competition. A Malay acquaintance commented on the difference between the attitude of Hitam and other villagers:

Of all these people, it is only Hitam who can work. He has the brains and the attitude. Last year, he planted vegetables and made 5,000 ringgit out of it. The others don't work as well as he does. What they get today, they spend it today. They don't think of tomorrow.

This difference between the attitudes of most of the residents of Air Bah and those of the competing leaders can also be seen as a difference between 'subsistence economy' and 'political economy' (Earle 1994). Others in the village work to fulfil their basic survival needs, while Hitam and Kecil are seeking opportunities to increase their production.

Nonetheless, the two leaders' elaborate schemes primarily emphasize competition, rather than the accumulation of wealth.[16] For those whose aim is to get rich, wealth is far easier to attain via external employment. Competing leaders, on the contrary, do not seem to be interested in wealth for its own sake, but only as a means to further their position within Air Bah. Even though they seek money and prestige, they are not the wealthiest in the village. That title belongs to Lopong, who works for the aboriginal police force in Kampung Dala. Despite having less land than others in the village (a little over an acre), his household is the most well-off, especially in the possession of commercial goods. The male members of Lopong's family are less oriented towards village politics than others. Lopong, although generously providing for his family, is absent most of time. His children have all been educated, and his boys all work on the Federal Land Development Authority (FELDA) plantations and, occasionally, in factories. At the same time, however, he lacks prestige, influence, and political consequence within the village. Being more acculturated and incorporated into the larger Malaysian society, he falls *outside* the framework of village politics. Unlike Lopong and his family, competing leaders increase their production and wealth because they compete *within* village politics.

Thus, it is important to differentiate between land accumulation as a self-aggrandizing strategy and land accumulation as a means of acquiring wealth.[17] That competing leaders are involved in the former, rather than the latter, is illustrated by their attitudes towards the output of their efforts. Although they both worked hard at planting paddy and other crops in all of their fields, they did not care whether they harvested all of their produce. Instead, in true Semang fashion, they abandoned parts of their harvest and cheerfully started to explore possibilities outside the village. This seems to indicate that, in spite of their self-aggrandizement, these leaders have not yet developed the 'asset consciousness' that is sometimes attributed to post-foragers (Cashdan 1984; Jolly 1996: 287; Blackburn 1996: 210).

Nonetheless, self-aggrandizement by these leaders has resulted in inequalities and the marginalization of certain individuals and families in Air Bah. According to Jeanne Arnold, marginalization 'indicates that rising leaders devise and accelerate socioeconomic changes and explicitly counters the position that leaders and followers ... are created by large-scale social processes beyond their control' (1995: 88–9, in Rousseau 2006: 22). Marginalization in Air Bah is similarly a consequence of self-aggrandizing leaders' securing land, resources, consumer goods, and the opportunities to generate these. In Air Bah this is facilitated by what Bailey refers to as 'incrementalism,' a process that implies that 'for the most part leaders try to meet new situations by forcing them into categories of familiar situations, or by making minimal adjustments to well-tried plans' (1969: 69). In Air Bah competing leaders have self-aggrandized by manipulating familiar rules of inheritance, ownership, and sharing.

Self-Aggrandizement, Incrementalism, and the Rules of Inheritance and Ownership

The first method for competing leaders in Air Bah to acquire land is through the manipulation of Lanoh inheritance rules. To understand how the leaders are able to do this, it is necessary to examine the nature of Lanoh inheritance rules, which are complex, ill-defined, and subject to contradictory interpretations. Among Lanoh rules of inheritance primarily apply to personal items (M. *pesaka*,[18] 'hereditary property'), including weapons, tools, and body ornaments, as well as land:

> Property in Lanoh means *bayaŋ* and even land is considered *bayaŋ*.[19] In the case of a deceased person, his or her property is divided among his family, according to the family member's position in the family and relationship with the deceased. Generally, fruit trees and other property are given to the eldest child of the deceased. If there are no children, they are given to the family member who is the closest, who had taken care of the person before he or she died.

Although in this interview excerpt inheritance clearly favours the eldest child, there is also evidence that, as much as possible, people try to distribute property equally and fairly (L. *ʔibuʔ samaʔ ʔisɛt samaʔ ʔisɛt*, 'equal as big as small'). As residents of Air Bah explained, this means that if a person gets a piece of property of a certain value, the others should get property of similar value. The items do not need to be similar in kind, nor equal in monetary value. If one person receives a motorcycle, the other may get a television set. According to one villager, an example of a distribution of goods violating this principle would be the following:

> if one gets an acre of land and the other gets a fruit tree then clearly it would not fulfil the 'sameness' expressed in the saying. In that case, the other should get twenty fruit trees to balance the acre of land.[20]

Such equality also seems to govern the division of property in the following particular cases, in which the rules, especially reference to primogeniture, explicitly intend to 'make up' for inequalities inherent in relationships, particularly in those of relative age:

(1) *The male family head dies*: All his property passes down to his wife, but this property is not given to her. At this stage, she is merely the custodian (*kasi jaga supaya boleh ʔog*, given the task to look after the property so that it can be divided) of the estate. The purpose of this is to share or divide the property equally among her children and herself. If the property of the deceased is substantial, the

distribution can be extended to siblings of the deceased and their children. In most cases, sharing is restricted to the deceased's immediate family. In some cases, the property (like land) would be claimed by the brother of the deceased, because sometimes an elder brother would 'lend' a piece of land to his younger brother. If the younger brother dies, the elder brother can repossess the land. The distribution of property, however, is not as straightforward in practice as it is in theory, because there is no way to prevent people from keeping property for themselves.

(2) *A man dies and he has no surviving wife*: His property passes down to his children. The property is divided depending on whether they are (a) all male children; (b) all female children; (c) male and female children. In the first case, the youngest son becomes the custodian of all property, which he divides among his siblings. This is because it is usually the youngest child who does not have property yet; passing it down to the youngest child ensures that he gets a fair and sufficient share of the property compared with his siblings. In the second case, the eldest daughter becomes the custodian and is responsible for dividing the property equally among her siblings; this usually means that she has to give more to those who have less, compared with the other siblings (for example, land). If one of the siblings does not have land, he or she will get it first, before the other siblings. In the third case, the rule is the same as in the first case.

(3) *A man dies and he has two wives*: The wife who is considered good (*bə?ɛt*) becomes the custodian.[21] Whichever wife becomes the custodian has the task of dividing the property equally between the two widows and their children.

(4) *A single person dies without children*: His property passes to his own family, the custodian being the oldest living member of that family, for instance, his father, mother, or eldest brother. The property is divided equally among them.

It would be easy to interpret these regulations for the equal distribution of property as evidence for an 'egalitarian ethic.' Yet, in light of the significance of non-violence for Lanoh, these examples could alternatively be efforts to minimize the conflict inherent in the distribution of property, especially those of different value, such as television sets, motorcycles, and expensive tools.

The distribution of such valuable goods often results in conflict and disagreement between relatives. A man from Air Bah, for example, got into a serious dispute with his half-brother in Tawai over the ownership of a generator. This man in Tawai alleged that his elder brother had bequeathed the generator to him before he died. However, when he came to Air Bah to claim it, his half-brother refused to give it up, arguing that 'one cannot claim anything from a dead person.' Such disputes are especially common when the claimants are widows with very young children and the custodian keeps the property. As a result, when someone dies today, people commonly seek the services of mediators (M. *orang tengah*, 'middlemen'), who are usually elders from both sides of the family. Although the majority of cases are resolved with the help of mediators, occasionally, no amount of mediation will bring peace. In those instances, the dispute will remain unsettled, as 'there is nothing [people] can do.' Thus, the apparent contradiction between rules of inheritance favouring the eldest child versus an equal distribution of property may reflect social change and the increasing potential of conflict when allocating property of equal value.

Change may also account for some people's desire to protect their property. Today people in Air Bah often measure, fence, and mark off family lands by spikes. As well, respective households now claim ownership of fruit trees and mark branches of fruit with plastic bags.[22] One could explain these changing attitudes towards ownership in Air Bah by the above-mentioned 'asset consciousness' which, as some have suggested, often develops among changing foragers as a result of limited access to resources (Cashdan 1984; Jolly 1996: 287; Blackburn 1996: 210). As discussed in earlier chapters, this condition certainly applies in Air Bah, as Lanoh today incessantly compete for land and resources. However, according to their own understanding, Lanoh protect their property to avoid conflict. The following episode involving an elder, Tenuk, who had just returned to Air Bah from Tawai with a measuring tape, explicitly supports this interpretation. Tenuk explained that he wanted to measure the exact acreage of his land and set up permanent boundaries as it borders on those of two other men. He suspected that one of them was encroaching on his land. However, he further added that although villagers constantly quarrelled over land, they never came together to measure it, so that they would not ever have to have disputes over boundaries again. He said he wanted to set an example to avoid further bickering. This, and similar remarks by others in the village regarding property markers, suggests that people in Air Bah began to set up boundaries not primarily because they are concerned with ownership, but because they are concerned with potential discord over the ownership of property.

These changing attitudes towards property may be consequential, but they cannot account for inequalities in land ownership. These inequalities are more likely to reflect the needs of elders in general, and those of competing leaders in particular, to expand their agricultural production. Different classes of elders (self-aggrandizers and non–self-aggrandizers) commonly achieve this by manipulating younger men's access to land. In the previous chapter, I indicated that people in Air Bah had access to different activities according to their age roles. In particular, I explained that elders of the village had limited access to certain types of forest collecting which was the primary reason for them to focus more on 'village work.' However, interviews also revealed that such a focus on village work was *only* available to elders. Younger men could not farm, as they lacked the necessary resources, such as money, time, tools, seeds, extra labour, and, most importantly, land.

In Air Bah young Lanoh men may only acquire land by three means: clearing, inheritance, and marriage. In the past people most often acquired land by independently clearing a tract of suitable forest. Today they are less able to do so, and not necessarily because of lack of space. Even though Air Bah is surrounded by government and private plantations, there is still room to clear secondary forest adjacent to existing farming land. Yet, as interviews on this subject revealed, younger men were explicitly prevented from doing so by elders (Dallos 2003).

As part of their strategy to control and manipulate resources for their own interests, elders in the village control younger men's farming efforts and land acquisition through an alleged knowledge of history and ownership. Reinforcing their positions as the possessors of information on tradition and customs, elders exercise a great deal of authority over deciding who can or cannot acquire land. Younger men, they contend, must ask for permission before clearing land, because most of the land in Air Bah 'already belongs to someone else.' When younger men ask for permission, they are usually denied with a claim that there is no available vacant land. Instead, elders urge young men to be patient and to continue to work on whatever land they already own. Elders also undermine the ability of young men to farm with accusations of being unprepared or of being 'lazy' and wanting to 'go out too much.' They advise them to cultivate their existing land properly before trying to acquire new land. Referring to a younger man, Busu, the village's *penghulu* (Kecil) comments:

[He] likes to complain. It happened before. He said, '*Penghulu* never gives people land.' Then I told him, 'At the time when people were clearing land, you didn't want [to do that]. You went away. When people planted paddy, you said you'd wait for next year.' So he always complains.

Self-aggrandizement is not the only reason for Lanoh elders to control land ownership by younger men. They may also regulate younger men's access to farming land in order to obtain as much help as possible with their own farms. This commonly applies to older and physically weaker individuals, especially older or middle-aged women and widows, who would exchange rights to work on their land for a share of the harvest and for support and care from their younger relatives.[23] In fact, receiving land (usually one or two acres) from their mothers- or fathers-in-law upon their marriage was one of the most common ways for young people to acquire land in Air Bah. Thus, manipulating younger men's access to land is a familiar situation for Lanoh, one that competing leaders only needed to minimally adjust for the purposes of self-aggrandizement.

Table 5.4, showing land ownership in Air Bah, supports the conclusion that these days elders further their ambition to acquire as much as possible from the village's limited land by preventing the acquisition of land by younger men.

Indeed, beyond the two acres every household head received upon resettlement, the two competing leaders accumulated their land by taking land from others, especially by disinheriting their younger relatives. Kecil, the *penghulu* of the village, refused his unmarried younger brother his share from their late father's large parcel of land (between six and eight acres), leaving the younger brother a meagre acre of land that he had to clear himself. Hitam not only claimed custody over the land of a cousin, who had moved away from the village, but also he kept his own father's land, allegedly for his young half-siblings. Many, however, doubt that these children, who are still in their teens, will ever receive their share. Thus, by exploiting familiar rules of inheritance and ownership, competing leaders in Air Bah were able to use farming as an arena for their competition.

Self-Aggrandizement, Incrementalism, and the Rules of Sharing

Among the practices of mobile hunter-gatherers, many consider sharing to be the most important in maintaining equality (Woodburn 1980;

Table 5.4 Land Ownership and Cultivation by Age in Air Bah

Age group (years)	Land owned (average no. of acres)	Land cultivated (average no of acres)
10–20	0	0
20–30	1.3	1
30–40	1.3	0.5
40–50	7	4.4
50–60	2	0

Gibson 1985, 1988; K.M. Endicott 1988; Kent 1993). Yet, in Air Bah, through incrementalism, competing elders were reinterpreting sharing rules for their own interest and thereby promoting the development of inequalities. Although ostensibly adhering to sharing like everyone else, they subtly modified rules to fit their ambitions. Lanoh rules of sharing generally conform to those among hunter-gatherers elsewhere. As hunter-gatherers elsewhere, Lanoh believe that one should share with neighbours and friends. While, as suggested earlier, people do not share money, they do share food purchased *with* money. They also share meat from the forest, especially that of larger game, as well as vegetables (although less frequently). The most important factor used to ensure compliance with sharing rules is visibility. As one Lanoh, for example, said:

> it cannot happen that others watch you [M. *tenggoh*] eating.

People in Air Bah continue to practise sharing and emphasize it in verbal statements, such as the following:

> I could sell game meat, *kijaŋ*, for RM 20 per kg, and some people do that … I never do that, but cut up the meat and give a portion to my neighbors. This is the Lanoh *adat* [custom, M.]. Whenever you have more of something, you share.

They also continue to instill the importance of sharing in young people, and use several methods to teach children to share from an early age. Women will, for instance, put a handful of chestnuts, or other foods, in the pocket of a little girl, and encourage her to walk around and distribute it among those present. On other occasions, people will ask a child to take an item such as a cigarette lighter, tobacco, or food from one grown-up to another, or from one house to another.[24] In yet other cases, people give children a favourite food, such as candy or a nut, and as the child wanders over to another grown-up with the food in hand, this other person would encourage and persuade the child to it give up, repeating 'give it to me [ʔɔg ʔiɲ, or miʔ ʔɔg ʔiɲ]' over and over again.

Letting go of possessions is similarly emphasized in the socialization of young men. As the following interview excerpt explains, young men are expected to exchange meat they hunt with their hunting partners. This custom not only facilitates working partnerships between younger men, but also teaches them to forgo their interests for the sake of others:

> My father taught me, 'If you have to go hunting, you must go with another person. When you get an animal, you cannot eat it, you have to give it to your friend and you have to take his [kill]. You have to make an exchange. You cannot take the animal that you hunted yourself.' The reason is this: when you hunt an animal for the first time and this is your first kill and then you bring it home and eat it, you'll never get that animal again because the animal can smell you. He'll know. You have to exchange it with a friend. You have to let go seventy-four[25] of every kind of animal you'll ever have. If you don't do that, it's going to be so hard for you to get the same animal, for example, a squirrel. You go into the forest for four or five days, maybe even for one month, and you'll only get one squirrel. So that is a taboo. That's what I'm doing now; I'm exchanging, exchanging animals I shoot with people. When you bring [the animal] home, you can let your family eat it and you just watch. You cannot eat it. That's taboo, too. If you eat the animal you just killed and you have not let pass seventy-four, the meat is bad and hard.

Even as young adults Lanoh are praised whenever they share food. In one instance, upon seeing two little girls coming out of the house of a young man with huge plates of cooked rice and handing these over to those sitting around outside, an old man remarked:

> This is the right way. Today, Rahim made some money and so he shares some of his fortune with family, neighbours, and friends.

Another old man nodded and said: 'Everybody in the village does that.' People in Air Bah do not perceive changes in their ability to adhere to general sharing after resettlement; in fact, they believe that they are continuously reinforcing it.

Yet, the same rules and practices today often produce different outcomes. While in the past sharing rules ensured that goods were distributed equally within a settlement, today these same regulations tend to result in restricted sharing. Researchers have long regarded restricted sharing as a predictable development in newly sedentary villages, and indeed, there are several points of consensus about restricted sharing among anthropologists. First, many agree that restricted sharing is often connected to settlement structure (e.g., Plog 1990). Second, some have suggested that this type of discriminative sharing is often associated with preferring kin over others among newly sedentary hunter-gatherers (e.g., Gurven et al. 2001). Finally, restrictions in sharing networks are also linked to emerging inequalities. Robert Hitchcock notes that after sedentism, among the Basarwa of eastern Botswana, 'sharing networks became more restricted, and status and wealth differences began to emerge' (1982: 255–6). This also relates to the structure of sedentary villages. As Stephen Plog suggests, while a disparity of wealth is absent in 'circular compounds ... differences in wealth appear early in villages' (1990: 198). Whereas the first two points on restricted sharing certainly apply, neither architecture nor kin preference can alone account for emerging inequalities in Air Bah. Arguably, restricted sharing is only relevant for inequality in the context of competitive self-aggrandizement.

It is correct that architecture and village structure in Air Bah promote limited sharing. The elongated rectangular-shaped settlement, with houses arranged in parallel rows, reduces visibility, and the solid wooden walls conceal activities. This spatial layout was unfamiliar to Lanoh. At the time of resettlement Lanoh occupied houses close to their families, and the village divided into family clusters. Since sharing is primarily determined by spatial proximity, as a result of this clustering, people in Air Bah began to share more with kin than with non-kin.[26] In this way, the rule, share with your neighbours and friends, has contributed to emerging kinship group boundaries. This process is further intensified by women, among whom frequent sharing of rice, raw vegetables, and vegetable dishes is an important way to reinforce kinship ties. However, such sharing by women, albeit conducive to delineating kinship group boundaries, hardly generates the 'post-distribution variation' that Plog identifies (1990). Such variation is the result of incrementalism, the reinterpretation of sharing rules by competing leaders in the interest of their self-aggrandizement.

These competing leaders have consciously modified and redefined sharing rules to introduce merit-based, restricted sharing that resulted in the marginalization of certain individuals and families in Air Bah.

In the following interview excerpt, Hitam offers his interpretation of sharing rules:

> You do not have to share all meals. You have to share once a day. Reciprocity is ensured by the custom that you give once, twice, three times, and if you do not get back anything, you stop giving. Sharing is called *jəheed*. People who like to give are called *mənihɛy*, and those who are stingy, *kəɲed*. Such people hoard things, do not give things to other people because 'they are afraid they would run out of things.' The amount of food given away has no significance. Everybody gives whatever he can afford to give. It is proportionate to how much one has. Sick people, unable to work and make money are given without any expectation of return. We either collect money for them or give them food; for instance, rice and sugar. If, however, a person does not work because he is lazy ... so that he only eats, sleeps, and plays, people stop giving things to him.

One of the best portrayals of the contrast between unconditional and conditional giving is provided in Bird-David's (1990) analysis of norms of distribution by Nayaka hunter-gatherers and Kurumba agriculturists in South India. While Lanoh sharing rules match the unconditional sharing of Nayaka, Hitam's explanation above resembles the conditional, merit-based providing among Kurumba (ibid.: 192). It not only sets a limit on giving ('you give once, twice, three times, and if you do not get back anything, you stop giving'), but also institutes conditions to giving ('If ... a person does not work because he is lazy ... people stop giving things to him'). Through village gossip and public censure competing leaders and their families marginalize certain individuals and families primarily by establishing claims that these people, indeed, meet the above conditions and thus should be excluded.

Invested with the authority to interpret and define rules and events, competing leaders often deliberately withhold goods from younger men, including those in their kinship groups. Marginalized individuals, families, or family groups were either younger, more distant offshoots of the competing leaders' clusters, or entire clusters headed by men who were younger than the competing leaders (Table 5.3). These individuals and families were easy targets because they were the most vulnerable in terms of support and status and, therefore, easiest to exploit through the manipulation of norms and rules. An example of this is described in the following account by Amat, a younger relative of Hitam, explaining how and why he was denied goods distributed to villagers by the JHEOA:

> Other projects, like fruits, like fertilizers, seedlings, all of those were for the ones with their names [on the list]. Our names were there too. The JHEOA had a long list. Everybody in the village had their names on the list. So they came with fruit seedlings; *rambutan*, *cempedak*, three or four seedlings each per person ... Then, when it came to distribution, it wasn't shared. This person got ten, that person twenty, another person thirty, another sixteen. I got nothing. And how many trips it has been already! I counted five times [that] the officers came. I didn't get anything ... I looked and my name was there. I can read my own name ... It was there, right at the bottom. Beside my name, there was the number 'ten,' and besides Hitam's name 'fifteen,' but I didn't get anything. When it comes to sharing, I don't get anything. So I asked them [the elders], my name was there, how come I didn't get anything? 'Oh,' they said, 'this is for Hitam this time.' So on and on, they distributed these trees, but I didn't get anything.

As a result of such restrictions competing leaders in Air Bah are able to hoard land, tools, and prestige items. Although, as established above, these leaders are not the wealthiest in the village, gaps in wealth between them and others have already begun to surface not only in the ownership of land, but also in that of consumer goods. Men in Air Bah tend not to have any articles of value beyond a few basic tools like a *parang* (machete), an axe, and a blowpipe. Yet, the personal possessions of the two competing leaders surpass those of other men. Not only do they both own motorcycles, television sets, and wristwatches, but in addition, Kecil erected a flashy extension to his house, while Hitam has acquired a VCR, as well as a series of household goods – clothes, carpets, and utensils in which other households are lacking. He further owns a few valuable tools and electronic equipment, such as a water pump and a chainsaw. It's clear that the self-aggrandizing schemes of these leaders, although aimed primarily at each other, evidently have the potential to transform temporal and transitory age differences into permanent inequalities.

Self-Aggrandizement and Elders' Rights in Egalitarian Politics

As suggested in the introduction of this book, there is an emerging consensus among scholars concerning the nature of egalitarianism in certain small-scale societies. This consensus is built on Woodburn's proposition in his article 'Egalitarian Societies' (1982) that equality among mobile hunter-gatherers is asserted in a conscious, egalitarian ethic and maintained through powerful levelling mechanisms. Based on this theory of equality, changing foragers are expected to resist self-aggrandizement and inequalities, and as suggested earlier, there have been indications that some do (Lee 1979; Woodburn 1980, 1982: 442; Bird 1982, 1983; Headland 1986: 416). Behaviour in Air Bah, however, seems to contradict these predictions; instead of resisting inequalities, villagers wholeheartedly support their respective kinship group leaders and even contribute to the marginalization of certain individuals and families. This is an intriguing departure from the general view of the nature of egalitarianism. In this respect, the response of Lanoh in Air Bah to the rise of aggrandizement deserves further scrutiny. By addressing why villagers in Air Bah act this way, we can begin to remove some of the main obstacles to understanding developing inequalities in previously egalitarian societies. It appears that people in Air Bah accept developing inequalities because they do not contradict the rights of elders to interpret and reinterpret rules and norms in egalitarian politics.

The Power to Persuade: The Foundation of Competing Leaders' Incrementalism

Different kinship group members in Air Bah not only accept developing inequalities, they also unconditionally support their kin leaders. Below, Hitam's younger brother, Ambok, explains village politics from the perspective of his kinship group. This excerpt also shows that he blames Kecil and his group and sees their actions against Hitam as motivated by jealousy:

> This village is divided into three groups: number one is organized around Hitam and Som; number two around Kecil and Tengah;[27] and number three around Leman's family. All the others try to be nice to all of them. Sometimes, they will support one group, sometimes another group. For instance, Tengah and Tambi will always quarrel but Tambi will always support Tengah in big meetings, even though Tambi's wife goes to Som a lot. That is why Tambi's wife never gets much food from Som, but still sometimes she would get some because Som pities her grandchildren. Kecil's and Tengah's group always tries to get everything for themselves first. They are always afraid that Hitam will get things from the outside,

and they are always afraid that Hitam will become the leader and that outsiders will trust him more. Amat supports them because he gets food from them. Leman has his family. He sometimes supports Kecil, sometimes he does not. His children sometimes support Kecil, sometimes Hitam. Musa supports Leman and Kecil.

This excerpt further reveals that people tend to see these two leaders as challengers and competitors, rather than as self-aggrandizers. Indeed, they consider them 'smart,' 'hard working,' and 'good providers,' who deserve their status and wealth. In the passage below, an older man, Kecil's uncle, expresses his approval of his nephew's hoarding of money:

> My nephew and his family are focusing on their own land. [He] wants to plant eight acres of paddy. He has a big family and he wants to make money and use that money to plant more. My nephew is the *penghulu* and it's no good for a *penghulu* not to have money. When my nephew has money, he can be generous and then people will like him.

Thus, this uncle regards his nephew's self-aggrandizement as entirely compatible with his role as village leader.

The prestige of competing leaders within their kinship groups derives from their status as elders. For instance, it appears that 'levelling mechanisms' designed to challenge self-aggrandizers, such as joking, shunning, meddling, demanding, and mocking, only apply when the perceived 'self-aggrandizer' is a younger man. Boasting or self-glorifying by competing elders, however, is tolerated, even approved. When Hitam, the charismatic leader, complained that people are jealous of him because he is smarter, wealthier, and more successful, people witnessing this, as a rule, members of his kinship group, nodded supportively in agreement. However, boasting, or 'big talk,' by younger men (or by the anthropologist) draws reproof. Younger men are also reprimanded when they take somebody else's property even if people in Air Bah still disregard claims to personal property and take things from others without asking. It is still common for them to walk into others' houses and pick up whatever they need, and most people in the village appear helpless against such invasions. For example, the younger man, Bulat, whose experiences with the auto mechanic course in Kuala Lumpur I recounted in an earlier chapter, complained to me about villagers 'borrowing' his tools:

> Look at my toolbox; I used to have a lot of tools. At one time, it was full,
> but now most of the tools are gone. People borrowed, but never returned
> them. They come when I'm not in the house. They take two or three. I
> don't even know who took them.

Divorced and without children, this man is politically inconsequential
and thus powerless against such invasions.

It is quite a different matter if the property is owned by one of the competing leaders. Although it is unlikely that anyone would enter either
of their houses and take something without their permission, occasionally their property is left out in public. In one such instance, a younger
man 'borrowed' the *penghulu*'s motorcycle. Although the motorcycle
was soon recovered, there was a public outrage, and the younger man
was sharply reprimanded. On a different occasion, another younger
man accidentally cut down one of Hitam's trees while clearing his land
and was subsequently scolded by the village elders.

It is quite evident that elders often label acts that would have been
considered 'sharing' in pre-resettlement times as 'stealing.' One elder,
commenting on the behaviour of a younger relative, remarked:

> He could help me work my land, because we are in-laws, but he just won't.
> Yet he will shamelessly accept rice from others. He steals, accepts, or asks
> for rice or whatever he needs from others.

People in Air Bah have evidently employed such different standards
towards the actions of younger men for a long time. In considering
people's recollections, it soon becomes apparent that Lanoh elders in
the past had substantial authority and privilege, including the right to
interpret rules and make sense of what was happening to the group.
This role manifests itself best in the persona of the Lanoh shaman (*səma?
hala?*).[28] As people in Air Bah explained, a 'shaman' is a person who can
'teach the young people stories and good things about the Lanoh.' Both
the prestige of today's elders in their kinship groups and the credibility
of Lanoh shamans in the past within *their* kinship groups derive from
age roles and age-based authority.[29] As indicated earlier, Lanoh men
only begin to show an interest in exploring esoteric matters and acquiring spiritual knowledge when they enter middle age or 'elderhood.'
Once an elder is recognized as having been endowed with the powers
of a 'shaman,' he would enjoy people's complete trust and support. It
is, for instance, entirely up to shamans' discretion to decide when they

need to erect a *pano?* (M. *bumbun*) hut to perform a community ritual. People in Air Bah affirmed that *pano?* can be built at any time, whenever the *hala?* feels there is the need for one. For instance, when there is an illness, conflict, or crisis in the village, 'It is up to the *hala?* to decide to build one.'

Lanoh shamans were not only influential in life, but also received privileged treatment after death. Villagers, describing the afterlife, explained:

> On the seventh day [after death], the dead person's soul is on his way back home. The soul will be met by his parents, mother and father, who died a long time ago. The mother will say, 'Oh my son has come home,' or 'My daughter has come home!' Our parents will take us to the village and there will be a lot of people like us; Lanoh. We will be happy there, celebrating with *sewang*. After we have our mother and father, we won't feel like going back to our own family anymore.

However, before one can proceed to the village of the dead, ordinary people must undergo a trial to determine whether 'they had lived a good life and did not contravene taboos.' Shamans, however, are exempt from this examination and advance directly to their final home:

> The land of the soul is a very flat land and there is a road. There is a tree on the road there. There is a junction on this road. To the right is the road which is taken by *səma? hala?* [shaman]. These are the people who are not like us. The *hala?* people go to the right on the road and there is a huge tree. They cut one part of the tree and they sit on the branches. And the branches break, but it is *ya?* [god] who makes the branches break. Then they jump from branch to branch and that is how they go on the road to their home.

In the past Lanoh shamans were also believed to possess invaluable powers. They could, for instance, talk to the elephant, the guardian father of the Lanoh, as well as guide people on spiritual trips. They often claimed to be able to communicate directly with god (*ya?*) and embrace, even mate with, the sun. Shamans possessed the power of divination and could cast spells, such as love charms or those that could make people invisible, enabling them to take something without getting noticed. People recounted that shamans were able to:

travel like a bird .... The *səma? hala?* can be here in Air Bah, and, at the same time, be in Tawai.

It is also clear that shamans in the past had considerable power over people's emotions. According to Lanoh a shaman was always 'a very good singer, so that everybody who listens to him feels calm and happy.' Most importantly, Lanoh shamans did not need any empirical validation for their claims and interpretations.

As mentioned earlier, among Lanoh religious knowledge and skills are hierarchical. While to achieve most levels of spiritual knowledge requires demonstrable ability and effectiveness, the most important one of these, the one that accords the highest prestige, depends on credibility alone. To become a shaman one does not need any tangible proof of skill. One can learn about medicine, healing, and incantations from others, but to become a shaman one must be chosen:

> You cannot train to be a [*hala?*]. You become a [*hala?*] when you are chosen to be one in a dream. Like the dream of being given or endowed by a spirit, woman, old man, or a talking animal. In the dream, he will be asked to do errands, go on a quest, or subject himself to mental and physical tests.

It is thus crucial that anyone who aspires to become a shaman can convince people that he has, indeed, been chosen to receive shamanic powers. As a result an elder who already possesses a measure of authority and respect within the community is more likely to be accepted as someone with special spiritual powers than a younger man.

The following two examples illustrate how important age is in determining one's credibility. One day, a young man, Rosli, recounted a dream of spiritual endowment and how he had failed to fulfil the requirements prescribed in the dream. Upon hearing about this incident, everyone agreed that the young man was '*not ready* to receive this gift of knowledge from the spirit world.' In the second instance, an older man, Leman, related a dream in which he was visited by a snake-woman, who promised him knowledge. Although he too admitted that he had failed to fulfil a set of requirements in the dream, he nonetheless persuaded the community that he was endowed in some way as a result. He explained that the fact that he was chosen to have the dream in the first place was proof that, from then on, he could foretell impending danger or sickness. People nodded in agreement, accepting this interpretation. It seems that the Lanoh are much more likely to entertain claims of spiritual endowment from an elder than from a younger person.

This discrepancy between the rights of elders and younger men to interpret dreams derives from the cognitive roles that Lanoh assign to younger men and elders. Categorical age roles among men are not only defined by the distinct economic roles discussed earlier, but also by a dichotomy of spontaneity versus deliberation. In this division, elders are seen to be wiser, more thoughtful, and more careful than their younger, more impetuous counterparts. Lanoh accentuate this difference symbolically in the contrasting notions of *kuy* and *yəl*. These concepts embody the difference between the rational and deliberate and the physical and spontaneous – in other words, the difference between elders and younger men.[30] *Kuy*, sometimes also referred to as *roway* (soul), resides in a person's throat and represents the person's cognitive faculties, such as speech, thought, and memory. *Kuy* gives a person voice, 'what we say, think, and remember.' *Yəl* (roughly, living dead), on the other hand, is a dumb, violent, shadowy spirit with a frightening, zombie-like appearance. After a person dies, his or her *kuy* abandons the body and travels to the land of the dead, leaving behind the potentially dangerous entity *yəl* which can be awakened by careless and thoughtless acts.

Correspondingly, elders in Air Bah aggressively control the verbal expressions of younger men. Lanoh, like hunter-gatherers elsewhere (e.g., Balicki 1989), attribute significant powers to language and verbal expressions. They believe that god gave people language. Before that they were motionless and speechless, unable to move, talk, or have will. Among Lanoh the elders desire above all others the mental powers that speech can confer. These powers not only include skills, such as those that come with knowledge of herbs, medicinals, healing, tool making, and house building, but also the power to influence others. Elders see the ability to persuade, to be able to 'convince anyone of anything,' to be the most advantageous.

As a result elders in Air Bah work hard to control younger men's verbal expressions in public settings. During demographic interviews, for instance, elders always insisted on being present when younger men were questioned. Similarly, elders in Air Bah monopolize decision-making. They argue that younger men are immature and 'hot-headed,' thus incapable of decision-making. This is why, they insist, it is imperative for younger men to ask for elders' advice before making important decisions.

The same foundation of credibility and the right to interpret rules have been used by Hitam and Kecil to manipulate the familiar Lanoh principles of sharing, ownership, and inheritance. Although leadership competition altered the meaning of this cognitive division between elders and younger men, competing leaders nonetheless reached for this construct in their rivalry against each other, and this explains why people in Air Bah consented so readily to their self-aggrandizement and the resulting inequalities.

Self-Aggrandizing Strategies and Their Implications for Emerging Inequalities

Since it is accepted, even expected, that elders interpret rules through rhetoric and verbal craftiness, discrimination is tolerated by all, even by those who are becoming disadvantaged as a consequence. Withholding goods and excluding others from sharing and work activities are seen to be well-deserved retributive or rehabilitative measures for past wrongdoings.[31] In other words, those who have been targeted at some point failed to share or cooperate with others, and their marginalization is a punishment for these earlier deeds.[32] Below is a piece of gossip justifying why some individuals simply do not deserve a share:

> If you eat the animal you just killed and you do not give up the first seventy-four of every species, the meat is bad and hard. For instance, Musa and Jalak … look at the meat when they hunt. The meat is bad. You cannot eat it. [That is] because they ate the animals they hunted for the first time. So they will never get good meat. Next time you take a look if they give you meat. After you cook it, the meat will look dark and hard like it's been shot, like when you hit your hand and it becomes blue and black, like that.

Families 'blacklisted' this way are not only excluded from government handouts, but also from the festive share of large game.[33] On more than one occasion, wild boar (*napag*) was brought back to be shared among the villagers. One household (Cluster 4 in Table 5.4), however, was regularly excluded from meat sharing. The head of this cluster is not only the youngest among all the leaders in Air Bah, but also an individual with a reputation of failing to share when he was younger. Members of this man's cluster were also excluded from the communal paddy-planting feast, as well as from work parties. Earlier, I suggested that in Air Bah a man's popularity determined his ability to participate in contract work groups. However, this popularity is rarely a function of personal attributes alone: increasingly, it depends on the person's family's status within the village. Female members of these marginalized families were similarly excluded from the women's work groups. Women in one of the benighted clusters explained that, when it came to recruiting, the *penghulu*'s wife, leader of the women's work group, exclusively picked her friends, family, and allies.

As a consequence of their marginalization these families are not only landless, but also gravely in need of cash. At harvest time they are the ones most likely to seek to work in the fields of the more ambitious and well-to-do people in Air Bah. They work for money, seeds, or a portion of the harvested paddy. One 'landowner' remarked:

> For people who don't have land, the best thing for them to do is to help us and we would surely give them some paddy. Those who don't help are really bad.

Are these accusations valid? Is it perhaps true that members of these marginalized families are simply not trying hard enough? My time-allocation survey indicates otherwise. It shows that the male members of these families work hard, often much harder, than other men in the village. They need to do so, as they rely on a smaller pool of support than the heads of larger family groups have. As noted earlier, Lanoh do not expect children younger than 13 years to work. However, I often observed children in these disadvantaged families doing household chores – minding younger siblings, scrubbing cooking pots, or washing clothes. Not surprisingly, in charting the development of the village's infants and children, members of the government's medical team found children in the two least popular families to be the most malnourished, in one instance even requiring hospital care.

Conclusion

I have emphasized the importance of identifying potential self-aggrandizers in terms of their structural attributes. In searching for the causes of emerging inequalities in small-scale societies, Peter Bogucki notes that 'if being an aggrandizer was the ticket to status, power, and wealth, then everyone would be an aggrandizer. Clearly that is never the case. Some other factors conspire against people and their kin to cause them to drop to second-class or third-class status' (1999: 209–10). The history and effects of leadership competition in Air Bah support Bogucki's suggestion that 'other factors' may be responsible for post-sedentary inequality. They also suggest that the most important of these may be the aggrandizer's position within the structure of egalitarian politics and that, ultimately, age status may be pivotal in determining who can self-aggrandize and who will be marginalized as a result. Furthermore, the developments described in this chapter appear to reinforce the suggestion made at the end of the previous chapter that Air Bah is becoming an increasingly integrated and segmented village community. In evaluating the extent to which this is indeed the case, in the next chapter I will once again shift focus away from structural attributes, such as categorical age, and back to hunter-gatherers' social organization and the way it has affected the development of social inequality in Air Bah.

6 Pre-resettlement Organization, Village Integration, and Self-Aggrandizing Strategies

In the previous chapters I reviewed numerous signs of integration in Air Bah. Elders have begun to promote village segregation, village boundaries, and village identity. They have attempted to control women's mobility and younger men's access to opportunities outside the village. At the kinship group level composite household clusters have apparently turned into factions, or as Boissevain has defined them, 'exclusive coalition[s] of persons (followers) recruited personally according to structurally diverse principles by or on behalf of a person in conflict with another person or persons within the same social unit over honour and/or over resources' (1968: 551). All of these developments support Elizabeth Brumfiel's conviction that 'all non-egalitarian societies, both ancient and modern, are shaped by the dynamics of factional competition' (1994: 3). However, we have yet to examine how the pre-resettlement organization of Lanoh has affected social integration in modern Air Bah.

By examining the way the organizational characteristics of immediate-return hunter-gatherers affect post-resettlement integration at the level of the household, kinship group, and village, we may learn more about the prospects of such social groups to become societies with a 'delayed-return' system of production. It is clear that Lanoh pre-resettlement 'immediate-return' social organization continues to impact this process of social change. In spite of elders' attempts to create greater cohesion, integration at most remains partial, as elders in Air Bah continue to exercise limited control over their younger male relatives. This, in turn, will affect, and ultimately determine, the self-aggrandizing strategies of those competing for leadership of the village.

Integration in Competing Leaders' Households

Even though household integration has long figured importantly in models of developing inequality, we still know relatively little about household integration among newly sedentary hunter-gatherers.[1] Scrutinizing the mechanisms involved in increasing household production and integrating different members of households into these groups is crucial not only for our understanding of household dynamics and emerging inequalities in these societies, but also for discovering the limitations to this process, especially among immediate-return hunter-gatherers. That is, by learning more about these limitations, we can also hope to better understand hunter-gatherers' social organization and what Gardner (1991) termed 'individual autonomy syndrome' among these hunter-gatherers. In Air Bah limitations deriving from pre-resettlement social organization presented an important obstacle to household integration. Although competing leaders have successfully integrated the female members of their households, their wives and daughters, they have had limited success with male members, their sons and sons-in-law.

Household integration in competing leaders' households can be approached from the perspective of increased production and the resulting scheduling conflicts. As noted in the last chapter, Kecil and Hitam, the two elders competing for leadership status, tried to extend and intensify their household production. In 1998 they were involved in several jobs and projects inside and outside the village, expanding their farming, working on a nearby Federal Land Development Authority (FELDA) rubber plantation, and conducting business transactions with outsiders. However, as Steadman Upham (1990b) has suggested, such production intensification often leads to scheduling conflicts, and household integration can be conceived as a measure to deal with such problems. Scheduling conflicts can be addressed, for example, by increasing specialization (ibid.: 113), which itself increases efficiency, an important goal in self-aggrandizement.

The first dimension of specialization in the competing leaders' households occurred between public and domestic engagements. Since the distinction between public and domestic domains as a rule is associated with the sexual division of labour, on the surface, this claim seems counterintuitive, because the sexual division of labour in the competing households actually appears *less* pronounced than elsewhere in Air Bah, where sedentism has resulted in the increased separation of men's and women's tasks.[2] To appreciate this discrepancy between competing and non-competing households, it is necessary to evaluate the effects of sedentism on the division of labour in post-resettlement Air Bah.

Cooperation between the sexes in Air Bah has been shaped by a number of factors, including sedentism, village structure, village population, task entailment, the decline of forest collecting, and men's increased involvement in contract work (Dallos 2003).[3] In most households the sexual division of labour increased, because women now spend more time taking care of their children, their larger houses, and their property than they did in the past. While in pre-resettlement times people would throw away bamboo utensils and burn lean-to shelters before abandoning camps, after sedentism households need to be maintained, clothes and containers washed, and areas in and around the house swept. As a result women in Air Bah spend a great part of their time on the upkeep of their homes and surroundings. These factors generally contribute to the increased separation of male and female realms. Nonetheless, how much time men and women spend together in leisure and work on overlapping tasks is also significantly influenced by demographic factors.

In Air Bah the sexual division of labour tends to be the lowest among younger and older couples with few dependent children. Such couples not only spend a significant amount of time together in leisure, but also they often work together on similar tasks, such as building an extension to their house. Likewise, younger couples often go together to the fields and beyond, to the forest, planting corn, gathering vegetables, and hunting together. Apparently, this was even more common in the past when Lanoh had fewer children. Then, it would have been customary for couples to spend weeks in temporary forest camps hunting and collecting vegetables and forest products for sale. One old man recalled that when he was young, he and his wife went on hunting trips in the forest lasting from one to two weeks. While he hunted his wife gathered wild herbs, vegetables, and roots. They consumed the meat on the spot and brought the gathered food, along with any useful products such as bamboo or aloewood back to the village.

Similarly, older couples whose children have already established independent households are once again able to spend more time together. Such couples often spend their days sitting side by side in their lean-to shelter. Therefore, younger and older couples have been less affected by resettlement than have middle-aged couples between the ages of 30 and 40, who normally have the largest number of dependent children.

Men in these households are often engaged in commercial collecting and contract work outside the village, while their wives are occupied with child care and household chores inside the village. Consequently, such middle-aged couples seem to live quite separate lives.

Contrary to other women, the competing leaders' wives are less confined to domestic tasks and spend more time in their fields and outside the village on contract jobs. The competing leaders each have one key ally, their wife, and these leaders and their wives spend more time together than other couples do, working on similar tasks, and they are often seen working side by side in the village fields as well as outside the village. Therefore, the tasks of these leaders and their wives overlapped more than those of husbands and wives in other households. For a few months in 1998, for instance, Hitam held a particularly well-paid job at a FELDA project, where his wife and one of their daughters regularly accompanied him. Similarly, Kecil's wife did not only work longer hours than other women of her age on their large family plot alongside her husband, but as leader of the women's work group at the vegetable farm, she also spent disproportionately more time working 'outside' the village than other women. Thus, as far as the division of labour is concerned, competing leaders and their wives displayed a pattern characteristic of older and younger, rather than of middle-aged couples. This was possible because, in both households, domestic tasks were assigned to the eldest unmarried daughters, thereby freeing the leaders' wives to engage in other activities.

Although older women in Air Bah have a lot of influence over the younger females of their households, directing activities and assigning chores, no other young women were as managed as the girls of the competing leaders' households.[4] While Hitam and his wife were out working on their land or at a plantation, they would instruct their unmarried daughter Puteh to stay at home to do the washing, cooking, and cleaning and to take care of her younger, disabled, brother. When asked to comment on this, Hitam said that 'she prefers to stay at home.' Similarly, in the *penghulu*'s household, Amoi, his elder unmarried daughter, supervised her younger siblings and was responsible for all domestic chores. Her father often praised her for being obedient and 'smart' with the broom.

In relieving scheduling conflicts these unmarried young women increased the efficiency of their parents' households, contributing to their families' advantage over others in the village. To understand this relationship we must first outline the process of scheduling work in

Lanoh households and the nature of female relationships in Air Bah, especially those between older and younger women.

Young women's relationships with their mothers or important mother figures are probably the most significant power relations that they endure. The influence of mothers over their daughters seems to be greater and more direct than that of fathers over their sons. While male elders could only carefully 'advise' younger men, older women 'tell' younger women, in no uncertain terms, what to do. The dependence of daughters on their mothers extends into adulthood. While Lanoh women tend to be independent from their husbands and strong in their marriages, they remain emotionally dependent on their mothers throughout their lives.[5] In the village permanent matrilocal residence has only enhanced this influence. Older women's power is evident in several respects. Not only have there been cases where women left their husbands under the counsel and guidance of their mothers, but these older women in Air Bah also have their way when allocating tasks among women.[6]

As noted in Chapter 2, it is customary for women in Air Bah to hold regular discussions to divide household chores. In any household these chores are divided among adult women (women above the age of 13). During these scheduling discussions older women usually have the first pick of the tasks. As well, they have sufficient power to influence the way their daughters spend their time. The following survey, designed to find out what factors influence women's participation in a particularly attractive two-week contract in the neighbouring village of Sumpitan, illustrates the influence of older women. This work opportunity was especially popular with women because it not only promised good wages but also a much-welcome chance for them to leave the village. Younger women were especially excited about going and anticipated having fun with their friends. Yet, despite these attractions, fourteen out of the twenty-two women interviewed chose not to participate in this contract opportunity. The reasons cited for not going included inconvenience (eight responses), a lack of alternative child care (five responses), and being asked by an older female relative to stay behind and look after the household (three responses). In the last case, the young women said they did not feel they could refuse the request from the older women. These power relations between women allowed competing leaders and their wives to exploit their eldest daughters' labour in the service of household production and task specialization.

Scheduling conflicts and the resulting pressure on younger women may occur even in households unaffected by leadership competition. Nearly all mothers and mother figures have sufficient power to exploit young women's time and labour, which they will use for their own convenience or for the smooth running of their household. In the following account Jenab, an older woman, uses this power to deal with a shortage of adult women in her household which at the time was comprised of two adult women (one of whom, Madu, was 15 years old), three adult men, an elderly man, an adolescent boy, and a 5-year-old girl. Jenab relied on the labour of the 15-year-old Madu to such extent that even friends of this girl remarked:

> Madu works all the time. You get up in the morning at seven and see her already doing the dishes, the laundry, carrying firewood.

By contrast, this girl's 13-year-old brother had no responsibilities and played with his friends all day long. Due to the surplus of adult men in his household, he could take his time growing up. In this instance making full use of the girl's help was an opportunistic solution to a practical problem, rather than a strategy for political advancement. In the households of the competing leaders, however, interfering with their eldest daughters' autonomy was a mechanism to manage and increase household production. This is evident from the way leaders and their wives interfered with their daughters' marriage plans.

For leaders and their wives to continue to utilize their daughters' help, it was imperative that these girls remain unmarried. Had they been married, their services would have been lost – even though daughters in Air Bah tend to stay near their parents' houses after marriage, the demands of their new independent families prevent these young women from providing further assistance to their parents' households. Upham (1990b) has suggested that scheduling conflicts can be relieved by increasing the size of households. While it is possible to increase the size of households by reproduction, or by employing servants or slaves, neither of these methods are viable in Air Bah. Instead, competing leaders increased the size of their households by retaining their eldest daughters.[7]

As a consequence, in Air Bah, where most girls are married by the age 20, these young women, both around the age of 25, were considered 'old maids.' To be sure, finding marriage partners is becoming more and more difficult in Air Bah. Since rules of exogamy prescribe that Lanoh cannot marry anyone 'too close,' the shortage of available partners has been affecting young people, especially young women. In the following interview excerpt, 19-year-old Timah explains the dilemma of young women in the village:

> I don't know when I will get married. Here in the village, I cannot find a mate because almost every young man is [closely related to me]. I think I will find a distant match, but I don't know how. There are many young Orang Asli men from other villages I can meet in town. Grik is one place. Lenggong is not good because only men from Bt. Sapi go there. They are all married or old. Grik is better. Many men from other villages will come to Grik on Saturdays. But [Grik] is not very good either because many of them are from Kemah, Dala, and the 'upstream' village [Ulu Grik]. The men there are not good. They marry women and leave them. Tawai men are all married. There was only one place where I went before which was good. It's Tanjung Rambutan, my father's village.[8] There are many young men there, they work in the factories, or are in secondary school. This is good. And they are also good people; they are not like people from Kemah. I know a boy there. I met him during the paddy harvest last season. I hope he will come to our harvest feast this year. But I'm in no hurry. I still want to *jalan-jalan* [wander around, hang out, stay single]. Here in the village the only boy I can marry ... he likes me, but I don't like him. Besides he has already *jalan* [go out] with [another girl]. There are really not many men here girls can marry. So they fight over the one or two men around.

Although the obstacles described above affect all the young people of Air Bah, they cannot explain why the eldest daughters of the competing leaders remained unmarried, as both of these girls were courted by younger men whom they evidently liked.

Anthropologists have long recognized that manipulating marriages via alliances is a mechanism of self-aggrandizement in small-scale societies (Lévi-Strauss 1969; Rubin 1975; van Baal 1975; La Fontaine 1978: 4; Ortner and Whitehead 1981; Collier and Rosaldo 1981; Collier 1988). Similarly, in Air Bah many believe that the competing leaders and their wives were reluctant to let their daughters marry the young men of their choice because they were waiting for a better match. These villagers suggested that the competing leaders 'would not want [their daughters] to marry anyone who is not well off.' The two leaders' actions, however, seem to contradict this assumption. Instead of waiting for a more prestigious suitor, they seemed intent on keeping their daughters at home as long as possible. This can be discerned from the way they handled their daughters' suitors. They did not openly reject any marriage proposal, but they remained evasive and non-committal to all potential suitors. As a result, they kept the interested young men in uncertainty for years. In the next interview excerpt, Jantan, one of the most eligible young men courting Kecil's daughter, expresses his frustration:

I have been waiting to marry the *penghulu*'s daughter for four years. During those four years, I have asked personally, as well as through emissaries. On all these occasions, I have been puzzled by the response of both father and daughter. The father's response was evasive. The *penghulu* merely said he would agree if his daughter did. I also asked his daughter, Amoi. Most often, she told me to wait and said, 'I will not go anywhere.' So I feel both of them are afraid to reject me but, at the same time, they are not really keen on accepting me either. The *penghulu* should see that this has gone on for four years and anybody else would have asked the daughter for a definite answer. I am willing to wait for one more year. I have no problem getting married. I can find other women in other villages easily. I just want to know if she wants me or not.

People in the village are just as puzzled as Jantan by this situation. They believe that Kecil's daughter likes Jantan, because 'she serves him food and washes his clothes for him.' According to one man:

during all this time, the girl has agreed and wanted to marry him. The only problem is her father. He has been evasive and non-committal. It seems that he doesn't want Jantan.

Another man, commenting on Jantan's affairs, said he did not understand why things were getting so complicated. He said he personally would not wait this long:

Waiting for a match is not like waiting for fruits. You know, the durian would be ripe and would fall. But a match is to be known immediately. There is no waiting for a match, unless, of course, the man is away for a long time. Even then, he would give signs that he is ready, like for example, sending gifts through somebody. When he returns, it would be known immediately.

And a third person said:

If they wait too long, they both become wrinkled and dry. How can a flower go to the bee? Jantan should be the one who approaches her.

One elder has even tried to act as mediator on Jantan's behalf, to no avail. He recounted his attempt to persuade the headman:

> I have gone to see [the *penghulu*] three times. The last time I actually called him to my house to talk about these young people. I told him that this was not good to let them go on like this, that he should say whether he agrees to have Jantan as his son-in-law or not. When I said that, the *penghulu* replied, 'I have no problems and it is the person concerned, my daughter, that you should ask.' After this, I asked the girl, 'Do you like this man, Jantan? Do you want to be his wife?' She said, 'Yes,' and according to custom, her father should then say, 'Yes, now we can have a meeting.' But you see the *penghulu* just kept quiet even after that. He pretended to have forgotten about it. So for me, it is as if he had said, 'No.' But because he did not say 'No' openly, we don't know whether it is a 'Yes' or a 'No.' I think this is very bad.

As the above excerpt shows, Kecil's behaviour is mystifying to people in Air Bah because it contradicts Lanoh marriage practices.[9] Yet, perplexing as they may seem, Kecil's and Hitam's actions towards these young men make sense in light of the difficulties they face in securing the help of younger men.

Competing leaders in Air Bah have made certain attempts to incorporate not only their daughters into the family enterprise, but also their sons, primarily by trying to 'educate' them. While most fathers in Air Bah are satisfied if their sons occasionally heed their advice, competing leaders actively 'groom' their sons for managerial tasks. Hitam's 17-year-old son Rosli not only participates in forest collecting and contract work, but also he is extensively 'advised' by his father on the merits of worthwhile pursuits. He works to earn cash and also to 'learn' or to gain experience. On one occasion his father sent him to work in a factory to 'widen his horizons.' As well, Rosli often acts as a guardian for the women's work group, because as his father explained, in this capacity, he 'learns' to negotiate and conduct business with outsiders.

Table 6.1 summarizes the three aspects of specialization in the household of the competing leaders. It shows that while men (fathers and sons) in these households generally perform more 'managerial' tasks, the women (mothers and daughters) are involved in more practical

Table 6.1 Specialization in Competing Leaders' Households in Air Bah

	Inside (Domestic)	Outside (Public)	Cognitive-Managerial	Practical (Executer)
Father	–	√	√ 'Decision-making'	–
Mother	–	√	–	√
Son	–	√	√ 'Apprenticeship'	√
Daughter	√	–	–	√

Table 6.2 Comparison of Gender Roles in Air Bah Households

	Self-Aggrandizing Households	Egalitarian Households
Domestic/public division	Overlap	Separate
Decision-maker/executer division	Separate	Overlap

roles. Paradoxically, despite the relative congruence in the tasks of leaders and their wives, they tend to be more separate in decision-making than other couples in the village. In most households, people reported that decisions were made cooperatively, in discussions between husband and wife. In the competing households, on the contrary, the household heads made every important decision. Thus, while the roles of the competing leaders and their wives overlap on the 'domestic/public' dimension, they are less equal than other couples' in the 'decision-maker/executor' dimension. This discrepancy between 'self-aggrandizing' and 'egalitarian' households is summarized in Table 6.2.

The rise of a cognitive/managerial household role is further indicated by the division of space in the competing leaders' households. In a 1995 paper Richard Blanton discusses the importance of ritual-symbolic division of space in households in societies with emerging social differentiation. A survey of living arrangements in Air Bah's plank houses indicates that, in the houses of competing leaders, the division of space may be more complex than elsewhere in the village. In most households men share sleeping space with their wives; however, in the competing leaders' houses, Kecil and Hitam maintain private spaces of their own.

Nonetheless, while it appears that Hitam and Kecil have succeeded in integrating members of their households, this integration is incomplete and asymmetrical, and their control over their young male relatives – sons and sons-in-law – remains limited. Although the sons of competing leaders may sometimes defer to their fathers' authority, they nonetheless move out of their parents' house when they reach late adolescence and are completely estranged from their natal households after they marry. As a result, instead of their sons, elders in Air Bah would rather put their faith in their sons-in-law.

In Air Bah sons-in-law are expected to support not only their wives and their children, but also the families of their wives. Even in pre-resettlement times there was an initial undefined period of matrilocal affiliation, and during this time young men were supposed to help their wives' parents. Lanoh consider this initial period of brideservice to be self-evident, especially when comparing the 'requirements' between Lanoh and Malay marriages:

> Of course they [young men] should pay something back; Lanoh marriage is free.[10] Why shouldn't they pay something back?

People in Air Bah believe it is good to have many daughters, because

> we can expect our sons-in-law to help us. They cannot forget that they are the pillars of the family.

This expectation makes courtship an especially critical period. Even though, in the past, Lanoh did not interfere with young people's marriage choices, courtship nonetheless allowed them to monitor a young man's ability and willingness to provide for his future wife's family. During courtship younger men demonstrate this willingness by giving gifts of food (usually meat) to their prospective bride, who then passes these on to her parents:

> We Lanoh are not like people from the village [Malays]. When the people here want to be in love [M. *nak bercinta itu*, making love], they go to the jungle together, to the shop together, joking and teasing. Like we will take fruits and throw at each other. That is being in love. That means we like each other. If she doesn't play with us like that, that means she's not interested. Then we go to the jungle together. Like we would say, 'Oh, I'm going to the jungle, do you want to come?' and she would say, 'Yes, I want to go to the jungle too, I'll go with you.' Then we would say, 'No, it's too far, you'd better not come.' And so we would go to the jungle together. Then we get food from the jungle; fruits or animals. We give these to her. So we will always have something for her, as well as for our family. So

it's that way. We bring one for our mother and we bring one for her. Then people would *know*. Her mother would ask, 'Who gave you this food?' But even if she doesn't say who gave the food, everybody *knows*. Then she cooks the food. She gives it to her family, but she would also give some to us, the person who gave her the food. She would then invite us to her house to eat. [After courting my wife for a while,] everybody had *seen us* together so much. So I would give her fruits and things I got from the jungle, like when I got a wild boar, she *didn't eat that*, but she *gave it to her family*. So we would give her fruits and food and people would ask, 'So what's going on between you two?' That's how we start the Lanoh way.

'Knowing' what is going on between young people therefore means that older people have an opportunity to watch, observe, and evaluate the abilities of younger men. This explains why the only time people reacted negatively to a match between young people in Air Bah was after they learned about a 'surprise' marriage. This was perhaps the only occasion that people appeared truly upset over someone else's conduct, as evidenced in the following account.

One day a young suitor, exasperated over the futility of courting Hitam's daughter Puteh, married another girl. Hearing about the news, people were bewildered:

When we came back from Sumpitan, we heard that Atan had married Aisah. We were astonished, because Atan liked Puteh and Puteh liked Atan . This is not the Lanoh way of doing this.

Then they proceeded to explain the 'Lanoh way' of getting married, using Amin, Hitam's oldest son, as an example:

Do you know how the *penghulu*'s daughter married Amin? Well, Amin did it the old Lanoh way. He went ahead and slept with his wife and then the next day he announced it to the *penghulu*, to his wife's family, and told the *penghulu* that if he, the *penghulu* did not announce it to the village, he would. After all, many people knew about it already. So the *penghulu* announced it to everybody. Many people were not surprised. They were smiling to themselves because they knew about it. What Amin did was all right, because that is our custom. We marry first, and then we tell people. But you should not do what Amat did. Amat's daughter Seri is married to Atan. Nobody knew about this, not even Atan's brother Musa. One night, Atan went to Amat's house and we saw them talking, late into the night.

A few days after that, we realized that Atan was living in Amat's house. When we asked Atan, he said he had married Amat's daughter. We were surprised. Why did he not tell us? Why did we have to ask? Atan said, Amat told him not to bother, but if anybody asked, it was Amat who told him to do it that way. I went to see Amat and asked him. He said, 'Yes, they were married. He is living in my house now.' I told Amat that is not the way to do it; even our grandfathers did not do it that way. He should have told us. He did not care.

As the above account demonstrates, it is important for elders to know about young people's courtship and intentions. Such knowledge offers them a sense of control, as well as the prospect of benefiting from the labours of young men in the future. Yet, these expectations are usually never realized, because, once married, sons-in-law become notoriously unreliable. Although fathers-in-law and sons-in-law occasionally work together in the forest, more often, elders, unable to count on these younger men, complain that their sons-in-law are quarrelsome, disrespectful, and are prone to 'borrowing' food that they never return. As a consequence, elders lament that their daughters continue to depend more on their parents than on their husbands. One man related:

My son-in-law never does anything. He loves to go to the forest, and never helps me in any way. I have to nag him to work on the land with me, but even nagging does not make much difference.

When a young couple decided to move further away from the wife's father's house, her father said, referring to her husband:

What's the point [of them living here]? He doesn't do anything anyway.

Since elders can only count on younger men while they are courting their daughters, it is therefore advantageous for competing leaders to keep their prospective sons-in-law in perpetual courtship. Most sons-in-law in Air Bah are famously untrustworthy, but Jantan, the young man aspiring to marry the *penghulu*'s daughter, has gone to great lengths over the years to prove himself worthy of her. He has helped the headman and his family with farming, performed different errands for them, and proven himself as a producer of large game. He even generated considerable income by hunting wild boar for Chinese merchants, which he then shared with the *penghulu*'s household. Once, during his five-year courtship, he even opened a village store in his father's house. Even though this venture eventually failed, it was the only time anyone has ever undertaken such an enterprise in Air Bah.

Thus, by guarding their elder daughters competing leaders not only ensured a source of additional labour within their households, they also secured the help of younger suitors. Although frustrated, Jantan had been available to the headman's household for five years by 1998, and he had done far more for them than any sons or sons-in-law would have. Nonetheless, as Jantan was becoming increasingly exasperated, his support was expected to be terminated, and his case would likely go down in the village's history as the exemption proving the rule that in Air Bah elders' power over younger men continues to be extremely limited. This limited power has had important implications not only for kinship group and village integration, but also for competing leaders' self-aggrandizing strategies.

Limitations on Kinship Group Integration

There is already a large and impressive literature in anthropology on the nature of factions in human society. Significantly less, however, has been written about how and why in some societies factions fail to develop. Yet, these questions are crucial to our understanding of integration processes among changing hunter-gatherers, especially those with an immediate-return system of production. From the following review of kinship group integration, it will be apparent that in Air Bah feuding kinship groups only superficially resemble factions. Due to the jobs and the opportunities that younger men pursue, they are far from 'exclusive coalition[s] of persons,' and consequently, elders can only count on their younger male relatives' moral, rather than actual, support.

In the previous chapter I reviewed the several ways in which kinship group boundaries are reinforced in Air Bah, encouraging the formation of factions. One of these was the spatial organization of the village, which limited interactions between different segments of the village and subsequently contributed to the emergence of restricted sharing, prompting people to share only within their kinship groups. Another was the rise of support for self-aggrandizing behaviour by competing group leaders and the marginalization of certain individuals and family groups that followed. Now I will introduce another, possibly even more telling sign of kinship group integration: the modification of Lanoh avoidance practices within the village.

Avoidance rules have changed in two distinct ways. First, people now manipulate avoidance rules to facilitate interactions between members of their kinship groups. I recorded two instances of young men addressing old women (their opposite-sex in-laws) using consanguinal relationship terms (aunt/elder sister), instead of affinal ones. Second, avoidance rules have been altered to demarcate and reinforce kinship groups. This seems to have been a result of the efforts of the competing leaders who, at the onset of their conflict, started to tell people that since they had become parents-in-law, they could no longer speak to each other.[11] Although Lanoh avoidance rules dictate that same-sex in-laws should not be 'too close,' they do not require full avoidance.[12] The competing leaders, using their authoritative positions within the village, were able to expand and exaggerate the opposite-sex in-law avoidance rule, thereby making communication between their kinship groups more difficult. They appear to have been successful; Hitam's younger brother, for example, explained to me that he himself was not supposed to be close to the headman's group, because the in-law avoidance between Hitam and Kecil extends to him as well.

Yet, in spite of these attempts, younger men's attitudes continue to undermine the ability of Hitam and Kecil to influence their respective kinship group members. As a result, while kin group boundaries are strengthened, kinship groups in Air Bah do not fulfil Boissevain's definition of 'factions.' They may be factions in every other respect, but kinship groups in Air Bah are *not* 'exclusive [coalitions] of persons.' Simply put, competing leaders have had considerable difficulty in controlling male group members, especially younger men. It appears therefore that Lanoh experience does not entirely support Jérôme Rousseau's contention that 'social exclusivity is one of the first steps toward complexification … [and exclusive] group membership radically transforms social interaction because it reduces the number of independent agents who interact with each other' (2006: 22). In Air Bah elders' attempts to create true factions were only partially successful, as younger men remain independent agents offering little tangible support to their cluster leaders.

The successful integration of female members into the leaders' kinship groups acts as a counterpoint to their inability to do the same with males. Women in Air Bah are not only more sedentary than men, but as suggested earlier, they seek social interaction based primarily on kinship affiliation. As a result of the rise of permanent matrilocal residences within the village, it is possible that ties among related women have become even stronger than in the past. Female relatives spend nearly every waking hour with each other, and they rarely associate with others, including other women, from outside of their kinship groups. As a result, women significantly contribute to the demarcation of kinship clusters, especially by helping competing leaders to marginalize individuals and families. This dynamic between competing leaders and their female relatives can be best illustrated by an incident in Hitam's kinship group. Amat, a distant relative of Hitam, when asked about his plans, told me the following:

> I have no plans other than to live like this. I have even asked for land. 'They' said 'No, there was no more land.' It's not that there is no land. There is land behind Hitam's house. They could have given that to me. If you want to know, some time ago, when there were still many rubber trees which belonged to Hitam. The land was Hitam's and the trees were his. It was Hitam who let me tap rubber. He said, 'Amat, this is for you,' but he also told me to work well and not to destroy the trees. So it was quite good. Then one evening, Amin's mother [Hitam's wife] told Amin to take all the rubber, then she went to Yang's place [at the other side of the village] and told the people there, 'I'm not giving Amat the trees anymore. Those trees belong to me.' So they took back that land that had been given to me by Hitam, to whom Senin had had given the land. So after that, I didn't have any land. I cannot do anything about it because the village elders agree with them. So what could I do? That is why I have to go into the jungle to work. Hitam didn't say anything. The one that complained a lot was his wife. She's the one who said I wasn't doing anything.

But while elders have enjoyed the full support of their affinal female relatives, their wives and their female kin, they have had considerably less success in securing the help of their younger male relatives, whose commitment or support rarely manifests itself in action. Due to the prospect of work outside the village, younger men in Air Bah are less dependent on elders than they would be in strictly agricultural communities with limited external ties. Still continuously exploring possibilities and visiting relatives and friends elsewhere, they are regularly exposed to opportunities over which elders in the village have no control. Consequently, the elders of Air Bah have not been able to create exclusive cooperative support groups composed of their kin.

An additional obstacle to faction building is that younger men regularly and obstinately associate across kinship group boundaries.

Elders, who have largely shifted to 'village work' and a sedentary life-style, seek social support through the strengthening of their kinship groups. Young men's occupations, on the contrary, call for instrumental and pragmatic partnerships rather than loyalties based on kin obligations. Especially in forest work, attributes such as character, skill, and work history continue to be more important than kin alliances. Men often complain how difficult it is to find good partners for forest work, and so they take particular care in selecting partners before embarking on trips into the deep forest. For elders, this is a significant problem. Spending time with non-kin, younger men may, perhaps inadvertently, pass confidential information to members of other kinship groups, and as a result, elders often do not trust their younger male relatives.

Furthermore, unlike women, younger men continue to share with each other. While, as described earlier, women in Air Bah reinforce kin group boundaries by the frequent sharing of rice and vegetables among female kin, younger men share across these boundaries both inside and outside the village to maintain solid relations with non-kin. This strategy limits the integration of factions in Air Bah because it makes competitive generosity, one of the primary mechanisms in furthering integration cross-culturally, a rather wasteful exercise.

The role of competitive generosity in enhancing a leader's status and strengthening his ties with his followers has been extensively studied and documented by anthropologists (Keesing 1968: 276; Sahlins 1972; Testart 1982: 526; Riches 1984: 245; van Bakel et al. 1986: 1; Rousseau 1990: 209 and 2006; Lederman 1990; Lepowsky 1990: 35; Lee 1990: 238; Brumfiel and Fox 1994). Especially in middle-range societies, the 'mobilization of foods, typically by virtue of ownership of the land, followed by their disbursement to provide subsistence for supporters' (Earle 1994: 953) is often used by self-aggrandizers to boost their position and power over their followers (see Emerson 1962: 31). By promoting allegiance to particular leaders, such competitive feasts also reinforce segmentation and the development of exclusive factions.

But while people in Air Bah expect leaders to be generous, younger men undermine the value of competitive generosity as a mechanism to build support groups. As a result, unlike the Temiar leader, described as 'the old man who shares out food' (Benjamin 1968: 4),[13] competitive leaders in Air Bah are often described as stingy, rather than generous:

The present *penghulu* is not a good *penghulu*. Besides being stupid and stubborn, he is also not generous. A headman should be generous and not stingy. A headman does not need to be stingy, because he will always get more than he gives out to people. He gives tea and cigarettes to people once in a while and people would work for him, whether village work or his own farm. Also, when he needs money to go to the JHEOA [Jabatan Hal Ehwal Orang Asli] or Kuala Lumpur, he could collect from people and people would give. But he has to give first. The *penghulu* gets RM 600 a year [as salary from the JHEOA]. This money should be used as a headman should use it, not just for his own consumption. The *penghulu* could use some money for tea and a pack of cigarettes during meetings. He could contribute a bit of food during *kenduri*, more than other people. When people work for the village, he should give refreshments too. But the *penghulu* does not do that. He is stingy.

In Air Bah, therefore, there are two impediments to kinship group integration: the autonomy of younger men and the way the elders have responded to it. By abandoning competitive generosity, elders do not only jeopardize their own efforts to build exclusive support groups, they also reduce their chances of recruiting young men for farming.

When it comes to organizing cooperative farming work, not much has changed since pre-resettlement times. In Chapter 2, I suggested that in the past Lanoh did not work their fields communally, instead cultivating much smaller plots as separate nuclear families. In 1998, during my time in Air Bah, elders attempted to organize communal working parties and failed, partly because of their inability to control younger men and partly as a result of their own attitudes. The following comments by a Temiar informant convey his frustration about communal work in Air Bah:

> Here there is the problem we talked about before. We don't want it [communal work]. The *penghulu* didn't want it because [the *royong*] begins with twenty people, at the end, there are only seven people. That's why we don't want it. Look at Pandak [a younger man], just now. Yesterday, one day only, he went to plant. Just now, he went looking for what, I don't know. Look at that: he came back late just now. That's why I don't want to help them. It's not really that I don't want to. If they did the real *royong*, I don't mind, I would. But they cheat. That makes me angry. That's why I'm trying [to farm] alone.

When criticized for not helping with farm work, sons and sons-in-law in Air Bah either get offended and refuse to work altogether, or simply ignore the 'advice' and go off to earn cash. One old man complained:

> I have given my land to my children but they want easy money. They go to work on contract to get RM 10 at the end of the day.

Apart from younger men's attitudes, however, communal farm work in Air Bah is also undermined by the behaviour of the elders.

Like everyone else, competing leaders' also act individually and, as a consequence, often forfeit their chances to create dependencies. The following three examples illustrate how the actions of leaders have subverted cooperation in farming. In the first example, the charismatic leader Hitam initiated and organized a *gotong royong* (communal work, M.). He did not, however, manage it in the dignified manner of a Temiar household leader. While he had sufficient authority and charisma to convince people to join him in the *royong*, and even managed to have it started on his field, he soon betrayed the trust of others in the work party by quitting as soon as his own field was done. After two to three days he gave up and the others followed soon after.

In the second example, Hitam again undermined cooperation by disregarding the needs of those lagging behind in a land-clearing work group. Although, as indicated earlier, farming is the one area in which cooperation and coordination are emphasized, as soon as his own land was cleared, Hitam went ahead to acquire ritual materials (M. *air jampi*) for the planting ritual from a shaman in another village to bless his field and begin planting. Ignoring the pleas from other Lanoh to wait until their land was also cleared, Hitam and his family started planting well ahead of anyone else. Hitam's refusal to wait for those who lagged behind is not an atypical response for an elder, and this lack of consideration on the part of elders does little to foster cooperation.

The third example involves the communal storage of food and resources, a practice of great importance in theories of inequality, as well in those concerning the shift from immediate- to delayed-return systems of production (Testart 1982; Woodburn 1982; Keeley 1988). Although Lanoh sell rather than store excess paddy, in the year of my fieldwork, there were extended discussions about possible arrangements for the drying and husking of paddy.[14] Due to rainy weather, harvested paddy could not be dried in the sun, and so people debated whether to build a big, communal, drying hut or several small ones in which the paddy could be spread on a platform and smoked dry with fire from underneath. When a Temiar man suggested that they build a communal ceremonial platform (*deŋ mənalɛy*) and use it to dry the village's paddy together, a Lanoh man, Ambok, disagreed, suggesting that everybody should take responsibility for his own paddy. He said people had lots of space in their houses, which they could use to dry their paddy, little by little. Another man suggested that they could use the mosque to dry paddy. At that point the *penghulu* interjected that he did not want to mix his paddy with that of others, effectively ending the discussion. Elders in Air Bah often focus on independent, rather than communal, goals, instead of taking actions that elders in delayed-return economies might use to create a sense of indebtness and dependency in others. In doing so they themselves reject and hinder the kinds of communal practices necessary for true factions to arise.

As a result of these obstacles to faction building, competing leaders in Air Bah are rather isolated from other men. They are often seen sitting on their porch alone, surrounded by women and children gossiping a small distance away. Disillusioned, these elders have withdrawn from the public domain and focus instead on extending and intensifying production within their nuclear households. This withdrawal, in turn, has had important consequences for village integration.

Limitations on Village Integration

As I outlined in the introduction of this book, conflict theories and social order theories have been the most influential in explaining developing inequality in small-scale societies. Conflict theories emphasize competition as the driving force behind inequality, and social order theories stress organizational challenges in sedentary villages as the factor impelling stronger leadership, invariably leading to inequality. Problematically, these theories have so far been mostly considered independently, and there has been little research on how the dynamics of these propositions might impact on each other. Harmonizing and amalgamating these theories would not only go a long way towards creating a unified model of social inequality, but also towards exposing contradictions between the two approaches. In Air Bah I found that while organizational requirements have indeed increased after sedentism, leadership competition seems to have instead undermined village integration.

As noted above, social order theories assign important public roles to leaders in sedentary villages. Several authors have suggested that sedentary villages with large populations have different organizational

requirements than smaller communities, as group size limits the efficiency of consensual decisions (Johnson 1982; Kent 1989; Plog 1990;
Brumfiel 1994). As a result mediators may emerge to deal with these
organizational challenges (Kent 1989; Hitchcock 1989b: 10; Plog 1990:
198). According to Susan Kent, in newly sedentary villages, 'leaders
with slightly different status (although not necessarily hierarchical status at first) are imperative for settling disputes and for generally ensuring the smooth running of sedentary aggregations' (1989b: 10).

In Air Bah sedentary village life has certainly resulted in organizational challenges that Lanoh were not likely to be confronted with in
their pre-resettlement villages and camps. The large village population
and the complexity arising from the interactions of the four kinship
groups have increased the probability of discord and conflict, precip-
itating the need for mediation. Given the composite structure of the
village, communal celebrations are less spontaneous and require more
planning and management today than they did in the past. Additionally, village administration and communication with outside authorities demand new forms of authority, foresight, and control on the part
of Lanoh leadership. People expect village leaders to see to development projects, such as the telephone, the water system, and the generator, as well as to organize transportation for schoolchildren. These
expectations on the part of the village present excellent opportunities
for the leaders to capitalize towards self-aggrandizement in the public
domain; however, there were a number of factors that prevented them
from taking advantage of these situations.

First, organizing public works and communal events presents an
insurmountable challenge because of the persistent individualism and
opportunism that characterize Lanoh society. Interpersonal relationships in Air Bah are generally contractual, thereby destabilizing ties
of dependency. It is expected, for example, that men provide for their
wives and children, yet these same men sometimes 'borrow' money
from their wives with a strict obligation to repay the sum in full.[15] People also expect to be paid for services rendered within households.
Mothers may ask their daughters to stay in the village and take care
of household chores while they are away on contract work, but it is
understood that, upon return, they would share their wages to com-
pensate. Knowledge is also treated as a commodity in Air Bah, rather
than a more fungible piece of social currency like prestige or authority.
Every incantation has a price, and it is customary for knowledgeable
elders and old men to demand payment for spiritual services. If people

consider this price 'too much,' they will simply refuse to turn to the old man in question with their problems.[16] At the same time, young relatives often seem disinclined to take care of their older relatives without compensation. Caring for old people is not seen as an obligation, but as an exchange:

> Old people will give their things, like their tools, when they cannot work anymore and then their children will take care of them.

On top of this, even when they are receiving help or support, older people capable of earning money for the household are expected to do so. Relatives of one of the old men in the village, for instance, often complained that, although he went 'out' all the time and sold things, he never brought anything back. This contractual relationship also extends to farming work. Whenever people help someone with farming, they expect to be paid. Even so, these 'helpers' continue to take every opportunity to serve their own self-interest. They often hide bundles of paddy or tie up larger bundles of their share of the harvest. These kinds of practices unsurprisingly undermine any larger-scale cooperation in the village.[17]

Another constraint to the success of any communal venture is the absence of communal consciousness among Lanoh. People in Air Bah often show an utter lack of consideration for the concerns of others and refuse to forgo their interests for the sake of the public good. A few examples related to the management of the village's water supply illustrate the difficulties leaders face in organizing communal projects. Air Bah receives its water from a waterfall in the forest via a gravitational system. However, the pipes leading from the waterfall to the village are constantly clogged, leaving villagers without water for days. When this happens, people need to walk for at least twenty minutes to reach the river. Yet, often, while most of the village is left without water, the water supply in houses closer to the source remains adequate. A more even supply could be ensured if, instead of leaving the water running, people upstream temporarily plugged their pipes. Yet, no matter how often the penghulu pleads with the owners of these houses, they simply shrug their shoulders, adding that what happens to people downstream is no concern of theirs.

This individualism is again apparent in the operation of work parties. For instance, during my stay in Air Bah whenever a work party was sent up to the water source to unclog the pipes, only a few of the men would actually be working, while the rest would watch, commenting on those who were working, and occasionally wandering off to look for fish in the pond. The disgruntled Temiar informant, mentioned earlier in this chapter, contrasted this lack of cooperation among Lanoh with the organization of communal work in his native village, Tanjung Rambutan:

> In T[anjun]g Rambutan, they built a *sewang* house that can sit two to three hundred people. They cut down huge logs to do that. It took them about a month and everybody worked on the project, the old, the young, the strong, the weak. If they are old, they cut and strip rattan to use as lashings. They did the *atap* [roofing] while the young and strong went into the forest and sometimes, some people contributed with tea or dessert. But here in Air Bah, nobody does that. Three people work, ten people watch it. He added, in Tanjung Rambutan, everybody listens to the *penghulu*, here nobody listens to Kecil.

In Air Bah older men never participate in communal projects. When, for example, during a discussion, someone suggested that older men could also contribute, an old man abruptly stood up and left without a word.

In addition to the prevailing attitude of Lanoh towards group efforts, cooperation in Air Bah is further stifled by a lack of an indigenous model for village leadership. In pre-resettlement times Lanoh household clusters and villages overlapped, and because of the fluidity of group membership, even the nature of the household cluster was ill-defined. Thus, today, the leadership of the segmented village does not follow naturally from an earlier notion of household cluster leadership. Temiar deal with this complexity by having *two* indigenous leadership positions with distinct roles and responsibilities. One is the household cluster leader, the head of the extended family, the person that others 'follow.' Household cluster leaders among Temiar are primarily responsible for projects concerning the kinship group, such as organizing house building and opening swiddens (Benjamin 1968). The other one is the village leader, who coordinates farming, leads war parties, 'acts as the symbolic guardian of the descent group's estate,' and mediates between household cluster leaders (ibid.: 29, 30–3). Lanoh fail to differentiate between these two levels of leadership, and consequently, they expect a household leader to fulfil the position of village leader, without a clear distinction regarding what such a role entails and what kind of legitimacy or authority it would require.

Accordingly, the disinclination among Lanoh to cooperate and the absence of an indigenous model for village leadership hinder communal projects in Air Bah. In addition to this, the attitudes and actions of the competing leaders only make the organization of village events even more difficult. Contrary to expectations that they would enhance their positions through organizing communal projects, leaders in Air Bah nearly completely withdraw from public life, often stifling, rather than facilitating, public events and cooperation. In 1998, for instance, both leaders stayed away from the large annual harvest feast. On the day of the celebration, people repeatedly asked the *penghulu* to join them, but he refused, instead staying out in his field and working late into the evening. Hitam not only remained absent from the same feast, he even tried to sabotage it. During the singing session (L. *pənloj*), he played his radio so loudly that people had to ask him to turn it down. He later explained that he had stopped caring about village affairs since the sale of the rubber trees, because instead of appreciating what he did for the village, people blamed him for getting paid less than they had expected. He assumed people were jealous because he had received the largest payment after the sale. After the incident he told everyone that he would not do anything for the village and that he would not be participating in communal events.

One way to interpret this withdrawal from public affairs is to see it as an extension of pre-resettlement conflict avoidance strategies. In the past people responded to conflict by physical withdrawal, moving away. Unable to physically remove themselves from an undesired situation, competing leaders respond instead with psychological withdrawal. Their frequent allegations of the use of black magic by others would indicate this as well.[18] Lanoh claim that prior to resettlement they avoided harmful magic and only used positive, healing practices. In the sedentary village, however, accusations of practising black magic have become more frequent. These claims are particularly suited to marginalizing people who have fallen out of favour with more powerful families and kinship groups. Yet, while these accusations turn villagers' attention away from the self-aggrandizement of the competing leaders, they also increase their isolation.

I encountered two instances of black magic accusations in Air Bah. In the first one an individual was accused of wearing a talisman (L. *cihoŋ*).

Cihoŋ were originally intended to offer good luck and protection. Made of a flower found on mountain peaks, they protected their wearers from disease. Nonetheless, this practice places the individual's interests in opposition to those of the community, because wearing a *cihoŋ* also brings rain and, as a consequence, may result in floods or landslides. In the year of my fieldwork unusually heavy rains in November interfered with the paddy harvest and were attributed to 'some people ... playing with their *cihoŋ*.' In the second instance Hitam alleged that certain individuals were using black magic to cause misfortune to him and his family. He claimed that, as a result, one of his sons became so ill that he was unable to walk and had to remain in the house at all times. Due to this black magic, Hitam has already moved residence three times, each time to increasingly peripheral and isolated locations away from the centre of the village. As well, since black magic is said to emit from the ground, to avoid contamination Hitam has been using his motorcycle to travel even the shortest distances in the village.

It is easy to see, therefore, why leaders in Air Bah are often seen as deterring, rather than facilitating the village's ability to cope with organizational challenges. Someone commenting on the headman's tendency to withdraw said:

> It is hard to deal with this man. He is a difficult man. [He] is prone to sulk.
> If anybody says something about him or to him that he feels is a criticism,
> he will withdraw and not speak to anyone for days.

Outsiders have also noted the difficulty the villagers of Air Bah have in dealing with their communal affairs. The following interview excerpt describes the case of a younger man in Air Bah who was accused of seducing a woman during a visit to Bukit Sapi. The villagers of Bukit Sapi expected Air Bah to take responsibility for this young man's actions. The assistant headman in Air Bah, who acted as mediator in this conflict, recounts the incident:

> This time [this young man] went to B[uki]t Sapi for some months. He
> went to disturb a woman there. That's why they wanted to fine him RM
> 2,000. He ran back here. Of course the people there want us to be respon-
> sible for this. They wanted to send the woman here and have a discussion
> between the headman from there and the headman from here. They pro-
> posed to meet. The problem, people over there said, is that people from
> here are not responsible for someone from here, because the headman here

didn't advise his people well. So I met their headman. He told me the case was this way and that way. I told him that the boy was really difficult and since he didn't listen to our advice, he was his problem. He could do whatever he wanted to do with him because that boy just doesn't listen to the elders of the village.

The dearth of village-level authority resulting from the withdrawal of Hitam and Kecil from public life potentially invites and increases the influence of outsiders in the village. As a result of their inability to organize communal projects, villagers in Air Bah have come to rely on outsiders to service the generator with fuel or to contribute to village feasts. During my stay in Air Bah, for instance, two contractors and the *ustad* (religious teacher) provided goods and money for the harvest feast.[19] Some younger people have tried to fill the vacuum created by the leaders' absence by forming a committee. However, composed of younger, single men and lacking in mediating power, this committee remained ineffectual.[20] As a result of all this, many in the village believe that village integration and the power of the household leaders have weakened compared with what was the case in the past. Leaders in the past, they recall, were stronger and had more authority and influence than leaders today:

> The Lanoh here do not have a leader like the Lanoh used to have. A Lanoh leader should be responsible for his group by knowing what everybody is doing. He should know who is sick and who is not. He should know who has food and who has not. But the present *penghulu* is not like that. He is the tail with the name of the head [M. *nama sahaja kepala, tapi dia itu buntut*] … He does not care who is sick or who has no food. He only cares about his family and himself.

An old man commenting on village affairs said that from his lean-to shelter he could see all the way to the *cempedak* tree[21] and that he did not like what he saw:

> Morning, day, evening, strong young men sit doing nothing, just chatting. This is not how things used to be when I was young. Young men would always have something to do. If they were not in the forest, they would be in the village, fixing their blowpipes or tools, making roofs for their houses, repairing their houses, clearing the undergrowth, bushes and getting rid of pests, such as smoking out hornets' nests … today people don't

listen to their elders and leaders. Leaders in my youth were strong. When I was young, whenever the headman came back from outside, he didn't have to call people to his house. They would already be there, waiting to hear what news or issues he had to tell them. Now, even when the *penghulu* had just returned from the JHEOA, nobody cares to know what his visit was about. Even if the *penghulu* called them to his house, only a few people came because people were not afraid or respectful of him.

Some people in Air Bah feel that the problems of the village can only be resolved by fission, by splitting up the village. Commenting on the possibility of moving to a larger resettlement village, one man said:

In a big village, there is more people, more trouble, more disagreement. The Lanoh are not used to that; we don't want that. Even Air Bah is already too big; we are having problems with too many heads, too many ideas.

Adding to this criticism, he noted:

You want to work alone, so there is no benefit in a big village.

He suggested that it would be far better to split Air Bah into two villages, where food would be easier to share.

Thus, we have seen that leadership competition in Air Bah has hindered, rather than fostered village integration. Earlier in this section I suggested that a study of community integration in Air Bah might have implications for the relationship between conflict and social order theories. Although observations of the process of social change in Air Bah seem to advance the principle that leadership competition weakens community integration, this conclusion is hardly applicable cross-culturally. As I proposed in the introduction of this book, both conflict theories and social order theories assume integration at some level. While conflict theories are based on integration on the faction/kinship group level, social order theories presume that integration will strengthen at the village level. These principles, however, are not at all mutually exclusive. If leadership competition develops in a society with a delayed-return system of production with dependencies between individuals, especially between younger men and elders, faction/kinship group members will actively support their respective kinship group leaders. As a consequence, in these cases competing leaders would presumably not isolate themselves within their households but instead compete openly in the public arena. Instead of hindering com-

Figure 6.1 Lanoh elders returning by raft from a visit to Cenawi.

munity celebrations, they would go out of their way to organize them. In a society with a delayed-return system of production, these actions would, in all likelihood, foster communal integration and village integration as well.

This implies that Air Bah is a special case with only limited implications for anthropological theories of inequality. First, prior to their resettlement, Lanoh had been hunter-gatherer collectors with an immediate-return system of production, and their social organization from that period continues to affect post-resettlement developments. Second, most of what I witnessed in 1998 would not have taken place without development, forced sedentism, and regroupment, events and processes specific to twentieth-century nation building in multiethnic Malaysia. Without this context, Lanoh would not have become sedentary, conglomerated in one village, or focused on farming.[22] Finally, without these developments, elders of the village would not have had alternative means for self-aggrandizement to make up for their inability to create internal ties and dependencies.

Implications for the Self-Aggrandizing Strategies of Competing Leaders

In Chapter 2, I outlined Geoffrey Benjamin's (1985a) theory about the 'outer orientation' of Malays and argued that some Orang Asli collectors, that is, northern Semang, have a similar 'outer orientation,' albeit an individualistic one. I also suggested that this outward orientation has implications for the intragroup relationships of these forest collectors. In this chapter we have so far seen that the quality of these intragroup relationships continues to influence processes of social change in Air Bah. I will next examine the implications of these internal limitations on integration for competing leaders' self-aggrandizing strategies and consider whether some of the residents of Air Bah are better poised to adjust to the changes of the late twentieth century. From this inquiry, it appears that competing leaders are less penalized for their cognitive and behavioural flexibility than others in the village and, paradoxically, are more able to retain their identity as 'collectors' than most others are, including other elders. While change has demanded that most people shift to an 'inner orientation,' Hitam and Kecil have retained the outer orientation of pre-resettlement Lanoh. As a result they are in a better position to adjust to change than are others in Air Bah.

In earlier chapters I outlined how people in Air Bah have become increasingly penalized for practices such as immediacy that were once highly beneficial for pre-resettlement interethnic relations, and how most of them, especially elders, withdrew from interethnic contact as a result. A clear exception to this, however, is the fact that Hitam and Kecil continue to emphasize contact with outsiders, and lacking internal support, they have built their political strength upon extra-community resources and alliances. These leaders have superior access to external resources and to the elders and leaders of other communities. Representing the village in important intergroup encounters, they have developed contacts with Orang Asli and non–Orang Asli businessmen, headmen, religious leaders, and government officials.

Yet, while both leaders rely extensively on outside contact, they emphasize different sources.[23] The headman of the village primarily relies on official resources, which naturally includes the JHEOA but also other related governmental and non-governmental organizations. One example is an Orang Asli cooperative, the 'Golden Deer' (M. *Kijang Emas*), set up by the JHEOA, whose representatives on one occasion approached the headman and his associates with a scheme to establish a palm oil plantation on village land. Kecil often used these official connections against his rival Hitam. For instance, after the rubber tree sale, Kecil asked for, and received, reassurance from the JHEOA that nothing could be done to Lanoh land without informing and consulting him first. Contrary to the headman, Hitam has relied primarily on unofficial external connections, such as Malay and Chinese businessmen and religious leaders. Hitam also maintains strong ties with important elders and leaders in Orang Asli villages, and he has used these connections to develop logging projects in several locations.

Development in Malaysia has largely contributed to these elders' ability to pursue such a strategy. While sedentism presents an obstacle to a number of activities, it does not prevent competing leaders from maintaining external contacts. First, outsiders now often come to Air Bah to seek out these leaders. Hitam shies from interactions within the community, yet he is often seen sitting on a log in front of his house deep in conversation with outside visitors. Second, the relatively accessible network of Orang Asli villages has created new opportunities that these leaders can exploit. Some of these opportunities are more suited to younger men than to elders with larger families, but improved methods of communication and travel, such as buses and the telephone (when it works), make it possible for elders to take advantage of these opportunities without having to move residence. For instance, sedentism did not prevent Hitam from visiting different Orang Asli villages, faraway cities like Ipoh and Kuala Lumpur, and even Thailand in pursuit of business connections and opportunities. Because of this continuing reliance on external relationships, these two competing leaders retain the outlook of pre-resettlement Lanoh, that of hunter-gatherer traders, to a far greater extent than do most people in the village.

On the surface there is little continuity between the self-aggrandizing schemes of the competing leaders and pre-resettlement collecting for trade. Both the scale and outcome of Hitam's and Kecil's transactions differ from the scale and outcome of collecting and trading activities by pre-resettlement Lanoh. Selling a bunch of medicinal herbs, a few turtles, or a pound of honey has far different ecological and political implications than selling a hillside worth of timber. Nonetheless, the principles (trading in forest resources) are quite similar and so are the strategies involved. Competing leaders approach these opportunities in the same way that their forefathers approached trading forest products with individual buyers, except that buyers today are no longer after minor forest products, but after the forest itself.[24]

As a consequence of their reliance on external relations, unlike other elders in the village, competing leaders still adhere to the tactics of 'strategic non-confrontation' so critical for maintaining the openness and fluidity of hunter-gatherer social networks. As suggested earlier, most people in the village are increasingly penalized for 'foragers' strategies,' such as individual autonomy, immediacy, and opportunism; the competing leaders, however, continue to benefit from these in their self-aggrandizement. As evident from previous discussions in this chapter, individualism and a reluctance to cooperate are continuing features of social life in Air Bah. Yet, Lanoh face intense pressure to cooperate and coordinate their activities, especially in the context of their relationships with contractors, middlemen, and employers from the outside. Competing leaders, however, evidently draw rewards for retaining forager-style relationships, not only in emphasizing extra-community ties but in operating individually and opportunistically as well. Secrecy, for example, is carried over from the organization of forest work and employed as a tactic in self-aggrandizement. Inhibitions to share information continue to shape the strategies of these leaders. They refuse to share their plans with others, sometimes even their closest relatives. The expectation that fellow villagers keep their intentions to themselves undoubtedly plays a role in the complacency of villagers in the face of cheating and secrecy by Hitam and Kecil, even if their schemes cause losses and aggravation.

Opportunism is similarly evident in the lack of commitment the competing leaders have for their plans. Typically, they juggle several projects at once, shifting and manoeuvring craftily. Rahim, a Malay with a long family history with Lanoh, and a previous business partner of Hitam, illustrates this point in the following incident:

Hitam cannot be trusted. He cheated me. We had applied for permits to extract timber from the Orang Asli reserve around Benum. Unlike in Air Bah, in Benum, land was already gazetted as an Orang Asli reserve. Hitam saw a business opportunity in the land in Benum and convinced a few people there to sell timber from the land. Hitam claimed he could get the agreement and signatures from everyone in the village. So we wrote many letters applying for all kinds of permits from different departments of the government. Hitam said he needed some money to convince officials as well as the people in the village. I managed to come up with 1,800 ringgit. We went to see the local officials and waited. Weeks later Hitam told me that the deal was off because, first, the people in the village did not agree, and second, this was Orang Asli reserve and could not be exploited. I then asked him about the money. He said that everything was spent on officials. Later I learned that the official in question had given the letter to Hitam a while ago, yet he did not receive any money from him at all. Still later I found out that Hitam approached two other Malays from Lawin who came up with capital for further administrative costs. Together, they went to Ipoh to obtain a letter of authorization from the Department of Forestry. He didn't say a word to me about this.

Competing leaders may successfully pursue these strategies because, even though development has destroyed a range of traditional sources of subsistence and trade, it has also produced several new ones as well. Accordingly, Hitam's and Kecil's attitudes towards people in other ethnic groups are different from those of other people in Air Bah. As noted earlier, people in the village often react to changing interethnic relations by emphasizing village identity and intercultural boundaries. Competing leaders, who benefit from these interethnic contacts more than others, instead continue to stress openness and a contextual identity. Although it is doubtful, for instance, that Hitam is more attuned to the doctrines of Islam than other villagers are, nonetheless, on several occasions he attended Friday prayers in the mosque in Kampung Sawa. He proclaims that he does not care about the ethnic differences of people and that he is ready to make friends with anyone. In this respect, he said, he is different from others in the village. While he is not afraid to get close to Malays, Indians, or Chinese, other people in Air Bah, because of their preconceived opinions of outsiders, shy away from outside contact and that is why they, in his eyes,

> do not get anywhere. They never go anywhere, so they don't learn about possibilities.

Hitam attributes Air Bah's inability to adapt to change to withdrawal and the growing emphasis on intergroup boundaries.

This discrepancy between the outlook and strategies of competing leaders and everyone else in Air Bah indicates that, because of their position, as well as the competition that provokes them to expand and explore, Hitam and Kecil are better adjusted to social change than are others in the village.[25] Severely restricted in their prospects, most Lanoh suffer the consequences of change in terms of a loss of opportunities, autonomy, and integrity, and as a result, rapidly approach the status of a 'demoralized rural lumpenproletariat' (Dentan et al. 1997: 159). Competing leaders, on the contrary, seem to thrive in the new circumstances. Perhaps this discrepancy is the most important indication that inequalities are truly developing in this previously egalitarian context.

Immediate- and Delayed-Return Societies

In the introductory part of this chapter I asked how pre-resettlement organization affects integration in Air Bah, and what the implications of this are for the difference between 'immediate-return' and 'delayed-return' systems of production. We have seen that pre-resettlement organization, especially the prevalence of individual autonomy, continues to impact both integration processes and the actions of self-aggrandizers in Air Bah. These organizational characteristics not only affect the integration of the competing leaders' households, but also the unity of kinship groups (factions) and the organization of the whole village. It is evident that, in spite of some indications to the contrary, Air Bah has failed to turn into an integrated village community. Most importantly, however, these results seem to indicate that the key to understanding the 'individual autonomy' of mobile hunter-gatherers may lie in the relationship between younger men and their elders. In the last part of this chapter I will address some implications we can draw from this concerning the difference between small-scale societies with immediate-return and delayed-return systems of production.

James Woodburn's distinction between immediate- and delayed-return systems is based on 'modes of production' (1982). He suggests that immediate-return hunter-gatherers subsist mainly on wild products and, consequently, obtain 'direct and immediate return from their labour' (ibid.: 432). This reasoning, however, contains certain inconsistencies. For instance, in spite of a number of similarities, certain mobile hunter-gatherers, such as Australian Aborigines, are excluded from the immediate-return category because they have generational structures that engender dependencies characteristic of delayed-return societies. One way to resolve this problem is to approach these two types of societies as organizationally, rather than economically different.

Raymond Firth conceptualizes organization as the 'change principle,' providing room for variation, while structure is the 'limitation to the range of alternatives possible' (1961: 39–40).[26] In this light immediate- and delayed-return systems can be conceptualized as organizational variations on a common structure deriving from age. These organizational variations depend on the varying strength of ties between younger men and elders. In small-scale delayed-return societies social organization supports categorical age differences, whereas in immediate-return societies, it undermines them. The result is that individualism, flexibility, and a lack of permanent leadership, precisely the principles that Woodburn observed in immediate-return societies, dominate.[27]

It follows that this pattern of organization should not be restricted to hunter-gatherers. Such a situation, in which the autonomy of younger men limits the authority of their elders, can be brought about by various historical circumstances. For instance, researchers have found a similar emphasis on alternatives, individualism, and opportunism among other nomadic and liminal populations commonly referred to as 'peripatetics' (Rao 1987; Casimir 1992). An organizational approach to immediate- and delayed-return systems could have other important implications as well. Attitudes that one would consider indicative of a delayed-return system of production, such as pre-resettlement farming and trading by Lanoh, their participation in a cash economy, and their practice of balanced reciprocity after resettlement, would not affect their 'immediate-return' status. According to the organizational definition of immediate- and delayed-return systems, the only criterion that would indicate a shift to a 'delayed-return' mode would be increased social integration and the development of interpersonal dependencies. As we have seen, attempts by elders to increase integration in Air Bah resulted in resounding failure. While leaders in a delayed-return society would have taken for granted that they could exploit their younger male relatives' services and labour, in Air Bah elders continued to exercise limited control over younger men and, consequently, had to fit their self-aggrandizing strategies to persisting organizational limitations.

This interpretation is compatible with Alan Macfarlane's argument in the final chapter of *The Origins of English Individualism: The Family, Property, and Social Transition* (1978). In that chapter Macfarlane considers the possibility that English individualism originates in the individualism of hunters and gatherers. Indeed, attitudes in Air Bah more closely resemble those of early English society than most historical cases of emerging social complexity. Macfarlane submits: 'The majority of ordinary people in England from at least the thirteenth century were rampant individualists, highly mobile both geographically and socially, economically "rational," market-oriented and acquisitive, ego-centered in kinship and social life' (1978: 163). This similarity is more than an interesting aside. As it may prompt new inquiries about the capitalist mode of production and what happens when these are superimposed on 'delayed-return' societies, it has obvious and important implications for theories of modernity, capitalism, and the processes that shape our contemporary global system.

The relationship between what is structurally desirable and organizationally possible may also be expressed through consideration of Frederick Bailey's (1969) notion of normative versus pragmatic rules. According to Bailey, normative rules are formal political rules, 'publicly-stated right and proper ways of reacting in specified situations,' while pragmatic rules tell the actor 'not what is the right or the good thing to do, but what will bring him the biggest pay-off as leader of a team' (ibid.: 61). Applied to the difference between immediate- and delayed-return societies, normative rules are similar in all age-based political systems, while pragmatic rules differ according to circumstances. In the mobile, flexible social formations of rainforest hunter-gatherers, these rules would reflect organizational limitations both before and after resettlement. In Air Bah competing leaders were allowed to self-aggrandize (the normative rule), but because they lacked sufficient internal support, they were forced to arrange for alternative means of external support (the pragmatic rule). In other words, while self-aggrandizing behaviour was tolerated on a normative level, it had to be adapted to the realities and constraints at the pragmatic level. This interpretation allows us to temporarily abandon organization, the source of variation, and refocus on age structure, the source of rights and privileges in small-scale societies. In the final chapter of this book, I will explore the implications of age structures for anthropological theories of equality and inequality.

7 Understanding Equality and Inequality in Small-Scale Societies

It would be difficult to deny that important changes have taken place in Air Bah since resettlement in the early 1980s. Historical data, ethnographies of Orang Asli groups, and the nature of interpersonal relationships in Air Bah indicate that in pre-resettlement times they had been mobile egalitarian foragers and forest collectors, but the change from mobile collecting to village life has been remarkable. The 'Negritos of Lenggong' that Evans (1937) described in the first part of the twentieth century would hardly be recognizable in the sedentary village population of Air Bah in 1998. The differences are apparent and striking, especially as inequality has begun to take hold, replacing equality.

In some respects developments in Air Bah confirm some existing models of social inequality. As theories of factional competition predict sedentism in Air Bah led to the formation of kinship clusters, whose members supported competing leaders (Bailey 1969; Bujra 1974; Clark and Blake 1994; Brumfiel and Fox 1994). These competing leaders gained increasing control of the most important resources in the area to enhance their political status. They also succeeded to a certain extent in controlling labour, the distribution of goods, and the marriages of their younger kin. Similarly, as theories of restricted sharing predict, the previously inclusive Lanoh kinship system has begun to shift towards exclusive group membership (Plog 1990). As social boundaries have emerged, certain families have become increasingly disadvantaged and often work for other families. Finally, as theories of household specialization predict, competing leaders have attempted to resolve scheduling conflicts by manipulating population dynamics and by increasing specialization within their households (Wilk 1991; Taylor 1996; Graves-Brown 1996; Bogucki 1999).

To some extent social change in Air Bah also provides an opportunity to evaluate the strength of conflict and social order theories, two dominant models of inequality that rely on internal factors for explanatory power. Social order theories, for example, see integration as a key step in the rise of inequality, but while inequalities have developed in Air Bah, integration has not. Even though there have been attempts by elders to tighten village cohesion and increase their control over younger men, these younger men still enjoy considerable autonomy, and the influence of elders over them remains limited. Theories based on competition fare better, because inequalities in Air Bah developed through leadership competition. Yet, as I suggested in the previous chapter, this study may only have limited direct relevance for theories of inequality as so many aspects of social change in Air Bah were influenced by development and modernization. Nonetheless, as I hope to show here, the way people have *responded* to leadership competition, self-aggrandizement, and rising inequality actually makes social change in Air Bah a broadly applicable situation.

Perhaps the most perplexing aspect of the political change in Air Bah is the lack of concern that villagers have with emerging inequality. Self-aggrandizing individuals freely enhance their production and hoard goods with very little resistance from their fellow villagers. There are, of course, conditions in which previously egalitarian people may be more receptive to emerging inequalities. Such conditions would include coercion, acculturation, or sufficient time for gradual changes to go unnoticed. In the case of coercive dominance, which according to Peter Richerson and Robert Boyd (2001), is one of the most frequent causes of social complexity, people may be able to do little but accept and go along with increased social differentiation. Similarly, acculturation, the adoption of the values of neighbouring agriculturist and pastoralists, may alter group values and render inequalities acceptable (Larrain 1979; Howell 1983; Kent 1995b). Finally, time often facilitates the acceptance of social differentiation in previously egalitarian communities. Eleanor Leacock, for instance, notes that after the fur trade, 'cooperative practices (among Montagnais-Naskapi) and attitudes continued to be important ... but *eventually* the "trading post band" ... superseded the previous socio-economic form' (1982: 160, emphasis added). Peter Bogucki similarly evokes an incubation period when accounting for developing inequalities in prehistoric societies: '[Self-aggrandizers] always existed, but in Pleistocene band society there were powerful social norms to keep them in check. The breakdown of band society which resulted in major social transformations among late foragers and early farmers provided the incubator for such individuals to emerge' (1999: 209).

However, while any of these conditions could explain a lack of resistance to developing inequality, none applied in Air Bah. Leaders who, at the most, carefully 'advise' others with the awareness that their counsel will be ignored, neither would, nor could, employ coercion. Similarly, although development and national politics have set the stage for social change, for now Lanoh have resisted acculturating the values of other groups around them. Finally, the transformation from equality to inequality occurred rapidly, within fifteen years of resettlement, without allowing for an incubation period or gradual adjustments. Yet, despite the lack of coercive force, acculturation, or time lag, people in Air Bah tolerated, even supported, self-aggrandizing leaders and the resulting inequalities. While there was a continuing emphasis on several aspects of the 'egalitarian ethic,' such as sharing, non-violence, and the use of public ostracism, gossip, and ridicule, people have failed to challenge the actions of self-aggrandizers. Instead, these self-aggrandizers and their supporters openly manipulated social structures and mechanisms commonly associated with the 'egalitarian ethic' to promote inequalities. This conspicuous lack of concern with emerging inequality indicates that our understanding of egalitarian politics is incomplete. These findings directly contradict the assumed ideological resistance to emerging social differentiation among changing foragers. Only by addressing this contradiction will we be able to build a new, comprehensive, and more parsimonious model of equality and inequality in small-scale societies and construct valid models of human evolution.

Theories of Equality and Inequality Revisited

The results of my fieldwork in Air Bah indicate that the notion of an 'egalitarian ethic' hinders our understanding of inequality. As I discussed in the introduction of this book, this theory, although popular among anthropologists, not only clashes with theories of inequality, but also contradicts the experience of Lanoh in Air Bah. As we will see, many have contended that the best way to address these inconsistencies is to get rid of the notion of the small-scale egalitarian society altogether. However, as I will argue, instead of eliminating the concept of egalitarian society, we ought to reassess it.

The incompatibility of theories of equality and inequality has been costly and frustrating for anthropologists (Upham 1990a: 16; Béteille 1996: 304). Jérôme Rousseau points out that, in anthropology, 'the study of inequality was split into two partially autonomous domains. Some researchers focused on the egalitarianism of hunter-gatherers, while others looked at inequality in complex societies' (2006: 31). As a consequence of this gap, there remains no comprehensive theoretical framework for the currently split realms of equality and inequality. A fix is desperately needed.

Many have proposed to bridge this gap between theories of equality and inequality by eliminating the concept of small-scale egalitarian society altogether and claiming instead that 'all societies are systems of inequality.' This would result in a comprehensive theory of social complexity, because, in this way, as Sylvia Yanagisako and Jane Collier suggested, 'we, as social scientists, are forced to explain not the existence of inequality itself but rather why it takes the qualitatively different forms it does' (1987: 40). This perspective has been voiced by anthropologists at least since the 1950s, when Marshall Sahlins noted that 'theoretically, an egalitarian society would be one in which every individual is of equal status, a society in which no one outranks anyone. But even the most primitive societies could not be described as egalitarian in this sense because of age, sex, and personal [differences]' (1958: 134, in Flanagan 1989: 246). This reasoning seems indisputable, especially after reviewing the evidence from Air Bah, where instead of overcoming the 'egalitarian' mechanisms in place, self-aggrandizers simply used them to manipulate others and support their own goals. Moreover, in this setting, the relatively easy shift from equality to inequality was based on the authority structure of age – an undisputedly non-egalitarian principle. All this seems to reinforce the claims for universal inequality, that is, that there are no truly egalitarian societies, only different degrees of inequality. Nonetheless, several aspects of the story of Air Bah described in this book indicate that this (universal inequality) is not an entirely satisfactory solution to our problem either.

First, the position of universal inequality is based on the weak assumption that age in small-scale societies is a principle of inequality. Second, it fails to address and account for the social phenomena that have been interpreted by researchers as 'egalitarian ethic.' Finally, the position of universal inequality is ill-equipped to deal with the structural change in political systems marking the transition from egalitarian to non-egalitarian politics, and from simple to complex social systems. In discussing the implications of social change in Air Bah, I will centre on these three issues.

Although the position of universal inequality has been popular, many researchers remain dissatisfied with simply doing away with the notion of egalitarian society. Instead, as Polly Wiessner (2002: 233, 252) suggests, we need to examine more critically the way equality is maintained. David Erdal and Andrew Whiten similarly note that 'egalitarianism in hunter-gatherer societies continues to present an evolutionary puzzle. It is not yet clear what social-psychological processes are responsible for keeping egalitarianism in place or how they evolved' (1994: 175; see also Wiessner 2002). I suggest that these processes are embedded in *categorical age*. A satisfactory theory of equality and inequality has to account for both the structural change marking the development of inequality and the continuity between egalitarian and non-egalitarian politics. To construct such theory, we need to re-examine the role of age in egalitarian political systems.

The Structure of Egalitarian Society

Although anthropologists disagree as to whether there are truly egalitarian small-scale societies, there is broad agreement in the discipline that differences of age, gender, skills, and charisma exist in all human societies (Sahlins 1958: 134; Fried 1967; Cashdan 1980; Woodburn 1982; Bloch 1983: 163; Yanagisako and Collier 1987; Knauft 1991; Clark and Blake 1994: 28; Erdal and Whiten 1994: 176–7; Feinman 1995; Barnard 1999: 304; Wiessner 2002; Rousseau 2006). In recent years, the notion that gender differences necessarily imply inequality has been challenged (e.g., Draper 1975a; Estioko-Griffin and Griffin 1981; Nowak 1986, 1988; K.L. Endicott 1999); nevertheless, most anthropologists do continue to hold the view that age is the most basic form of social differentiation in small-scale societies. Thus, whether they believe in egalitarianism or dispute it, anthropologists tend to agree that age in small-scale societies constitutes a form of natural inequality (Fried 1967; Bloch 1983: 163; Béteille 1983: 32; Flanagan 1988, 1989; Shennan 1996; Trigger 1998). In all appearances, leadership competition in Air Bah reinforces this interpretation. In the previous chapters I have argued that leadership competition and inequalities in Air Bah were built on age politics and that people tolerated self-promotion by competing leaders because their actions were compatible with age roles and, as a result, were not perceived as violations of Lanoh values. However, the fundamental problem with views that associate age relations with inequality in small-scale societies is that they fail to contemplate the implications of 'natural' age differences, and thus they fail to appreciate the effect of complementary age roles in these social and political systems. Although, as the developments in Air Bah indicate, social inequality is clearly rooted in categorical age differences, categorical age has a contrary connotation in simple egalitarian societies. In this section, I intend to show that instead of reflecting natural age differences (which, indeed, constitute the basis for dominance hierarchies in primate societies) categorical age successfully counters inequalities deriving from 'natural' age. Thus, in small-scale societies, categorical age ought to be conceived of as a principle of equality, rather than of inequality.

The distinction between categorical age and natural age differences while rarely made is extremely important. Natural age differences in small-scale societies would most certainly result in the dominance of younger men, while categorical age differences prevent this from happening. In Chapter 5, I reviewed some important differences between the age relations of men and women and suggested that in small-scale societies, compared with the 'natural' age relations of women, those of men tend to be constructed and organized into the structure of categorical age. Categorical age, defined here as ideological work that elders in small-scale societies expend, promotes equality at least in two respects: first, by endorsing cognitive/cultural power displays against spontaneous displays of violence, and second, by ensuring that elders are favourably, or at least equally, provided for.

This reinterpretation of categorical age as an agent of equality allows for further adjustments to our theories of equality and inequality. For one, we can continue to work with data revealing 'egalitarian ethic,' as opposed to disregarding these as incorrect and irrelevant, as it would be the logical implication of the theory of universal inequality. Over the years anthropologists have supported the notion of an 'egalitarian ethic' with an abundance of reliable data (Lee 1979; Ten Raa 1986; K.M. Endicott 1988; Headland 1987; Persoon 1989; Bird-David 1990, 1992b; Peterson 1991; Grinker 1992; Lee 1992; Rushforth 1994; Silberbauer 1996; Hewlett 1996; Lewis-Williams 1996). In these studies researchers often convincingly describe how actions of self-aggrandizers are vigorously resisted by their fellow group members (Fox 1953: 248; Meillassoux 1973; Lee 1979; Woodburn 1980, 1982; Rai 1982; Bird 1982, 1983; Boehm 1993: 236; Erdal and Whiten 1994: 178). Rather than dismissing all these reports by all these anthropologists, we should confront discrepancies in data and theory by reinterpreting their observations.

Based on this understanding of egalitarian society, we will now also be able to reconceptualize behaviours and attitudes commonly interpreted as 'egalitarian ethic' in the literature on small-scale societies, especially that on hunter-gatherers, as manifestations of beliefs and practices associated with categorical age in contexts where the power of elders is otherwise extremely limited. As discussed earlier, these societies, where 'egalitarian ethic,' or counterdominance, has been recorded, tend to be immediate-return hunter-gatherers (Woodburn 1982). As seen in Air Bah, the social organization of such hunter-gatherers is characterized by an autonomy of younger men (see 'individual autonomy syndrome') derived from the alternatives they may pursue independently of elders' influence, and this results in the limited power of elders in these groups. In the following I will argue that what has commonly been interpreted as 'egalitarian ethic' is, in fact, a manifestation of ideologies associated with categorical age. I am going to base this argument on two often-cited attributes of the value system and practices among immediate-return hunter-gatherers, non-violence, and 'egalitarian' sharing.

Cognitive/Cultural Power Displays Balancing 'Natural' Inequalities

Age is a deeply entrenched concept in anthropology, but little work has been done on the question of how elders in human societies prevent a loss of status as they age. A good place to start is a comparison of the implications of aging in primate and human political systems. This comparison reveals that, while dominance systems based on physical displays are devastating for aging individuals among primates, among humans, categorical age offsets the threat to elders as their strength declines, primarily by promoting cultural, as opposed to physical, displays of dominance.[1]

Anthropologists sometimes comment with wonderment on the relative equality of younger men vis-à-vis elders in certain small-scale societies. For instance, Keith and Kertzer write: 'Even in societies where political supremacy is the prerogative of elders, there are ways in which younger men may gain the upper hand' (1984: 47; also see Goody 1976: 122–3; La Fontaine 1978: 14–15). This statement is based on observations of the often overwhelming power of elders in small-scale societies. However, once we consider the structural foundation of the relationship between younger men and elders and realize that in small-scale societies categorical age is indispensable in balancing out 'natural' age differences between men, we cannot help but marvel at the power of elders, instead.

Another prevailing view obscuring the significance of categorical age is the assumption that social inequality among humans is of the same kind as tendencies of dominance among primates. Boehm suggests that 'the African great apes ... have marked social dominance hierarchies with authoritative leadership, and so do humans living in chiefdoms, kingdoms, and states' (1993: 227; Erdal and Whiten 1994). In the same vein, Knauft assumes that in middle-range societies the primate tendency for social dominance reappears in the form of 'marked male dominance hierarchies' (1994: 181 and 1991: 397). This implies that equality may only be accomplished by vigilantly countering these long-standing dominance tendencies through ideological equality, or an 'egalitarian ethic' (Woodburn 1982; Schubert 1991: 35; Boehm 1993: 235, 227 and 1999: 252–3; Erdal and Whitten 1994: 176–7; Knauft 1994: 181 and 1991: 397; Trigger 1998: 216; Wiessner 2002: 233). Those assuming that primate and human dominance hierarchies are of the same kind, however, fail to consider that in all human political structures primate-type dominance is countered, and the basis of primate dominance – spontaneous physical advantage – is replaced with cognitive/cultural advantage as the basis for political leadership and power. This transformation of the foundation of political power occurs with the development of categorical age based on the ideological regulation of relationships between younger men and elders. To appreciate this difference between primate and human politics, we only have to consider the implications of dominance hierarchies based on physical displays for aging individuals in primate politics.

In spite of growing evidence for the role of social alliances in primate politics, most primatologists agree that dominance among primates is fundamentally based on displays of physical strength. Jane Goodall writes: 'Like many other primates, chimpanzees are exceptionally emotional mammals, easily aroused and not quite so easily pacified ... [and] many of the aggressive acts performed by males during other forms of intense social excitement can be interpreted as status rivalry' (1991: 118, 121).[2]

Knauft similarly notes that in primate social groups 'genuine challenges at the top of the hierarchy frequently result in severe wounds and permanent injuries' (1991: 396). This violent foundation has important implications for the age of dominant individuals. In systems of political dominance 'ultimately based on the ability to fight' (Washburn and De Vore 1961: 100), the status of aging males is usually in decline. Goodall observed that among chimpanzees aging was the single most important reason for an individual to lose rank. Chimpanzee males tend to achieve their highest rank in their physical prime, between the ages of 25 and 30 years, and their status gradually declines when they start to age (Goodall 1986: 415 and 1991: 127). Although displays of physical power continue for a while, these threats are pure 'bluff,' and soon the once-dominant male loses fights even to late-adolescent males (ibid. 1986: 414–30). Thus, Goodall suggests, old chimpanzee males are 'very low ranking during the last few years of life' (ibid.: 415). In human social groups it is equally true that very old men often lose their status. Yet, this is not because of loss of their physical strength, but because of decline in their cognitive and persuasive powers. Indeed, among humans, men manage to retain their status far beyond their physical prime. In fact, as the leadership structure of small-scale societies suggests, elders arrive at the top of their political career just as their physical strength is in decline.

Thus, although dominance based on physical displays is devastating for aging primates, among humans, practices and mechanisms derived from categorical age contribute to the maintenance of elders' status even as they weaken physically. This, however, requires constant ideological reinforcement on the part of elders. Among the ideologies that promote equality in small-scale societies, internal non-violence is one of the most important. By discouraging internal violence, elders in human societies reduce the likelihood of spontaneous aggressive dominance displays, particularly by younger men, bolstering a political system based instead on the cultural/cognitive superiority of elders.

The importance of non-violence is more readily recognized in societies where the power of elders is extremely limited, as in several peaceful foraging and horticulturist societies (Dentan 1968; Benjamin 1968; Gibson 1985; K.M. Endicott 1988: 37; Knauft 1991; Kent 1993: 487; Boehm 1993: 231). Nonetheless, in-group non-violence is universally emphasized, even in warlike societies. Many anthropologists, who still assume that in human warfare male aggression is freely displayed, fail to appreciate this.[3] Yet, this perception of human warfare as a manifestation of spontaneous aggression has been contested over and over again, perhaps most memorably by Marshall Sahlins (1976) who, in critiquing vulgar sociobiology, pointed out that in wars men do not fight as individuals, but as members of social structures. To this, we may add that in all human societies the structures to which Sahlins refers are rooted in age ideologies that carefully manage male aggression and discourage, even punish, in-group violence.

Peaceful and warlike small-scale societies are therefore similar in preventing spontaneous internal displays of physical violence. Whether elders merely discourage such displays or channel younger men's aggressions towards external threats depends on their control, as well as on the group's interethnic context. Among mobile hunter-gatherers with an immediate-return system of production, elders have limited power, and these groups tend to benefit more from amiable external relations than from enforced territorial boundaries and boundary defence. In warlike societies, on the contrary, elders not only have sufficient power to mobilize younger men against external enemies, but they may also use territorial boundary defence to protect resources and to build internal political strength. Needless to say, warfare is a far more potent tool in self-aggrandizement than is pacifism.

Whether immediate- or delayed-return, in small-scale societies categorical age promotes cultural displays of power and ensures parity between elders and physically fitter younger men.[4] In small-scale societies, especially in those in which they have limited power, elders have reason to be concerned with the physical displays of younger men.[5] In these settings younger men have the advantage in virtually any task requiring physical strength and ability including most economic activities. In previous chapters I discussed the physical requirements of farming, contract work, and forest collecting among Lanoh. Although evidence is inconclusive, younger men may also be more efficient in hunting. Kelly, discussing the effect of aging on hunter-gatherers, suggests that 'foragers' capabilities are a product of a number of factors: their age and physical/mental condition, whether they have children with them on a foray, whether women are breastfeeding infants, and so forth' (1995: 99). Although middle-aged Ache men appear to have higher return rates than either younger or older men, and in general, 'foragers go through a period of proficiency at their subsistence tasks ... and then enter a period of time as they age when they are not so proficient. For male hunters, hunting success decreases over the age of forty due to eye problems and arthritis' (ibid., 179; also see Dwyer 1983; Ohtsuka 1989; Howell 1986; Hart and Pilling 1960: 34, as cited in Kelly, ibid., 355).[6]

Given younger men's tendency for violence, and to express dominance through physical displays, it makes sense for elders in these societies to discourage boasting by young hunters.[7] Indeed, incidents that have been taken as evidence for the existence of an egalitarian ethic can alternatively be interpreted as discouraging physical dominance displays by younger men. The following excerpt by Richard Lee, for instance, widely quoted in support of egalitarian ideology, contains clearly recognizable references to both the age of the boaster and the concern with violence:[8]

> But ... why insult a man after he has gone to all that trouble to track and kill an animal and when he is going to share the meat with you so that your children will have something to eat?.'.. 'Arrogance,' was his cryptic answer. 'Arrogance?' 'Yes, when a *young man* kills much meat he comes to think of himself as a chief or a big man, and he thinks of the rest of us as his servants or inferiors. We can't accept this. We refuse one who boasts, for someday his pride will make him *kill* somebody. So we always speak of his meat as worthless. This way we cool his heart and make him gentle. (1993: 188, emphasis added)

Beyond a mere physical activity, hunting carries sexual symbolism and connotations likely to drive young hunters to strive aggressively. By 'cooling' younger men's hearts, elders reduce the likelihood of spontaneous power displays and thus diminish or neutralize the greatest threat to their authority.

To 'cool' a younger man's heart, elders mainly use cognitive tools.[9] The rhetoric employed by elders in small-scale societies is aimed at explicitly establishing a structural quality in the form of oppositional roles in their relationship with younger men.[10] They emphasize the structural opposition between roles and status through concepts and, in particular, categorical differences. In light of the above argument, it is expected that some of the most important among these categorical differences would emphasize the distinction between physical and cognitive advantages, between spontaneous and deliberate displays, and between nature and culture.

In the past, the nature-culture distinction has been commonly interpreted as an expression of gender ideologies. Probably the most widely cited example of this is Sherry Ortner's (1974) model of women's association with nature and men's association with culture. Since Ortner's paper, however, the universality of the link between gender relations and the nature-culture distinction has been questioned (e.g., Strathern 1980; Harris 1980; Piña-Cabral 1986). Some critics, however, have suggested that just as often the opposition between nature and culture defines the structural relationship between younger men and elders and, as Marilyn Strathern (1981) has so excellently demonstrated, women could merely be caught up in the contest of power between men. Indeed, the way cognitive power, *kuy*, is juxtaposed to physical power, *yəl*, among Lanoh, and the way this distinction is applied, reinforces the interpretation that the nature-culture distinction may be more about regulating categorical age relations among men than it is about gender relations.

In Chapter 5, I noted that, among Lanoh, *kuy* is representative of the qualities that make us human. It symbolizes a person's ability to think, speak, and remember, while *yəl*, the dumb, violent, shadow spirit, stands for spontaneous violent behaviour. *Yəl* is what is left of humans when their rational faculties, the ability to speak and to think, are removed. We may further recall that while *kuy* is primarily associated with elders, *yəl* is associated with younger men. As Schebesta suggests, 'the *yurl* [*yəl*] of a bachelor is particularly evilly disposed and will kill anyone' (1929: 235–6, in Evans 1937: 264). Similarly, the careless, thoughtless acts that can awaken *yəl* are associated with younger men susceptible to displaying youthful, spontaneous, disrespectful behaviour. This is why, according to Lanoh elders, acts associated with such behaviour, such as whistling, talking, urinating, or splashing water during forest work, are discouraged, and younger men, who 'cannot be trusted,' are continuously monitored and disciplined. In controlling such actions, Lanoh elders set 'culture,' notably the powers of reason and rationality, against threatening displays of spontaneous, 'natural,' violence by younger men.

The universality that Claude Lévi-Strauss famously attributed to binary categories, such as 'nature' and 'culture,' has been frequently challenged. Ingold, for instance, suggests that 'the rigid division that Western thought and science draws between the worlds of society and nature, of persons and things, does not exist for hunters and gatherers' (1999: 409). Similarly, some have expressed the opinion that deliberation and self-control have only recently gained emphasis in Western history as it became necessary to manage complex technology in industrial societies (Elias 1982: 88, in Trigger 1998: 218). However, based on the preceding argument, I posit that an emphasis on deliberation and self-control may actually be among the defining characteristics of *Homo sapiens sapiens*. The Lanoh division between *kuy* and *yəl* is but a reminder that, time and again, researchers discover distinctions between nature and culture, spontaneous and deliberate, animal and human, in the most unexpected places, including among mobile egalitarian hunter-gatherers. For instance, in the same volume where Ingold questions the universal validity of the nature-culture distinction, Richard Lee (1999) calls attention to a shared attribute in the cosmology of hunter-gatherers; he suggests that hunter-gatherers commonly differentiate between two states, before and after human, and that in the after-human state, the distinction between nature and culture is analogous to that between animals and humans (also see Balikci 1989). Indeed, if the structural basis of human politics is universal, it follows that the binary categories supporting it would be as well.

This reasoning should also prompt us to reconsider some of our convictions about the relationship between moral judgments and inequality. Yanagisako and Collier, in stressing that 'values entail evaluation ... [and] consequently, a society is a system of social relations in which all things and actions are not equal,' (1987: 39) voice a common assumption, according to which inequalities are embedded in value systems, judgments, and comparisons. Whether this is true would depend on the context. As competing leaders in Air Bah demonstrated, the manipulation of societal values may indeed support self-aggrandizement and contribute to emerging inequalities. Nonetheless, *in egalitarian societies*, moral systems support categorical age and, as such, would seem to contribute to maintaining elders' equality. Thus, while Yanagisako and Collier suggest that we separate 'justice (moral rightness)' from 'equality (the state of being equal)' (ibid.) in egalitarian societies, counterintuitive as it may seem, 'moral rightness' contributes to 'the state of being equal.' Among such egalitarian peoples, morality not only reinforces self-control, deliberation, and rationality against spontaneous displays of violence, but also promotes an 'equality of outcome,' that is, it ensures that elders are provisioned beyond their means.

Production Systems Balancing 'Natural' Inequalities

Production systems are among the most unique and significant of human institutions. There have been numerous attempts to understand human production in its various contexts; most, however, have inexplicably ignored the politics of small-scale societies. This especially applies to studies of production among mobile hunter-gatherers. Since humanity has spent about 90 per cent of its time subsisting as hunters and gatherers (Lee and Daly 1999), there has been considerable effort to understand patterns of production and distribution in hunting-and-gathering societies. Here I will review and evaluate four main approaches to this inquiry: pair bonding, sexual selection, and social and ecological models of hunter-gatherer production. In general, pair bonding theories ignore the social context of production, because they are too narrowly focused on understanding pair bonding in the framework of the nuclear family.[11] Sexual selection theories, although highly critical of pair bonding models, do not fare much better, because they are based on female choice and disregard the structure of political relations among men in human societies. For their part, social theories focus on organization and interpersonal relations while often overlooking the political structures of hunter-gatherer societies, and ecological theories simply brush aside the human context altogether. After reviewing these approaches and their weaknesses, it will be apparent that human production systems, including those of immediate-return hunter-gatherers, can only be comprehensively understood within the framework of categorical age.

One of the most common anthropological frameworks for analysing production systems in small-scale societies is the ecological or 'adaptationist' approach. Adaptationist theorists aim to reach back to the strict basics: evolution, behavioural ecology, and subsistence behaviour. As Kelly suggests, 'we have to start someplace ... [and] an understanding of human interaction with the environment ... is the most straightforward task before anthropology at present' (1995: 36–7). Guided by this reasoning, these theorists assume the existence of a purely rational *homo economicus* who makes decisions for maximum personal benefit (Headland 1986: 30; Kelly 1995). Second, they posit that models developed from studies of animal foraging can sufficiently account for the actions of this *homo economicus*. These adaptationist approaches, with their strict focus on natural selection, have been heavily criticized in anthropology. Lacking an appreciation of human sociality in its full complexity, they have often been deemed inadequate in explaining human production.

Tim Ingold (1988) has been one of these critics. In his criticism of ecological approaches he raises several important points; he suggests that in applying models of animal foraging to human behaviour these approaches neglect human relationships, and he emphasizes that people in hunter-gatherer societies are producers, just as people in so-called food producing societies. As a reminder of the fundamental differences between animal foraging and human producing, Ingold suggests that we replace 'foraging mode' with 'hunting-gathering mode' (ibid.). Nurit Bird-David similarly critiques the implications of ecological studies of hunting and gathering behaviour. She suggests that these 'conversations on "subsistence"... consigned hunter-gatherers to a liminal position – the border area between animal and human realms, evolutionary and present times' (1994: 600).

Ingold (1988) calls attention to a further difference between animal foraging and human hunting and gathering; in human production, he suggests, social goals may be far more important than maximizing food intake. Monica Minnegal (1997) reinforces this claim by arguing that distribution may in fact be the very rationale for subsistence production. Ingold is thinking along similar lines when urging anthropologists to realize the uniqueness of human hunting and gathering and to distinguish it from animal foraging. He argues that the purpose of hunter-gatherer production is 'the aggregation and transport of foodstuffs to a central place... The operations entailed in gathering are classed as such because they are... governed by an intention concerning the foodstuff's future distribution and consumption' (1988: 271; see also Bird-David 1994: 600). That is, for Ingold, human hunting and gathering and animal foraging are differentiated mainly by the *intent* of human hunter-gatherers: when hunter-gatherers leave their camp, they leave with a plan to bring back food.[12] While this is an important point, gathering and transporting food to a central place is an insufficient trait for distinguishing human production as several animal species, from wild dogs to vampire bats, bring back food to a base to share with offspring, co-parents, and alternative caretakers (Wilkinson 1984: 182, in Binmore 2001).[13] Instead, the difference between human production and animal foraging may be that human hunters are primarily motivated by prestige behaviour.

Indeed, ecological/adaptationist models, especially optimal foraging theories, have been further criticized on the grounds that hunters may exploit particular resources for reasons other than gaining nutrients. As has been pointed out, hunting behaviour is modified not only by cultural rules like food taboos (Mithen 1989; Silberbauer 1981), but also by prestige seeking (Dwyer 1974, 1985a, 1985b). Kelly, in an attempt to rebut these criticisms, states:

> Foraging models do not claim to duplicate reality; instead, they claim to model reality at some level of specificity if hunter-gatherers are behaving according to a model's set of goals and conditions. Optimization models are heuristic; they do not provide a priori answers and explanations. By predicting which resources a forager will take if resources are ranked only in terms of their search costs and post-encounter return rates ... optimal-

foraging models flag those resources that are treated for reasons other
than energetic. (1995: 109)

Yet, as I shall demonstrate, apart from extreme conditions, and apart
from a individuals hunting for their own on-the-spot consumption, eco-
logical/adaptationist frameworks will never be sufficient in explaining human hunting behaviour, because human hunting behaviour can
never be separated from prestige seeking.

Kristen Hawkes similarly connects production and status seeking
when, in recent discussions on the topic, 'Why Hunter-Gatherers Work,'
she assumes that status seeking by hunter-gatherers can be understood
within a sexual selection framework (Hawkes 1993; see also Marlowe
1999; Dwyer 1974, 1985a, 1985b). The answer to this question about
hunter-gatherers' production has long been taken for granted. Early
researchers were convinced that hunter-gatherers worked to provide
for members of their nuclear family (Barnes 1973: 72–3; Sahlins 1972:
196, in Wilk 1989: 26; Steele and Shennan 1996: 10). Lately, this utilitari-
an model of parental cooperation and provisioning has been challenged
on several grounds (Hawkes 1996; Graves-Brown 1996; Marlowe 1999,
2000; Hawkes et al. 2001). First, as Edward Miller (1994) reasons, in
warm climatic regions with abundant vegetation for females to gather,
paternal provisioning is not absolutely necessary for offspring survival.
Second, the theory of parental provisioning has been challenged on the
basis of sex-specific reproductive interests. Hawkes (1996) and Paul
Graves-Brown (1996) argue that male and female hunter-gatherers pursue different strategies according to their distinct reproductive interests
– while females collect for their child's benefit, males hunt to 'show off.'
By focusing on these sex-specific interests, sexual competition models
successfully address the phenomenon of overproviding by younger
men which natural selection and paternal provisioning models, as the
next quote by Kelly reveals, have been unable to explain: 'One might
expect that married men do the most foraging since they have more
dependents than single men. However, this is not the case: single Ache
men produce the most and are the most consistent in their production.
They share the most and receive the least in return. What do they gain
from this?' (1995: 177). Still, by assuming that younger men want to
'show off' to impress women, these models of 'female choice' omit the
political framework of human production. The fact is that even among
hunter-gatherers with an immediate-return system of production it is
elders who seem to benefit the most from younger men's work.

The pair bonding model, according to which men primarily produce for members of their nuclear family, has ultimately been challenged on the recognition that since hunter-gatherers share meat widely the producer's own nuclear household may actually benefit little from his or her superior hunting skills (Hawkes et al. 2001). Indeed, focusing on the nuclear family as the primary context for the evolution of human production obscures the fact that, instead of providing for co-parents and offspring, providing for members of ascending generations is the most unique aspect of human production.[14] Human production systems not only increase offspring survival, they are also exceptionally beneficial for the survival and longevity of elders. To underline this, even among hunter-gatherers with an immediate-return system of production, elders are entitled to be cared and provided for. Referring to a paper by Harriet Rosenberg (1990), Richard Lee writes about elders' entitlement among the Dobe !Kung: 'I prefer to … use the term "entitlement" to account for the ways in which !Kung elderly were cared for by relatives and non-relatives alike, such that no one, not even childless people, would be denied access to support in old age. This was part of a general phenomenon in !Kung society in which everyone claimed, and was recognized as being "entitled" to, the necessities of life, by right of being a member of the society' (1993: 175). Although Lee considers this to be a manifestation of 'primitive communism,' interpreting entitlement as a manifestation of age ideology is a far more parsimonious explanation. In small-scale societies, age roles not only balance 'natural' differences in physical strength, they also ensure equal access to resources. In short, they ensure an 'equality of outcome.'

Equality of outcome has always figured importantly in discussions of egalitarian society. Jill Nash, for instance, notes that in small-scale egalitarian societies, 'the material base and the relations of production do not lend themselves to the development of inequalities' (1987: 150). Similarly, Eleanor Leacock (1982) argues that in mobile hunter-gatherer societies there is equal access to forces of production. However, it is important to recognize that neither an equality of outcome, nor equal access to resources, would be possible without ideologically contrived age differences. Without age ideology acting as an equalizer between young and old, elders would most likely be able to provide for themselves less successfully. Thus, in the absence of these age roles, elders in small-scale societies could not be equal to younger men.

It follows that the division of labour into producers and consumers is an inherently derived aspect of human production. Like age, the division of labour, or role specialization, is assumed to be a source of inequality in small-scale societies, something that runs contrary to 'egalitarian' beliefs and practices, such as egalitarian sharing. As Upham notes, for instance, the separation of producers and consumers 'presents a unique challenge to any decision-making system, and especially to those predicated on egalitarian patterns of sharing' (1990b: 114). However, on the contrary, the preceding discussion indicates that there would not likely be human production without this division of labour, that is, without this separation of producers and consumers. Furthermore, even though the division of labour into producers (younger men) and consumers (elders) may eventually become a basis of social hierarchy, it is evidently a source of equality in small-scale egalitarian societies.

To appreciate this point, and to consider the 'natural' status implications of being consumers, we must turn, once again, to primate research. This research indicates that younger males in their physical prime tend to be more efficient hunters not only among humans but also among great apes, where hunting success often elicits 'begging' from other members of the group. In chimpanzee troops, the most efficient hunter and the most dominant individual often coincide. Jane Goodall describes how young, dominant males hand out pieces of meat to subordinate males, as well as to females, after a hunt: 'Begging ... is the way most chimpanzees try to get some meat for themselves ... Those who beg may reach out to touch the meat, often glancing at the face of the possessor as they do so, as though to gauge his mood – or they hold out a hand, palm up, toward him' (1986: 300). However, among chimpanzees, such begging implies submission, subservience, and low status. Among humans, age ideology and entitlement ensure that elders receive subsistence without servility, without having to ask, and without debasing their status as a consequence.

Chimpanzee begging resembles 'demand sharing' among human hunter-gatherers. Nicholas Peterson (1993) has pointed out that, as with chimpanzees, articles and assets are often shared because people demand them. Demand sharing is also common among Lanoh. Women, children, and low-status individuals would frequently ask for, and receive, food, money, and tobacco. Yet, despite this widespread practice, elders, mindful of the negative implications of demand sharing on their status, never ask. And they do not need to: age roles ensure that they are well-provided for.

So if young hunters are not the most dominant individuals, and if hunting success does not automatically translate to leadership, why do younger men fulfil the role of 'net providers,' and what does status seeking mean among hunter-gatherers? My answer to these questions is that status seeking ought to be understood within the framework of age relations. Apart from female choice, the theory of sexual selection also entails male competition, and this facet ought to be emphasized more when inquiring into the origins of human production. Thus, while the general model of sexual competition applies, I contend that in human societies younger men primarily produce to impress elders rather than women, because producing, acting as 'net providers,' paves their way to becoming an 'elder,' the ultimate status in egalitarian politics.

Hopefully, this review has cogently demonstrated that an age-based political framework is likely to be a more satisfactory one in explaining human systems of production. Returning to the sharing practices of immediate-return hunter-gatherers, where the autonomy of younger men limits elders' power, this basic structure of production is still clearly identifiable; sharing among mobile hunter-gatherers can be understood in terms of age structures and the limiting effects of organization.

Sharing, occasionally confounded with generalized reciprocity, is one of the most controversial and most often discussed topics in the literature on hunter-gatherers.[15] It has been first and foremost interpreted to be an ideology and a mechanism to attain and maintain equality (Woodburn 1982: 431; Kaplan and Hill 1985; Kent 1993: 480). Apart from examining its role in social relationships, researchers have often analysed sharing from an ecological and evolutionary perspective. Within this framework sharing has been interpreted as risk reduction, tolerated theft, permission granting, and variance reduction (Testart 1982; Blurton Jones 1984, 1987; Kaplan and Hill 1985; Kelly 1995; Kameda et al. 2002). Lately, even group selection models have resurfaced as explanations for hunter-gatherer sharing (Boehm 1996; Wilson and Sober 1994; Wilson 1998; Jones 2000).[16] Despite this assortment of proposed interpretations, however, the phenomenon of sharing continues to elude explanation.

These varied perspectives could be effectively reconciled if sharing is considered to be a particular manifestation of the above-discussed relationships entailed in production. From this perspective, it is evident that, like non-violence, sharing compensates for younger men's physical superiority and reinforces elders' status in egalitarian societies. Consequently, similar to other levelling mechanisms, sharing can be understood within the context of the age system. It is not an ill-defined, indistinct submission of the individual to 'communal solidarity,' but a practice brought about by ideologies of categorical age (e.g., Gibson 2005: 249–50).[17] To fully appreciate this, we must, once again, consider the difference between the power relations of elders and younger men in societies with immediate- and delayed-return systems of production.

The extent to which elders are provided for in small-scale societies depends on their control over different phases of production. This, in turn, is usually determined by their power over younger men. As I have argued in previous chapters, among mobile hunter-gatherers with an immediate-return system of production, individual autonomy severs dependencies between younger men and elders. In these social groups, production is less efficiently controlled by elders than in small-scale egalitarian societies with a delayed-return system of production. Consequently, among these immediate-return hunter-gatherers, the provisioning of elders by particular younger men is generally unpredictable. In these groups, it is easier for younger men to avoid cooperation than in societies with a delayed-return system of production. Younger men may move away, for example, or avoid contributing by 'hiding, secretive behavior and lying' (Peterson 1993: 864; Turnbull 1972: 130). In Air Bah, for instance, smaller animals, such as squirrels, are often eaten by the hunter on the spot. In these cases, when questioned later, the hunter flatly denies that his hunt was successful.

It is conceivable, therefore, that sharing rules among these hunter-gatherers are so sweepingly 'general' so as to make up for the unreliability of relationships between particular individuals.[18] Thus, although several authors have suggested these sharing patterns to be responsible for individual autonomy (Gardner 1991; Bird-David 1996), the relationship may in fact be the reverse. Instead of individual autonomy being caused by sharing, it appears that it is individual autonomy that leads to general sharing practices because, in conditions of extreme individualism, they best guarantee the provision of elders. On the contrary, in egalitarian societies with a delayed-return system of production, where kinship obligations are strong, there is no compelling need for such general sharing rules, because providing for elders is inherent in the authority structure of continuous relationships and interpersonal dependencies. General sharing thus can be interpreted as a minimal case of the tribute to elders in small-scale delayed-return societies. To some extent it makes up for severed ties between younger men and elders in the context of a social organization associated with immediate-return production. To appreciate this point, we only need to imagine conditions in hunter-gatherer camps.

It is not accidental that sharing rules among hunter-gatherers empha-size spatial proximity, visibility, and inclusion. In hunter-gatherer camps, people eat and sleep together in a small, open, circular area, and once food is brought back to camp, because of the high visibility of any activity, it is difficult to avoid sharing (Stearman 1989: 225–7; K.M. Endicott 1988: 117; Turnbull 1972). Thus, mobile hunter-gatherers com-pensate for the unreliability of particular interpersonal ties by saying, 'share with whoever happens to be in camp.' This interpretation is rein-forced by Bird-David's observation that, if social cohesion is managed through shifting ties, it is maximized when 'the courses of these social circuits are random and constantly changing' (1987: 162).

This connection between interpersonal ties and forms of distribution among immediate-return hunter-gatherers further allows for a revision of the presumed relationship between sharing (generalized reciproc-ity) and balanced reciprocity. In Chapter 6, I suggested that balanced reciprocity among Lanoh does not necessarily imply that they have developed a delayed-return system of production. Here I would like to elaborate on this argument. In light of the above discussion on shar-ing, I will question the legitimacy of regarding generalized reciprocity and balanced reciprocity as opposites. Anthropologists have not only regarded generalized reciprocity and balanced reciprocity as mutually exclusive practices, but also as practices that sit along an evolutionary sequence (Sahlins 1972: 193–4).[19] In Air Bah general sharing and bal-anced reciprocity are simultaneously practised, yet they are not viewed as contradictory. This is because both sharing and balanced reciprocity assume similarly discontinuous and unreliable interpersonal relation-ships.[20] In balanced reciprocity this lack of trust is straightforwardly expressed. We will recall that in Air Bah people expect to be repaid for every favour, good turn, or service to others, even within their nuclear families. Although the cash economy has certainly enhanced this ten-dency, Lanoh mistrust in interpersonal relationships is likely to have originated earlier, in pre-resettlement individualistic trade with Malay villagers.

However, it is important to realize that, similar to balanced reciproc-ity, general sharing among these foragers may also be rooted in the fluidity of relationships and weak interpersonal obligations. The dif-ference between balanced reciprocity and hunter-gatherers sharing is that balanced reciprocity relates to temporal aspects of these relations while sharing relates to spatial aspects. Thus, balanced reciprocity can be conceptualized as a diachronic – and general sharing a synchronic –

expression of unreliable interpersonal relations among immediate-return hunter-gatherers. Balanced reciprocity occurs because mobile hunter-gatherers rarely know when they will see each other again and, as a result, want to ensure that transactions reach a closure before parties go on their separate ways.[21] In general sharing people are similarly uncertain who will be in camp at any one time. Thus, people share with whoever happens to be in camp, irrespective of closeness or the nature of their relations. Elders in hunter-gatherer camps can never be sure that younger men related to them in particular, prescribed ways will be around to provide for them. However, because of general sharing rules, they can reasonably expect to be provided for by any young man who happens to share his camp. This complementary relationship between balanced reciprocity and general sharing may explain why, on the one hand, people in Air Bah freely enter each other's houses to take things while, on the other hand, they reciprocate favours as soon as possible.

Although general sharing among hunter-gatherers is likely to reflect their unreliable interpersonal relations, this does not alter the fact that sharing, like other forms of distribution, is part of an institution conceived within the structure of categorical age. As suggested earlier, in spite of organizational limitations on elders' control over younger men, even among mobile hunter-gatherers, elders usually end up receiving the bulk of meat. This is not immediately apparent because the first responsibility of any hunter is to provide for members of his nuclear family, his wives and children. Likewise, among Lanoh, there is a strong obligation for men to provide for their families. As discussed earlier, Lanoh women have a right to their husband's earnings and this allows them to save money. It is therefore considered important for a woman to have a 'good man' who would take care of her, and young men are encouraged to become good providers from the time they begin to hunt. People consider men who 'eat a lot … two plates of rice, a jug of tea,' to be bad husband material because a man's primary responsibility is to be concerned with the well-being of his families. There are also taboos to further ensure that men fulfil their responsibilities. For instance, animals hunted while looking for forest products are not to be cooked, because that would imply 'changing one's intention,' which would anger the spirit of the forest product in question. Instead, men are supposed to bring back the game they hunt during collecting trips. For this reason, young men are directed only to hunt at the end of collecting trips.

Because of these strong expectations, men are uncomfortable when placed in a situation when they cannot provide for their families. For instance, when they attended feasts where food is served freely, men from Air Bah would always pack up a large portion of their food to bring home. A man's ability and willingness to provide for his family is also the most important condition for approval by the community if he intends to take a second wife. Lanoh believe that 'a man may have two wives, three wives, but he has to be able to provide for all his wives.' The strong obligation for men to provide for their families seems to support the view that this is their primary motivation for 'producing.' When it comes to distributing money and goods, this is undoubtedly the case. As sharing rules do not apply to money, money and purchased goods usually stay in the household and find their way to women.[22]

However, when it comes to distributing meat, the hunter's own nuclear household benefits little from his efforts. This is not only because hunters share meat widely, but also because menstrual taboos (*salantap*) forbid women from consuming meat. Menstrual taboos connected to meat consumption in Air Bah are idiosyncratic, and informants' accounts about these taboos vary significantly. Minimally, menstruating women are 'not allowed to eat salt, edible oil, and fish for a week; they can only eat vegetables,' but towards the end of the week they are allowed food they were previously denied. At this time they must eat alone, refraining from sharing their food with anyone. In practice, these taboos are much stricter, effectively preventing women from consuming the meat of any large game. No woman in Air Bah, for instance, cooks or consumes the meat of wild boar, the largest game hunted by Lanoh. In fact, many people were of the opinion that, just to be on the safe side, women should refrain from eating meat altogether.

If women do consume meat, it is only of smaller game such as monkeys, birds, and animals that they can obtain themselves. Thus, women's menstrual taboos not only overlap with sharing rules, they reinforce them: they are allowed to eat the meat of small game, generally shared only within the nuclear family, but are not allowed to eat the meat of large animals that could be shared more widely. Older men, when asked about women's menstrual taboos, said that women do not eat the meat of wild boar because they 'do not like to eat large animals.' When pressed to elaborate, they offer:

> They have their menstruation taboos and they don't know when they are going to have their period, they might get it at night, so it is advisable for them to refrain from eating meat altogether.

They further justify this caution by noting the adverse health consequences of eating meat among women. If a woman, for instance, eats
forbidden food, especially meat, in the presence of a menstruating
woman, the latter will develop chest pain (*tiyɔʔ*). During my stay in
Air Bah, a young woman was treated for this illness because, while
she was menstruating, her sister-in-law ate turtle in her presence. Concerned with each other's well-being, pre-menopausal women rarely
consume meat in Air Bah. The implications of these food taboos are
further extended to children, and if a woman refrains from eating the
meat of an animal, she is not likely to feed it to her children either. As a
result, most women and children in Air Bah subsist on vegetables, rice,
tapioca, and fish. Significantly, however, these meat taboos are lifted
after menopause:

> Old women can eat all those things, because they can no longer have
> babies.[23]

This reinforces the point that even among hunter-gatherers elders,
including older women, are the primary consumers of meat.

Lanoh are not unique among hunter-gatherers in applying these regulations to female meat consumption. According to John Speth, among
Australian hunter-gatherers, women are similarly restricted (1990,
in Kelly 1995: 166). Thomas Gibson (1988) has compiled examples of
comparable rules among hunter-gatherers elsewhere. Richard Lee also
observes that 'the !Kung believe that the women must never eat the
men's part of the animals or hunting success will drop to zero' (1979:
247, in Gibson 1988: 177). Likewise, among the Hadza, 'if a woman or
child approaches close to the men when they are eating the sacred meat,
then the men may decide to take action against the offender: mass rape
is said to be a possibility' (Woodburn 1979: 254, in Gibson 1988: 177).
These examples illustrate that rules and regulations concerning the
sharing of food increase the benefits that elders accrue from the hunting success of younger men.

On the one hand, this argument implies that values and practices
commonly interpreted as 'egalitarian ethic' among immediate-return
hunter-gatherers are indeed responsible for equality, but not in an
ambiguous philosophical sense. Rather, categorical age in these groups
accomplishes equality through concrete, negotiated relations between
younger men and elders, as it also does in small-scale delayed-return
societies. The difference, and hence the 'extreme' egalitarianism of

immediate-return foragers, is in elders' power to influence younger men. The reduced power of elders in these settings results in the perfect power balance between younger men and elders that anthropologists recorded in their ethnographies and interpreted as the rare occurrence of philosophical egalitarianism of hunter-gatherers reinforcing the Marxian concept of 'primitive communism' (e.g., Lee 1990).

On the other hand, this analysis on the underlying structure of hunter-gatherer sharing also underscores that organization alone is inadequate to comprehensively explain the motives and objectives of production. To fully understand hunter-gatherer sociality, we need to reverse the trend of overemphasizing organization in hunter-gatherer studies. Since the beginning of hunter-gatherer studies, researchers have sustained continuing fascination with their subjects by stressing their uniqueness among human societies. It started with Julian Steward's emphasis on hunter-gatherers' 'primal' relationship with their environment (1936, in Helms 1978: 176), and continued with Richard Lee and Irven De Vore's (1968) efforts to highlight their evolutionary role. Still later, attention shifted to hunter-gatherers' unique relationship to time and space, as in Marshall Sahlins' notion of the 'original affluent society' (1972), and, from the 1980s on, to highlighting unique qualities of hunter-gatherers' social relationships (e.g., Woodburn 1982; Bird-David 1987; Kent 1996a; Myers 1986; Gardner 1991; Ross 1993; Norström 2001: 42–3). Since the exceptional nature of hunter-gatherers' sociality lies in social organization, researchers have accordingly focused on flexibility, fluidity, mobility, opportunism, and individual autonomy at the expense of structural relations (Woodburn 1982; Gibson 1988: 167; Boehm 1993, 1996, 1999; Gardner 2000).[24]

This trend culminated in postmodern challenges to earlier ecological/adaptationist frameworks, including phenomenological descriptions of hunter-gatherers' relationships with their environment (Pedersen and Waehle 1988; Smith 1988; Griffin 1989; Kelly 1995; Minnegal 1996; Rocha 1996; Ingold 1996; Lye 1998) and social approaches focusing on 'we relationships' and 'shared perspectives' (Bird-David 1994: 584). Bird-David, for example, has called for 'a renewed conversation on the (human) quality' of hunter-gatherers' social relationships (ibid.: 600). Yet, if 'human quality' refers to the shared elements of all human societies, proponents of these social approaches have fared only slightly better than their ecological predecessors. Their predominant focus on unique organizational patterns has prevented them from considering the structural attributes that mobile hunter-gatherers share with delayed-return societies. Moreover, while this focus on the extraordinary has admittedly produced important insights into the dynamics of the social life of mobile hunter-gatherers, as well as provided continuous justification for hunter-gatherer studies, it has also set in place a wall of incommensurability between theories of social equality and inequality.

In their focus on the uniqueness of hunter-gatherer social organization, proponents of the 'social approach' have gone so far as to question whether the concept of 'society' can even be applied to the flexible networks of mobile hunter-gatherers (Burch 1994; Bird-David 1987, 1994; Ingold 1999). Ingold, for instance, proposes that 'the distinctiveness of hunter-gatherer sociality lies in its subversion of the very foundations upon which the concept of society, taken in any of its modern senses, has been built' (1999: 399). In developing his argument, Ingold claims that hunter-gatherer sociality is characterized by immediacy, personal autonomy, and sharing, contradicting three common definitions of 'society': as a community, as a set of strategic interactions between individuals, and as a social structure. Yet, this only seems so if one focuses selectively on the centrifugal, decentralizing effects of organization (such as immediacy, opportunism, and individual autonomy), while ignoring the centripetal, integrative force of age-based authority. Ernest Burch highlights the importance of this conceptual debate by suggesting that until we resolve the 'society' issue, 'hunter-gatherer studies will not contribute much in the way of a general theory of social science as a whole' (1994: 451). I propose that the 'society' issue can be resolved by viewing hunter-gatherer sociality as an interplay of structural and organizational factors and hunter-gatherer organization as a particular manifestation of structural characteristics common to all human societies. Such an approach offers significantly more theoretical promise than dissociating mobile hunter-gatherers from the concept of 'society' entirely. Furthermore, only by redirecting our attention to the structure of hunter-gatherer society will we be able to construct a more powerful and persuasive model of structural complexity.

The Structure of Complex Society

An understanding of equality in small-scale societies as resulting from categorical age differences between men allows for a new parsimonious model of social evolution, one that has two advantages over older models. First, by acknowledging that categorical age is responsible for equality in egalitarian societies, while at the same time it is the structure on which systems of inequality are founded, this new model renders egalitarian and non-egalitarian systems commensurable because in it both egalitarian and hierarchical systems centre on the same structure, categorical age. Second, and here I will once again address the notion of universal inequality, this new model allows us to keep egalitarian and non-egalitarian societies analytically separate. Thus, I will argue that the distinction between egalitarian and non-egalitarian, simple and complex societies is, indeed, meaningful, because simple egalitarian and complex hierarchical societies are structurally different.

Debates about social inequality are older than anthropology, yet our notions of simple and complex society have so far been imprecise, descriptive, and impressionistic. More often than not anthropologists have employed the idea of social 'complexity' to indicate large populations, social differentiation, and heterogeneity – role specialization – the common hallmarks of chiefdoms and state societies (Bender 1989; Rowlands 1989; Stewart 2001).[25] However, with the advent of complexity theory, social complexity can be more exactly defined, and concepts of egalitarian and non-egalitarian societies can be elevated to the level of a theoretical model. Complexity theory, along with chaos theory, has been developed in the natural sciences to analyse processes in systems far from equilibrium, that is, in systems which cannot be described using linear equations. Its potential to reconcile structure and agency, scientific and humanistic approaches, as well as order and randomness, has been increasingly recognized in the social sciences, including anthropology (Mosko 2005). These attributes make complexity theory eminently applicable in studies of social evolution, allowing scholars to move away from older linear, reductionist explanations while continuing to aspire for general models of social change.[26]

Applying complexity theory in modelling the process of social evolution from egalitarian to non-egalitarian social systems will resolve a further contradiction pertaining to the argument of this chapter in earlier theories. Michael Rowlands summarizes this contradiction: 'The contrast between simple and complex social forms has been used to describe cumulative development as well as the discontinuities of social change. In the former, increasing differentiation is seen as a smooth, unfolding process in which earlier forms are present in later developed forms ... In the latter, a savage-barbarist social form is seen as the inversion and negation of its civilized counterpart' (1989: 31).[27] Clearly, an ideal model of social change would be able to capture both continuity and structural change at the same time. Such a model can be conceived within the framework of complexity theory, because it contains principles that are able to grasp both of these aspects of social change. After all, as Harvey and Reed explain, '[social systems] consist of nested and emergent levels of increasing complexity' (1996, in Stewart 2001: 339). The idea of self-similar nesting systems (and dependence on initial conditions) addresses continuity,[28] while the notion of emergence and phase transition[29] calls attention to the important structural change occurring during the transformation from simple to complex society.[30] Principles of complexity theory apply to social change in Air Bah in more than one way.

Proponents of the universal inequality argument are undoubtedly right in pointing out continuities in egalitarian and non-egalitarian politics. After all, as the case of Air Bah has also illustrated, systems of inequality do build on structures of differentiation found in the previous egalitarian system. Complexity theory recognizes that even in extreme, radical structural changes previous structural states will have a significant effect on the proceeding structure. Complexity theory predicts that, although change in systems far from equilibrium may take different directions depending on variations in key parameters at bifurcation points, it is, nonetheless, contingent on previous states (Byrne 1998). As John Clark and Michael Blake note, 'changes result from the purposive action of individuals pursuing individual strategies and agendas within the structural constraints of their cultural system' (1994: 28).[31] In Air Bah competing leaders used incrementalism to appropriate the constraints of egalitarian politics and age relations for self-aggrandizement. In spite of this continuity, however, the relatively smooth transition from egalitarian to non-egalitarian social relations in Air Bah has masked an underlying structural change, resulting in a political system distinct from what came before in important and recognizable ways. This change indicates above all that the contrast between egalitarian and non-egalitarian politics is valid.

The structural transformation from egalitarian to non-egalitarian politics is first of all indicated by a change in leadership structure. Raymond Firth suggests that when structural change occurs, 'the observer can recognize that the former basic relation has lost its magnitude, its force, its frequency' (1964: 84). This certainly applies to developments in Air Bah, where the desire to defeat one another has eclipsed all former political goals that Hitam and Kecil once had. Regardless of organization, the goal of egalitarian politics is to regulate the relationship between younger men and elders and to ensure that in spite of younger men's physical superiority, the status of elders is continually maintained. In non-egalitarian politics, however, the goal of certain elders is no longer primarily to negotiate their power relations with younger men, but to defeat other elders in similar structural positions. These competitors are no longer satisfied with the rewards of egalitarian politics, but strive to be first among elders. Competition and changing leadership goals lead to cultural elaboration. While this connection may seem self-explanatory, the lack of political motivation to create elaborate culture in egalitarian societies sometimes remains underappreciated, as for instance in the following quote by Marshall Sahlins. Contemplating the culture of a group of Australian Aborigines, Sahlins writes: 'The failure of Arnhem Landers to "build culture" is not strictly from want of time. It is from idle hands' (1972: 20). It is important to stress, however, that 'idle hands' in egalitarian societies relate to political motivation. The goals of egalitarian politics are not conducive to cultural elaboration; the goals of complex politics are.

As well, and this is a further indication of structural change when inequality develops, in the shift to non-egalitarian politics the nature of the political elite changes drastically and, perhaps, irrevocably. In *Stratagems and Spoils: A Social Anthropology of Politics*, Frederick Bailey defines a political elite as those within a community 'entitled to compete for honours and power … who are qualified by the rules of the political structure to take an active part in political competition' (1969: 23–4). In egalitarian politics, this includes every man.[32] With leadership competition, however, political elite becomes more differentiated. While most men continue to compete for the 'honours and power' of eldership within the old framework of egalitarian age politics, in the new system, a new, considerably narrower, elite emerges, one restricted to those elders who happened to be heads of their kinship groups at the time of conflict. In Air Bah no other men but the two competing family cluster leaders were 'entitled to compete for the honours and power' that village leadership represents. These changes in leadership structure show that the emergence of a new political elite in Air Bah fulfils the definition of complexification as an aspect of social evolution that implies 'an increase in the number of social roles and statuses' (Rousseau 2006: 22, 248).

Furthermore, and this, again, indicates social change, the emergence of a new political elite in Air Bah resulted in a gap between the two competing household leaders and other men, which may also turn out to be irreversible.[33] Through self-aggrandizement, Hitam and Kecil have acquired advantages and increased their families' wealth in ways that have led to enduring inequalities in the village and the rise of a power elite composed of these leaders and their families. These developments may even transform achieved status in egalitarian politics into the ascribed status of hierarchical societies. While leadership positions in egalitarian politics are transitory and impermanent, because sooner or later most young men become elders, with leadership competition, a potential for a permanent elite has emerged.

Thus, the rise of inequality involves an important structural change, a phase transition, and non-egalitarian societies have emergent qualities that are different from egalitarian ones. Egalitarian societies have simple structures; they cannot be broken into smaller, still meaningful components. As such, the foundational unit of human politics, 'the *atomic* [unit] of social structure' (Morava 2005: 61, original emphasis) would appear to be categorical age. While simple egalitarian societies usually contain one such unit, complex politics contain several of these simple component units. Complexity theory posits that complex structures emerge from interactions between simple structures; in this case, as a result of political competition between simple age-structured units. One could, therefore, argue that, in a very small scale, the emerging political system in Air Bah has the basic qualities of a structurally complex society.[34]

Below, I present graphic representations of the model of equality and inequality outlined in this chapter. These figures have been developed based on the notion of 'self-similarity,' an attribute of fractals. In fractal structures subsystems and the whole are proportionally equivalent. Benoît Mandelbrot explains that 'a fractal object looks the same when examined from far away or nearby – it is self-similar' (1990). Emerging complex political systems have such a fractal structure, with simple structures embedded (nested) within them. Figures 7.1 to 7.4 show this relationship between simple, egalitarian social structures and complex hierarchical ones. This nested structure resembles a Sierpinski gasket, a simple fractal produced by breaking up a triangle. In Figure 7.1a, point A represents an elder, while points B1 and B2 are younger men. The arrows pointing from younger men to elders characterize their support and their aspiration to become elders themselves. In this relationship categorical age balances with the physical advantage of younger men, resulting in structural equality. The dependency relations implied in this structure, however, are only intact in small-scale societies with a

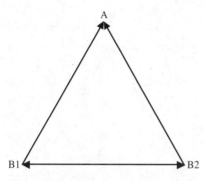

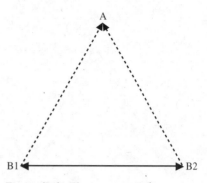

Figure 7.1a The structure of delayed-
return egalitarian society.

Figure 7.1b The structure of
immediate-return egalitarian society.

delayed-return system of production. In Figure 7.1b the broken lines
indicate younger men's limited support of elders and elders' limited
power over younger men in immediate-return societies. In Figures 7.1a
and 7.1b the horizontal arrows between younger men (B1 and (B2) indicate competition for the 'honours and power' of egalitarian politics, or
eldership.

Figures 7.2a and 7.2b depict the structure of emerging inequality.
They show that the attention of (certain) elders (A1 and A2) is now
focused primarily on each other (albeit, because complex structures
consist of embedded simple ones, they also continue to control younger
men). The horizontal arrow between elders illustrates their competition and the vertical arrows their self-aggrandizement. These figures
also show that the ambitions of younger men (B1, B2, B3, and B4) have
remained the same. They still, above all, aspire to become elders.[35] In
Figure 7.2a leadership competition develops in an egalitarian society
with a delayed-return system of production. In this setting competing
leaders are able to rely on younger men for support in self-aggrandizement. Figure 7.2b shows the situation when, as in Air Bah, leadership
competition develops in an egalitarian society with an immediate-
return system of production. In this case, as it was demonstrated in the
ethnography portion of this book, competing leaders would not be able
to rely on their younger male relatives in self-aggrandizement.

Figure 7.3 shows the embedded structures and self-similarity of an
emerging complex society. Point C represents the new 'goal' of political
competition. In Air Bah this was the position of village leader.[36]

This pattern of self-similarity may lead to increasing levels of social

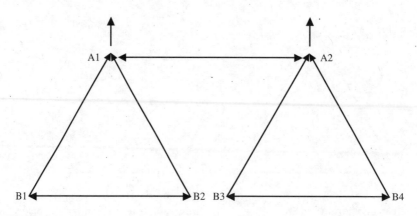

Figure 7.2a The structure of emerging inequality (in delayed-return society).

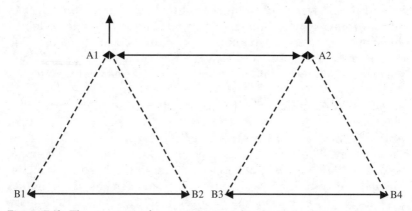

Figure 7.2b The structure of emerging inequality (in immediate-return society).

complexity. Figure 7.4 shows that at these levels complex structures will be embedded within other complex structures.

Regardless of scale, however, at all levels of complexity, non-egalitarian societies have an essentially similar structure that emerges through similar mechanisms (competition at the 'top' of the base structure). Although, in its initial phase, structural complexity evolves from simplicity, the structure of complex, hierarchical societies is nonetheless fundamentally different from the structure of simple egalitarian societies. Based on this analysis, it seems that equality, inequality, simplicity, and complexity are concepts future anthropologists should continue to

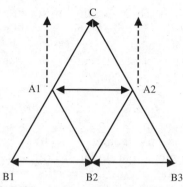

Figure 7.3 Embedded, self-similar structure of complex society.

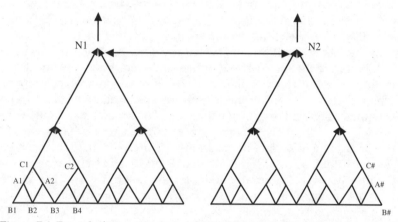

Figure 7.4 Fractal of increasingly complex embedded structures.

find useful, especially if consolidated with developing analytical devices, such as complexity theory. In the remainder of this chapter I will consider the implications of this argument for further studies on the evolution of egalitarian society.

Further Research on the Evolution of Egalitarian Society

In this chapter I developed a common framework for simple and complex societies by identifying a key component, categorical age, for explaining both. We cannot leave this discussion without considering one further implication. The preceding argument, especially the comparison of human and non-human political systems, strongly suggests that the emergence of categorical age relations, which is essentially the same as the emergence of egalitarian politics, ought to figure prominently in theories of human evolution.

There are two imaginable approaches to studying the evolution of egalitarian society. The first is to continue to try and model the organization of the first human societies of anatomically modern humans. However, if we insist on engaging in such an exercise, we ought to question the assumptions that undergird this approach. One of these is the insistence that the first human societies had a social organization similar to modern immediate-return hunter-gatherers. In spite of revisionist arguments that have cautioned against modelling prehistoric society on contemporary ones, this continues to be a common feature of theories of human evolution (e.g., Bogucki 1999; Boehm 1999; Rousseau 2006). However, this assumption, originating in Richard Lee's !Kung studies of the 1960s and which has since become the backbone of evolutionary theorizing about hunter-gatherers, may prove misleading. For one thing, research has shown time and again that a shift from a delayed-return to an immediate-return egalitarian society may be easier than a shift in the opposite direction. For another, we should consider whether it is likely that age-based authority would have evolved in a society where social organization and interpersonal relationships constantly undermine it. It follows that delayed-return egalitarian societies may be a more accurate model for the first human societies, one that is also better able to account for variations in pre-historic and historical social organization.

Instead of focusing on social organization, an even better strategy for the study of the evolution of egalitarian society would be to focus on understanding the evolution of age structure, its role in human evolution, and the shift from primate-like dominance to human-like dominance. This focus, although admittedly less straightforward, could open up new questions and new directions for the study of human evolution, providing the field with an entirely new angle in investigating the origins of human culture and social institutions. Understanding the emergence of human institutions has long been considered one of the most important tasks in evolutionary anthropology. As Robert Foley (2001) suggests, human evolutionary research most of all needs to find out how multi-male, multi-female groups also found among chimpanzees and bonobos could evolve into communities with a capacity for human-like institutions. It is not unreasonable to think that our institutions have their common root in this complementary structural relationship between younger men and elders and that, therefore, the evolution of our species most likely entailed a structural change of politics. The new political structure had emergent properties not evident in the properties of primate-like politics from which it developed. This recognition further requires us to pay more attention to the role of social processes and transformations in species evolution.[37]

In this newly emerging structure, elders retained their position by promoting cultural behaviour. This structural definition offers a new way to conceptualize culture as a fundamentally political concept. While, especially lately, we have produced a multitude of studies on how culture and power manifest themselves in different contexts, we have rarely considered the structural foundation of this relationship and what this structure implies for the character and development of human culture. However, we are unlikely to ever understand the relationship between culture and politics without considering this foundation and its implications in a human evolutionary framework. Conceiving of culture as an attribute of structural relationships deriving from categorical age should also contribute to the resolution of recent heated debates about differences between animal culture and human culture (McGrew 1998; Bosch 2003; Laland and Hoppitt 2003). Since the age structure of politics is unique to our species, human culture deriving from it is bound to be similarly unparalleled and distinct from social learning and other 'cultural' sources of intraspecific variation in animals.

This structural model of human culture would allow anthropologists to construct more plausible models of cultural evolution as well. One of the most important questions in evolutionary culture theory concerns cultural transmission and modification. The model outlined in this chapter could be fruitfully integrated with the ideas developed in this field, for instance, by William Durham who, in *Coevolution: Genes, Culture, and Human Diversity* (1991), inquires into the role of power structures in processes of cultural transmission. In considering the role of decision-making, including the imposed (or negotiated) decisions of 'powerful individuals or groups,' he begins to bring social structure and asymmetrical power relations into contemplating the evolutionary dynamics of cultural change (ibid.: 198). The ideas in this chapter are well suited to further inquiries in the same vein.

Finally, an investigation into the evolution of categorical age could also help us understand its relationship to cognitive-behavioural and organizational changes that accompany it.[38] Particularly important and interesting would be to examine the co-evolution of political structures and human conceptual mechanisms. Such an inquiry would allow us to discover the way political processes, the shift from physical to cognitive/cultural dominance displays, and cognitive processes, the development of conceptual language and categorical thought, co-evolved and reinforced each other in human evolution. A further examination of the relationship between complementary age roles and binary categories could also breathe new life into the Lévi-Straussian project, and address the common postmodern criticism of Lévi-Straussian structural analysis that it is sterile and unconcerned with power relations.

There is one important caveat to the research programs outlined here. They can only be executed through increased collaboration between the subfields of anthropology. Only by focusing equally on the linguistic, biological, and social aspects of this structural change from physical dominance to cultural dominance can we hope to understand our species. This collaboration, in turn, can only be established if we, representatives of the different subfields, recognize and appreciate the common interests, questions, and problems concerning the humanity we all share. Advocating a processual sense of holism, Marvin Harris suggests:

> Anthropology does not seek holistic perspectives as an end in itself. Rather, anthropologists use that perspective because it has been found to be crucial for solving the major riddles of human existence. In broadest terms, these riddles have to do with the origins and spread of hominids; the origins and spread of *Homo sapiens*; the causes and effects of human biological polymorphism; the origin of human linguistic capacity and the origins and spread of human languages; the emergence of human consciousness; the origin of human society and culture; and the causes of the divergent and convergent evolution of human sociocultural systems. (1997: 25–6)

Complexity theory may prove to be just the tool to integrate these problems disjointed by subdisciplinary boundaries. Perhaps complexity theory even has a potential to rekindle the holistic spirit in anthropology and a new excitement about our very oldest questions and interests.

Language Notes and Glossary

Pronunciation Guide

In this work, Lanoh words have been transcribed by a near-phonemic, IPA-derived system of orthography currently used in Mon-Khmer linguistics. For a more complete description of this system see Benjamin (1985c, 1986a). The following guide supplies approximate English equivalents to different phonemes occurring in Lanoh.

Vowels
i p<u>i</u>t
e h<u>a</u>te
ɛ g<u>e</u>t
ə butt<u>er</u>
a h<u>a</u>t
u l<u>oo</u>t
o h<u>o</u>le
ɔ f<u>o</u>rt
ʉ f<u>oo</u>t (with lips rounded), or Scottish h<u>u</u>s ('house')

Consonants
k s<u>k</u>ip
c <u>ch</u>urch
ɲ o<u>ni</u>on
ŋ si<u>ng</u>er
ʔ glottal stop[1]

---

1 Ashby suggests that with glottal stop, 'what we hear is actually a brief interval of silence, with a characteristic abrupt termination of the proceeding speech sound and a similarly abrupt onset of whatever sound follows' (1995: 17).

Lanoh and Malay Glossary, as well as Acronyms[2]

adat	custom, tradition (M.)
batin, penghulu	village head, headman (M.)
atap	*Nipa fruticans.*, roofing, thatch
baka?	family, relatives
bayaŋ	thing, property
bə?ɛt	good, beautiful, happy
bətay	*petai (Parkia speciosa)*
bisat	child's spouse's parent (in-laws)
bisey	share (e.g., food)
blaw	blowpipe
bood	bored, 'fed up'
boy	monkey
cancaŋ	aphrodisiac root; probably from *kencang* ('to erect,' M.)
COAC	Center for Orang Asli Concerns
cənɔy	invisible, spirit
cənoy	younger brother-in-law; younger brother of wife/husband; younger sister's husband
Dakwah	Muslim missionary activity
datok	honorary title (M.)
dayah	blood
deŋ	house
deŋ lɛ?loy/walwa?	traditional Lanoh lean-to shelter
dusun	orchard (M.)
Emergency	Civil war with communist insurgents (1948–1960)
FELCRA	Federal Land Consolidation and Rehabilitation Authority
FELDA	Federal Land Development Authority
gaharu	*Aquilaria spp.* eaglewood, aloewood; inner part of tree trunk; used in perfume manufacture
gɔs	alive

---

2 This list is not exhaustive, but it contains the most commonly occurring terms in the text. Throughout the text, we can assume that non-English words are in Lanoh, unless otherwise specified. Malay words are identified with in abbreviation, e.g., *semangat* ('soul,' M.).

gob	outsider, mostly Malay in most Orang Asli languages
gotong royong	community work (M.)
gutta percha	*Dichopsis gutta*, indigenous rubber
ʔɔŋ	drink, water, river (*ʔɔŋ bluum*, Perak River)
ʔɔg	give
Haji	Muslim holy man, who has been on the *Haj*, the religious pilgrimage to Mecca
halal	permissible according to Muslim rule
haram	forbidden by Muslim religious law
humaʔ	dry paddy field
jagoʔ	corn
jahad	evil, bad (*jahat*, M.)
jampiʔ	spell, incantation
jənampiʔ	medicine man
JHEOA	Jabatan Hal Ehwal Orang Asli (Department of Orang Asli Affairs)
kampuʔ	village (kampung, M.)
kancɔʔ	grandchild
kenduri	communal feast (M.)
kədɔy	wife
kəloŋ	centre, in, inside
kənuyiʔ	feast (kenduri, M.)
kəɲɛd	stingy
kuy	head, language, voice, word, say, decide
Merdeka	Malaysia's Independence (1957)
mənalɛy	ceremonial platform
mənihɛy	generous, person who likes to share
mənuwaʔ	discussion
mənwaʔ	word(s), speak, talk
mɔy	other, different (*lain*, M.)
napag	wild boar
nɔh, nanɔh	here, this (word from which exonym, 'Lanoh,' i.e., 'nanɔh' derives)
Orang Asli	Indigenous Peoples of Malaysia
panoʔ	shaman's ceremonial hut (*bumbun*, M.)
parang	cleaver, chopper (M.)
pənloj (sewang)	ceremonial session
petai	*Parkia speciosa*. Bean species with medicinal qualities

*ple*ʔ	Temiar (e.g., *kuy ple*ʔ, 'Temiar language')
POASM	Persatuan Orang Asli Semenanjung Malaysia (Peninsular Malaysia Orang Asli Association)
Polis Hutan	Forest Police
raja	king, queen, prince (M.)
RELA	People's Voluntary Corporation Malaysia
ringgit (RM)	Malaysian currency
roway	soul
*saka*ʔ	original (*asal*, M.)
Senoi Praaq	Orang Asli paramilitary force, under the Police Field Force
*səhɛlo*ʔ	blowpipe (verb; hunt with a blowpipe)
səlantap	taboo
*səma*ʔ	people (Orang, M.; ethnonym: Lanoh (person) *səma*ʔ *bluum*)
*səma*ʔ *hala*ʔ	shaman
sənyoŋ	cave
sumpit, sumpitan	blowpipe (M.)
surau	mosque, Muslim prayer-hall (M.)
təgtɛɛg	marry, sleep together
təluy	banana
*tiyɔ*ʔ	chest pain
towkay	(mostly Chinese) middleman
tulah	sin (*dosa*, M.)
ustad	Muslim religious teacher
*ya*ʔ	grandmother, grandparent's female sibling, god (*pɛ*ʔ also means god)
yəl, yəl gɔs	spirit, ghost, live ghost
yəway (*roway*)	soul (e.g., *yəway səma*ʔ *kəsbəs*, 'soul of the dead')

Notes

1 Equality, Inequality, and Changing Hunter-Gatherers

1 It is customary to divide Orang Asli peoples into three main sub-catego-
ries, according to linguistic, and, instead of racial, increasingly ecological
criteria: (1) Semang (Kensiu, Kintak, Jahai, Lanoh, Mendrik, and Batek)
and Semaq Beri foragers; (2) Upland and Lowland Senoi (Temiar, Semai,
Jah Hut, Mah Meri, Chewong, Temok, and Semelai); and (3) Austronesian-
speaking farmers (Temuan and Jakun) and sea nomads (Orang Laut and
Orang Seletar) (Walker 1995). The older literature referred to Semang as
'Negritos,' and indigenous Austronesian speakers as 'Proto-Malays.' As
it has been pointed out (e.g., by K.L. Endicott 1979; K.M. Endicott 1979;
Nicholas 2000; and Gomes 2007), the term 'Semang' has a pejorative connotation, and, throughout this study, it is used to indicate a cultural pattern (Benjamin 1985a, 1985b, 1985c, 2003), not an ethnic group.
2 Evans, an early researcher of Lanoh, noted this similarity with other
Semang. He remarked that Lanoh he encountered were 'speakers of what
is termed a Sakai dialect, as against the "Negrito dialects" of other groups,
though in blood they are pretty pure Negritos, as also in culture' (1937:
26–7).
3 Scholars have linked the development of distinct Semang and Senoi
lifestyles to specialization following the arrival of Austronesian populations in the region about 2,000 years ago. Robert K. Dentan (1989: 11)
suggests that this event signalled an increase in slave raiding, to which
indigenous populations developed different responses. The ancestors of
Senoi withdrew into the interior hills, consciously maintaining a distance
between Malays and themselves by making their settlements inaccessible to Malays, employing devices such as man-traps, and fighting back.

Thus, they have become known as the 'wild' races (K.M. Endicott 1983: 229, 233). The ancestors of Semang, on the contrary, combined a 'non-shy readiness to have dealings with outsiders' with a tactic of '[pulling] out at a moment's notice and [moving] on' (Benjamin 1985a: 241; also K.M. Endicott 1983: 224–8). It must also be noted that Senoi populations differ in the degree to which they are isolated. For instance, east Semai are more isolated, while west Semai often live closer to Malay and Chinese settlements (Dentan 1968).

4 One of the Semang groups, the Batek, is one of Woodburn's (1982) examples of hunter-gatherers with an immediate-return system of production. He describes Batek as foragers who 'positively value movement,' who have extremely low population densities, and most importantly, who appear to be practically self-sufficient (1980: 99–100; 1982: 433).

5 Anthropologists often differentiate between two types of egalitarianism: 'egalitarianism of opportunity' and 'egalitarianism of outcome.' According to David Riches, 'egalitarianism of opportunity' is where 'initial equivalent access to resources and power is stipulated as the prerequisite for people's individual transactions; but these transactions will lead to inequalities' (2000: 670). 'Egalitarianism of outcome,' on the contrary, refers to situations 'whereby social equivalence is stipulated as the result desired from individual transactions' (ibid.). According to several theorists, for instance, Woodburn, the egalitarianism of hunter-gatherers corresponds to this latter form. That is, people in these societies 'positively value social equality and maintain some practices that favour it' (Endicott and Endicott 2008: 7; see also Widlok 2005).

6 Lanoh in Air Bah today still maintain such contact with Malay villagers in Kampung Sawa and Gelok, as well as with the Chinese villagers of Air Kala.

7 The relative isolation of Senoi groups is also indicated by their linguistic developments. According to Geoffrey Benjamin, '[Temiar were] buffered from linguistic contact with Malay by the Aslian languages that surrounded it' (2003: 12).

8 While realizing that changing names is not always sufficient to protect the identity of sources, I nonetheless opted for using pseudonyms in most cases throughout this book.

9 This historical relationship between Lanoh and Temiar will be explored in the next chapter.

10 The name 'Lanoh' is probably a derivative of the Temiar expression, 'those who say *noh* for "here"' (Benjamin 1980: 32). Occasionally, Schebesta also refers to Lanoh as '*Sabubn*' (1929). My experience in trying to trace this

latter name among Lanoh in Air Bah and Tawai has been similar to that of Evans. He writes: 'Schebesta marks all the Perak Valley from Leng-gong to Grik as being occupied by the *Sabubn*. I have absolutely (1935 and previously) failed to trace the name among the Negritos of Lenggong and Kuala Kenering, but I got ample confirmation for the two names for the Lenggong people that I have mentioned above' (1937: 26–7). Evans also recalls that Lanoh of Lenggong suggested that *sabubn* meant 'black.' Evans inferred that Schebesta could not have heard the name '*Sabubn*' from Lanoh, but from Jahai or Temiar (1937: 26–7).

11 The name of the Perak River in Lanoh is *ʔɔŋ bluum*, with *ʔɔŋ* meaning 'water' or 'river.'

12 Even today, the Lanoh population does not exceed two hundred individu-als. The population of Air Bah in January 1998 was 125. There are also a few Lanoh individuals living in the villages of Tawai, Cenawi, Bukit Sapi, Baling, Kroh, and Dala. These people, as a rule, moved into these villages after marriage.

13 This corresponds to the numbers recorded by Karen Endicott (1992: 282), who describes the composition of Batek forest camps as containing five to eight nuclear families, with an average camp population of thirty-four.

14 Notable exceptions are small-scale research projects by Shuichi Nagata, and, later, Anthony Walker and their students. Most of these student reports were circulated as Provisional Papers by the Universiti Sains Malaysia, School of Comparative Social Sciences, Social Anthropology Section (e.g., Ahmad Ezanee bin Mansor 1972; Mohd. Razha b. Hj. Abd. Rashid, Syed Jamal Jaafar, and Tan Chee Beng 1973; Abdul Razak Yaa-cob 1974). Nonetheless, in spite of early interest in 'Negritos' (Skeat and Blagden 1906; Evans 1923, 1924, 1927a, 1927b, 1937; Schebesta 1929, 1952, 1954, 1957), later ethnographic work tended to focus more on horticultur-ist Senoi than on hunters and gatherers (e.g., Benjamin 1967, 1968, 1987; Dentan 1965, 1970, 1978, 1983; Gomes 1986; Roseman 1987, 1991; Juli 1990; Giano 1990; Jennings 1995). Notable exceptions are the Batek, who have been extensively studied by Karen Endicott (1979, 1981, 1984, 1992) and Kirk Endicott (1969, 1974, 1979, 1984, 1988, 1995), and more recently, by Lye Tuck-Po (1998, 2005).

15 Shortly after my arrival, I began taping life history interviews both in Air Bah and during visits to other, nearby Orang Asli communities with strong ties to the village. These interviews were mostly unstructured and informal. In Air Bah they were conducted by inviting people to my house and simply asking them to tell stories about their past, their childhood – anything they remembered and chose to share with me. If the sitting

was particularly successful and the informant appeared to be willing to elaborate on certain themes, these visits were repeated on other occasions. The stories were transcribed and analysed at a later date. The context of the interviews was initiated by Lanoh themselves. Early in the fieldwork, they suggested that talking to everyone on an individual basis would be the best way of getting to know people.

16 Life histories also helped me trace patterns of current social interactions. When interviewed regarding contemporary events, Lanoh are generally reluctant in expressing opinions about interpersonal relations directly. Ever suspicious, they are inclined to be protective and secretive, especially about economic information. Since accusations of being a 'spy' or informant are easily allotted, people tend to be cautious in expressing their opinions of each other's attitudes and actions. However, in life history interviews, people were relieved to talk about themselves, because they felt they owned their life story. As well, they consider past events, because they are no longer relevant, 'easy' topics. Yet, indirectly, these life history interviews also elicited attitudes towards social change, contemporary events, and group dynamics in the present.

17 Volumes by Dentan et al. (1997), Jumper (1997, 1999), and Colin Nicholas (2000) review the problems of Orang Asli in Peninsular Malaysia and their struggle for self-determination.

18 Some Lanoh did not return to the neighbourhood of Air Bah, but instead moved to other resettlement villages like Bukit Sapi, Tawai, Cenawi, and Kampung Dala.

19 The village is about two hours walking distance from the main road and it takes about twenty minutes to reach the nearest water source, the river. Air Bah was first occupied in the 1960s and was considered to be a temporary paddy-planting site from which people planned to move on after the paddy season. In the late 1970s, elders of the time evidently decided to stay, because the Jabatan Hal Ehwal Orang Asli (JHEOA) promised land to those who become sedentary. At that time, twenty-five Lanoh families, who stayed in Air Bah, received fifty acres of land (two acres per family).

20 These proselytizers are members of a *Dakwah* group, a religious Islamic group from Sebarang Prai, Penang. They visit Air Bah twice a month 'to make sure that people follow the right way.'

21 Today, as in the past, people completely recycle materials in Air Bah primarily because they cannot be wasteful. Paper is used to start fires and organic material is fed to chicken, cats, and dogs. Plastic and metal are applied to reinforce blowpipes or built into house furniture. Plastic bottles are collected and used for carrying water or as drinking cups. As well,

Lanoh rarely buy ready-made tools. Instead, store-bought blades are fitted with bamboo handles.

22 Often more expensive commercial goods, such as television sets and motorcycles are purchased on lottery winnings. Among the four television sets and three motorcycles in Air Bah, one television set and one motorcycle were obtained this way.

23 The amount of debt was obtained in conversation with the Indian vendor.

24 Out of the 125 regular residents of Air Bah in January, 1998, six (7.5%) were older than 50 years, and seventy-two (58%) were younger than 20. In comparison, Karen Endicott describes the composition of Batek forest camps as containing five to eight nuclear families, with an average camp population of thirty-four. This population consists of eleven men, nine women, and fourteen children below the age of 15 (1992: 282).

25 Middle-aged (35- to 50-year-old) couples in Air Bah today have between six and eight children (6.66 on average). The increase in the number of children per family from three to five to six to ten after sedentism is also likely to be because of higher infant survival rates as a result of improved medical care. While not so long ago administering medical care to people in Air Bah was difficult because people would run off to the forest, nowadays health care in Air Bah includes regular monthly checkups of infants and pregnant women, as well as malaria tests. Yet, Lanoh in Air Bah still give birth in the village with the help of Lanoh midwives. Moreover, while official procedure states that parents of sick children are supposed to inform the headman who, in turn, is supposed to contact the JHEOA so that the child can be taken to a hospital, in practice, this never happens. As well, Gomes provides an alternative explanation for why women have more children in resettlement villages. He suggests that while the incidence of some diseases has declined, other illnesses, especially tuberculosis, respiratory diseases, and malnutrition are still common (2007: 158–9; also see Endicott and Dentan 2004: 36), and that between 1978 and 1998 the birthrate among resettled Menraq increased to compensate for increased mortality rates (Gomes 2007: 88). Finally, it must also be noted that Temiar have an impact on this increased family size in Air Bah. Temiar tend to have more children per family than Lanoh, and families with the largest number of children in the village are those with a Temiar parent. In one such family, with a Temiar father, there were eleven unmarried children, four of whom were raised by the wife's childless sister.

26 Parents in Air Bah have mixed feelings about sending their children to school. Although they miss them and worry about the religious pressure placed on them in school, they also welcome the government subsidy for

schoolchildren, usually in the form of allowances for clothing, books, and meals. Yet, regardless of parents' preference, it is unheard of for either parents or the government to pressure children to attend school. Children decide whether to attend school depending on whether their friends or older siblings would be there as well.

27 Karen Endicott describes the forest camps of Batek hunter-gatherers as follows: 'Families erect lean-tos at random locations, rarely more than a few yards from each other. These shelters are open on three sides, thus exposing the activities of camp members to the full view of everyone else in camp … [In these camps,] family members sleep, cook, eat, store their goods, relax, and do much of their work and childcare in and immediately in front of the lean-to' (1992: 283).

28 For discussions of emerging social inequality among hunter-gatherers elsewhere see, e.g., Meillassoux (1973: 197, in Rowley-Conwy 2001: 55–6); Hitchcock (1982: 255–6); Cashdan (1987); Altman and Peterson (1988); Howell (1983); and Gomes (2007).

29 For discussions of different forms of inequality see, e.g., Tilly (2001a) or Verdery (2001).

30 Slamet-Velsink similarly suggests that ethnographic material is useful in the 'elucidation of certain aspects of prehistoric cultures and the processes of stratification and state formation which must have taken place in prehistoric societies, as long as suggestions are made with the necessary caution and reserve' (1995: 4).

31 For the role of demographic change and sedentism in theories of social differentiation see, e.g., Boserup (1965, 1981); Kuyit and Morris (2002: 363); Feinman (1995: 274); Hayden (1995: 15–16, 23); Rousseau (2006: 8, 29, 31).

32 Marcus (2008: 253) also comments on the difficulty for archaeologists to incorporate agency in their studies.

33 Models of inequality developed by psychologists since the 1960s also support integration theory. Especially influential has been Emerson's (1962) power-dependence model, which has since been developed by others (Molm 1985: 812; Das and Cotton 1988). This model emphasizes the link between inequality and interpersonal dependence resulting in differential power relations between people.

34 The debate, whether individualism or social integration is responsible for social inequality, has a long history in Western political thought. Dumont, for instance, just as Tocqueville before him, associates equality with individualism. Contrasting *homo hierarchicus* and *homo aequalis*, he states that 'hierarchy is the social expression of … "holism," and equality … of individualism' (in Béteille 1986: 123). Against this, Béteille argues that

'individualism, when combined with a high value on achievement, creates and legitimizes a structure of unequal rewards' (1983: 9). On the other hand, an equally strong tradition associates individualism with inequality, and researchers in hunter-gatherer studies often attribute egalitarian social relations in these groups to individual autonomy. For instance, in arguing women's autonomy among egalitarian hunter-gatherers, Karen Endicott writes that, in these groups, 'adults of both sexes are free to decide their own movements, activities, and relationships; among adults no individual holds authority over others; and neither group has power through economic, religious, or social advantage' (1992: 282).

35 Whether anthropologists envision the process of social evolution as a transition from 'hunter-gatherers' to 'farmers' (Childe 1936), from 'bands' or family-level organizations to 'tribes' or local group organizations (Service 1962; Johnson and Earle 1987), from 'head man' to 'big man' (Sahlins 1963; Earle 1978), or finally, from 'immediate' to 'delayed-return' systems (Woodburn 1982), initial transformation in most cases includes social integration.

36 The study forming the basis of this book consisted of a year-long period of ethnographic fieldwork conducted primarily in the main Lanoh resettlement village of Air Bah. My fieldwork in Air Bah lasted altogether for fourteen months, between December 1997 and January 1999. Air Bah, my main fieldwork site, is located about forty-five kilometres south of the district centre of Ulu Perak, Grik. I also spent time in another Orang Asli village with a predominantly Lanoh population, Tawai, located about sixteen kilometres south of Grik. Originally a Temiar village just north of the Lanoh area, Tawai seems to have been 'overtaken' by Lanoh through marriage (M. 'Orang Lanoh dengan kahwin Orang Tawai lama-lama Orang Tawai jadi macam Orang Lanoh. Lama-lama Orang Lanoh ambil kuasa Orang Tawai. Macam itu Tawai jadi Lanoh'). Tawai not only reminded people in Air Bah of villages of the old days in terms of population size and village structure, but also in terms of patterns of activities. In 1998, for reasons discussed later, men in Tawai were more involved in forest collecting than were men in Air Bah. As a result, they often left, and for longer periods, than men in Air Bah. When trying to illustrate past lifestyle, people often brought up Tawai as an example. Tawai no longer exists; due to frequent conflicts with nearby Malay villagers, its inhabitants were transferred to Air Bah in 2000. In 1998 people from Air Bah maintained extremely close relationships with those in Tawai, many of whom were originally from Air Bah. In analysing processes of transition among newly sedentary hunters and gatherers, the greatest difficulty lies in the circumstances of sedentism (involuntary,

prompted by force, development, and modernization). In Tawai, although history, ethnic background, social organization, and the circumstances of sedentism were similar to those in Air Bah, people's responses to change were often significantly different. Thus, throughout my research, I benefited considerably from comparing events and processes in these two settings. Like most ethnographic research in anthropology, mine also centred on participant observation, which I supplemented with demographic, household, and genealogical surveys during the first part of my fieldwork. Although my research was mostly conducted in Malay, which most Lanoh speak fluently, in an effort to learn Lanoh, throughout the fieldwork, I compiled a vocabulary list.

37 Time allocation by villagers in Air Bah was observed and recorded during six consecutive months, beginning in June 1998 and ending in December 1998. Although observing a full-year economic cycle would have been desirable, because of time restrictions, I was unable to complete a full year. The study, which recorded the activities of randomly selected individuals at randomly selected times, was executed in the following manner. I randomly selected nine days of each month. In each of these days, I randomly selected five hours out of the fourteen daytime hours (from 8 a.m. to 9 p.m.) for observation. During each of these hours, I observed the activities of five individuals, whom I had randomly selected out of a pool of sixty-three. This method resulted in information about twenty-five individuals in each such day. The sample of sixty-three included adult (aged 13 years or older) inhabitants of Air Bah. When I visited the individuals selected for a particular hour, I recorded their activity, and the location and social context in which the activity occurred. I made every effort to carry out the study of time-allocation in an unobtrusive manner, as part of my everyday checking in with people. Admittedly, it was only possible to directly record observations of people who happened to be in the village. With regard to the activities of people outside the village, I relied on information from family and neighbours. In later months, I employed two villagers as research assistants to perform these surveys when I was outside the village. I had chosen this solution when faced with the possibility that, due to my absence from the village, there would be a gap in the data. Netting et al. summarize the advantages of involving indigenous assistants in ethnographic surveys: '[Local enumerators] can conduct quite extensive interviews using their own linguistic skills, rapport, and fund of cultural knowledge, thereby reaching a broader cross-section of the population than the investigator could.' (1995: 61). In my study of time allocation in Air Bah, contributions by local assistants have proven similarly invaluable.

Unmarried but middle-aged, they were in a position to visit most people in the community less obtrusively than I could. Moreover, the background information they possessed about people's whereabouts and activities produced especially detailed and sensitive data. Despite the time limit, this record keeping resulted in 1,270 observations, allowing for valid inferences about a range of phenomena pertinent to my research topic. Because of the large enough number of observations, the survey allowed for inferences about the sexual and age division of labour in Air Bah (percentages of time were calculated by dividing the number of observations of a given activity by the total number of observations). There were also sufficient numbers of observations to support claims about time spent inside and outside the village by men and women. Even more importantly, this systematic observation ensured that even individuals who were less visible were represented in fieldnotes. Yet, perhaps most importantly, time allocation helped me recognize patterns of association, directing my attention to aspects of field data that I might have otherwise overlooked. They not only highlighted the relative strength, or permeability, of different social units, but also revealed emerging inequalities within and between these units. Thus, the study of time allocation in Air Bah has proven invaluable in supplementing qualitative data and prompting analysis.

38 *Lɛ?loy* in Lanoh means 'good, appropriate, or proper,' as in *bʉd lɛ?loy*, 'good and warm.'

39 The Temiar-style dwellings are not longhouses, but nuclear family-sized, and in 1998, there were five of them in Air Bah.

40 For instance, in 1998, younger male members of an extended family cluster, who had just moved back from Sumpitan where they had spent two sessions planting paddy and collecting forest products, occupied one wooden house, around which their parents and two married sisters erected a semi-circle of lean-to shelters each with its own separate hearth.

41 In the sedentary village, the initial matrilocal residence Lanoh practised in the past has become permanent.

42 In one household, for instance, a widow was raising two of her widowed nephew's children, as well as two of her uncle's teenage children. Also affiliated with this household were three unmarried men: the widow's young son, the above-mentioned nephew and father of one set of the children, as well as a third, divorced nephew. While these men lived in a separate 'bachelor's house' on the opposite side of the road, they regularly contributed to the widow's household. She, in turn, provided them with meals and clean clothes.

43 It must be also noted that, in spite of an emphasis on individual autonomy

among mobile hunter-gatherers, there has been considerable confusion regarding the role of individual autonomy versus communality in maintaining equality among these hunter-gatherers. This confusion regarding the individualism and communalism of hunter-gatherers is evident not only in the notions of 'communal mode' and 'primitive communism,' but also in different conceptions of 'egalitarian sharing' (Woodburn 1982; Kaplan and Hill 1985; Testart 1989: 4; Lee 1990: 245; Hastorf 1990; Knauft 1991: 395; Kent 1993: 480; Gibson 2005). One of the central concepts in theories of equality is that, among egalitarian hunter-gatherers, cooperation, collectivism, and sharing promote 'distributive justice' (Béteille 1986) by reducing individual competition for food. Kent expresses this relationship between egalitarianism, communalism, and sharing by stating that 'egalitarianism is necessary for the cohesiveness ... and sharing is necessary for egalitarianism' (1993: 503). Richard Lee similarly writes: 'Despite our seeming adaptation to life in hierarchical societies, there are signs that humankind retains a deep-rooted egalitarianism, a deep-rooted commitment to the norm of reciprocity, a deep-rooted desire for what Victor Turner has called communitas, the sense of community' (1990: 245). Thus, on the one hand, people in mobile egalitarian hunter-gatherer societies are supposed to manifest a 'love of autonomy,' while, on the other hand, they are thought to possess a readiness to sacrifice this autonomy to the interests of the group. This contradiction has rarely been recognized or addressed in hunter-gatherer studies. While Woodburn claims, for instance, that the extreme equality of immediate-return hunter-gatherers is due to an absence of 'dependence on specific others,' he also suggests that meat sharing is imposed on hunters by the community (1982: 439, 441).

44 Using the guidelines provided by Gladwin (1989), I collected complete data about three subsistence decisions: (1) why fourteen men participated in a planting contract while others opted for forest collecting; (2) why certain men planted more hill paddy than they and their family consumed while others planted just for subsistence, or even less; and (3) why certain women participated in a ten-day contract job away from the village while others stayed behind? Apart from these completed inquiries, I also started and later aborted additional lines of inquiry, such as the decision to join the Persatuan Orang Asli Semenanjung Malaysia (Peninsular Malaysia Orang Asli Association or POASM) or reasons for listening to 'Radio 7,' the Orang Asli radio program. These topics were later abandoned because they proved less revealing than originally anticipated. Towards the end of the fieldwork, I also tentatively initiated a study of women's decisions concerning their use of contraceptive/fertility medicine, but because of

a lack of time, as well as the women's unwillingness to discuss topics of a sexual nature, this inquiry was subsequently abandoned. Nonetheless, interviews were later included in fieldnotes and were analysed as such. These interviews, even on those topics that were later abandoned, revealed unexpected, often surprising, reasons for people's actions in Air Bah. Most importantly, they taught me about the way Lanoh ordered their values and priorities.

45 It must be also emphasized, however, that group discussions do not necessarily imply a consensus in decision-making. While Lanoh men frequently came together for discussions, as they had done in pre-resettlement times, they rarely reached consensus as a result of these gatherings, and at the end, most often than not, everyone went on to carry out his own individual plans.

2 Interethnic Trade and the Social Organization of Pre-resettlement Lanoh

1 In a 1985 paper, Benjamin makes several further references to Lanoh sedentism. For instance, he says that 'recent Semang populations,' Lanoh and Batek Nong, 'have usually been reported as living in semipermanent villages' (1985a: 262). He suggests that Lanoh and Mendriq are more sedentary than other Semang and that Lanoh 'have been fairly sedentary for some time' (ibid.: 244). In an unpublished paper, he further notes that Lanoh 'have long been farily sedentary part-farmers along the banks and major tributaries of the accessible Perak River between Lenggong and Grik, which is an area of quite dense peasant Malay settlement' (1980: 31).

2 This lack of boundaries between hunters and farmers is also supported by the fact that, in Malaysia, horticulturist Senoi regularly substitute subsistence farming with hunting.

3 Benjamin summarizes the most important factors in the emergence of these distinct cultural patterns as follows: (1) new external influences (trade, civilization centres); (2) increasing commitment to one of three modes of subsistence (foraging, horticulture, forest collecting); and (3) dissimilation from neighbouring cultures 'to maximize the advantages of following complementary environmental orientations' (1985a: 239). A shifting emphasis on different aspects of kinship rules and affiliations has also resulted in distinct social organizations of the three cultural patterns of the peninsula. For a comparison of indigenous cultural patterns of Peninsular Malaysia see, e.g., Benjamin (1986b: 9).

4 According to Benjamin, these 'mixed' cultures developed because, living at the boundaries of distinct subsistence modes (foraging, horticulture,

and forest collecting), they faced 'too many attractions' (1980: 8; 1986b: 31). As a consequence, Northern Semang are more nomadic, while Southern Semang (Batek Nong and Lanoh) retained a more generalized Hoabinhian attitude (Benjamin 1985a: 259, 262).

5 'Some 80,000 [of about 133,000] Orang Asli speak Aslian languages; the remainder speak Malay dialects' (Benjamin 2004: 47).

6 The Aslian subfamily is divided into the Northern Aslian (or Jahaic), Central Aslian (or Senoic), and Southern Aslian (or Semelaic) subgroups (Benjamin 2004: 46). In 1906 Blagden separated the subfamily into Northern Sakai (Temiar, Lanoh), Central Sakai (Semai), Southern Sakai (May Meri, Semelai, Temoq), and Eastern Sakai (Semaq Beri) speakers (in Benjamin 1976: 39).

7 According to Benjamin (1986b: 33), glottochronological evidence suggests that the Temiar-Lanoh language split occurred between 2300 BP and 2030 BP

8 Today Lanoh, as well as other northern Orang Asli, continue to use Temiar as a lingua franca. Temiar is also the language of the indigenous radio broadcasts (Benjamin 2003: 12 and 2004).

9 In this respect, Benjamin indicates that there is a difference even between Lanoh subdivisions. He suggests that *sabɯm*, those who live closer to Temiar, maintain that marriage is possible between siblings-in-law – yet no joking or avoidance is tolerated. Contrary to *sabɯm, sɜmnam* insist on joking between siblings-in-law (1980: 32).

10 Lanoh define siblings as 'those from the same hearth.' This category, however, also often includes first and second cousins, and is important for determining potential marriage partners, as those from the same hearth cannot marry each other.

11 Another expression sometimes used for *yaʔ* is *pɛʔ* – for instance, Lanoh refer to the village of the dead as *kampuʔ pɛʔ*.

12 Lanoh perform two types of rituals to dispel thunder. The first method involves cutting one's lower leg and collecting blood in a cup, which is then mixed with water. Following this, one takes a bamboo rod, digs a pit in the ground, mixes in the blood-water concoction, bangs it hard with the rod, throws a little towards the sky, and covers the pit. The second, communal, method involves collecting a piece of hair from everyone present and, using the roots of a *kasəy* tree (in Lanoh; *cinuus*, in Temiar), working the hair into a ball. The ball is smolked over a fire and, as the smoke goes up to the sky, hit with a rod. Lanoh further draw blood to treat *tiyɔʔ* (chest pain) caused by breaking menstruation taboos. The blood is collected in a cup and a *jampiʔ* (incantation) is recited. The blood is then rubbed on the chest and neck and some of it is drunk.

13 Evans, for instance, records that two groups of Negritos (Semang), Lanoh of Kuala Kenering-Lenggong, and the 'Menik Semnam' of the Grik area, speak a Senoi language. He further notes that those in the Girk area live nearest to Pleh, 'the half-breed Negrito-Sakai of the Upper Perak hills' (1937: 283). Earlier, however, Wilkinson referred to both of these groups as 'Sakai Jeram' (1926: 13). Benjamin classifies Lanoh into four subgroups: Semnam, Lanoh Jengjeng, Lanoh Yir, and Sabum (1976: 57, in Howell 1984: 6). My own attempt to repeat this exercise produced the same uncertain results. People I consulted about this matter in Air Bah and elsewhere were unable to recall the meaning of any of these different names.

14 However, as a result of social change, regroupment, and resettlement, these subdivisions may have gained new, albeit considerably different, significance, particularly for the inhabitants of Air Bah. These developments will be discussed in Chapter 4.

15 Benjamin contradicts this claim by suggesting that there are, indeed, differences in the degree to which people observe avoidance relations in different Lanoh subdivisions. He suggests, for instance, that *sabɨm*, who live closer to Senoi Temiar, maintain that marriage is possible between siblings-in-law. At the same time, they do not have either avoidance or joking relationships. According to Benjamin contrary to *sabɨm*, *səmnam* insist on a joking relationship between siblings-in-law (1980: 32). I was only able to collect data among Lanoh *jəram*, people in Air Bah, on this topic. As suggested earlier, people there maintain that in the past marriage between pairs of siblings was frequent, that it was almost the norm, and village demographics reinforce this observation. A further difference Benjamin has noted between dialect groups is in the rate of borrowing from Malay. He contrasts the loan rate of *səmnam* from Malay (10) with that of *sabɨm* and Lanoh (5) versus Temiar (2) (2003: 13). These loan rates indicate the dialect groups' distance from agricultural populations and their frequency of interactions with them.

16 For evidence of Semang farming, see Skeat and Blagden (1966 [1906]: 178–9), Schebesta (1929: 273), Evans (1937: 53, 55, 58, 61), Lye (2005), and Nagata (personal communication).

17 *Petai*, a bean species with medical properties, is much sought after by Orang Asli, as well as outsiders. In its season, *petai* is one of the main sources of income for Lanoh.

18 Semang villages today also contain individuals from different linguistic groups because of resettlement schemes (Nagata, personal communication).

19 As Benjamin notes, 'Lanohs are usually considered to be somatically "Negritos," like other Semang' (2003: 10).

20 In the early twentieth century, Schebesta recorded a sample of a dialect which he described as 'intermediate between Temiar and Lanoh.' He referred to this group as 'Ple-Temer,' but subsequent researchers have been unable to identify its speakers (Benjamin 2003: 15–16).

21 For evidence of 'immediacy' in Semang farming see Lye (2005: 93).

22 Porath notes that the Meniq also abandon swiddens to collect produce for trade (2001: 125).

23 Lanoh continue to farm opportunistically. In 1998, after a ten-year hiatus, several people engaged in farming in Air Bah, but only because their land was cleared by a logging company that bought their old, unproductive rubber trees. Most of these individuals planned on planting rubber tree seedlings, and resumed rubber tapping as soon as possible.

24 Headland (1987) believes that hunter-gatherers resist agriculture to avoid direct competition with neighbouring farmers. In another place, Headland (1986) argues that hunters and gatherers, like the Agta, have not become farmers because they were excluded from farming by their more powerful neighbours.

25 A number of researchers have questioned the validity of contrasting ecological and social approaches to the study of hunter-gatherers, emphasizing instead that social and ecological phenomena are closely intertwined (Pedersen and Waehle 1988; Smith 1988; Griffin 1989; Kelly 1995; Minnegal 1996; Rocha 1996). Ingold, in particular, conceives of social relations as a part of ecology, suggesting that 'there can ... be no radical break between social and ecological relations; rather, the former constitute a subset of the latter' (1996: 150).

26 Lye (2005: 93) similarly acknowledges the association between the 'immediate-return' characteristics of Semang (Batek), but assumes that social organization preceded trade and that trade is pursued because it fits with their unique pattern of organization.

27 It must be noted that lately a broader, more inclusive, conception of Semang 'hunting and gathering' has become more common. Gomes, for instance, who still attributes Semang social organization to hunting and gathering when noting that 'nomadism is ... a social and cultural adaptation to hunting and gathering' (2007: 95), also includes trade and barter activities in his conception of 'hunting and gathering.' Similarly, in a more recent chapter, Benjamin states that Semang 'forage off *anything* that comes their way, including the Malay state' (2003: 34, original emphasis).

28 Benjamin mentions periodical taboos concerning farming-related activities among Temiar, pushing people to hunt, gather, and fish 'sometimes in whole family groups' (1985a: 263). Such communal hunting and gathering

would not likely occur among Lanoh. People only gather food in family groups in Air Bah during the fruit season.

29 Lanoh believe that things in nature are rare, so they have to be taken as a gift upon encounter, or one will never find the particular resource again, no matter how hard one looks.

30 The information Williams-Hunt obtained from Lanoh in the 1950s concerning the afterlife is different in some respects from what I found in Air Bah. While he was told that men and women went to different places after they died, I was assured that men and women were, indeed, going to the same place. Although I did not participate in a funeral, I was also informed that while both men and women may be present at funerals, women, as a rule, do not want to participate.

31 This extreme opportunism and readiness to change plans may nowadays also signal a greater dependence on money (Nagata, personal communication).

32 In the next chapter, I will discuss why it was vital for pre-resettlement Lanoh to trade with their Malay neighbours.

33 Air Boh is a forest location, not to be confused with Air Bah.

34 Temiar, like other swidden cultivators, are semi-sedentary and move infrequently, according to the requirements of swidden farming.

35 For a detailed description of these ceremonies, see Dallos (2003).

36 This incantation ceremony was performed by volunteers. Although there are several knowledgeable elders and old men in the village, in 1998 Air Bah had no esteemed shaman (L. *səma? hala?*). For the main harvest ceremony, villagers approached a familiar Malay shaman (M. *bomoh*) to bless the sacred (M. *jampi*) water. Later, for the end of the harvest feast, they invited a Lanoh shaman, a relative, from Tawai.

37 This temporal synchronicity is an attempt to coordinate people's activities; the reference to the calendar reflects the Lanoh's contact with outsiders, especially Malays.

38 As we will see later, although most work associated with farming is performed by women, men are indispensable during paddy planting. During planting, men dig holes in the ground into which women, who follow them, distribute the seeds.

39 Norström (2001: 37) has recorded a similar pattern in Paliyan farming, stating that Paliyan farming, typically performed on a small land, 'fitted patterns of Paliyan social and economic organization.' This means that Paliyan, just as Lanoh, cultivated their land by working in small families.

40 This interpretation seems to be reinforced by Williams-Hunt (1952: 60, cited in Gomes 2007: 99), who, as Gomes notes, 'attributes the abandonment

of the bow and the increased use of blowpipes to changes in the social and ecological situations among the Menraq.' Gomes further argues that 'as a hunting weapon, the blowpipe is only effective for small tree-dwelling game such as squirrels, monkeys, bats, and birds, and for this reason alone its use is restricted to the forest' (ibid.).

41 However, as Gomes suggests, these days, trade may have become primary as a result of development and modernity. He notes that 'in economic terms, [commodity production] ... led to a decline in subsistence-oriented foraging as people devote more time and effort to growing cash crops and participating in other market-oriented activities' (2007: 93). As a result of logging and the depletion of forest resources, foraging ceased to be a 'viable or rewarding economic option,' and this increases Menraq (Semang) dependence on market economy (ibid.).

42 Admittedly, priorities could have shifted, as today, because of a greater reliance on cash, commercial trade may be more lucrative than it once was. However, as I argue in the next chapter, there is a similarly strong reason to believe that interethnic trade was equally important in pre-resettlement times, albeit for different reasons.

43 The most important animals regularly consumed by Lanoh are monkeys, wild pheasants, different rat and squirrel species, frogs, monitor lizards, and tortoises.

44 Lye similarly suggests that the 'Batek are fundamentally outward-oriented people' (2005: 96).

45 Dunn notes that among rainforest hunter-gatherers, collecting for trade is an 'almost entirely male pursuit' (1975: 80). Endicott confirms this, suggesting that although, occasionally, some women participate in collecting, it is mostly those who either have no children or whose children are 'old enough to help or are grown up' (1992: 284). Children among the Batek are never involved in rattan collecting. Instead, they usually accompany women on their vegetable collecting trips (ibid.). In Air Bah, women started collecting palm leaves, which were stripped, made into brooms, and sold in a Malay store in Grik for RM 1.5–2 apiece. However, even in this case, the brooms were taken to town and traded by men. The other exception, *petai* and fruit, are usually collected in mixed-sex groups. Presumably, this is because *petai* is collected for sale as well as for people's own consumption.

46 This could explain why early researchers of indigenous peoples in the area noted that there was a 'shortage of women' in Lanoh camps. Evans could have stumbled upon a temporary forest camp when taking the following note: 'one certainly does notice considerably more men and boys about the camps than women and girls' (1937: 14).

47 This method is further necessitated by buyers' specifications. For instance, the most commonly collected species, *rotan pasong*, needs to be at least thumb-sized in diameter and sixteen feet in length. Rattan smaller than this is left to grow to be revisited a few years later.

48 It must be noted, however, that greater mobility in the past likely resulted in a more varied diet than today. As well, an increasing reliance on rice, which is today often bought in the store, has reduced the need for mobility, because it acts as a substitute for wild tubers in the Lanoh diet.

49 In pre-resettlement times, Lanoh postmarital residence was uxoribilocal, that is, ambilocal-neolocal, with an initial matrilocal bias. In the sedentary village of Air Bah, where this initial matrilocal residence has become permanent, women spend most of their time in the company of their female relatives, mothers, aunts, sisters, cousins, daughters, and nieces, who now make up the most important social network in women's lives.

50 Yet, as a consequence, children today do not learn about the ways of the forest, at least not until they are about 13 years old, around when they can start to perform adult chores.

51 Because of birth spacing and infant mortality, in the past, it seems there were often considerable age differences between siblings.

52 The toy, *main tɛndroy*, is associated with a liminal being, *tɛndroy*. Originally, *tɛndroy* was a person. While everyone had somebody, *tɛndroy* was left alone without a partner, a liminal being: neither man, nor woman, neither human, nor animal. The appearance of *tɛndroy* – ugly, with long unkempt hair hanging down – reflects its loneliness. It is the appearance of a person who is not cared for by anyone. *Tɛndroy* is responsible for people getting lost in the forest. There are two ways to outsmart *tɛndroy*. First, by calling its name and teaming up with it (this makes sense, because both *tɛndroy* and the lost person are alone). Second, one could make a *main tɛndroy*, solve it, leave it on the spot, and walk away. *Tɛndroy*, attracted to the game, will play with it, and while it plays, the spell breaks and the lost person finds his or her way. Pak Lang goes from place to place testing people's smarts by challenging them to solve *main tɛndroy*.

53 Although this conclusion does not undermine claims for women's autonomy among rainforest hunters and gatherers (K.L. Endicott 1999; Endicott and Endicott 2008), it should be a reminder that personal autonomy among hunters and gatherers is a complex matter. As is common among mobile hunter-gatherers, pre-resettlement Lanoh women were free to make choices about their bodies, their mobility, and their life circumstances. Nonetheless, these choices were circumscribed by constraints outside their control.

54 Schebesta also claimed that the Kintak Bong and Jahai knew aphrodisiacs, as well as contraceptives (abortion medicine), although the Jahai claimed not to use them, only to sell them to Malays (1929: 102, 228–9, in Evans 1937: 215, 245–7). Even though the actual effectiveness of the medicine (*susuak ayam, berana gajah, ham, pəniya?, limaw, tasan,* and *simpot*) that Lanoh use for birth control has not been tested as part of this project, the emphasis in this discussion is on women's volition. Semang women's use of contraception is also confirmed by Alberto Gomes, who notes that 'to control births, Menraq … used several kinds of traditional contraceptives and abortifacients' (2007: 87).

55 There are several reasons for Lanoh marriages to have become more stable compared with the past (Dallos 2003). One of the most consequential ones among these is that transportation makes up to some extent for residential mobility and thus, unlike in the past, men no longer need to actually move away to gather resources.

56 At present, the interbirth interval (IBI) among Lanoh in Air Bah is about two years. This is lower than the four years reported for certain groups of hunter-gatherers, like the !Kung (Lee 1979), but higher than the IBI of several large resettlement villages, such as Kampung Dala or Kampung Kroh, where women give birth every year (Dr Tiam, physician of mobile medical unit, Grik, personal communication). This two-year IBI is likely due to nursing practices. Lanoh women still do not interfere with the nursing of infants (i.e., nursing is frequent and on-demand), and Pennington suggests that lactation can postpone fertility for two years (2001: 189). In addition, Lanoh women claim that what changed in terms of practices, compared with the past, is the degree to which different methods of contraception are employed.

57 This obviously does not mean that communities are unable to farm and participate in trade at the same time, something that has been accomplished by other Orang Asli groups (see Dunn 1975). What I mean to say is that once social organization is adjusted to better suit the organizational requirements of trade, as seems to be the case for Semang, the society becomes ill-adapted to practising efficient swidden cultivation.

3 The Changing Context of Interethnic Relations: From Power Balance to Power Imbalance

1 Although ethnicity does not necessarily imply inequality, the way many anthropologists formulate the ethnic identity of foragers – as oppressed minorities – it certainly does.

2 This claim is naturally limited to pre-modern interactions between hunter-gatherers and food producers. In changed circumstances, these frameworks may be entirely valid, such as, when, for instance, Motzafi-Haller (1986, 1994) applies a Marxist interpretation to the marginality of the Basarwa serfs living as permanent residents in a Tswana village. In this case, Basarwa themselves would presumably agree that, having been incorporated into the hierarchical relations of farmers, they occupy the bottom tier of a social hierarchy.

3 Food producing is used here as a descriptive label. Ingold (1988) has very convincingly argued that hunter-gatherers are food producers as is everyone else.

4 This limited focus is all the more curious when considering the long theoretical insistence in anthropology that intergroup relations are to be analysed considering their social, political, as well as material, implications (e.g., Sahlins 1972).

5 See also Bowdler (2002: 175), who similarly remarks that it is simplistic to perceive trade relations between foragers and farmers in purely economic terms.

6 In 1997 Orang Asli, with a population of 106,131, comprised only 0.5 per cent of the total population of Malaysia (22.7 million), and the Semang comprised 'a little over three per cent of the Orang Asli population' (*The Star*, 24 Dec.1999; JHEOA 1997, in Nicholas 2000: 3, 13).

7 For the role of Orang Asli in slave trade see Sullivan (1982: 42) and Leary (1995: 19).

8 Although people in Air Bah consider metal tools, such as *parang* (Malay for the machete-like long instrument used in the region) and axe, valuable and convenient, they also suggested that these were far from indispensable, because these would be easy to replace with instruments made of material extracted from the forest. These, people suggested, although perhaps not quite as efficient as metal tools, would still be sufficient to perform tasks for which Lanoh now use metal tools. Moreover, forest collectors, like the Lanoh, did not necessarily need to 'trade' to obtain some of these items, for instance, metal tools. It seems that often, they 'collected' these, like they would collect anything else. Thus, as people in Air Bah related, 'in the old days, parang and axe were very expensive, so we would often just take them. Whenever we were near Malay and Chinese farms, we would pick up tools left by these people.'

9 Malay shamanistic beliefs assigned magical and supernatural attributes to many rare jungle products, such as yellow bamboo, metal ores, and precious stones (Skeat 1965).

10 In a diagram, Sullivan (1982: 41) summarizes the economic and political relationships in nineteenth-century Perak. Focusing on the mining economy, he only depicts the flow of jungle produce from aborigines to local market and from there to 'Orang Besar' (District Chiefs), and Malay villages and Orang Asli as interacting only indirectly through local markets. Thus, he fails to indicate the direct relationships between aborigines and Malay village families. Since, on the basis of informants' accounts, such relationships between collectors and Malay farmers were frequent and significant, it is also possible that even individual Malay farmers played an important part in maintaining the flow of goods from the forest to local markets and from there to larger collection points.

11 To some extent Sullivan challenges this bias for placing Malay settlements exclusively on riverbanks. He suggests that several Malay villages were more commonly found in the jungle interiors than it is generally acknowledged and that 'jungle tracks … were an important adjunct to river travel' (1982: 22). He writes: 'Certainly the riverbanks harboured the greater proportion of the Malay population, and the rivers carried the greater proportion of traffic; still, a significant number of Malays living in the interior and linked to river settlements by jungle tracks tended to be ignored simply because colonial observers found access to inland areas difficult, and the population of these areas of relatively little interest' (ibid.: 20). Nonetheless, in Malay literature and history, the jungle is the place one goes to meditate for special powers or get lost as punishment (see, e.g., the 'legend of the Princess of Mt. Ophir – *Kisah Putri Gunong Ledang*' in Skeat 1965: 164).

12 Marie-Andrée Couillard has drawn the same conclusion, suggesting that the Malay–Orang Asli relationship, characterized today by voluntary dependency and antagonism, used to be an equal trading partnership (1984, in Leary 1995: 21).

13 The influx of Chinese migrants also affected Orang Asli livelihoods. Harper (1997), for instance, notes that even before the Second World War Chinese infringed/encroached on Orang Asli areas in search of land. Occasionally, they chased Orang Asli away from their *ladang* and planted there themselves (ibid.; see also Holman 1984).

14 *Panglima* ('commander,' M.) is a military title as well as an administrative position. It is a titular position used by Malay rajas.

15 The Malayan Emergency (1948–1960) was an especially disruptive time for Orang Asli, particularly those in the northern states. Nonetheless, people in Air Bah did not indicate that their lifestyle was significantly upset as a result of these events. Although they had encounters with communist insurgents, who approached them for food and help, and were monitored

and questioned by authorities about these encounters, unlike many other groups, they were not regrouped or resettled during this time by the British colonial administration.

16 People here used the expression, 'Catch-22,' in English.

17 As Norström (2001: 47) suggests, licences and regulations concerning forest products also reduce foragers' and post-foragers' bargaining power in other areas, such as wage labour and contract work.

18 For a related discussion of organizational discrepancy see Norström (2001).

19 Although Lanoh often share food bought with money, they do not share their earnings.

20 Even though Lanoh are also in contact with Indian and Chinese contractors and employers, such employers tend to be more cautious in their dealings with Orang Asli because they perceive them to be protected by the government.

21 It would fill a separate volume to record the instances when Lanoh were cheated, shortchanged, offended, or abused by outside employers. Different authors have extensively documented mistreatment of Orang Asli by outsiders (e.g., Rashid 1995; Dentan et al. 1997; Nicholas 2000). Here, my main concern is to understand the implications of these incidents for internal relationships among Lanoh.

22 Although the Emergency officially ended in 1960, the northern part of the country remained a restricted area until the late 1960s (Nagata, personal communication).

23 This cave system, comprising Gua Badak (Rhinoceros cave), Gua Teluk Melaka (Melaka Bay cave), Gua Ular (Snake cave), Gua Tarzan (Tarzan cave), Gua Tasik (Lake cave), and Gua Kajang (Roof cave) is also the location of important archaeological sites. These caves have been occupied since prehistory by hunter-gatherers. One of the most important sites containing the remains of the Perak man in Gunung Runtuh (Caved-in Mountain cave) has been investigated by a team of Malay archaeologists (Zuraina Majid 1994, 1998, 2005).

24 The names Gluk and Lenggong both derive from Lanoh words. While gəluk refers to a river passing through the area, Lenggong (now the name of a town) is said to originate in the Lanoh expression, ŋen ʔɔŋ, 'they are drinking.'

25 Although kajang in Malay means palm-frond roofing and atap (terkajang means 'roofed under shelter'), people in Air Bah claim that the cave's Malay name, Gua Kajang, actually stems from the Lanoh word, kaja? which is the name of a plant growing in swamps, ləmaja?, layaw in Lanoh, or paya, in Malay.

26 For an analysis of the common occurrence of the flood myth among Mon Khmer speakers, see Dang (1993).

27 The Aboriginal Peoples Act of 1974 is a revision of the Aboriginal Peoples Ordinance of 1954, originally devised to prevent communists during the Malayan Emergency of 1948–1960 from getting Orang Asli help and winning Orang Asli to their cause (Nicholas 2000: 82). The principles of the original Aboriginal Peoples Ordinance were laid down on the initiative of H.D. Noone in the Aboriginal Tribes Enactment of 1939 (ibid.).

28 Here, the narrative related by people in Air Bah becomes inconsistent. It is likely that, at this point, they received some pay for the land they were to abandon to the Chinese vegetable farmer.

29 Ironically, this farmer hired Lanoh as contract labourers, and Lanoh women continue to work on this farm to this day.

30 At the same time, however, because of the constant clash with Malays over their diet, diet may be currently gaining in importance for Lanoh ethnic identity as a symbol of resisting Islam.

31 Sociologically, the category includes peoples with 'divergent political structure, land tenure, kinship and ritual systems' (Walker 1983: 459). Linguistically, they are divided into Austroasiatic and Austronesian speakers, the latter differing from Malays only in their religion. Finally, a few of these groups arrived at their present habitat from Indonesia, later than Malays, approximately four hundred years ago (ibid.: 455–6).

32 In calling attention to an apparent contradiction in the philosophy of the native movement in relation to a segment of the population on which the movement has impact, I do not intend to question or decry fellow anthropologists' sincerity and good intentions, neither the seriousness of their concerns. The questions I propose to investigate are important precisely because of these considerations. Instead of breaking the impetus of the aboriginal movement, I would like to contribute factors that would sensitize it to concerns of its less well-known and cared-for members.

33 Established in 1976, the Peninsular Malaysia Orang Asli Association (POASM) was fairly inactive until 1987, when it was revived under the presidency of Bah-Tony Williams (Nicholas 2000: 153). After an 'active membership drive' and aggressive media campaign in 1989, POASM membership started to grow until in 2000 the organization counted more than 17,000 members (ibid.: 154, 179n10).

34 Yet, as Colin Scott (personal communication) has pointed out, it is likely that one of the greatest paradoxes of the situation of contemporary hunter-gatherers today is that, without developing a more corporate, ethnic type of identity and corresponding strategy, there is little hope that hunting/fishing territories and economic opportunities can be maintained.

35 There is a possibility, however, that since ethnic identity is based on selected features of culture while identity becomes ethnicized, underlying traditional strategies, habitus, perceptions, and modes of interaction remain intact (Scott, personal communication).

36 This conclusion is supported by the small population of Semang compared with the majority Orang Asli groups. See n6 above.

37 Note, however, that there are signs that since my research in the late 1990s the situation has changed considerably. Gomes (2007: 169–70) reports that Rual Menraq received assistance and legal representation from the Centre for Orang Asli Concerns (COAC) during the 'Jeli incident.'

38 This regional identification also used to characterize Malays. Before independence and nation building, in the absence of central government, people distinguished each other according to their state of origin, as Orang Johor, Orang Perak, or Orang Kelantan.

39 The late Cornelia van der Sluys conducted extended ethnographic field research among the Jahai and was well known by all Orang Asli in the Grik area.

40 In December 2002 Colin Nicholas invited representatives from Air Bah to participate in the Suhakam workshop in Kuala Lumpur. In spite of promises, the Lanoh failed to show.

41 Alberto Gomes seems to be reinforcing this perception when describing that, in spite of the general failure of the JHEOA educational program among Orang Asli, there is now a new 'class' of more educated Orang Asli, who put up an air, behave like Malays, and 'play politics' (*main politik*): 'One could say that they have attained a modern sense of self and personhood' (2007: 146).

4 Withdrawal from Contact and the Development of Village Identity

1 This lack of interest in age-specific responses to change by hunter-gatherers is curious, especially given that, next to gender, age is considered the second important source of social differentiation in small-scale societies.

2 For now, this discussion will be restricted to age-differentiated responses by men. As noted by researchers of the topic, the age trajectories of men and women are quite different (Gutmann 1977: 303; Keith and Kertzer 1984: 28), and this difference definitely applies in Air Bah. In subsequent chapters, I will elaborate more on these distinctions.

3 It is important to note that throughout this work 'elder' is used as an etic category. Among Lanoh, as among most Orang Asli, middle-aged men constitute an 'unmarked' category (Nagata, personal communication; this point was also raised by an anonymous reviewer of the manuscript). In

'Leadership in a Resettlement Village of the Orang Asli in Kedah, Malaysia,' Nagata translates the concept, *bidog*, as 'elder' (2004: 99–102), but in the Lanoh usage, *bidog* would most often refer to old men, past maturity, rather than to men in leadership positions. Benjamin relates that Temiar use the word *tawa?*, which derives from the Malay word, *'tua'* for 'an elder' (along with the word *tuŋgɔ?*), mostly to refer to 'authority-holding in the context of extra-village relationships' (1968: 3–4).

4 For a classification and extensive list of forest products see Dunn, who suggests that several products that today are considered minor 'were among the major products exported from the Malay Peninsula prior to the twentieth century' (1975: 87).

5 Although in principle women can also be shamans, and there is reference to female shamans in Lanoh mythology, today there are no female shamans in Air Bah, and no one could name powerful female shamans in the past. In 1998, however, there were four older women in the village whose skills as midwives were respected by all.

6 Nicholas (2000: 19) similarly suggests that older people are more likely to participate in agriculture.

7 Patani rubber workers' quarters were situated halfway between Air Bah and the main road, and one day they sent representatives to Air Bah to find out if the missing child came to the village or if people had seen the child somewhere in the forest.

8 During my fieldwork, I only learned of two teenagers ever working in factories, and even these engagements only lasted for a few weeks.

9 Due to inclusive kinship reckoning, 'brother' might actually mean sibling, half-sibling, or cousin of any degree.

10 One young man was known to have paid RM 150 to his bride's father upon marriage. In view of the general resistance of Lanoh to Malay customs, however, such instances could be interpreted more as opportunism on the part of fathers-in-law than as adherence to Malay-Muslim marriage protocol.

11 According to Karen Endicott, rattan collecting is 'generally carried out by men and by women who do not yet have children or whose children are old enough to help or are grown up' (1992: 284). Thus, although among Batek some women may participate in rattan collecting, it is not typical, because children as a rule are not involved in this activity. Instead, children usually accompany women on their vegetable-collecting trips (ibid.: 287).

12 Estioko-Griffin (1986) observed that Agta women had gender-specific weapons, but Marshall (1976) notes that !Kung women were not allowed to carry weapons at all. Tabet suggests that 'it is not the hunt that is for-

bidden to women but rather the weapons (ce n'est pas la chasse qui est interdit aux femmes, c'est les armes)' (1979: 28, in Quraishy 2001: 195; also see Testart 1982). In summing up this evidence, Quraishy (2001) comments that the sexual division of labour is a result of gendered technologies.

13 This list is not exhaustive. Some cultivars, for instance, paddy, are planted by both men and women.

14 This protection was extended to the ethnographer as well. People did not want me to stay in a house alone, or go anywhere outside by myself. They especially warned me off certain Malays.

15 Lanoh no longer perform the *pano?* ceremony in the way described in this excerpt. This account was transcribed from a life history interview.

16 Although beneficial from an elder's perspective, this limited contact with outsiders is detrimental for women's independence and autonomy because it increases their dependence on men. Women's access to earnings in Air Bah is not only limited, because less demanding jobs also tend to pay less (while a group of nine women earned RM 200 building cucumber frames in ten days, for example, a group of ten men earned RM 600 clearing land in four days) but also because women work in large groups and thus need to divide their earnings between more people. In addition, limited contact with outsiders also limits women's ability to speak Malay, which, in turn, affects their confidence in dealing with outsiders. Today, when many of their children are in school, this may even affect their efficiency and competence as mothers, because they cannot consult officials and fear they do not fully comprehend what their children need.

17 Outsiders may have also played a role in this crystallization of ethnic categories. Early resettlement schemes focused on regrouping Orang Asli according to ethnicity. For instance, at the time of earliest Lanoh resettlement in 1965, people from Tawai were excluded, because this village, with its Jahai, Kensiu, Temiar, and Lanoh inhabitants, was considered to be ethnically 'mixed' as opposed to 'pure' Lanoh.

18 As noted earlier, opinions about the origin of different dialect groups varied considerably. Nonetheless, with regard to the spatial associations of different Lanoh subdivisions, the following summary can be discerned from interviews. People of the first of these divisions, Lanoh *koba?*, used to live in Lasa and Baung, but nowadays they inhabit the areas of the Dala and Piah rivers. The original territory of Lanoh *jinjɛŋ* was at Kuala Kenderung near Sungai Papan, but today, along with Lanoh *mandəray* who originally inhabited Ijok Selama (see Evans 1937), they can mostly be found in Ulu Grik, an Orang Asli resettlement village near the town of Grik. Lanoh

məndərəy shared this area with Kensiu and Kintak Bong who subsequently moved to Baling and Kelian Intan. In addition, about seven people in the resettlement village of Bukit Sapi are said to be Lanoh *ləpey*. According to people in Air Bah, Lanoh *ləpey* are originally from an island called Pulau John in the area of Sungai Siput and Labit, near the Perak Dam.

19 For instance, they say, Lanoh *kobaʔ* pronounce the word *'wal'* as *'waal,'* while Lanoh *jinjɛŋ* 'drag' their words, and do *kobaʔ*. Lanoh *məndərəy* are also known as Lanoh *yir* because they pronounce the word *'yay'* (two of us) as *'yir.'*

20 'Perceived' must be emphasized here, because I collected some of the most valuable information about Lanoh history in other villages.

21 It appears that preserving community identity is also an important concern in the refusal of Lanoh to move to larger resettlement villages. When asked about his opinion of POASM, a man voiced the following concern. He said people in Air Bah were afraid that POASM wants to organize Orang Asli together and move them into large villages like Dala and Kemah. In these big villages not only would Lanoh have to mix with other Orang Asli, but also there would be a 'big chief' in charge of a central organization, and their own leaders would become 'small chiefs.' In those villages, they would have to get approval for everything they wanted to do from the central leadership, as well as synchronize their activities with the majority. For instance, they would have to plant what they were told to plant. If others planted rubber, they too would have to plant rubber. In those villages, they would not be free and their leadership and community (*suku*, M.) would disappear.

22 Certain aspects of changes described in this chapter, especially increased control of women's sexuality, could be seen as aspects of acculturation to Malay/Islamic values. However, the resistance of Islam and the values it represents challenges such an interpretation.

23 Gomes details the effect of acculturation on Menraq forager-collectors: 'There are several salient features of quintessentially and recognizably Malay *adat* which appear to have been advocated and promoted as part of the resettlement package to "modernize" the Menraq.' These include 'culinary styles, home decoration, planting of home gardens, village grounds maintenance, and the village hall (*balai*) as a centre of social interactions' (2007: 146–7). Many of these effects are also present in Air Bah. Nonetheless, as I argue in this chapter, Lanoh manage to maintain their identity in some important respects.

24 For further (and overlapping) reasons for Orang Asli's reluctance to become Muslim see Gomes (2007: 149–50).

25 For a fuller discussion of Islamization of Orang Asli in Malaysia see

Nobuta (2008).

26 An *ustad* is a Muslim religious teacher accorded an '*istaz*' or '*istazah*,' a recognition akin to a diploma. One such teacher visits Air Bah for a few days
a month from Kampung Dala to teach children not enrolled in boarding
school about religion, grammar, and basic arithmetic.

27 A similar 'going along attitude' characterizes Lanoh in every situation where they are forced to take some action or are cornered in other
ways. Such an occasion was the Malaysian Emergency, when they were
approached by the government and the communists and ended up 'going
along' with the requests of both.

28 Testart, for instance, noted that Australian hunter-gatherers rejected 'the
bow ... horticulture ... [and] ... techniques for preserving meat' (1988:
12), and, according to Galaty, the Dorobo vehemently reject drinking milk
(1986: 123).

29 Even though violence is common among changing foragers, Peter Gardner
(2000) reports similar retention of non-violent values among newly sedentary Paliyan.

30 It is conceivable to interpret this refusal of alcohol consumption in Air Bah
in light of Islamic prohibitions concerning alcohol consumption, or fears of
retribution from authorities. However, *haram* food is similarly prohibited
by Islam, yet people in Air Bah have no objections to consuming such food
daily.

31 Several layers of meaning have been attributed to the Semang refusal to
kill and eat domestic animals. Cornelia van der Sluys, for instance, suggests that pets raised by Jahai are not eaten because 'they share soul-sub-
stance with their owners' (2000: 441).

32 The way Orang Asli were once seen as animals by neighbouring Malays
has been commented on by researchers of Orang Asli (Evans 1937).
Similarly, this note reveals that Orang Asli perceive their neighbours to be
animals as well.

33 Although nobody knows exactly how long each cycle would last, according to Lanoh, in the present cycle, four epochs have already passed: the
time of the great flood, the beginning of Lanoh history; the time of the
mythical leader, Tok Agong, who led the Lanoh against the Thai (Siam);
the epoch of British rule; and finally, the present epoch of Malay rule.

5 Leadership Competition, Self-Aggrandizement, and Inequality

1 In Malay-type social systems, such as Melayu and Southern Orang Asli,
relative age is transferred to gender relations, and 'the husband-wife rela-

tion ... tends to be assimilated to the relation between older and younger "sibling/cousin'" (Benjamin 1985a: 246). Among Lanoh, such transfers do not apply.

2 The importance of relative age is symbolically accentuated in farming. One is expected to be observant when planting paddy and corn together, because paddy is the elder and corn the younger brother. Corn can only be harvested *after* paddy, because 'one always has to wait for the elder brother.' To avoid breaking this rule, Lanoh usually refrain from planting these two crops together.

3 An additional difference between men's and women's age status is the way they are influenced by marriage. No matter how old, unmarried men had no political influence in Air Bah, while women's status did not seem to be affected by marriage in a similar way.

4 Som, the eldest sister of Hitam's wife, is possibly the most powerful and influential woman in the village. She spends most of her time socializing with the female members of her kinship group, including Hitam's wife and daughters. As a result, even though she and Hitam are in avoidance relationship, thus unable to talk to each other, they nonetheless synchronize their actions via the mediation of these female relatives.

5 As Gomes notes, 'regroupment is a euphemism in Malaysian government rhetoric for resettlement. It is, however, a slightly more accurate term than resettlement, as such schemes involve the amalgamation of several villages to form a composite village located in the vicinity of the original settlements' (2007: 178n).

6 The Lanoh term for an avoidance rule is *tulah*. Among Malays, *tolah* means 'a calamity consequent upon sacrilege or extreme presumption' (Coote 1976, in Howell 1989). According to Endicott, the Batek use *tolah* for 'a large number of social disruptive and disrespectful acts, especially those that are directed towards older people' (1979: 81, in Howell, ibid.).' Among Chewong, like among Lanoh, *tolah* signifies avoidance relationships between affines (ibid.).

7 This is one of the reasons that people often send their children to deliver items to other people.

8 In this respect, foragers with an immediate-return system of production are not at all different from small-scale egalitarian societies with a delayed-return system of production. Among Temiar, a small-scale egalitarian society with a delayed-return system of production, it was likely that one elder, accompanied by his extended family, would occupy a river valley. Even though Benjamin disputes this claim, Carey argues that large Temiar family groups tended towards fission with the junior line moving

upstream from the senior group (1961, in Benjamin 1968). The difference between foragers' and horticulturists' social organization in this respect is that among foragers individual mobility discouraged even the aggregations of extended families.

9 Although in the literature on hunter-gatherers' mobility is often emphasized as a means of conflict resolution, as I suggested earlier, trade opportunities could sufficiently account for the mobility and individual autonomy of Lanoh in the past. In Air Bah people occasionally moved away to resolve conflict, and as we will see, moving away certainly played a role in conflict resolution in Tawai; however, people more likely turned to this solution to resolve intergenerational conflicts. That is, young people would occasionally move away to assert their independence from their parents, but rarely moved to assert their independence in relationships governed by relative age. Instead, as outlined above, younger siblings usually make an effort to stay close to their older siblings – even *against* the atomizing implications of economic activities.

10 When asked if he would like to be a headman, even an unpopular man said he preferred to remain a 'commoner' instead. (He used the word *kuli*, or 'coolie,' meaning unskilled labourer.)

11 According to Lanoh, the position of headman (*penghulu* or *to? batin*) is not necessarily inherited by the headman's son. The criterion is always the ability of the person chosen. If it happens that the son of the headman has all the abilities and characteristics of a good headman, such as skill in organizing village and jungle work, the ability to negotiate successfully with outside communities, honesty, patience, humility, and affability, the headman's son will be made the new headman. If not, another candidate with all of these abilities will be made headman.

12 Earlier, I suggested that the number of children per household has increased after sedentism. This, however, has not impacted all households equally. Middle-aged couples tend to have the greatest number of dependent children, and this renders them quite immobile compared with other households.

13 The fact that the headman of the village had no idea how long it would take to plant his eight acres shows the novelty of large-scale farming among Lanoh. He had predicted that it would take him three days to plant his eight acres. In the end, it took him three weeks.

14 These interviews were conducted with fourteen people, eight of whom planted below subsistence, three 'just enough to eat,' and three beyond subsistence. Although originally I had meant to interview both men and women, it became clear early in the process that women have little input in

determining how much paddy is planted – because this depends on the size of cleared land, and the initial task of land clearing is performed by men.

15 It has been noted that agricultural expansion, although a convenient avenue for self-aggrandizement in sedentary societies with a tradition of farming, is but one of many possible ways to increase prestige and power. Bruce Trigger (1998: 163–4), for instance, cites examples in which social complexity developed independently of an economic base: in Florida, chiefdoms were founded on intensive collecting, and in Peru power was based on monumental architecture *before* the development of intensive agriculture. Similarly, in Air Bah competing leaders grabbed every opportunity to prove themselves against their opponent. Agricultural expansion was selected opportunistically partly because, at present, in Malaysia land development is a likely candidate for expansion and partly because land was cleared and available due to the sale of the rubber trees.

16 Others, such as Beidelman (1971: 24), have also pointed out that the extensive acquisition of land by leaders is often not primarily to increase wealth, but to increase prestige.

17 The full extent of leaders' opportunism will be explored in Chapter 6. Unfortunately, I was unable to ascertain whether eventually other villagers profited from Hitam's and Kecil's expanded farming strategy by harvesting the crop for themselves, because my fieldwork ended in January 1999, when some villagers were still harvesting.

18 Kirk Endicott refers to *pesaka* with regard to places with which individuals have a special relationship (1988: 113). It is quite possible that in the past there was a similar relationship between landscape, identity, and inheritance among Lanoh.

19 This word is a derivative of the Malay word *barang* (commodity, thing).

20 People can only claim ownership of fruit trees that they planted themselves. As mentioned above, similar to the Batek De' (Endicott 1988), Lanoh deny having individual or group ownership claims to resources in the wild, such as fruit trees or poison trees. Yet, these days in Air Bah people claim ownership of such trees. Although fruit from the village's trees will be shared, it cannot be taken without the owner's permission.

21 The informant was not able to say exactly what *baʔɛt* means in this case. Yet, he described a wife who was considered *baʔɛt* as one who 'took care of the deceased more' and 'took care of the children better, whether these children were actually hers or not.' Whether a wife is considered *baʔɛt* also depends on the opinion of the deceased's siblings.

22 See n21 above.

23 The influence of older women is also enhanced by bilateral inheritance.

Bilateral inheritance has been noted to have a positive effect on the status of women in small-scale societies, for instance, as among Semai (Gomes 1991). Similar to Semai women, Lanoh women in Air Bah inherit property. As a result, these older widows sometimes own as much land as, or even more, than some men.

24 Kent (1999: 118) describes similar methods in Kutse, where children are asked to carry goods from one household to another.

25 Traditionally, Lanoh did not count beyond two. 'Seventy-four' in this case, is presumably used to indicate a 'reasonably' large number or a 'reason-ably' long time (i.e., the time it would take for an average hunter to hunt seventy-four of each animal species).

26 Exceptions to this are communal feasts, such as those following planting or the beginning of harvest, in which everyone in the village is supposed to take part, and where there is the distribution of large game. On such occasions, sharing goes beyond kinship clusters.

27 Tengah, the headman's younger brother-in-law, acts as 'assistant headman' in the village.

28 Today, although there are medicine men, there are no shamans in Air Bah. Significantly, the last Lanoh shaman was Senin, whose death in 1996 induced the leadership conflict in Air Bah.

29 The initial phases of developing inequality have been long associated with religious rites and religious specialists (e.g., Brumfiel 1994; Shennan 1996; Woodburn 2005; Gibson 2005). Although, as noted earlier, in 1998 there was no shaman in Air Bah, in this discussion I am focusing on age-based authority as the common denominator between the right of religious mediators to interpret rules among pre-resettlement Lanoh and the right of competing leaders to self-aggrandize in post-resettlement Air Bah.

30 Schebesta made a similar association between yəl and younger men when, writing of Jahai, he said (1929: 235–6, in Evans 1937: 264): 'the soul of a dead person, yurl, goes to the place by the setting sun where all yurl meet … The yurl of a bachelor is particularly evilly disposed and will kill any-one, being angry because he died without having a wife and, therefore, has no wife in the afterworld.'

31 The didactic element in this formulation also indicates the role of age.

32 Kent explains such 'sharing isolates' in Kutse in more neutral terms, by the asocial tendencies of certain people (1999: 118): 'Whereas it is somewhat unusual for a household not be part of a sharing network … there are a few regular sharing isolates at Kutse … Such isolates are perceived as simply being less social than others.'

33 People used the English expression 'blacklisted' here.

6 Pre-resettlement Organization, Village Integration, and Self-Aggrandizing Strategies

1 For discussions of the relationship between household integration and inequality see Woodburn (1980), Upham (1990b), Wilk (1991), Brumfiel (1992), Blanton (1995), Taylor (1996), Graves-Brown (1996), Bogucki (1999), and Rousseau (2006); and for discussions of household integration among changing hunter-gatherers see, e.g., Draper (1975a, 1975b), Kent (1989, 1995a, 1995b, 1999), and Thambiah (1997).
2 It is generally acknowledged that among mobile hunter-gatherers the sexual division of labour is tenuous (K.L. Endicott 1979, 1981, 1992; Draper 1975b; Nowak 1986, 1988; Gomes 1991; Kent 1996a).
3 For a discussion of the respective impact of sedentism, acculturation, and commercial trade on changing hunter-gatherers see Kent (1995b: 531–2), Howell (1983: 79), and Gomes (2007: 135–6).
4 The manipulation of daughters is a common practice cross-culturally when increasing household production (Beidelman 1971).
5 For detailed discussions of how social change affected women's status in Air Bah see Dallos (2003, 2006).
6 This power discrepancy between younger and older women has also been documented by other researchers. Victoria Burbank (1994), for instance, refers to acts of intragender aggression in Aboriginal Australia as 'disciplinary aggression.'
7 Employing servants and slaves is another means to increase the size of the household.
8 Timah's situation is uncharacteristic because her father is a Temiar from Tanjung Rambutan. As a Temiar, he has maintained strong ties with his kin in his native village and was able to send Timah there for a few months to work in a factory and try to get to know young men there. However, most other young women in the village have had no such opportunities.
9 Hitam offered the following justification for not letting his daughter Puteh marry Atan, the young man she liked. He explained that, a few years back, his daughter and the *penghulu*'s eldest daughter broke an important taboo (*səlantap*) by refusing to marry a Semai shaman who cured the *penghulu*'s son. In exchange for curing the young man, this shaman asked to marry these two girls who, however, refused him. As a consequence, now they are cursed, and nobody can marry them. Other people, when asked about this, reinforced Hitam's interpretation: 'Yes, we are afraid that those girls became spellbound, because Hitam said that Semai are notorious for black magic.' In accounting for his and the *penghulu*'s behaviour, Hitam relied on

people's memories of the 1965 cholera epidemic, which was thought to be caused by a young girl similarly refusing to marry an older man.

10 This is a reference to bride-price, or *antaran*, in Malay marriage.

11 Two years earlier, Hitam's eldest son married one of Kecil's daughters. This young couple were living behind the headman's house in a newly built Temiar-style home.

12 Benjamin suggests that among Semang, only cross-sex relations are marked by avoidance, while 'the economically more important same-sex relations are unrestricted' (1980: 11).

13 Elsewhere, Benjamin (1968: 32) somewhat contradicts this statement, noting that the 'distribution of meat and other foods throughout the village is on a purely *ad hoc* basis and anyone may do the sharing.' Nonetheless, he also posits that the headman acts as a redistributor of gifts from outside (ibid.).

14 Lanoh in Air Bah do not try to store excess paddy because of damage from rodents and insects. While keeping seeds for the following year's planting, those planting paddy beyond subsistence sold their surplus for RM 60–70 per bag. This proved easy, as their hill paddy was much sought after by outsiders for its fragrance. Around harvest time, the village was besieged by outsiders requesting *gantangs* (one *gantang* is four *cupak*; one *cupak* is the capacity of half a coconut shell) of paddy. In addition, the JHEOA also offered to buy excess paddy as seed for Orang Asli villages elsewhere.

15 Admittedly, most women's husbands do not earn enough money to cover all their household expenses, and these women often spend their earnings on everyday necessities such as food or clothing. Nonetheless, this has enabled women, especially older women, to save up considerable sums that they may dispose of as they please. On one occasion, for instance, a man borrowed RM 300, quite a large sum in the context of the Lanoh economy, from his wife to start a vegetable farm. This asymmetry in expectations, in spite of the fact that women earn less cash than men, contributes to women's continuing independence in Air Bah (Dallos 2003, 2006).

16 These contractual relationships between people had unexpected implications for my fieldwork. People in Air Bah were unwilling to teach me Lanoh as a favour; they requested that I teach them English in return. As well, as one old man suggested, *jampi* ('incantation') collected by white people in the past were all 'fake,' because 'every Orang Asli knows that nobody gives *jampi* away for free.'

17 It is open to argument whether this 'balanced reciprocity' in Air Bah results from recent changes – modernization and the introduction of a money economy – or whether it is inherent in relationships of trade. It is

most likely that while the medium of exchange is relatively new, balance, the quality that this medium facilitates, is inherent in the individual bartering that Lanoh have been conducting with Malays for hundreds of years.

18 Lanoh use the Arabic-Malay expression, *ilmu*, as in *pakai ilmu*, to refer to black magic, or, alternatively, they talk about people 'getting them' (*kenakan*).

19 The contractors gave 5–15 ringgit to each person working for them, while the *ustad* gave the village 80 ringgit, as well as meat.

20 Bailey (1969: 32) calls such individuals 'referees,' that is, those who are 'clearly and unambiguously not one of the players: [and who] can never win the prize.'

21 The *cempedak* tree is a large tree in the middle of the village under which communal meetings of men are usually held.

22 It is likely that in 1998 competing leaders could only expand their farming production because their land had been cleared during the rubber tree sale, and because they received seeds, fertilizers, and tools from the JHEOA. Especially in the first phase of farming, land clearing, the contribution of younger men was critical. Without such help, Hitam and Kecil would probably not have been able to clear and cultivate more than one or two acres of land.

23 This is compatible with Boissevain's suggestion that competing factions, although equally strong, often have asymmetrical resource bases and employ differing strategies (1968: 551).

24 Selling the forest for timber apparently contradicts the idea of 'indigenous stewardship' (e.g., Dentan and Ong Hean Chooi 1995). Yet, it is unjustified to adopt romantic Western notions of environmental protection to indigenous environmental management (see Brosius 1997). Although Lanoh never destroy resources carelessly and unnecessarily, they refrain from doing so not out of a moral imperative but because they intend to postpone exploitation until these resources are mature.

25 Couillard (1980: 20) similarly observed that among the Jah Hut the first person to start producing for market was the headman, a powerful shaman.

26 Semang (e.g., Lanoh) and Senoi (e.g., Temiar) provide good examples for organizational variations for similar age structures. For further discussions of social structure versus organization see, e.g., Barnard (1996: 510), who notes that in the history of anthropology '"social organization" has tended to be used loosely to refer to the sum total of activities performed in a given social context … [while] "social structure" has usually been employed for the social context itself, or more precisely for the set of social

relations which link individuals in a society.' In general, anthropologists who focus on social action (e.g., Firth) tend to write about organization, while those focusing on the 'more formal relations between people' (e.g., Radcliffe-Brown) refer to structure (ibid.). The latter further distinguish between 'structure' (the relations between individual people) and 'structural form' (the positions that individuals occupy in relation to one another). Barth (1966: 2) envisions social structure to be 'related to a set of moral constraints' and social organization to be regularities of 'actions and interrelations of human beings,' which affect, '[restrict,] and [canalize] the possible course of events.' This latter formulation approximates most my understanding of the difference between social structure and organization. Thus, even though anthropologists have often used the concepts of social structure and organization interchangeably (Barnard, ibid.), the distinction between them is useful in accentuating the difference between immediate- and delayed-return egalitarian social systems.

27 This means that the concept of 'immediacy,' as singled out by Woodburn is a creation of this organizational difference, rather than its creator. This notion will become more apparent in the context of the argument in the final chapter of this book.

7 Understanding Equality and Inequality in Small-Scale Societies

1 Recent studies of *Ardipithecus ramidus* dentition have suggested non-violent tendencies and increased cooperation among the earliest hominins (Lovejoy 2009; Suwa et al. 2009). Although these findings may raise questions regarding certain aspects of the argument presented in this chapter, they do not conclusively contradict it. Further examination and analysis on related research in various disciplines will provide insights into still less than fully understood aspects of human evolution.

2 Even though Power (1995) questions the validity of Goodall's data on the basis that the group she studied was artificially fed and thus more prone to aggression, her work overwhelmingly shows that the basic style of dominance display among non-human primates is physical (Galdikas 1979; Tutin 1979; Nishida 1979; Fossey 1979; Nishida et al. 1985; Rodman and Mitani 1987; Schubert 1991: 35).

3 For instance, Sanday suggests that 'when a people's identity is formed in adverse circumstances, they may become heavily dependent on the aggressive acts of men' (1981: 11).

4 It is also important to recognize that this shift from physical to cultural dominance has defined human politics. When social inequality devel-

ops, as in Air Bah, human self-aggrandizing leaders do not revert back to physical competition and physical displays of power, but enhance their position via competitive cultural displays; schemes, plans, and plots. In other words, self-aggrandizers rely on the cognitive/cultural advantage of eldership, which forms the basis of egalitarian politics. Thus, while in primate politics, physical displays restrict competition to an extremely narrow range of possibilities, the possibilities of cognitive competition, of the 'planned schemes of leaders' (Hastorf 1990: 173), are practically limitless.

5 Studies by the psychologist Richard Tremblay and his colleagues have countered the view that boys learn to be violent in adolescence by showing that aggressive behaviour in young men surfaces in early childhood and must be curbed by socialization (Tremblay 1999, 2000; Tremblay et al. 1999; Seguin et al. 1995; Schaal et al. 1996). Incidentally, these studies excellently corroborate Miller's (1999) notion of cognitive power displays among humans. Tremblay and his colleagues found that among adolescent boys high testosterone levels were associated with social dominance, but not necessarily with physical aggression. In fact, boys with high physical aggression tended to have lower testosterone levels. Furthermore, boys with a history of physical aggression performed worse in tasks associated with cognitive executive functions (self-control) than did boys with no such history (Tremblay 1999; Tremblay et al. 1999; Schaal et al. 1996; Seguin et al. 1995).

6 But see Walker et al. (2002), who note that among Ache hunting abilities reach their peak surprisingly late, significantly after peaks in strength.

7 Although Woodburn (1982: 436) emphasizes that among mobile hunter-gatherers everyone has access to lethal hunting weapons, differences in physical strength may still be consequential.

8 Readers will remember that Richard Lee was a young man in his 20s at the time of this incident. One can only wonder if his 'boasting' would have been equally ridiculed had he been an 'elder' in his 40s.

9 While, of course, the relationship between oratory, authority, and social control has long been acknowledged in anthropology (e.g., Bloch 1975; Brenneis and Myers 1984; Gal 1991; Povinelli 1991), in the context of the present discussion, I am trying to emphasize that oratory and verbal manipulation have a role in maintaining *equality* in small-scale societies by discouraging displays of physical power.

10 As Peter Stewart (2001: 345) notes, 'theorists such as Luhmann and Zygmunt Bauman argue that institutions and systems of society are devices of simplification and order.'

11 In a 2009 paper, Owen Lovejoy outlines a more plausible explanation based on the notion of adaptive suite for the early origin of pair bonding and paternal provisioning (see also Suwa et al. 2009).

12 This realization implies that all human production systems, *by definition*, are 'delayed-return,' and consequently, 'delay' in consumption is an inexact way to differentiate between social types.

13 Vampire bats are known to share blood with neighbours who shared with them in the past (Wilkinson 1984: 182, in Binmore 2001).

14 Anthropologists working in the area of human life histories often neglect this fact. In reviewing the distinctive characteristics of human life histories, Kaplan et al. (2000), for instance, list four such attributes: (1) exceptionally long lifespan; (2) extended period of juvenile dependence; (3) support of reproduction by older post-reproductive individuals; and (4) male support of reproduction by provisioning of females, while overlooking a fifth one: the provisioning of post-reproductive individuals.

15 Although 'sharing' and 'generalized reciprocity' are often used interchangeably, in the hunter-gatherer literature there have been initiatives to distinguish between hunter-gatherers' sharing from generalized reciprocity. For instance, Jérôme Rousseau has pointed out that apart from altruistic sharing, or generalized reciprocity, demand sharing is also part of immediate-return hunter-gatherers' economy (2006: 46–7). According to Rousseau, demand sharing predates generalized reciprocity. The distinction between the two is that altruistic sharing, i.e., generalized reciprocity, entails moral obligations. Thus, he suggests that 'meat sharing is not reciprocity because sharing is obligatory and disconnected from the right to receive. Donors often persist in giving more than they receive' (ibid.: 47). In a different argument, Nurit Bird-David proposes that hunter-gatherers' mode of distribution (sharing) is to be differentiated from reciprocity, because 'they view their environment as giving, and their economic system is characterized by modes of distribution and property relations that are constructed in terms of giving, as within a family, rather than in terms of reciprocity, as between kin' (1990: 189).

16 For critiques see, e.g., Palmer et al. (1997) and Okasha (2001).

17 According to Gibson, 'the meat of large game animals is subject to the most elaborate rules of sharing and it comes to symbolise the submission of the individual to the group. By contrast, the plants and small animals gathered by women are only shared within the domestic group and come to symbolise factional loyalty. Even in the most egalitarian hunter-gatherer societies, the division of labour between male and female provides a basis for a symbolic association of men with communal solidarity and of women

with factionalism' (2005: 249–50).

18 There is an inherent contradiction in the personal relationships of Lanoh. On the one hand, it is considered important to have people around at all times – hence the extreme fear of loneliness described in Chapter 2. On the other hand, relationships with particular individuals are notoriously unreliable. The rules of general sharing cater to this contradiction. Due to flexibility and individual autonomy, it is impossible to trust that one will be helped or supported by particular others. People move around a lot and young people do not listen to their elders. Hence the emphasis that one is *generally* helpful in *whatever* social context, *whichever* camp. While insisting on interpersonal obligations would be unrealistic, general sharing rules more closely match the realities of Lanoh social life and organization.

19 Kent refers to balanced reciprocity as 'intense sharing' (1999: 118).

20 Jérôme Rousseau (2006: 60ff) considers 'accountable reciprocity,' a term he prefers to 'balanced reciprocity,' to be the basis of a delayed-return system of production and thus a step towards the evolution of middle-range society. Unlike generalized reciprocity (the form of distribution among hunter-gatherers with an immediate-return system of production), in accountable reciprocity, accounts are kept. With this, he suggests that there is an assumption of being able to count on people over time: 'If I give you something with the expectation of an equivalent return, I need you to be there later to reciprocate' (ibid.: 63). Accordingly, Rousseau's account of the development of delayed-return systems assumes exclusivity and reduced individual autonomy. Although, as seen earlier, there have been attempts by elders to develop such exclusivity in Air Bah, the elders have not been successful. Because of continuing resistance to social integration, the conditions of 'delayed-return' organization have failed to develop. In this context, balanced reciprocity still expresses uncertainty about the longevity of interpersonal relationships, although this uncertainty could have been greater in pre-resettlement times when the Lanoh were still mobile.

21 This interpretation of balanced reciprocity among immediate-return hunter-gatherers reinforces Kent's terminology, where she refers to balanced reciprocity as 'intense sharing' (1999: 118).

22 In this respect, the shift to a money economy seems to have had a positive effect on the status of women in Air Bah. Lanoh are not unique in this. Gomes, for instance, notes that Semai women 'can claim a share of the commodity production income despite the fact that they spend considerably less time on such production than men' (1991: 189).

23 Similarly, restrictions are lifted for male elders. In Chapter 5, I described how young Lanoh men are taught to share by being made to give up the

meat they acquire. Significantly, this rule only applies to the first 'seventy-four of every kind of animal.' This means that by the time a hunter reaches middle age, 'after a long time, when a hunter has become more experienced,' this requirement no longer applies.

24 Structure associated with age has only been emphasized in discussions of hunter-gatherers where generational (and resultant gender) inequalities are more pronounced, as in Aboriginal groups in Australia.

25 According to Michael Rowlands, 'although differentiation is observed at all stages, the term "complex society" is most strongly associated with a stage of evolution in which notions such as the state, cities, writing, social stratification, bureaucratic administration, craft specialization and long-distance trade figure prominently' (1989: 32).

26 Although the application of complexity theory in the study of social complexity is increasingly common, these applications are not always successful in enhancing our understanding of social processes. As, for instance, Peter Stewart suggests, 'there ... have been an increasing number of attempts to use the concepts – and sometimes the cosmology – of complexity theories for social analysis ... Paradoxically, these investigations are rather simple processes with a bit of a twist; they involve fairly easy questions of quantification; they relate to rule-bound behavior and situations with low levels of personal interaction' (2001: 329).

27 For further discussion of continuous and discontinuous change also see Byrne (1998: 18) and Rousseau (2006: 229–331).

28 A similar emphasis on continuity is expressed by Fredrik Barth when he states: 'Change implies a difference of a very particular kind: one that results from an alteration through time and is determined by the constraints of what has been, or continues, in a situation' (1967: 664).

29 Jérôme Rousseau defines phase transition as 'the kind of change that brings about a transformation into a radically different system' (2006: 25).

30 As Byrne notes, 'the idea that systems are nonlinear means exactly that changes happen in them which are discontinuous and represent transformations of kind' (1998: 2).

31 It must be noted here that, although this discussion focuses on structural transformation, the application of complexity theory to social change in Air Bah can also highlight the interaction between structure and agency. An important tenet of complexity theory is an 'extreme sensitivity to initial conditions' (Byrne 1998). This means that small differences in the early phases of change result in large differences later in the process. In Air Bah small differences in age, life history, and personality, as well as minute historical accidents, have resulted in perhaps irreversible structural change.

32 Although in small-scale societies leadership positions tend to be occupied by men, there is also evidence that among 'natural leaders,' individuals to whom people look for guidance, there might be more women than previously recognized (e.g., K.M. Endicott and K.L. Endicott 2008: 6, 64).

33 This gap is evident in several excellent studies of factions and factional competition focusing on vertical and horizontal cleavages in complex class systems (e.g., Brass 1965; Nicholas 1968; Bailey 1968; Boissevain 1977; Attwood 1977). Salisbury and Silverman, for instance, write: 'Followers from less privileged groups attach themselves to leaders who are members of the elites. But the conflicts giving rise to factions really concern only the interests of the elite leaders' (1977: 14). This observation equally applies to Air Bah and the way competing elders' goals and interests differ from those of others in the village.

34 This statement is not meant to predict the outcome of leadership competition in Air Bah in terms of transforming the political system. Only a follow-up study could accurately determine the long-term effects of this competition.

35 For the sake of simplicity, omitted from these figures are elders who are not involved in the competition. Their main goals remain the same as those of elders in egalitarian politics: to balance and regulate their relationships with younger men.

36 It must be noted, however, that this 'price' does not automatically signal the development of complex social structure. In some egalitarian delayed-return societies, such as Senoi Temiar or Semai, the functions of household leader and village leader have traditionally been separate (Benjamin 1968). These separate leadership functions, however, did not mean that Temiar or Semai social groupings were 'complex' or hierarchical. In Air Bah, competition for village leadership signalled a structural change towards greater complexity, because contesting this position led to competition and self-aggrandizement.

37 There is still an insufficient amount of work on the relationship between social and biological processes in evolution. The study of human evolution would seem exceedingly suited to seriously entertain the possibility and implications of these connections.

38 This line of inquiry allows us to reconsider a range of behavioural and cultural characteristics commonly associated with the appearance of anatomically modern humans, such as the ability for reasoning, complex tool use, and morality. While many have recognized the significance of the 'invention of a symbolic environment ... [and] symbolic categories' in restraining 'simple dominance' (Fried 1967: 251), the relationship between

the symbolic and cognitive systems of humans and age roles among men has not been sufficiently emphasized. A possible exception is Miller (1999); not only does he emphasize the prominence of cognitive dominance displays among humans, but also his findings indicate that these cognitive dominance displays are related to age.

References

Abdul Razak Yaacob. (1974). *A Batek Negrito Resettlement Area in Ulu Kelantan.* Penang: Universiti Sains Malaysia, School of Comparative Social Sciences, Social Anthropology Section.

Ahmad Ezanee bin Mansor. (1972). *Kampong Lubok Legong: A Negri to Resettlement Community in Kedah.* Penang: Universiti Sains Malaysia, School of Comparative Social Sciences, Social Anthropology Section.

Altman, J., and N. Peterson. (1988). 'Rights to game and rights to cash among contemporary Australian hunter-gatherers,' in T. Ingold, D. Riches, and J. Woodburn (eds.), *Hunters and Gatherers*, vol. 2, *Property, Power, and Ideology.* Oxford: Berg, 75–94.

Andaya, Barbara W., and Leonard Y. Andaya. (1982). *A History of Malaysia.* London: Macmillan.

Anderson, Benedict. (1991). *Imagined Communities: Reflections on the Origins and Spread of Nationalism.* 2nd ed. London: Verso.

Andrews, Elizabeth F. (1994). 'Territoriality and land use among the *Akulmiut* of Western Alaska,' in E.S. Burch Jr and L.J. Ellanna (eds.), *Key Issues in Hunter-Gatherer Research.* Oxford: Berg, 65–95.

Arnold, Jeanne E. (1995). 'Social inequality, marginalization, and economic process,' in T.D. Price and G.M. Feinman (eds.), *Foundations of Social Inequality.* New York: Plenum, 87–103.

Ashby, Patricia. (1995). *Speech Sounds.* London: Routledge.

Attwood, D.W. (1977). 'Factions and class conflict in rural Western India,' in M. Silverman and R.F. Salisbury (eds.), *A House Divided? Anthropological Studies of Factionalism.* Toronto: University of Toronto Press, 171–96.

Bahuchet, Serge. (1992). 'Spatial mobility and access to resources among the African pygmies,' in M.J. Casimir and A. Rao (eds.), *Mobility and Territoriality: Social and Spatial Boundaries among Foragers, Fishers, Pastoralists and Peripatetics.* New York and Oxford: Berg, 205–37.

Bailey, F.G. (1968). 'Parapolitical systems,' in M.J. Swartz (ed.), *Local Level Politics*. Chicago: Aldine.

Bailey, F.G. (1969). *Stratagems and Spoils: A Social Anthropology of Politics.* Oxford: Blackwell.

Bailey, R.C., G. Head, M. Jenike, B. Owen, R. Rechtman, and E. Zechenter. (1989). 'Hunting and gathering in tropical rain forest: Is it possible?' *American Anthropologist* 92: 59–82.

Balikci, Asen. (1989). *The Netsilik Eskimo*. Prospect Heights: Waveland.

Bamberger, Joan. (1974). 'The myth of matriarchy: Why men rule in primitive society?' in M. Rosaldo and L. Lamphere (eds.), *Woman, Culture and Society*. Stanford: Stanford University Press, 263–80.

Barnard, Alan. (1983). 'Contemporary hunter-gatherers: Current theoretical issues in ecology and social organization.' *Annual Review of Anthropology* 12: 193–214.

Barnard, Alan. (1996). 'Social structure and social organization,' in A. Barnard and J. Spencer (eds.), *Encyclopedia of Social and Cultural Anthropology*. London: Routledge, 510–11.

Barnard, Alan. (1999). 'Modern hunter-gatherers and early symbolic culture,' in R. Dunbar, C. Knight, and C. Power (eds.), *The Evolution of Culture: An Interdisciplinary View*. New Brunswick, NJ: Rutgers University Press, 50–71.

Barnard, Alan. (2000). *History and Theory in Anthropology*. Cambridge: Cambridge University Press.

Barnes, J.A. (1973). 'Genetrix: genitor: : nature: culture,' in J. Goody (ed.), *The Character of Kinship*. Cambridge: Cambridge University Press, 61–73.

Barr, Pat. (1978). *Taming the Jungle: The Men Who Made British Malaya*. Devon: Newton Abbot.

Barth, Fredrik. (1966). *Models of Social Organization*. Glasgow: Robert MacLlehose (reprinted in 1969 by Richard Madley, London).

Barth, Fredrik. (1967). 'On the study of social change.' *American Anthropologist* 69(6): 661–9.

Beidelman, T.O. (1971). *The Kaguru: A Matrilineal People of East Africa*. New York: Holt, Rinehart and Winston (reissued in 1983 by Waveland Press, Prospect Heights).

Bell, Duran. (1995). 'On the nature of sharing: Beyond the range of methodological individualism.' *Current Anthropology* 36: 826–30.

Bellwood, Peter. (1985). *Prehistory of the Indo-Malaysian Archipelago*. Sydney: Academic Press.

Bellwood, Peter. (1999). 'Archaeology of Southeast Asian hunters and gatherers,' in R.B. Lee and R. Daly (eds.), *The Cambridge Encyclopedia of Hunters and Gatherers*. Cambridge: Cambridge University Press, 284–339.

Bender, Barbara. (1989). 'The roots of inequality,' in D. Miller, M. Rowlands, and C. Tilley (eds.), *Domination and Resistance*. London: Unwin Hyman, 83–95.

Bender, Barbara. (1990). 'The dynamics of nonhierarchical societies,' in S. Upham (ed.), *The Evolution of Political Systems: Sociopolitics in Small-Scale Sedentary Societies*. Cambridge: Cambridge University Press, 247–64.

Bender, B., and B. Morris. (1988). 'Twenty years of history, evolution, and social change in gatherer-hunter studies,' in T. Ingold et al. (eds.), *Hunters and Gatherers*, vol. 1, *History, Evolution and Social Change*. Oxford: Berg, 4–14.

Benjamin, Geoffrey. (1967). 'Temiar Religion.' Unpublished Ph.D. thesis, Cambridge University.

Benjamin, Geoffrey. (1968). 'Headmanship and leadership in Temiar society.' *Federation Museums Journal* 13: 1–43.

Benjamin, Geoffrey. (1973). 'Introduction,' in P. Schebesta, *Among the Forest Dwarfs of Malaya*. Kuala Lumpur: Oxford University Press, 1–10.

Benjamin, Geoffrey. (1974). 'Prehistory and ethnology in Southeast Asia: Some new ideas.' Working Paper 25, Department of Sociology, University of Singapore.

Benjamin, Geoffrey. (1976). 'Austroasiatic subgroupings and prehistory in the Malay Peninsula,' in P.N. Jenner (ed.), *Austroasiatic Studies*. Hawaii: University of Hawaii Press.

Benjamin, Geoffrey. (1979). 'Indigenous religious systems of the Malay Peninsula,' in A.L. Becker and Aram A. Yengoyan (eds.), *The Imagination of Reality: Essays in Southeast Asian Coherence Systems*. Norwood: Ablex, 9–27.

Benjamin, Geoffrey. (1980). 'Semang, Senoi, Malay: Culture-history, kinship and consciousness in the Malay Peninsula.' Unpublished Manuscript.

Benjamin, Geoffrey. (1985a). 'In the long term: Three themes in Malayan cultural ecology,' in K.L. Hutterer, A.T. Rambo, and G. Lovelace (eds.), *Cultural Values and Human Ecology in Southeast Asia*. Ann Arbor: Center for South and Southeast Asian Studies, University of Michigan, 219–78.

Benjamin, Geoffrey. (1985b). 'Achievements and gaps in Orang Asli research.' *Akademika* 35(7–45): 25.

Benjamin, Geoffrey. (1985c). 'On pronouncing and writing Orang Asli languages: A guide for the perplexed,' Part 1. *Orang Asli Studies Newsletter* 4: 4–16.

Benjamin, Geoffrey. (1986a). 'On pronouncing and writing Orang Asli languages: A guide for the perplexed,' Part 2. *Orang Asli Studies Newsletter* 5: 4–29.

Benjamin, Geoffrey. (1986b). *Between Isthmus and Islands: Reflections on Malayan Paleo-sociology*. Working Paper 71, Department of Sociology, University of Singapore.

Benjamin, Geoffrey. (1987). *Process and Structure in Temiar Social Organisation*. Working Paper 82, Deptartment of Sociology, University of Singapore.

Benjamin, Geoffrey. (2003). 'The current situation of the Aslian languages,' in H. Steinhauer and J.T. Collins (eds.), *Endangered Languages of Southeast Asia*. London: SOAS.

Benjamin, Geoffrey. (2004). 'Aslian languages,' 'Aslian: Characteristics and usage,' in Asmah Haji Omar (ed.), *The Encyclopedia of Malaysia*, vol. 12, *Languages and Literatures*. Kuala Lumpur: Archipelago Press, 46–9.

Benjamin, Geoffrey, and Cynthia Chou (eds.). (2003). *Tribal Communities in the Malay World: Historical, Cultural and Social Perspectives*. Singapore: Institute of Southeast Asian Studies.

Bern, John. (1987). 'Is the premise of egalitarianism inequality?' *Mankind* 17: 212–23.

Béteille, André. (1983). *The Idea of Natural Inequality and Other Essays*. Delhi: Oxford University Press.

Béteille, André. (1986). 'Individualism and equality.' *Current Anthropology* 27: 121–8.

Béteille, André. (1996). 'Inequality,' in A. Barnard and J. Spencer (eds.), *Encyclopedia of Social and Cultural Anthropology*. London: Routledge.

Binford, Lewis R. (1980). 'Willow smoke and dogs' tails: Hunter-gatherer site systems and archaeological site formation.' *American Antiquity* 45: 4–20.

Binmore, Ken. (2001). 'How and why did fairness norms evolve?' in W.G. Runciman (ed.), *The Origin of Human Social Institutions*. Oxford: Oxford University Press, 149–71.

Bird, Nurit. (1982). '"Inside" and "outside" in kinship usage: The hunter-gatherer Naiken of South India.' *Cambridge Anthropology* 7(1–2): 47–57.

Bird, Nurit. (1983). 'Wage-gathering: Socio-economic change and the case of the Naiken of South India,' in P. Robb (ed.), *Rural South Asia: Linkages, Changes and Development*. London: Curzon, 57–86.

Bird-David, Nurit. (1987). 'Single persons and social cohesion in a hunter-gatherer society,' in P. Hockings (ed.), *Dimensions of Social Life: Essays in Honour of David Mandelbaum*. Berlin: Mouton.

Bird-David, Nurit. (1988). 'Hunter-gatherers and other people: A reexamination,' in T. Ingold et al. (eds.), *Hunters and Gatherers*, vol. 1. Oxford: Berg, 17–31.

Bird-David, Nurit. (1990). 'The giving environment: Another perspective on the economic system of gatherer-hunters.' *Current Anthropology* 31: 189–96.

Bird-David, Nurit. (1992a). 'Beyond the "the original affluent society."' *Current Anthropology* 33(1): 25–47.

Bird-David, Nurit. (1992b). 'Beyond the hunting and gathering mode of subsistence: Observations on Nayaka and other modern hunter-gatherers.' *Man* 27(1): 19–44.

Bird-David, Nurit. (1994). 'Sociality and immediacy: Or, past and present conversations on bands.' *Man* 29: 583–603.

Bird-David, Nurit. (1996). 'Hunter-gatherer research and cultural diversity,' in S. Kent (ed.), *Cultural Diversity among Twentieth-Century Foragers*. Cambridge: Cambridge University Press, 297–305.

Bishop, Charles A. (1989). 'Comment on Headland and Reid 1989.' *Current Anthropology* 30: 52–3.

Blackburn, Roderic H. (1996). 'Fission, fusion, and foragers in East Africa: Micro- and macroperspectives of diversity and integration among Okiek groups,' in S. Kent (ed.), *Cultural Diversity among Twentieth-Ccentury Foragers*. Cambridge: Cambridge University Press, 188–213.

Blagden, C.O. (1906). 'Language' and 'Comparative vocabulary of Aboriginal dialects,' in Skeat and Blagden, *Pagan Races of the Malay Peninsula*, vol. 2, 379–472; 481–775.

Blanton, Richard E. (1995). 'The cultural foundations of inequality in households,' in T.D. Price and G.M. Feinman (eds.), *Foundations of Social Enequality*. New York: Plenum, 105–27.

Bloch, Maurice. (1983). *Marxism and Anthropology: The History of a Relationship*. Oxford: Oxford University Press.

Bloch, Maurice (ed.). (1975). *Political Language and Oratory in Traditional Society*. New York: Academic Press, 1–29.

Blurton Jones, N. (1984). 'A selfish origin for human food sharing: Tolerated theft.' *Ethnology and Sociobiology* 5: 1–3.

Blurton Jones, N. (1987). 'Tolerated theft: Suggestions about the ecology and evolution of sharing, hoarding, and scrounging.' *Social Science Information* 26: 31–54.

Bodley, John H. (1992). 'The Tasaday debate and indigenous peoples,' in T. Headland (ed.), *The Tasaday Controversy: Assessing the Evidence*. Washington: American Anthropological Association, 197–200.

Boehm, Christopher. (1982). 'The evolutionary development of morality as an effect of dominance behavior and conflict interference.' *Journal of Social and Biological Structures* 5: 413–22.

Boehm, Christopher. (1993). 'Egalitarian behavior and reverse dominance hierarchy.' *Current Anthropology* 34: 227–54.

Boehm, Christopher. (1996). 'Emergency decisions, cultural-selection mechanics, and group selection.' *Current Anthropology* 37(5): 763–93.

Boehm, Christopher. (1997). 'Impact of the human egalitarian syndrome on Darwinian selection mechanics.' *American Naturalist* 150: S100–S121.

Boehm, Christopher. (1999). *Hierarchy in the Forest: The Evolution of Egalitarian Behavior*. Cambridge: Harvard University Press.

Bogucki, Peter. (1999). *The Origins of Human Society*. Oxford: Blackwell.

Boissevain, Jeremy. (1968). 'The place of non-groups in the social sciences.' *Man* 3: 543–56.

Boissevain, Jeremy. (1977). 'Of men and marbles: Notes towards a reconsideration of factionalism,' in M. Silverman and R.F. Salisbury (eds.), *A House Divided?* Toronto: University of Toronto Press, 99–111.

Bosch, C. (2003). 'Is culture a golden barrier between human and chimpanzee?' *Evolutionary Anthropology* 12(2): 82–91.

Boserup, Esther. (1965). *The Conditions of Agricultural Growth*. Chicago: Aldine.

Boserup, Esther. (1981). *Population and Technological Change: A Study of Long-Term Trends*. Chicago: University of Chicago Press.

Bowdler, Sandra. (2002). 'Hunters and traders in northern Australia,' in K.D. Morrison and L.L. Junker (eds.), *Forager-Traders in South and Southeast Asia: Long-Term Histories*. Cambridge: Cambridge University Press, 167–85.

Brass, P.R. (1965). *Factional Politics in an Indian State*. Berkeley: University of California Press.

Brenneis, D.L., and F.R. Myers (eds.). (1984). *Dangerous Words: Language and Politics in the Pacific*. New York: New York University Press.

Brody, Hugh. (2000). *The Other Side of Eden: Hunters, Farmers and the Shaping of the World*. Vancouver: Douglas & McIntyre.

Brosius, J. Peter. (1991). 'Foraging in tropical rain forests: The case of the Penan of Sarawak, East Malaysia. (Borneo).' *Human Ecology* 19: 123–50.

Brosius, Peter. (1997). 'Endangered forest, endangered people: Environmentalist representations of indigenous knowledge.' *Human Ecology* 25(1): 47–69.

Brown, Paula. (1990). 'Big men, past and present: Model, person, hero, legend.' *Ethnology* 29: 97–117.

Brumfiel, Elizabeth M. (1992). 'Distinguished lecture in archaeology: Breaking and entering the ecosystem – gender, class, and faction steal the show.' *American Anthropologist* 94: 551–67.

Brumfiel, Elizabeth M. (1994). 'Factional competition and political development in the New World: An introduction,' in E.M. Brumfiel and J.W. Fox (eds.), *Factional Competition and Political Development in the New World*. Cambridge: Cambridge University Press, 3–15.

Brumfiel, E.M. and J.W. Fox (eds.). (1994). *Factional Competition and Political Development in the New World*. Cambridge: Cambridge University Press.

Brunton, Ron. (1989). 'The cultural instability of egalitarian societies.' *Man* 24: 673–81.

Buckley, Thomas. (1982). 'Menstruation and the power of Yurok women: Methods in cultural reconstruction.' *American Ethnologist* 9(1): 47–60.

Bujra, Janet M. (1974). 'The dynamics of political action: A new look at factionalism.' *American Anthropologist* 75: 132–52.

Bulbeck, F. David. (2003). 'Hunter-gatherer occupation of the Malay Peninsula from the Ice Age to the Iron Age,' in J. Mercader (ed.), *Under the Canopy: The Archaeology of Tropical Rain Forests*. New Brunswick, NJ: Rutgers University Press, 119–61.

Burbank, Victoria K. (1994). 'Women's intra-gender relationships and "disciplinary aggression," in an Australian Aboriginal community.' *Journal of Cross-Cultural Gerontology* 9: 207–17.

Burch, Ernest S. Jr. (1994). 'The future of hunter-gatherer research,' in E.S. Burch and L.J. Ellana (eds.), *Key Issues in Hunter-Gatherer Research*. Oxford: Berg, 441–56.

Byrne, David. (1998). *Complexity Theory and the Social Sciences: An Introduction*. New York: Routledge.

Carey, Iskandar. (1961). *Tengleq kui serok: A Study of the Temiar Language, with an Ethnographic Summary*. Kuala Lumpur: Dewan Bahasa dan Pustaka.

Carey, Iskandar. (1976). *Orang Asli: The Aboriginal Tribes of Peninsular Malaysia*. Kuala Lumpur: Oxford University Press.

Cashdan, Elizabeth. (1980). 'Egalitarianism among hunters and gatherers.' *American Anthropologist* 82: 116–20.

Cashdan, Elizabeth (ed.). (1984). 'G//ana territorial organization.' *Human Ecology* 12: 443–63.

Cashdan, Elizabeth. (1987). 'Trade and its origins on the Botletli River, Botswana.' *Journal of Anthropological Research* 43: 121–38.

Cashdan, Elizabeth. (1990). *Risk and Uncertainty in Tribal and Peasant Economies*. Boulder: Westview.

Casimir, Michael J. (1992). 'The dimensions of territoriality: An introduction,' in M.J. Casimir and A. Rao (eds.), *Mobility and Territoriality*. Oxford: Berg, 1–27.

Chayanov, A.V. (1966). *The Theory of the Peasant Economy*. Homewood: Richard Irwin.

Chee Heng Leng. (1995). 'Health and nutrition of the Orang Asli: The need for primary health care amidst economic transformation,' in Razha Rashid (ed.), *Indigenous Minorities of Peninsular Malaysia: Selected Issues and Ethnographies*. Kuala Lumpur: INAS, 48–74.

Childe, V.G. (1936). *Man Makes Himself*. London: Watts.

Clark, John E., and Michael Blake. (1993). 'The power of prestige: Competitive generosity and the emergence of rank societies in lowland Mesoamerica,' in E. M. Brumfiel and J.W. Fox (eds.), *Factional Competition and Political Development in the New World*. Cambridge: Cambridge University Press, 17–30.

Collier, Jane Fishburne. (1988). *Marriage and Inequality in Classless Societies*. Stanford: Stanford University Press.

Collier, Jane F., and Michelle Z. Rosaldo. (1981). 'Politics and gender in simple societies,' in S.B. Ortner and H. Whitehead (eds.), *Sexual Meanings: The Cultural Construction of Gender and Sexuality*. Cambridge: Cambridge University Press, 275–329.

Collier, J., and S.J. Yanagisako (eds.). (1987). *Gender and Kinship: Essays towards a Unified Analysis*. Stanford: Stanford University Press.

Cooper, John M. (1940). 'Andamanese-Semang-Eta cultural relations.' *Primitive Man* 13(2): 29–47.

Coote, E. (1976). *Malay-English, English-Malay Dictionary*. Kuala Lumpur: Macmillan.

Couillard, Marie-Andrée. (1980). *Tradition in Tension: Carving in a Jah Hut Community*. Pulan Pinang: Penerbit Universiti Sains Malaysia.

Couillard, Marie-Andrée. (1984). 'The Malays and the Sakai: Some comments on their social relations in the Malay Peninsula.' *Kajian Malaysia: Journal of Malaysian Studies* 2: 81–108.

Cowlishaw, G. (1988). *Black, White or Brindle: Race in Rural Australia*. Cambridge: Cambridge University Press.

Curtis, Richard. (1986). 'Household and family in theory on inequality.' *American Sociological Review* 51: 168–83.

Dahlberg, Frances. (1981). 'Introduction,' in F. Dahlberg (ed.), *Woman the Gatherer*. New Haven and London: Yale University Press, 1–33.

Dallos, Csilla. (1998). 'Media, identity, and opportunity: A study of decision making among Lanoh semi-sedentary foragers of Peninsular Malaysia.' Paper presented at the 8th International Conference on Hunting and Gathering Societies [hereafter CHAGS], Osaka, Japan, Oct.

Dallos, Csilla. (2003). 'Identity and Opportunity: Asymmetrical Household Integration among the Lanoh, Newly Sedentary Hunter-Gatherers and Forest Collectors of Peninsular Malaysia.' Unpublished Ph.D. thesis, McGill University, Montreal.

Dallos, Csilla. (2006). 'Estructure de la autoridad y relaciones de género entre los Lanoh de la Península Malaya: Implicaciones de un caso de sedentarización reciente. (Authority structure and gender relations among newly sedentary Lanoh of Peninsular Malaysia).' *Revista Colombiana de Antropología* 42: 99–129.

Dang Nghiem Van. (1993). 'The flood myth and the origin of ethnic groups in Southeast Asia.' *Journal of American Folklore* 106: 421.

Das, G.S., and C.C. Cotton. (1988). 'Power-balancing styles of Indian managers.' *Human Relations* 41: 533–51.

Denbow, J.R. (1984). 'Prehistoric herders and foragers of the Kalahari: The Evidence for 1500 years of interaction,' in C. Schrire (ed.), *Past and Present in Hunter-Gatherer Studies*. Orlando: Academic Press, 175–93.

Denbow, J.R., and E. Wilmsen. (1986). 'Advent and the course of pastoralism in the Kalahari.' *Science* 234: 1509–1515.

Dentan, Robert K. (1965). 'Some Semai Senoi Dietary Restrictions: A Study of Food Behavior in a Malayan Hill Tribe.' Unpublished Ph.D. thesis, Yale University, New Haven.

Dentan, Robert K. (1968). *The Semai: A Nonviolent People of Malaya.* New York: Holt, Rinehart and Winston (2nd ed. 1978).

Dentan, Robert K. (1970). 'Labels and rituals in Semai classification.' *Ethnology* 9: 16–25.

Dentan, Robert K. (1975). 'If there were no Malays, who would the Semai be?' in J.A. Nagata (ed.), *Pluralism in Malaysia: Myth and Reality.* Leiden: Brill, 50–64.

Dentan, Robert K. (1978). 'Notes on childhood in a nonviolent context: The Semai case,' in A. Montague (ed.), *Learning Non-Aggression: The Experience of Non-Literate Societies.* New York: Oxford University Press, 94–143.

Dentan, Robert K. (1979). 'Identity and ethnic contact: Perak Malaysia, 1963,' in Tai S. Kang (ed.), *Nationalism and the Crisis of Ethnic Minorities in Asia.* Westport: Greenwood, 81–8.

Dentan, Robert K. (1983). *A Dream of Senoi.* Buffalo: State University of New York Press.

Dentan, Robert K. (1988). 'Band-level Eden: A mystifying chimera.' *Cultural Anthropology* 3: 276–84.

Dentan, Robert K. (1989). 'Untitled.' Unpublished ms.

Dentan, Robert K. (1991). 'Potential food sources for foragers in Malaysian rainforest: Sago, yams and lots of little things.' *Bijdragen tot de Taal-, Land- en Volkenkunde* 147: 420–44.

Dentan, Robert K. (1992). 'The rise, maintenance, and destruction of peaceable polity: A preliminary essay in political ecology,' in J. Silverberg and J.P. Gray (eds.), *Aggression and Peacefulness in Humans and Other Primates.* Oxford: Oxford University Press, 214–69.

Dentan, Robert K. (1993). Comment on Boehm, Christopher, "Egalitarian Behavior and Reverse Dominance Hierarchy."' *Current Anthropology* 34: 227–54.

Dentan, Robert K. (1995). 'Bad day at Bukit Pekau.' *American Anthropologist* 97(2): 226–31.

Dentan, Robert K. (2008). *Overwhelming Terror: Love, Fear, Peace, and Violence among Semai of Malaysia.* Lanham: Rowman & Littlefield.

Dentan, Robert Knox, Kirk Endicott, Alberto Gomes, and M.B. Hooker (eds.). (1997). *Malaysia and the 'Original People': A Case Study of the Impact of Development on Indigenous Peoples.* Boston: Allyn and Bacon.

Dentan, Robert K., and Ong Hean Chooi. (1995). 'Stewards of the green and beautiful world: A preliminary report on Semai aboriculture and its policy implications,' in R. Talib and Tan Chee-Beng (eds.), *Dimensions of Tradition and Development in Malaysia*. Selangor: Pelanduk, 53–125.

Department of Statistics, Malaysia. (1997). *Profail Orang Asli di Semenanjung Malaysia / Profile of the Orang Asli in Peninsular Malaysia*. Population Census Monograph Series 3, April, Kuala Lumpur.

Dodge, Nicolas N. (1981). 'The Malay-Aborigine nexus under Malay rule.' *Bijdragen tot de Taal-, Land- en Volkenkunde* 137: 1–16.

Dolhinow, Phyllis. (1984). 'The primates: Age, behavior, and evolution,' in D.I. Kertzer and J. Keith (eds.), *Age and Anthropological Theory*. London: Cornell University Press, 65–82.

Draper, Patricia. (1975a). 'Cultural pressure on sex differences.' *American Ethnologist* 2: 602–16.

Draper, Patricia. (1975b). '!Kung women: Contrasts in sexual egalitarianism in foraging and sedentary contexts,' in R.R. Reiter (ed.), *Toward an Anthropology of Women*. New York: Monthly Review Press, 77–110.

Draper, Patricia. (1992). 'Room to maneuver: !Kung women cope with men,' in D. Counts et al. (eds.), *Sanctions and Sanctuary: Cultural Perspectives on the Beating of Wives*. Boulder: Westview, 43–63.

Dunn, Frederick L. (1975). *Rain-Forest Collectors and Traders: A Study of Resource Utilization in Ancient and Modern Malaya*. Kuala Lumpur: Malaysian Branch of the Royal Asiatic Society.

Durham, William H. (1991). *Coevolution: Genes, Culture, and Human Diversity*. Stanford: Stanford University Press.

Dussart, Françoise. (2000). *The Politics of Ritual in an Aboriginal Settlement: Kinship, Gender, and the Currency of Knowledge*. Washington: Smithsonian Institution.

Dwyer, Peter. (1974). 'The price of protein: Five hundred hours of hunting in the New Guinea Highlands.' *Oceania* 44: 278–93.

Dwyer, Peter. (1983). 'Etolo hunting performance and energetics.' *Human Ecology* 11: 145–74.

Dwyer, Peter. (1985a). 'A hunt in New Guinea: Some difficulties for optimal foraging theory.' *Man* 20: 243–53.

Dwyer, Peter. (1985b). 'Choice and constraint in a Papua New Guinea food quest.' *Human Ecology* 13: 49–70.

Dyson-Hudson, Rada, and Eric Alden Smith. (1978). 'Human territoriality: An ecological reassessment.' *American Anthropologist* 80(1): 21–41.

Earle, Timothy. (1978). *Economic and Social Organization of a Complex Chiefdom: The Halelea District, Kaua'I, Hawaii*. Ann Arbor: University of Michigan Press.

Earle, Timothy. (1994). 'Political domination and social evolution,' in T. Ingold (ed.), *Companion Encyclopedia of Anthropology*. London: Routledge, 940–62.

Earle, Timothy. (1997). *How Chiefs Come to Power: The Political Economy in Pre-history*. Stanford: Stanford University Press.

Eder, James F. (1988). 'Hunter-gatherer/farmer exchange in the Philippines: Some implications for ethnic identity and adaptive well-being,' in A.T. Rambo, K. Gillogly, and K.L. Hutterer (eds.), *Ethnic Diversity and the Control of Natural Resources in Southeast Asia*. Ann Arbor: University of Michigan Press, 37–57.

Elias, Norbert. (1982). *The Civilizing Process*, vol. 2, *State Formation and Civilization*. Oxford: Blackwell.

Ellen, Roy. (1988). 'Foraging, starch extraction and the sedentary lifestyle in the lowland rainforest of central Seram,' in T. Ingold et al. (eds.), *Hunters and Gatherers*, vol. 1. Oxford: Berg, 117–35.

Emerson, R.M. (1962). 'Power-dependence relations.' *American Sociological Review* 27: 31–41.

Endicott, Karen L. (1979). 'Batek Negrito Sex Roles.' Unpublished M.A. Thesis, Australian National University, Canberra.

Endicott, Karen L. (1981). 'The conditions of egalitarian male-female relationships in foraging societies.' *Canberra Anthropology* 4(2): 1–10.

Endicott, Karen L. (1984). 'The Batek De' of Malaysia: Development and egalitarian sex roles.' *Cultural Survival Quarterly* 8(2): 6–8.

Endicott, Karen L. (1992). 'Fathering in an egalitarian society,' in B.S. Howlett (ed.), *Father-Child Relations: Cultural and Biosocial Contexts*. New York: Aldine de Gruyter, 281–95.

Endicott, Karen L. (1999). 'Gender relations in hunter-gatherer societies,' in R.B. Lee and R. Daly (eds.), *The Cambridge Encyclopedia of Hunters and Gatherers*. Cambridge: Cambridge University Press, 411–19.

Endicott, Kirk M. (1969). 'Negrito blowpipe construction on the Lebir River, Kelantan.' *Federation Museums Journal* 14: 1–36.

Endicott, Kirk M. (1974). 'Batek Negrito Economy and Social Organisation.' Unpublished Ph.D Thesis, Harvard University.

Endicott, Kirk M. (1979). *Batek Negrito Religion: The World-View and Rituals of a Hunting and Gathering People of Peninsular Malaysia*. Oxford: Clarendon.

Endicott, Kirk M. (1983). 'The effects of slave raiding on the Aborigines of the Malay Peninsula,' in A. Raid and J. Brewster (eds.), *Slavery, Bondage and Dependency in South East Asia*. Brisbane: University of Queensland Press, 216–45.

Endicott, Kirk M. (1984). 'The economy of the Batek of Malaysia: Annual and historical perspectives,' in B.L. Isaac (ed.), *Research in Economic Anthropology*. Greenwich: JAI Press, 29–53.

Endicott, Kirk M. (1987). 'The effects of government policies and programs on the Orang Asli of Malaysia,' in B.R.O'G. Anderson (ed.), *Southeast Asian Tribal Groups and Ethnic Minorities*. Cambridge: Cultural Survival Inc., 47–51.

Endicott, Kirk M. (1988). 'Property, power and conflict among the Batek of Malaysia,' in T. Ingold et al. (eds.), *Hunters and Gatherers*, vol. 2. Oxford: Berg, 110–29.

Endicott, Kirk M. (1993). 'Semang,' in P. Hockings (vol. ed.), *Encyclopedia of World Cultures*, vol. 5, *East and Southeast Asia*. New York: G.K. Hall, 233–6.

Endicott, Kirk M. (1995). 'Seasonal variation in the foraging economy and camp size of the Batek of Malaysia,' in Rokiah Talib and Tan Chee-Beng (eds.), *Dimensions of Tradition and Development in Malaysia*. Selangor: Pelanduk, 239–59.

Endicott, Kirk M. (1997). 'Batek history, interethnic relations, and subgroup dynamics,' in R.L. Winzeler (ed.), *Indigenous Peoples and the State: Politics, Land, and Ethnicity in the Malayan Peninsula and Borneo*. New Haven: Yale University Press, 30–50.

Endicott, Kirk M. (1999a). 'Introduction: Southeast Asia,' in R.B. Lee and R. Daly (eds.), *The Cambridge Encyclopedia of Hunters and Gatherers*. Cambridge: Cambridge University Press, 275–84.

Endicott, Kirk M. (1999b). 'Batek,' in R.B. Lee and R. Daly (eds.), *The Cambridge Encyclopedia of Hunters and Gatherers*. Cambridge: Cambridge University Press, 298–303.

Endicott, Kirk M. (2000). 'The Batek of Malaysia,' in L.E. Sponsel (ed.), *Endangered Peoples of Southeast and East Asia: Struggles to Survive and Thrive*. Westport: Greenwood, 101–22.

Endicott, Kirk M. (2002). 'The significance of trade in immediate-return societies.' Paper presented at the 9th CHAGS, Edinburgh, Scotland.

Endicott, Kirk. (2005). 'The significance of trade in immediate-return society: The Batek case,' in T. Widlok and W.G. Tadesse (eds.), *Property and Equality*, vol. 2, *Encapsulation, Commercialisation, Discrimination*. New York: Berghahn, 79–90.

Endicott, Kirk, and Peter Bellwood. (1991). 'The possibility of independent foraging in the rain forest of Peninsular Malaysia.' *Human Ecology* 19: 151–85.

Endicott, Kirk M., and Robert K. Dentan. (2004). 'Into the mainstream or into the backwater? Malaysian assimilation of Orang Asli,' in C.R. Duncan (ed.), *Civilizing the Margins: Southeast Asian Government Policies for the Development of Minorities*. Ithaca: Cornell University Press, 24–55.

Endicott, Kirk M. and Karen L. Endicott. (1986). 'The question of hunter-gatherer territoriality: The case of the Batek of Malaysia,' in M. Biesele (ed.), *The Past and Future of !Kung Ethnography*. Hamburg: Helmut Buske, 137–62.

Endicott, Kirk M., and Karen L. Endicott. (2008). *The Headman Was a Woman: The Gender Egalitarian Batek of Malaysia*. Long Grove: Waveland.

Erdal, David, and Andrew Whiten. (1994). 'On human egalitarianism: An evolutionary product of Machiavellian status escalation?' *Current Anthropology* 35: 175–83.

Estioko-Griffin, Agnes. (1986). 'Daughters of the forest.' *Natural History* 5: 37–42.

Estioko-Griffin, A., and P.B. Griffin. (1981). 'Woman the hunter: The Agta,' in F. Dahlberg (ed.), *Woman the Gatherer*. New Haven: Yale University Press, 121–51.

Evans, Ivor H.N. (1914). 'Notes on the Aborigines of Lenggong and Kuala Kenering, Upper Perak.' *Journal of the Federated Malay States Museum* 5: 64–74.

Evans, Ivor H.N. (1924). 'Some beliefs of the Lenggong Negritos.' *Journal of the Federated Malay States Museum* 12: 17–23.

Evans, Ivor H.N. (1927a). 'Further notes on the Lenggong Negritos.' *Journal of the Federated Malay States Museum* 12: 101–4.

Evans, Ivor H.N. (1927b). 'Negrito cave drawings at Lenggong Upper Perak.' *Journal of the Federated Malay States Museum* 12: 105–7.

Evans, Ivor H.N. (1937). *The Negritos of Malaya*. Cambridge: Cambridge University Press (reprinted 1968 by Frank Cass, London).

Fardon, R. (1990). 'Malinowski's precedent: The imagination of equality.' *Man* 25: 569–87.

Feinman, Gary M. (1995). 'The emergence of inequality: A focus on strategies and processes,' in D. Price and G.M. Feinman (eds.), *Foundations of Social Inequality*. New York: Plenum (reprint, 2005), 255–81.

Feit, Harvey A. (1992). 'Waswanipi cree management of land and wildlife: Cree ethno-ecology revisited,' in B. Cox (ed.), *Native People, Native Lands: Canadian Indians, Inuit and Métis*. Ottawa: Carleton University Press, 75–91.

Firth, Raymond. (1961). *Elements of Social Organization: Josiah Mason Lectures Delivered at the University of Birmingham*. London: Watts.

Firth, Raymond. (1964). *Essays on Social Organization and Values*. London: Athlone.

Flanagan, J.G. (1988). 'The cultural construction of equality on the New Guinea Highlands' Fringe,' in J.G. Flanagan and Steve Rayner (eds.), *Rules, Decisions, and Inequality in Egalitarian Societies*. Aldershot: Avebury, 164–81.

Flanagan, J.G. (1989). 'Hierarchy in simple "egalitarian" societies.' *Annual Review of Anthropology* 18: 245–66.

Flannery, K.V., and J. Marcus. (1993). 'Cognitive archaeology.' *Cambridge Archaeological Journal* 3: 260–70.

Foley, Robert. (1988). 'Hominids, humans and hunter-gatherers: An evolutionary perspective,' in T. Ingold et al. (eds.), *Hunters and Gatherers*, vol. 1. Oxford: Berg, 207–21.

Foley, Robert. (2001). 'Evolutionary perspectives on the origins of human social institutions,' in W.G. Runciman (ed.), *The Origin of Human Social Institutions*. Oxford: Oxford University Press, 171–97.

Fossey, Dian. (1979). 'Development of the mountain gorilla (Gorilla gorilla beringei): The first thirty-six months,' in D.A. Hamburg and E.R. McCown (eds.), *The Great Apes*. Menlo Park: Cummings, 139–84.

Fox, Richard G. (1969). 'Professional primitives: Hunters and gatherers of nuclear South Asia.' *Man in India* 49: 139–60.

Fox, Robert B. (1953). *The Pinatubo Negritos: Their Useful Plants and Material Culture*. Manila: Bureau of Printing.

Fricke, Thomas E. (1990). 'Elementary structure in the Nepal Himalaya: Reciprocity and the politics of hierarchy in Ghala-Tamang marriage.' *Ethnology* 29: 135–59.

Fried, Morton. (1967). *The Evolution of Political Society*. New York: Random House.

Friedman, Jonathan. (1994). *Cultural Identity and Global Process*. London: Sage.

Gal, Susan. (1991). 'Between speech and silence: The problematics of research on language and gender,' in M. di Leonardo. (ed.), *Gender at the Crossroads of Knowledge*. Berkeley: University of California Press, 175–204.

Galaty, John. (1986). 'East African hunters and pastoralists in a regional perspective: An ethnoanthropological approach,' in F. Rottland and R. Vossen (eds.), *Sprache und Geschichte in Afrika*. Hamburg: Helmut Buske, 105–32.

Galdikas, Biruté M.F. (1979). 'Orangutan adaptation at Tanjung Putting reserve: Mating and ecology,' in D.A. Hamburg and E.R. McCowen (eds.), *The Great Apes*. Menlo Park: Cummings, 195–233.

Gardner, Peter M. (1991). 'Foragers' pursuit of individual autonomy.' *Current Anthropology* 32: 543–59.

Gardner, Peter. (2000). 'Respect and nonviolence among recently sedentary Paliyan foragers.' *Journal of the Royal Anthropological Institute* 6: 215–36.

Giano, Rosemary. (1990). *Semelai Culture and Resin Technology*. New Haven: Connecticut Academy of Arts and Sciences.

Gibson, Thomas. (1985). 'The sharing of subsistence versus the sharing of activity among the Buid.' *Man* 20: 391–411.

Gibson, Thomas. (1988). 'Meat sharing as a political ritual: Forms of transaction versus modes of subsistence,' in T. Ingold et al. (eds.), *Hunters and Gatherers*, vol. 2. Oxford: Berg, 165–81.

Gibson, Thomas. (2005). 'From humility to lordship in Island Southeast Asia,' in T. Widlok and W.G. Tadesse (eds.), *Property and Equality*, vol. 2. New York: Berghahn, 231–53.

Gladwin, Christina H. (1989). *Ethnographic Decision Tree Modeling*. Newbury Park: Sage.

Gomes, Alberto G. (1986). 'Looking-for-Money: Simple Commodity Production in the Economy of the Tapah Semai of Malaysia.' Unpublished Ph.D. thesis, Australian National University, Canberra.

Gomes, Alberto G. (1991). 'Commoditification and social relations among the Semai of Malaysia,' in N. Peterson and T. Matsuyama (eds.), *Cash, Commoditisation and Changing Foragers*. Osaka: National Museum of Ethnology, 163–99.

Gomes, Alberto G. (2004). *Looking for Money: Capitalism and Modernity in an Orang Asli Village*. Subang Jaya, Malaysia: COAC Trans Pacific Press.

Gomes, Alberto G. (2007). *Modernity and Malaysia: Settling the Menraq Forest Nomads*. London and New York: Routledge.

Goodall, Jane. (1986). *The Chimpanzees of Gombe: Patterns of Behavior*. Cambridge: Cambridge University Press.

Goodall, Jane. (1991). 'Gombe Chimpanzee Politics,' in G. Schubert and R.D. Masters (eds.), *Primate Politics*. Carbondale and Edwardsville: Southern Illinois University Press, 105–38.

Goody, Jack. (1976). *Production and Reproduction: A Comparative Study of the Domestic Domain*. Cambridge: Cambridge University Press.

Gottlieb, Alma. (2005). 'From pollution to love magic: The new anthropology of menstruation,' in C.B. Brettell and C.F. Sargent (eds.), *Gender in Cross-Cultural Perspective*. Upper Saddle River: Prentice-Hall, 256–68.

Graves-Brown, Paul. (1996). 'Their commonwealths are not as we supposed: Sex, gender and material culture in human evolution,' in J. Steele and S. Shennan (eds.), *The Archaeology of Human Ancestry: Power, Sex and Tradition*. London: Routledge, 347–61.

Griffin, Marcus B. (1984). 'Forager resource and land use in the humid tropics: The Agta of northeastern Luzon, the Philippines,' in C. Schrire (ed.), *Past and Present in Hunter-Gatherer Studies*. Orlando: Academic Press, 95–121.

Griffin, Marcus B. (1989). 'Hunting, farming, and sedentism in a rain forest foraging society,' in S. Kent (ed.), *Farmers as Hunters: The Implications of Sedentism*. Cambridge: Cambridge University Press, 60–71.

Griffin, Marcus B. (1996). 'The cultural identity of foragers and the Agta of Palanan, Isabela, the Philippines.' *Anthropos* 91: 111–23.

Griffin, Marcus B. (2000). 'Homicide and aggression among the Agta of Eastern Luzon, the Philippines,' in P.P. Schweitzer, M. Biesele, and R.H. Hitchcock (eds.), *Hunters and Gatherers in the Modern World: Conflict, Resistance and Self-Determination*. New York: Berghahn, 94–110.

Grinker, Roy Richard. (1992). 'History and hierarchy in hunter-gatherer studies.' *American Ethnologist* 19: 160–5.

Grinker, Roy Richard. (1994). *Houses in the Rain Forest: Ethnicity and Inequality among Farmers and Foragers in Central Africa*. Berkeley: University of California Press.

Guddemi, Philip. (1992). 'When horticulturalists are like hunter-gatherers: The Sawiyano of Papua New Guinea.' *Ethnology* 31: 303–14.

Guenther, Mathias. (1986). 'From foragers to miners and bands to bandits: On the flexibility and adaptability of Bushman band societies.' *Sprache und Geschichte in Afrika* 7: 133–59.

Guenther, Mathias. (1996). 'Diversity and flexibility: The case of the Bushmen of Southern Africa,' in S. Kent (ed.), *Cultural Diversity among Twentieth-Century Foragers*. Cambridge: Cambridge University Press, 65–87.

Gurven, Michael. (2004). 'To give and give not: The behavioral ecology of human food transfers.' *Behavioral and Brain Sciences* 27(4): 543.

Gurven, M., W. Allen-Arave, K. Hill, and A.M. Hutardo. (2001). 'Reservation food sharing among the Ache of Paraguay.' *Human Nature: An Interdisciplinary Biosocial Perspective* 12: 273–97.

Gutmann, David. (1977). 'The cross-cultural perspective: Notes toward a comparative psychology of aging,' in J.E. Birren and K. Warner Schaie (eds.), *Handbook of the Psychology of Aging*. New York: Van Nostrand, 302–26.

Harper, T.N. (1997). 'The politics of the forest in colonial Malaya.' *Modern Asian Studies* 31(1): 1–29.

Harris, Marvin. (1997). 'Anthropology needs holism; Holism needs anthropology,' in C.P. Kottak et al. (eds.), *The Teaching of Anthropology: Problems, Issues, and Decisions*. London: Mayfield, 22–9.

Harris, Olivia. (1980). 'The power of signs: Gender, culture, and the wild in the Bolivian Andes,' in C.P. MacCormack and M. Strathern (eds.), *Nature, Culture and Gender*. Cambridge: Cambridge University Press.

Hart, C., and A. Pilling. (1960). *The Tiwi of North Australia*. New York: Holt, Rinehart and Winston.

Harvey, D.L., and M. Reed. (1996). 'Social science as the study of complex systems,' in L.D. Kiel and E. Elliot (eds.), *Chaos Theory in the Social Sciences: Foundations and Applications*. Ann Arbor: University of Michigan Press, 295–323.

Hastorf, Christine A. (1990). 'One path to the heights: Negotiating political Inequality in the Sausa of Peru,' in S. Upham (ed.), *The Evolution of Political Systems*. Cambridge: Cambridge University Press, 146–77.

Hayden, Brian. (1995). 'Pathways to power: Principles for creating socio-economic inequalities,' in D. Price and G.M. Feinman (eds.), *Foundations of Social Inequality*. New York: Plenum, 15–87.

Hayden, B., and R. Gargett. (1990). 'Big man, big heart? A Mesoamerican view of the emergence of complex society.' *Ancient Mesoamerica* 1: 3–20.

Hawkes, Kristen. (1992). 'On sharing and work.' *Current Anthropology* 33: 404–7.

Hawkes, Kristen. (1993). 'Why hunter-gatherers work: An ancient version of the problem of public goods.' *Current Anthropology* 34: 341–51.

Hawkes, Kristen. (1996). 'Foraging differences between men and women: Behavioural ecology of the sexual division of labour,' in J. Steele and S. Shennan (eds.), *The Archaeology of Human Ancestry*. London: Routledge, 283–306.

Hawkes, K., J.F. O'Connell, and N.G.B. Jones. (1997). 'Hadza women's time allocation, offspring provisioning, and the evolution of long postmenopausal life spans.' *Current Anthropology* 34(4): 551–77.

Hawkes, K., J.F. O'Connell, and N.G.B. Jones. (2001). 'Hunting and nuclear families: Some lessons from the Hadza about men's work.' *Current Anthropology* 42: 681–709.

Headland, Thomas N. (1986). 'Why Foragers Do Not Become Farmers: A Historical Study of a Changing Ecosystem and Its Effects on a Negrito Hunter-Gatherer Group in the Philippines.' Unpublished PhD thesis, Department of Anthropology, University of Hawaii.

Headland, Thomas N. (1987). 'The wild yam question: How well could independent hunter-gatherers live in a tropical rainforest ecosystem?' *Human Ecology* 15: 465–93.

Headland, Thomas, and Lawrence Reid. (1989). 'Hunter-gatherers and their neighbors from prehistory to the present.' *Current Anthropology* 30: 43–66.

Helliwell, C. (1995). 'Autonomy as natural equality: Inequality in "egalitarian" societies.' *Journal of the Royal Anthropological Institute* 1: 359–76.

Helms, Mary W. (1978). 'On Julian Steward and the nature of culture.' *American Ethnologist* 5(1): 170–83.

Hewlett, Barry. (1996). 'Cultural diversity among African pygmies,' in S. Kent (ed.), *Cultural Diversity among Twentieth-Century Foragers*. Cambridge: Cambridge University Press, 215–45.

Hitchcock, Robert K. (1982). 'Patterns of sedentism among the Basarwa of eastern Botswana,' in E. Leacock and R. Lee (eds.), *Politics and History in Band Societies*. Cambridge: Cambridge University Press, 223–69.

Holman, Dennis. (1984 [1953]). *Noone of the Ulu*. Oxford: Oxford University Press.

Howell, N. (1986a). 'Demographic anthropology.' *Annual Review of Anthropology* 15: 219–46.

Howell, N. (1986b). 'Feedbacks and buffers in relation to scarcity and abundance: Studies of hunter-gatherer populations,' in D. Coleman and R. Schofield (eds.), *The State of Population Theory*. Oxford: Blackwell, 156–87.

Howell, Signe. (1983). 'Chewong women in transition: The effects of monetization on a hunter-gatherer society in Malaysia,' in *Women and Development in Southeast Asia*. Canterbury: Centre of Southeast Asian Studies, 46–80.

Howell, Signe. (1984). *Society and Cosmos: Chewong of Peninsular Malaysia.* Singapore: Oxford University Press (2nd edition, 1989, by University of Chicago Press, Chicago and London).

Howell, Signe. (1985). 'Equality and hierarchy: Chewong classification,' in R.H. Barnes and D. De Coppet (eds.), *Context and Levels*. Oxford: JASO.

Howell, Signe. (1989). 'To be angry is not to be human, but to be fearful is,' in S. Howell and R. Willis (eds.), *Societies at Peace: An Anthropological Perspective*. London: Routledge and Kegan Paul, 45–59.

Ingold, Tim. (1986). *Evolution and Social Life*. Cambridge: Cambridge University Press.

Ingold, Tim. (1987). *The Appropriation of Nature: Essays on Human Ecology and Social Relations*. Iowa City: University of Iowa Press.

Ingold, Tim. (1988). 'Notes on the foraging mode of production,' in T. Ingold et al. (eds.), *Hunters and Gatherers*, vol. 1. Oxford: Berg, 269–86.

Ingold, Tim. (1996). 'Hunting and gathering as ways of perceiving the environment,' in R. Ellen and K. Fukui (eds.), *Redefining Nature: Ecology, Culture and Domestication*. Oxford: Berg.

Ingold, Tim. (1999). 'On the social relations of the hunter-gatherer band,' in R.B. Lee and R. Daly (eds.), *The Cambridge Encyclopedia of Hunters and Gatherers*. Cambridge: Cambridge University Press, 399–411.

Jennings, Sue. (1995). *Theatre, Ritual and Transformation: The Senoi Temiars*. London: Routledge.

Jensen, Knud-Erik. (1978). 'Relative age and category: The Semaq Beri case.' *Folk* 19–20: 171–81.

JHEOA. (1997). 'Deraf data Kelasifikasi Kampung Perkampungan Orang Asli.' Kuala Lumpur.

Johnson, A. (1975). 'Time allocation in a Machiguenga community.' *Ethnology* 14(3): 301–10.

Johnson, Gregory A. (1982). 'Organizational structure and scalar stress,' in C. Renfrew, M.J. Rowlands, and B.A. Segraves (eds.), *Theory and Explanation in Archaeology*. New York and London: Academic Press.

Johnson, A., and T. Earle. (1987). *The Evolution of Human Societies: From Foraging Group to Agrarian State*. Stanford: Stanford University Press.

Jolly, Pieter. (1996). 'Symbiotic interaction between black farmers and south-eastern San: Implications for Southern African rock art studies, ethnographic analogy, and hunter-gatherer cultural identity.' *Current Anthropology* 37: 277–88.

Jones, D. (2000). 'Group nepotism and human kinship.' *Current Anthropology* 41: 779–809.

Juli, Edo. (1990). *Tradisi Lisan Masyarakat Semai* [The Oral Traditions of Semai Society]. Bangi, Selangor: Penerbit Universiti Kebangsaan Malaysia.

Juli, Edo. (2003). 'Traditional alliances: Contact between the Semais and the Malay state in pre–modern Perak,' in G. Benjamin and C. Chou (eds.), *Tribal Communities in the Malay World: Historical, Cultural and Social Perspectives.* Singapore: Institute of Southeast Asian Studies, 137–60.

Jumper, Roy D.L. (1997). *Power and Politics: The Story of Malaysia's Orang Asli.* Lanham: University Press of America.

Jumper, Roy D.L. (1999). *Orang Asli Now: The Orang Asli in the Malaysian Political World.* Lanham: University Press of America.

Junker, Laura L. (2002a). 'Part II, Southeast Asia: Introduction,' in K.D. Morrison and L.L. Junker (eds.), *Forager-Traders in South and Southeast Asia: Long-Term Histories.* Cambridge: Cambridge University Press, 131–67.

Junker, Laura L. (2002b). 'Economic specialization and inter-ethnic trade between foragers and farmers in the prehispanic Philippines,' in K.D. Morrison and L.L. Junker (eds.), *Forager-Traders in South and Southeast Asia: Long-Term Histories.* Cambridge: Cambridge University Press, 203–42.

Kameda, T., M. Takezawa, R.S. Tindale, and C.M. Smith. (2002). 'Social sharing and risk reduction: Exploring a computational algorithm for the psychology of windfall gains.' *Evolution and Human Behavior* 23: 11–33.

Kaplan, Hillard, and Kim Hill. (1985). 'Food sharing among Ache foragers: Tests of explanatory hypotheses.' *Current Anthropology* 26: 223–45.

Kaplan, H., K. Hill, J. Lancaster, and A.M. Hurtado. (2000). 'A theory of human life history evolution: Diet, intelligence, and longevity.' *Evolutionary Anthropology* 9: 156–85.

Karim, Wazir Jahan. (1995). 'Malaysia's indigenous minorities: Discrepancies between nation–building and ethnic consciousness,' in R. Rashid (ed.), *Indigenous Minorities of Peninsular Malaysia.* Kuala Lumpur: INAS, 18–36.

Keeley, Lawrence H. (1988). 'Hunter-gatherer economic complexity and "population pressure": A cross-cultural analysis.' *Journal of Anthropological Archaeology* 7: 373–411.

Keeley, Lawrence H. (1991). 'Ethnographic models for late glacial hunter-gatherers: A cross-cultural survey,' in N. Barton, A.J. Roberts and D.A. Roe (eds.), *The Late Glacial in Northwest Europe.* London: Council for British Archaeology, 179–90.

Keen, Ian. (1994). *Knowledge and Secrecy in an Aboriginal Religion*. Oxford: Oxford University Press.

Keen, Ian. (2001). 'Theories of Aboriginal cultural continuity and Native Title applications in Australia,' in I. Keen and J. Tanaka (eds.), *Identity and Gender in Hunting and Gathering Societies*. Papers presented at the 8th CHAGS. Osaka: National Museum of Ethnology, 163–83.

Keesing, R.M. (1968). 'Chiefs in a chiefless society.' *Oceania* 38: 276–80.

Keith, Jennie, and David I. Kertzer. (1984). 'Introduction,' in D.I. Kertzer and J. Keith (eds.), *Age and Anthropological Theory*. Ithaca: Cornell University Press, 19–65.

Kelly, Robert I. (1992). 'Mobility/sedentism: Concepts, archaeological measures, and effects.' *Annual Review of Anthropology* 21: 43–66.

Kelly, Robert. (1995). *The Foraging Spectrum: Diversity in Hunter-Gatherer Lifeways*. Washington: Smithsonian Institution.

Kent, Susan. (1988). 'Food use and nutrition in a hunting and gathering community in transition, Peninsular Malaysia.' *Man and Culture in Oceania* 4: 1–30.

Kent, Susan. (1989). 'And justice for all: The development of political centralization among newly sedentary foragers.' *American Anthropologist* 91: 703–12.

Kent, Susan. (1990). 'Kalahari violence in perspective.' *American Anthropologist* 92: 1015–17.

Kent, Susan. (1993). 'Sharing in an egalitarian Kalahari community.' *Man* 28: 479–514.

Kent, Susan. (1995a). 'Unstable households in a stable community: The organization of a recently sedentary Kalahari community.' *American Anthropologist* 97(2): 293–313.

Kent, Susan. (1995b). 'Does sedentarization promote gender inequality? A case study from the Kalahari.' *Journal of the Royal Anthropological Institute* 1: 513–36.

Kent, Susan. (1996a). 'Cultural diversity among African foragers: Causes and implications,' in S. Kent (ed.), *Cultural Diversity among Twentieth-Century Foragers*. Cambridge: Cambridge University Press, 1–19.

Kent, Susan. (1996b). 'Comment on Boehm 1996.' *Current Anthropology* 37(5): 780–1.

Kent, Susan. (1999). 'Sharing: The adhesive that binds households in the Kalahari,' in D.B. Small and N. Tannenbaum (eds.), *At the Interface: The Household and Beyond*. Lanham: University Press of America, 113–29.

Kertzer, D.I. (1979). 'Generation and age in cross-cultural perspective,' in M.W. Riley, R.P. Abeles, and M.S. Teitelbaum (eds.), *Aging from Birth to Death*, vol. 2, *Sociotemporal Perspectives*. Boulder: Westview.

Knauft, B.M. (1990). 'Violence among newly sedentary foragers.' *American Anthropologist* 92: 1013–15.

Knauft, B.M. (1991). 'Violence and sociality in human evolution.' *Current Anthropology* 32: 391–428.

Knauft, B.M. (1994). 'Comment on Erdal, D. and A. Whiten, "On human egalitarianism: An evolutionary product of Machiavellian status escalation?"' *Current Anthropology* 35: 181–2.

Knight, C., R. Dunbar, and C. Power. (1999). 'An evolutionary approach to human culture,' in R. Dunbar, C. Knight, and C. Power (eds.), *The Evolution of Culture: An Interdisciplinary View.* New Brunswick, NJ: Rutgers University Press, 1–15.

Kuchikura, Yukio. (1987). *Subsistence Ecology among Semaq Beri Hunter-Gatherers of Peninsular Malaysia.* Sapporo: Hokkaido University.

La Fontaine, J.S. (1978). 'Introduction,' in J.S. La Fontaine (ed.), *Sex and Age as Principles of Social Differentation.* London: Academic Press, 1–23.

Laland, Kevin, and William Hoppitt. (2003). 'Do animals have culture?' *Evolutionary Anthropology* 12: 150–9.

Larrain, Jorge. (1979). *The Concept of Ideology.* Athens: University of Georgia Press.

Layton, Robert, Robert Foley, and Elizabeth Williams. (1991). 'The transition between hunting and gathering and the specialized husbandry of resources: A socio-ecological approach.' *Current Anthropology* 32: 255–74.

Layton, Robert H. (2001). 'Hunter-gatherers, their neighbours and the nation state,' in C. Panter-Brick, R.H. Layton, and P. Rowley-Conwy (eds.), *Hunter-Gatherers: An Interdisciplinary Perspective.* Cambridge: Cambridge University Press, 292–322.

Leacock, Eleanor. (1982). 'Relations of production in band society,' in E. Leacock and R. Lee (eds.), *Politics and History in Band Societies.* Cambridge: Cambridge University Press, 159–71.

Leary, John D. (1994). 'Orang Asli contacts with the Malays, Portugese and Dutch in Peninsular Malaya from 1400 to 1700.' *Asian Studies Review* 18: 89–104.

Leary, John D. (1995). *Violence and the Dream People: The Orang Asli and the Malayan Emergency, 1948–1060.* Athens: Ohio University Press.

Lederman, Lena. (1990). 'Big men, large and small? Towards a comparative perspective.' *Ethnology* 29: 3–17.

Lee, Richard B. (1969). 'Eating Christmas in the Kalahari.' *Natural History* (Dec.): 14–22, 60–3.

Lee, Richard B. (1979). *The !Kung San: Men, Women, and Work in a Foraging Society.* Cambridge: Cambridge University Press.

Lee, Richard B. (1981). 'Is there a foraging mode of production?' *Canadian Journal of Anthropology* 2: 13–19.

Lee, Richard B. (1990). 'Primitive communism and the origin of social inequality,' in S. Upham (ed.), *The Evolution of Political Systems*. Cambridge: Cambridge University Press, 225–47.

Lee, Richard B. (1992). 'Art, science or politics? The crisis in hunter-gatherer studies.' *American Anthropologist* 94: 31–54.

Lee, Richard B. (1993). *The Dobe Ju/'Hoansi*. Fort Worth: Harcourt Brace (1st ed. published as *The Dobe !Kung*, 1984).

Lee, Richard B. (1999). 'Hunter-gatherer studies and the millennium: A look forward (and back).' Paper presented as a keynote address, at the 8th CHAGS. In P.J. Matthews et al. (eds.), *8th International Conference on Hunting and Gathering Societies: Foraging and Post-Foraging Societies* (reprinted from *Bulletin of the National Museum of Ethnology* 23(4): 821–45).

Lee, Richard B. (2005). 'Power and property in twenty-first century foragers: A critical examination,' in T. Widlok and W.G. Tadesse (eds.), *Property and Equality*, vol. 2. New York: Berghahn, 16–32.

Lee, Richard B., and Richard Daly (eds.). (1999). *The Cambridge Encyclopedia of Hunters and Gatherers*. Cambridge: Cambridge University Press.

Lee, Richard B., and Irven DeVore. (1968). 'Problems in the study of hunters and gatherers,' in R.B. Lee and I. DeVore (eds.), *Man the Hunter*. Chicago: Aldine, 3–13.

Lee, Richard B., and M. Guenther. (1991). 'Oxen or onions? The search for trade (and truth) in the Kalahari.' *Current Anthropology* 32: 592–603.

Lepowsky, Maria. (1990). 'Big men, big women and cultural autonomy.' *Ethnology* 29: 35–50.

Lévi-Strauss, C. (1969). *The Elementary Structures of Kinship*. Boston: Beacon Press.

Lewis-Willams, J. David. (1996). 'Comment on Jolly 1996.' *Current Anthropology* 37: 289–291.

Lightfoot, K.G., and G.M. Feinman. (1982). 'Social differentiation and leadership development in early pithouse villages in the Mogollon region of the American Southwest.' *American Antiquity* 47: 64–86.

Lovejoy, C. Owen. (2009). 'Reexamining human origins in the light of *Aridipithecus ramidus*.' *Science* 326(2 Oct.): 74. DOI 10. 1126/science. 1175834.

Lye, Tuck-Po. (1998). '*Hep*: The significance of forest to the emergence of Batek knowledge in Pahang, Malaysia.' Paper presented at the 8th CHAGS.

Lye, Tuck-Po. (2005). *Changing Pathways: Forest Degradation and the Batek of Pahang, Malaysia*. Petaling Jaya: SIRD.

Macfarlane, Alan. (1978). *The Origins of English Individualism: The Family, Property, and Social Transition*. Oxford: Blackwell.

Mandelbrot, B.B. (1990). 'Fractals – a geometry of nature' *New Scientist*, 15 Sept.1990, Issue 1734. Available at http: //www.fortunecity.com/ema-chines/e11/86/mandel.html.

Marcus, Joyce. (2008). 'The archaeological evidence for social evolution.' *Annual Review of Anthropology* 37: 251–66.

Marlowe, F. (1999). 'Showoffs or providers? The parenting effort of Hadza men.' *Evolution and Human Behavior* 20: 391–404.

Marlowe, F. (2000). 'Paternal investment and the human mating system.' *Behavioural Processes* 51: 45–61.

Marlowe, Frank W. (2003). 'A critical period for provisioning by Hadza men: Implications for pair bonding.' *Evolution and Human Behavior* 24(3): 217–29.

Marshall, Lorna. (1976). *The !Kung of Nyae Nyae*. Cambridge: Harvard University Press.

Marshall, Lorna. (1979). 'Sharing, talking, and giving: Relief of social tensions among the !Kung,' in R.B. Lee and I. DeVore (eds.), *Kalahari Hunter-gatherers: Studies of the !Kung San and Their Neighbors*. Cambridge: Harvard University Press, 349–72.

McGrew, W.C. (1998). 'Culture in nonhuman primates?' *Annual Review of Anthropology* 27: 301–28.

McGuire, Randall. (1983). 'Breaking down cultural complexity: Inequality and heterogeneity.' *Advances in Archaeological Method and Theory* 6: 91–142.

Means, Gordon P. (1985/1986). 'The Orang Asli: Aboriginal policies in Malaysia.' *Pacific Affairs* 58(4): 637–52.

Meillassoux, Claude. (1973). 'On the mode of production of the hunting band,' in Pierre Alexandre (ed.), *French Perspectives in African Studies*. London: Oxford University Press, 187–200.

Miller, Edward M. (1994). 'Paternal provisioning versus mate seeking in human populations.' *Personality and Individual Differences* 17: 227–55.

Miller, Geoffrey F. (1999). 'Sexual selection for cultural displays,' in R. Dunbar, C. Knight, and C. Power (eds.), *The Evolution of Culture: An Interdisciplinary View*. New Brunswick, NJ: Rutgers University Press, 71–92.

Miller, Richard W. (1991). 'Class, politics and family organization in San Cosme Xalostoc, Mexico,' in F. McGlynn and A. Tuden (eds.), *Anthropological Approaches to Political Behavior*. Pittsburgh: University of Pittsburgh Press, 181–99.

Minnegal, Monica. (1996). 'A necessary unity: The articulation of ecological and social explanations of behaviour.' *Journal of the Royal Anthropological Institute* 2: 141–58.

Minnegal, Monica. (1997). 'Consumption and production: Sharing and the social construction of use-value.' *Current Anthropology* 38: 25–48.

Mithen, Steven J. (1989). 'Modeling hunter-gatherer decision making: Complementing optimal foraging theory.' *Human Ecology* 17: 59–83.

Mithen, Steven J. (1990). *Thoughtful Foragers: A Study of Prehistoric Decision Making*. Cambridge: Cambridge University Press.

Molm, L.D. (1985). 'Relative effects of individual dependences: Further tests of the relation between power imbalance and power use.' *Social Forces* 63: 810–37.

Morava, Jack. (2005). 'From Lévi-Strauss to chaos and complexity,' in M.S. Mosko and F.H. Damon (eds.), *On the Order of Chaos: Social Anthropology and the Science of Chaos*. New York: Berghahn, 47–64.

Morrison, Kathleen. (2002a). 'Historicizing adaptation, adapting to history: Forager-traders in South and Southeast Asia,' in K.D. Morrison and L.L. Junker (eds.), *Forager-Traders in South and Southeast Asia: Long-Term Histories*. Cambridge: Cambridge University Press, 1–21.

Morrison, Kathleen. (2002b). 'Pepper in the hills: Upland-lowland exchange and the intensification of the spice trade,' in K.D. Morrison and L.L. Junker (eds.), *Forager-Traders in South and Southeast Asia*. Cambridge: Cambridge University Press, 105–31.

Mosko, Mark S. (2005). 'Introduction: A (re)turn to chaos: Chaos theory, the sciences, and social anthropological theory,' in M.S. Mosko and F.H. Damon (eds.), *On the Order of Chaos: Social Anthropology and the Science of Chaos*. New York: Berghahn, 1–47.

Motzafi, Pnina. (1986). 'Whither the "True Bushmen": The Dynamics of Perpetual Marginality.' *Sprache und Geschichte in Afrika* 7: 295–328.

Motzafi-Haller, Pnina. (1994). 'When Bushmen are known as Basarwa: Gender, ethnicity, and differentiation in rural Botswana.' *American Ethnologist* 21: 539–63.

Murphy, Robert F., and Julian H. Steward. (1956). 'Tappers and trappers: Parallel processes in acculturation.' *Economic Development and Cultural Change* 4: 335–55.

Myers, Fred. (1986). *Pintupi Country, Pintupi Self*. Washington: Smithsonian Institution.

Myers, Fred. (1988). 'Critical trends in the study of hunter-gatherers.' *Annual Review of Anthropology* 17: 261–82.

Nagata, Judith. (1974). 'What is a Malay? Situational selection of ethnic identity in a plural society.' *American Ethnologist* 1(2): 331–50.

Nagata, Shuichi. (1992). 'Changing Sources of Subsistence and the Control of Sexuality and Fertility.' Paper presented at the International Symposium on 'The Environment and the Regeneration of Outline': Perspectives of Gender,

Family, Ethnicity and State, Women and Human Resource Studies Unit, Universiti Sains Malaysia and UNESCO.

Nagata, Shuichi. (1997a). 'The origin of an Orang Asli Reserve in Kedah,' in R.L. Winzeler (ed.), *Indigenous Peoples and the State: Politics, Land and Ethnicity in the Malayan Peninsula and Borneo*. New Haven: Yale University Press, 84–303.

Nagata, Shuichi. (1997b). 'Working for money among the Orang Asli in Kedah, Malaysia.' *Contributions to Southeast Asian Ethnography* 11: 13–31.

Nagata, Shuichi. (1999). 'Conjugal families and the non-circulation of children in a resettlement community of foragers in West Malaysia,' in L.V. Aragon and S.D. Russell (eds.), *Structuralism's Transformations: Order and Revision in Indonesian and Malaysian Societies*. Papers Written in Honor of Clark E. Cunningham. Tempe: Arizona State University Press, 37–67.

Nagata, Shuichi. (2004). 'Leadership in a resettlement village of the Orang Asli in Kedah, Malaysia.' *Contributions to Southeast Asian Ethnography* 12: 95–126.

Nash, Jill. (1987). 'Gender attributes and equality: Men's strength and women's talk among the Nagovisi,' in M. Strathern (ed.), *Dealing with Inequality*. Cambridge: Cambridge University Press, 150–73.

Needham, Rodney. (1964). 'Blood, thunder, and mockery of animals.' *Sociologus* 14(2): 136–49.

Needham, Rodney. (1966). 'Age, category and descent.' *Bijdragen tot de taal-, land- en volkenkunde* 122: 1–35.

Netting, Robert McC. (1990). 'Population, permanent agriculture, and polities: Unpacking the evolutionary portmanteau,' in S. Upham (ed.), *The Evolution of Political System*. Cambridge: Cambridge University Press, 21–62.

Netting, Robert McC., Glenn D. Stone, and M. Priscilla Stone. (1995). 'The social organization of agrarian labor,' in E.F. Morgan (ed.), *The Comparative Analysis of Human Societies*. London: Lynne Rienner, 55–75.

Nicholas, Colin. (2000). *The Orang Asli and the Contest for Resources: Indigenous Politics, Development and Idenity in Peninsular Malaysia*. Copenhagen: IWGIA.

Nicholas, Ralph W. (1968). 'Structures of politics in the village of Southern Asia,' in M. Singer and B.S. Cohn (eds.), *Structure and Change in Indian Society*. Chicago: Aldine.

Nishida, Toshisada. (1979). 'The social structure of chimpanzees of the Mahale mountains,' in D.A. Hamburg and E.R. McCown (eds.), *The Great Apes*. Menlo Park: Cummings, 73–121.

Nishida, Toshisada, Mariko Hiraiwa-Hasegawa, Toshikazu Hasegawa, and Yukio Takahata. (1985). 'Group extinction and female transfer in wild chimpanzees in the Mahale National Park, Tanzania.' *Zeitschrift für Tierpsychologie* 67: 284–301.

Nobuta, Toshihiro. (2008). *Living on the Periphery: Development and Islamization among the Orang Asli.* Kyoto: Kyoto University Press, and Melbourne: Trans Pacific Press.

Noone, H.D. (1936). 'Report on the settlements and welfare of the Ple-Temiar Senoi of the Perak-Kelantan watershed.' *Journal of the Federated Malay States Museums* 19(1): 1–85.

Noone, R.O.D. (1954–55). 'Notes on the trade in blowpipes and blowpipe bamboo in North Malaya.' *Federation Museums Journal* 1 and 2: 1–18.

Norström, Christer. (2001). 'Autonomy by default versus popular participation: The Paliyans of South India and the proposed Palni Hills Sanctuary,' in I. Keen and J. Tanaka (eds.), *Identity and Gender in Hunting and Gathering Societies.* Papers presented at the 8th CHAGS. Osaka: National Museum of Ethnology, 27–53.

Norström, Christer. (2003). *They Call for Us: Strategies for Securing Autonomy among the Paliyans, Hunter-Gatherers of the Palni Hills, South India.* Stockholm: Stockholm University.

Nowak, Barbara. (1986). 'Marriage and Household: Btsisi' Response to a Changing World.' Unpublished Ph.D. thesis, State University of New York at Buffalo.

Nowak, Barbara. (1988). 'The cooperative nature of women's and men's roles in Btsisi' marine extracting activities,' in J. Nadel-Klein and D. Lee Davis (eds.), *To Work and to Weep: Women in Fishing Economies.* St John's: Memorial University of Newfoundland, 51–72.

Ohtsuka, R. (1989). 'Hunting activity and aging among the Gidra Papuans: A biobehavioral analysis.' *American Journal of Physical Anthropology* 80: 31–9.

Okasha, S. (2001). 'Why won't the group selection controversy go away?' *British Journal for the Philosophy of Science* 52: 25–50.

Ortner, Sherry B. (1974). 'Is female to male as nature is to culture?' in M.Z. Rosaldo and L. Lamphere (eds.), *Woman, Culture, and Society.* Stanford: Stanford University Press.

Ortner, Sherry B., and Harriet Whitehead. (1981). 'Introduction: Accounting for sexual meanings,' in S.B. Ortner and H. Whitehead. (eds.), *Sexual Meanings.* Cambridge: Cambridge University Press, 1–29.

Palmer, C.T., B.E. Fredrickson, and C.F. Tilley. (1997). 'Categories and gatherings: Group selection and the mythology of cultural anthropology.' *Evolution and Human Behavior* 18: 291–308.

Pandaya, V. (1993). *Above the Forest: A Study of Andamanese Ethnoanemology, Cosmology and the Power of Ritual.* Delhi: Oxford University Press.

Park, R.E. (1950). *Race and Culture.* Glencoe: Free Press.

Pauketat, T.R. (1996). 'The foundations of inequality within a simulated Shan community.' *Journal of Anthropological Archaeology* 15: 219–36.

Paynter, R., and R.H. McGuire. (1991). 'The archaeology of inequality: Material culture, domination, and resistance,' in R.H. McGuire and R. Paynter (eds.), *The Archaeology of Inequality*. Oxford: Blackwell, 1–27.

Pedersen, Jon, and Espen Waehle. (1988). 'The complexities of residential organization among the Efe (Mbuti). and the Bamgombi (Baka): A critical view of the notion of flux in hunter-gatherer societies,' in T. Ingold et al. (eds.), *Hunters and gatherers*, vol. 1. Oxford: Berg, 75–91.

Pennington, Renee. (2001). 'Hunter-gatherer demography,' in C. Panter-Brick, R.H. Layton, and P. Rowley-Conwy (eds.), *Hunter-Gatherers: An Interdisciplinary Perspective*. Cambridge: Cambridge University Press, 170–205.

Persoon, Gerard. (1989). 'The Kubu and the outside world. (South Sumatra, Indonesia): The modification of hunting and gathering.' *Anthropos* 84: 507–19.

Peterson, Jean Treloggen (1978). 'Hunter-gatherer/farmer exchange.' *American Anthropologist* 80: 335–51.

Peterson, Nicholas. (1991). 'Cash, commoditisation and authenticity: When do Aboriginal people stop being hunter-gatherers?' in Peterson, N. and T. Matsuyama (eds.), *Cash, Commoditisation and Changing Foragers*. Osaka: National Museum of Ethnology, 67–91.

Peterson, Nicholas. (1993). 'Demand sharing: Reciprocity and the pressure for generosity among foragers.' *American Anthropologist* 95: 860–74.

Peterson, N., and T. Matsuyama (eds.). (1991). *Cash, Commoditisation and Changing Foragers*. Osaka: National Museum of Ethnology.

Piña-Cabral, J. de. (1986). *Sons of Adam, Daughters of Eve*. Oxford: Clarendon.

Plog, Stephen. (1990). 'Agriculture, sedentism, and environment in the evolution of political systems,' in S. Upham (ed.), *The Evolution of Political Systems*. Cambridge: Cambridge University Press, 177–203.

Porath, Nathan. (2001). 'Foraging Thai culture: A performing tribe of South Thailand,' in D.G. Anderson and K. Ikeya (eds.), *Parks, Property, and Power: Managing Hunting Practice and Identity within State Policy Regimes*. Papers Presented at the 8th CHAGS. Osaka: National Museum of Ethnology, 117–39.

Povinelli, Elizabeth A. (1991). 'Organizing women: Rhetoric, economy, and politics in process among Australian Aborigines,' in M. di Leonardo (ed.), *Gender at the Crossroads of Knowledge*. Berkeley: University of California Press, 235–57.

Power, Margaret. (1995). 'Gombe revisited: Are chimpanzees violent and hierarchical in the "free" state?' *General Anthropology* 2(1): 5–9.

Pryor, Frederic L. (2003). 'Economic systems of foragers.' *Cross-Cultural Research* 37(4): 393–426.

Quraishy, Zubeeda Banu. (2001). 'Gender politics in the socio-economic organization of contemporary foragers: A case study from India,' in I. Keen and J. Tanaka (eds.), *Identity and Gender in Hunting and Gathering Societies.* Papers presented at the 8th CHAGS. Osaka: National Museum of Ethnology, 195–207.

Rai, Navin K. (1982). 'From Forest to Field: A Study of Philippine Negrito Foragers in Transition.' Unpublished Ph.D. thesis, University of Hawaii, Honolulu.

Rambo, A. Terry. (1988). 'Why are the Semang? Ecology and ethnogenesis of aboriginal groups in Peninsular Malaysia,' in A.T. Rambo, K. Gillogly and K. Hutterer (eds.), *Ethnic Diversity and the Control of Natural Resources in Southeast Asia.* Ann Arbor: University of Michigan Press.

Rao, Aparna. (1987). 'The concept of peripatetics: An introduction,' in A. Rao (ed.), *The Other Nomads: Peripatetic Minorities in Cross-Cultural Perspective.* Cologne: Böhlau, 1–32.

Rashid, Razha (ed.). (1995). *Indigenous Minorities of Peninsular Malaysia: Selected Issues and Ethnographies.* Kuala Lumpur: INAS.

Rashid, Mohd. Razha b. Hj. Abd., Syed Jamal Jaafar, and Tan Chee Beng. (1973). *Three Studies on the Orang Asli in Ulu Perak.* Penang: Universiti Sains Malaysia, School of Comparative Social Sciences, Social Anthropology Section.

Richerson, Peter J., and Robert Boyd. (2001). 'Institutional evolution in the Holocene: The rise of complex societies,' in W.G. Runciman (ed.), *The Origin of Human Social Institutions.* Oxford: Oxford University Press, 197–235.

Riches, David. (1984). 'Hunting, herding, and potlatching: Towards a sociological account of prestige.' *Man* 19: 234–51.

Riches, David. (2000). 'The holistic person; or, the ideology of egalitarianism.' *Journal of the Royal Anthropological Institute* 6(4): 669–85.

Robarchek, Clayton A. (1977a). 'Frustration, aggression, and the nonviolent Semai.' *American Ethnologist* 4(4): 762–79.

Robarchek, Clayton A. (1977b). 'Semai Nonviolence: A Systems Approach to Understanding.' Unpublished Ph.D. thesis, University of California at Riverside.

Robarchek, Clayton A. (1979a). 'Learning to fear: A case study of emotional conditioning.' *American Ethnologist* 63(3): 555–67.

Robarchek, Clayton A. (1979b). 'Conflict, emotion, and abreaction: Resolution of conflict among the Semai Senoi.' *Ethos* 7(2): 104–23.

Robarchek, Clayton A. (1989). 'Hobbesian and Rousseauan images of man:

Autonomy and individualism in a peaceful society,' in S. Howell and R. Willis (eds.), *Societies at Peace: Anthropological Perspectives*. London: Routledge, 31–45.

Robarchek, Clayton A., and R.K. Dentan. (1987). '"Blood drunkenness" and the bloodthirsty Semai: Unmaking another anthropological myth.' *American Anthropologist* 89(2): 356–65.

Rocha, Jorge M. (1996). 'Rationality, culture and decision making.' *Research in Economic Anthropology* 17: 13–41.

Rodman, Peter, and John C. Mitani. (1987). 'Orang utans: Sexual dimorphism in a solitary species,' in B.B. Smuts et al. (eds.), *Primate Societies*. Chicago: University of Chicago Press, 146–54.

Roseman, Marina. (1987). 'Inversion and conjuncture: Male and female performance among the Temiar of Peninsular Malaysia,' in *Women and Music in Cross-Cultural Perspective*. New York: Greenwood.

Roseman, Marina. (1991). *Healing Sounds from the Malaysian Rainforest*. Berkeley: University of California Press.

Rosenberg, Harriet G. (1990). 'Complaint discourse, aging, and caregiving among the !Kung San of Botswana,' in J. Sokolovsky (ed.), *The Cultural Context of Aging*. New York: Bergin and Garvey, 19–41.

Rosenberg, M. (1998). 'Cheating at musical chairs: Territoriality and sedentism in an evolutionary context.' *Current Anthropology* 29: 653–81.

Ross, Marc. (1993). *The Management of Conflict: Interpretations and Interests in Comparative Perspective*. New Haven: Yale University Press.

Rousseau, Jérôme. (1990). *Central Borneo: Ethnic Identity and Social Life in a Stratified Society*. Oxford: Clarendon.

Rousseau, Jérôme. (1998). *Kayan Religion: Ritual Life and Religious Reform in Central Borneo*. Leiden: KITLV.

Rousseau, Jérôme. (2006). *Rethinking Social Evolution: The Perspective from Middle-Range Societies*. Montreal: McGill-Queen's University Press.

Rowlands, Michael. (1989). 'The question of complexity,' in D. Miller, M. Rowlands, and C. Tilley (eds.), *Domination and Resistance*. London: Unwin Hyman, 28–40.

Rowley-Conwy, Peter. (2001). 'Time, change and the archaeology of hunter-gatherers: How original is the "Original Affluent Society"?,' in C. Panter-Brick et al. (eds.), *Hunter-Gatherers*. Cambridge: Cambridge University Press, 39–73.

Rubin, Gayle. (1975). 'The traffic in women: Notes toward a political economy of sex,' in R. Reiter (ed.), *Toward an Anthropology of Women*. New York: Monthly Review Press, 157–210.

Rushforth, Scott. (1994). 'Political resistance in a contemporary hunter-gatherer society: More about Bearlake Athapaskan knowledge and authority.' *American Ethnologist* 21(2): 335–52.

Sahlins, Marshall. (1958). *Social Stratification in Polynesia*. Seattle: University of Washington Press.

Sahlins, Marshall. (1963). 'Poor man, rich man, big man, chief: Political types in Melanesia and Polynesia.' *Comparative Studies in Society and History* 5: 285–303.

Sahlins, Marshall. (1968). *Tribesmen*. Englewood Cliffs: Prentice-Hall.

Sahlins, Marshall. (1972). *Stone Age Economics*. Chicago: Aldine-Atherton.

Sahlins, Marshall. (1976). 'Introduction and critique of the vulgar sociobiology,' in *The Use and Abuse of Biology*. Ann Arbor: University of Michigan Press, 3–26.

Salisbury, R.F., and M. Silverman. (1977). 'An introduction: Factions and dialectic,' in M. Silverman and Salisbury R.F. (eds.), *A House Divided?* Toronto: University of Toronto Press, 1–21.

Salzman, P.C. (1999). 'Is inequality universal?' *Current Anthropology* 40: 31–61.

Sanday, Peggy R. (1981). *Female Power and Male Dominance: On the Origins of Sexual Inequality*. New York: Cambridge University Press.

Schaal, Benoit, Richard E. Tremblay, Robert Toussignan, and Elizabeth J. Susman. (1996). 'Male testosterone linked to high social dominance but low physical aggression in early adolescence.' *Journal of the American Academy of Child and Adolescent Psychiatry* 35(10): 1322–30.

Schebesta, Paul. (1929). *Among the Forest Dwarfs of Malaya*. Translated by A. Chambers. London: Hutchinson (reprinted, 1973, with and introduction by G. Benjamin, Oxford University Press, Kuala Lumpur).

Schebesta, Paul. (1952). *Die Negrito Asiens: Gesichte, Geographie, Umwelt, Demographie und Anthropologie der Negrito*. Vienna: St Gabriel Verlag.

Schebesta, Paul. (1954). *Die Negrito Asiens: Wirtschaft und Soziologie*. Vienna: St Gabriel Verlag.

Schebesta, Paul. (1957). *Die Negrito Asiens: Religion und Mythologie*. Vienna: St Gabriel Verlag.

Schrire, Carmel. (1980). 'An inquiry into the evolutionary status and apparent identity of San hunter-gatherers.' *Human Ecology* 8(1): 9–32.

Schrire, Carmel (ed.). (1984). *Past and Present in Hunter-Gatherer Studies*. Orlando: Academic Press.

Schubert, Glendon. (1991). 'Introduction: Primatological Theory,' in G. Schubert and R.D. Masters (eds.), *Primate Politics*. Carbondale and Edwardsville: Southern Illinois University Press, 29–37.

Seguin, Jean R., Robert O. Pihl, Philip W. Harden, and Richard E. Tremblay.

(1995). 'Cognitive and neuropsychological characteristics of physically aggressive boys.' *Journal of Abnormal Psychology* 104(4): 614–24.

Sellato, Bernard J.L. (1994). *Nomads of the Borneo Rainforest: The Economics, Politics, and Ideology of Settling Down.* Honolulu: University of Hawaii Press.

Service, Elman. (1962). *Primitive Social Organization: An Evolutionary Perspective.* New York: Random House.

Shennan, Stephen. (1996). 'Social inequality and the transmission of cultural traditions in forager societies,' in J. Steele and S. Shennan (eds.), *The Archaeology of Human Ancestry.* London: Routledge, 365–80.

Shnirelman, Victor A. (1994). 'Hunters and gatherers in the modern context.' Report on the 7th CHAGS, Moscow, 1993. *Current Anthropology* 35: 298–301.

Shnirelman, Victor A. (2001). 'Ethnicity in the making: The Tlingits of southeast Alaska on the eve of the 21st century,' in I. Keen and J. Tanaka (eds.), *Identity and Gender in Hunting and Gathering Societies.* Papers presented at the 8th CHAGS. Osaka: National Museum of Ethnology, 53–69.

Shoocongdej, Rasmi. (2000). 'Forager mobility organization in seasonal tropical environments of Western Thailand.' *World Archaeology* 32(1): 14–40.

Shostak, Marjorie. (1981). *Nisa: The Life and Works of a !Kung Woman.* Cambridge: Harvard University Press.

Silberbauer, George. (1981). *Hunter and Habitat in the Central Kalahari Desert.* Cambridge: Cambridge University Press.

Silberbauer, George. (1996). 'Neither are your ways my ways,' in S. Kent (ed.), *Cultural Diversity among Twentieth-Century Foragers.* Cambridge: Cambridge University Press, 21–65.

Skeat, Walter W. (1965). *Malay Magic: An Introduction to the Folklore and Popular Religion of the Malay Peninsula.* London: Frank Cass.

Skeat, Walter W., and Charles O. Blagden. (1906). *Pagan Races of the Malay Peninsula.* London: Frank Cass, 2 vols. (reprinted in 1966, by Barnes and Noble, New York).

Slamet-Velsink, Ina E. (1995). *Emerging Hierarchies: Processes of Stratification and Early State Formation in the Indonesian Archipelago: Prehistory and the Ethnographic Present.* Leiden: KITLV.

Smith, Eric Alden. (1988). 'Risk and uncertainty in the "Original Affluent Society": Evolutionary ecology of resource-sharing and land tenure,' in T. Ingold et al. (eds.), *Hunters and Gatherers,* vol. 1. Oxford: Berg, 222–51.

Solway, J.S., and R.B. Lee. (1990). 'Foragers, genuine or spurious?' *Current Anthropology* 31(2): 109–46.

Speth, John. (1990). 'Seasonality, resource stress, and food sharing in so-called "egalitarian" foraging societies.' *Journal of Anthropological Archaeology* 9: 148–88.

Spielmann, Katherine A., and James F. Eder. (1994). 'Hunters and farmers: Then and now.' *Annual Review of Anthropology* 23: 303–23.

Spitulnik, Debra. (1993). 'Anthropology and mass media.' *Annual Review of Anthropology* 22: 293–315.

Stearman, A.M. (1989). 'Yuqui foragers in the Bolivian Amazon: Subsistence strategies, prestige, and leadership in an acculturating society.' *Journal of Anthropological Research* 45: 219–44.

Steele, James, and Stephen Shennan. (1996). 'Introduction,' in J. Steele and S. Shennan (eds.), *The Archaeology of Human Ancestry: Power, Sex and Tradition.* London: Routledge, 2–43.

Steward, Julian. (1936). 'The economic and social basis of primitive bands,' in R. Lowie (ed.), *Essays in anthropology presented to A.L. Kroeber.* Berkeley: University of California Press, 331–50.

Stewart, Frank Henderson. (1977). *Fundamentals of Age-Group Systems.* New York: Academic Press.

Stewart, Peter. (2001). 'Complexity theories, social theory, and the question of social complexity.' *Philosophy of the Social Sciences* 31: 323–60.

Strassmann, B.I. (1992). 'The function of menstrual taboos among the Dogon: Defense against cuckoldry?' *Human Nature* 3: 89–131.

Strathern, M. (1980). 'No nature, no culture: The Hagen case,' in C.P. Mac-Cormack and M. Strathern (eds.), *Nature, Culture, and Gender.* Cambridge: Cambridge University Press.

Strathern, M. (1981). 'Self-interest and the social good: Some implications of Hagen gender imagery,' in S.B. Ortner and H. Whitehead (eds.), *Sexual Meanings: The Cultural Construction of Gender and Sexuality.* Cambridge: Cambridge University Press, 166–91.

Sullivan, Patrick. (1982). *Social Relations of Dependence in a Malay State: Nineteenth-Century Perak.* Kuala Lumpur: Art Printing Works.

Suwa, Gen, Reiko T. Kono, Scott W. Simpson, Berhane Asfaw, C. Owen Lovejoy, and Tim D. White. (2009). 'Paleobiological implications of the *Ardipithecus ramidus* dentition.' *Science* 326(2 Oct.): 69. DOI 10: 1126/science. 1175824.

Tabet, P. (1979). 'Les Mains, les outils, les armes' *L'Homme* 19: 3–62.

Taylor, Michael. (2001). 'Narratives of identity and assertions of legitimacy: Basarwa in northern Botswana,' in D.G. Anderson and K. Ikeya (eds.), *Parks, Property, and Power.* Papers presented at the 8th CHAGS. Osaka: National Museum of Ethnology, 157–83.

Taylor, Timothy. (1996). *The Prehistory of Sex.* New York: Bantam.

Ten Raa, E. (1986). 'The acquisition of cattle by hunter-gatherers: A traumatic experience in cultural change.' *Sprache und Geschichte in Afrika* 7(1): 369–89.

Testart, Alain. (1982). 'The significance of food storage among hunter-gatherers: Residence patterns, population densities, and social inequalities.' *Current Anthropology* 23: 523–30.

Testart, Alain. (1988). 'Some major problems in the social anthropology of hunter-gatherers.' *Current Anthropology* 29: 1–31.

Testart, Alain. (1989). 'Aboriginal social inequality and reciprocity.' *Oceania* 60: 1–17.

Thambiah, Shanti. (1997). 'Household formation and egalitarian gender relations among the Bhuket of central Borneo.' *Asian Journal of Women's Studies* 3(3): 101–26.

Tilly, Charles. (2001a). 'Introduction: Anthropology confronts inequality.' *Anthropological Theory* 1(3): 299–306.

Tilly, Charles. (2001b). 'Relational origins of inequality.' *Anthropological Theory* 1(3): 355–72.

Tremblay, Richard E. (1999). 'When children's social development fails,' in D.P. Keating and C. Hertzman.(eds.), *Developmental Health and the Wealth of Nations: Social, Biological, and Educational Dynamics*. New York: Guilford, 55–71.

Tremblay, Richard E. (2000). 'The development of aggressive behavior during childhood: What have we learned in the past century?' *International Journal of Behavioral Development* 24(2): 129–41.

Tremblay, Richard E., Christa Japel, Daniel Perusse, Pierre McDuff, Michel Boivin, Mark Zoccolillo, and Jacques Montplaisir. (1999). 'The search for the age of "onset" of physical aggression: Rousseau and Bandura revisited.' *Criminal Behaviour and Mental Health* 9(1): 8–23.

Trigger, Bruce G. (1990). 'Maintaining economic equality in opposition to complexity: An Iroquoian case study,' in S. Upham (ed.), *The Evolution of Political Systems*. Cambridge: Cambridge University Press, 119–46.

Trigger, Bruce G. (1998). *Sociocultural Evolution: Calculation and Contingency*. Oxford: Blackwell.

Turnbull, Colin M. (1965). *Wayward Servants: The Two Worlds of the African Pygmies*. Garden City: Natural History Press.

Turnbull, Colin M. (1972). *The Mountain People*. New York: Simon & Schuster.

Turner, Victor. (1980). 'Social dramas and stories about them.' *Critical Inquiry* 7(1): 141–68.

Tutin, Caroline E. (1979). 'Mating patterns and reproductive strategies in a community of wild chimpanzees.' *Behavioral Ecology and Sociobiology* 6: 29–38.

Tuzin, Donald. (2001). *Social Complexity in the Making: A Case Study among the Arapesh of New Guinea*. London: Routledge.

Upham, Steadman. (1990a). 'Decoupling the process of political evolution,' in S. Upham (ed.), *The Evolution of Political Systems*. Cambridge: Cambridge University Press, 1–20.

Upham, Seadman. (1990b). 'Analog or digital? Toward a generic framework for explaining the development of emergent political systems,' in S. Upham (ed.), *The Evolution of Political Systems*. Cambridge: Cambridge University Press, 87–119.

van Baal, J. (1975). *Reciprocity and the Position of Women*. Amsterdam: Van Gorcum.

van Bakel, M.R., Hagesteijn, R., and P. van de Velde. (1986). 'Introduction,' in M.R. van Bakel, R. Hagesteijn, and P. van der Velde (eds.), *Private Politics: A Multi-Disciplinary Approach to 'Big-Man' Systems*. Leiden: E.J. Brill.

van der Sluys, Cornelia. (1993). 'Peace and tranquility in Jahai social life,' in Hood Salleh, Hasan Mat Nor, and Kamaruddin M. Said (eds.), *Orang Asli: An Appreciation*. Kuala Lumpur: International Convention Secretariat, Prime Minister's Office.

van der Sluys, Cornelia. (2000). 'Gifts from the immortal ancestors: Cosmology and ideology of Jahai sharing,' in M. Biesele, R. Hitchcock, and P. Schweitzer (eds.), *Hunters and Gatherers in the Modern World*. New York: Berghahn.

Verdery, Katherine. (2001). 'Inequality as temporal process.' *Anthropological Theory* 1(3): 373–92.

Walker, Anthony R. (1983). 'In mountain and Ulu: A comparative history of development strategies for ethnic minority peoples in Thailand and Malaysia.' *Contemporary Southeast Asia* 4(4): 451–85.

Walker, Anthony R. (1995). 'From the mountains and the interiors: A quarter of a century of research among Fourth World peoples in Southeast Asia (with special reference to Northern Thailand and Peninsular Malaysia).' *Journal of Southeast Asian Studies* 26(2): 326–65.

Walker, R., K. Hill, H. Kaplan, and G. MacMillan. (2002). 'Age-dependency in hunting ability among the Ache of Eastern Paraguay.' *Journal of Human Evolution* 42(6): 639–57.

Washburn, Sherwood L. (1981). 'Longevity in primates,' in J.L. McGaugh and S.B. Kiesler. (eds.), *Aging: Biology and Behavior*. New York: Academic Press.

Washburn, Sherwood, and Irven DeVore. (1961). 'The social behavior of baboons and early man,' in S. Washburn (ed.), *Social Life of Early Man*. Chicago: Aldine, 91–105.

Widlok, Thomas. (1999). *Living on Mangetti: 'Bushman' Autonomy and Namibian Independence*. Oxford: Oxford University Press.

Widlok, Thomas. (2005). 'Introduction,' in T. Widlok and W.G. Tadesse (eds.), *Property and Equality*, vol. 1, *Ritualisation, Sharing, Egalitarianism*. New York: Berghahn, 1–17.

Wiessner, Polly. (2002). 'The vines of complexity: Egalitarian structures and the institutionalization of inequality.' *Current Anthropology* 43(2): 233–71.

Wiessner, Polly. (2005). 'Norm enforcement among the Ju/'hoansi Bushmen: A case of strong reciprocity?' *Human Nature: An Interdisciplinary Biosocial Perspective* 16(2): 115–45.

Wilk, Richard. (1989). 'Decision making and resource flows within the household: Beyond the black box,' in R.R. Wilk (ed.), *The Household Economy: Reconsidering the Domestic Mode of Production*. Boulder: Westview, 23–55.

Wilk, Richard. (1991). 'The household in anthropology: Panacea or problem?' *Reviews in Anthropology* 20: 1–12.

Wilkinson, G. (1984). 'Reciprocal food-sharing in the vampire bat.' *Nature* 308: 181–4.

Wilkinson, R.J. (1910). *Papers on Malay Subjects.* Kuala Lumpur: F.M.S. Government Press.

Wilkinson, R.J. (1926). *The Aboriginal Tribes.* Kuala Lumpur: F.M.S. Government Press.

Williams-Hunt, Anthony. (1995). 'Land conflicts: Orang Asli ancestral laws and state policies,' in Razha Rashid (ed.), *Indigenous Minorities of Peninsular Malaysia*. Kuala Lumpur: INAS, 36–47.

Williams-Hunt, P.D.R. (1954–55). 'A Lanoh Negrito funeral.' *Federation Museums Journal* 1–2: 64–74.

Wilmsen, Edwin N. (1983). 'The ecology of illusion: Anthropological foraging in the Kalahari.' *Reviews in Anthropology* 10(1): 9–20.

Wilmsen, Edwin N. (1986). 'Historic process and the political economy of San.' *Sprache und Geschichte in Africa* 7(2): 413–32.

Wilmsen, Edwin N. (1989). *A Land Filled with Flies.* Cambridge: Cambridge University Press.

Wilmsen, Edwin N. (ed.). (1989). *We Are Here: Politics of Aboriginal Land Tenure.* Berkeley: University of California Press.

Wilson, D.S. (1998). 'Hunting, sharing, and multilevel selection: The tolerated-theft model revisited.' *Current Anthropology* 39: 73–97.

Wilson, D.S., and E. Sober. (1994). 'Reintroducing group selection to the human behavioral sciences.' *Behavioral and Brain Sciences* 17: 585–608.

Wolcott, Harry F. (2008). *Ethnography: A Way of Seeing.* 2nd ed. Lanham: AltaMira Press.

Woodburn, James. (1979). 'Minimal politics: The political organization of the Hadza of North Tanzania,' in W.A. Shack and P.S. Cohn (eds.), *Politics and Leadership: A Comparative Perspective*. Oxford: Clarendon, 244–66.

Woodburn, James. (1980). 'Hunters and gatherers today and reconstruction of the past,' in A. Gellner (ed.), *Soviet and Western Anthropology*. London: Duckworth, 95–117.

Woodburn, James. (1982). 'Egalitarian societies.' *Man* 17(3): 431–51.

Woodburn, James. (1988). 'African hunter-gatherer social organization: Is it best understood as a product of encapsulation?' in T. Ingold et al. (eds.), *Hunters and Gatherers*, vol. 1. Oxford: Berg, 31–64.

Woodburn, James. (2005). 'Egalitarian societies revisited,' in T. Widlok, and W.G. Tadesse. (eds.), *Property and Equality*, vol. 2. New York: Berghahn, 18–32.

Yanagisako, Sylvia J., and Jane F. Collier. (1987). 'Toward a unified analysis of gender and kinship,' in J.F. Collier and S.J. Yanagisako (eds.), *Gender and Kinship*. Stanford: Stanford University Press, 14–50.

Zuraina Majid. (1994). *The Excavation of Gua Gunung Runtuh and the Discovery of the Perak Man in Malaysia*. Kuala Lumpur: Malaysia Museums Journal.

Zuraina Majid. (1998). 'Radiocarbon dates and culture sequence in the Lenggong Valley and beyond.' *Malaysia Museums Journal* 34: 241–9.

Zuraina Majid (ed.). (2005). *The Perak Man and Other Prehistoric Skeletons of Malaysia*. Pinang: Penerbit Universiti Sains Malaysia.

Index

Ache, 220, 226

age, as natural inequality, 215

age roles: categorical versus relative age, 141–4; difference between men's and women's, 144; ensuring equal access to resources, 227. *See also* categorical age

agency, in hunter-gatherer studies, 16

aging, implications of in primate versus human politics, 217

Agta, 18, 30, 274n12

Ahmad Ezanee bin Mansor, 22

Air Bah: fieldwork in, 257n36; regroupment and resettlement in, 254n19

Andrews, E., 97

'asset consciousness' and changing hunter-gatherers, 159. *See also* property

avoidance rules: stricter than that of Temiars, 32, 146; demarcating kinship groups, 190; restricting the composition of pre-resettlement camps, 145–6

Bahuchet, S., 65

Bailey, F., 148, 210, 239, 284n20

Bailey, R., 70

Barnard, A., 284n26

Barth, F., 285n26, 289n28

Batek, 37, 97, 274n11

'begging,' among chimpanzees, 228

Bellwood, P., 52

Benjamin, G., 31–2, 40, 48, 50, 53, 145, 203–4, 261nn1–4, 263n15, 264nn27–8, 283nn12–13

Bird-David, N., 20, 22, 165, 224, 235, 287n15

birth control, before versus after resettlement, 63–4

black magic accusations in Air Bah, 199–200

Blake, M., 238

Boehm, C., 18, 26, 48, 218

Bogucki, P., 29, 57, 174, 212

Boissevain, J., 150, 176, 285n23

Bowdler, S., 269n5

Boyd, R., 212

Brumfiel, E., 176

Bulbeck, D., 40, 52

Burbank, V., 282n6

Burch, E., 236

Byrne, D., 289n30

Cashdan, E., 18

categorical age: as basis for culture,

ANTHROPOLOGICAL HORIZONS

Editor: Michael Lambek, University of Toronto

Published to date: